Fundamentals *of* Government Information

SECOND EDITION

Fundamentals *of* Government Information

Mining, Finding, Evaluating, and Using Government Resources

CASSANDRA J. HARTNETT

ANDREA L. SEVETSON

ERIC J. FORTE

Neal-Schuman

An imprint of the American Library Association

CHICAGO 2016

Extensive effort has gone into ensuring the reliability of the information in this book; however, the publisher makes no warranty, express or implied, with respect to the material contained herein.

ISBNs
978-0-8389-1395-6 (paper)
978-0-8389-1418-2 (PDF)
978-0-8389-1419-9 (ePub)
978-0-8389-1420-5 (Kindle)

Library of Congress Cataloging-in-Publication Data
Names: Forte, Eric J., 1967- author. | Hartnett, Cassandra J., 1964- author. | Sevetson, Andrea, author.
Title: Fundamentals of government information : mining, finding, evaluating, and using government resources / Cassandra J. Hartnett, Andrea L. Sevetson, Eric J. Forte.
Description: Second edition. | Chicago : ALA Neal-Schuman, an imprint of the American Library Association, 2016. | Includes bibliographical references and index.
Identifiers: LCCN 2015040001| ISBN 9780838913956 (print : alk. paper) | ISBN 9780838914182 (pdf : alk. paper) | ISBN 9780838914199 (epub : alk. paper) | ISBN 9780838914205 (kindle : alk. paper)
Subjects: LCSH: Government information—United States. | Government publications—United States. | Electronic government information—United States. | Libraries—Special collections—Government publications. | Government publications—Bibliography—Methodology.
Classification: LCC ZA5055.U6 F67 2016 | DDC 025.17/34—dc23 LC record available at http://lccn.loc.gov/2015040001

Cover design by Kimberly Thornton. Image © Kim Seidl/Shutterstock, Inc.

Text design and composition by Kirstin McDougall in the Bembo Std, Meta Pro, and Roboto Condensed typefaces.

♾ This paper meets the requirements of ANSI/NISO Z39.48–1992 (Permanence of Paper).

Printed in the United States of America
20 19 18 17 16   5 4 3 2 1

This book is dedicated to all those who love learning about
and using government information.

Contents

PART I
Overview of Key Government Information Resources

CHAPTER 1
Introduction: The People's Information *Eric Forte*

CHAPTER 2
How to Think Like a Government
Documents Librarian *Andrea Sevetson*   **25**

CHAPTER 3
Congressional Publications *Cassandra Hartnett* 49

CHAPTER 4
Introduction to Law *Eric Forte and Peggy Roebuck Jarrett* 77

CHAPTER 5
Public Laws and the *U.S. Code*   Peggy Roebuck Jarrett   **83**

CHAPTER 6
Regulations   Cassandra Hartnett   **101**

CHAPTER 7
Case Law and the Judicial Branch   *Peggy Roebuck Jarrett*   **123**

CHAPTER 8
The President   *Andrea Sevetson*   **141**

Part II
Government Information in Focus

CHAPTER 9
The Executive Branch   *Cassandra Hartnett*   **165**

CHAPTER 10
Statistical Information   *Amy West and Eric Forte*   189

CHAPTER 11
Health Information   *Ann Glusker*   **211**

CHAPTER 12
Education Information   *Susan Edwards*   **235**

CHAPTER 13
Scientific and Technical Information   *Kathryn W. Tallman*   255

CHAPTER 16

Census   *Eric Forte, Kelly Smith, and Annelise Sklar*   **313**

CHAPTER 17
Patents, Trademarks, and Intellectual Property   *Martin K. Wallace*   **335**

CHAPTER 18
Historical and Archival Information   *Cassandra Hartnett*   **363**

Figures

Preface to the Second Edition

CASSANDRA HARTNETT AND ANDREA SEVETSON

For decades, librarians in all settings have known that government information is an integral part of their work. Examples include public librarians who assist users with consumer questions, job seeking, special queries at tax and election time, or applying for government benefits; community college librarians who discover that the Congressional Research Service offers the best concise overviews of controversial topics; academic librarians who are often amazed that a high percentage of their grand collections are in fact government holdings; law librarians who help users find government cases, legislation, and regulations; and medical librarians who have built an entire intellectual framework around the government-produced PubMed database.

Our ardent belief is that greater knowledge of government resources can strengthen the skills of any librarian. *Fundamentals of Government Information: Mining, Finding, Evaluating, and Using Government Resources* (2nd edition) introduces librarians, library and information science students, educators, and information seekers of all kinds to the world of government material. Far from dry, dusty documents, today's government offerings are deep, far-reaching, and ultimately essential to an informed citizenry, a true democracy, and outstanding library collections and services.

The book provides the reader with the following:

- models and techniques for discovery of government information
- insight into the popular and research value of government publications
- experience acquiring new skills in a simple, sequential manner, reinforced by exercises

Above all else, we aim to help you, the reader, become comfortable with the everydayness of government information. We will encourage you to look for basic evidence of government in your daily life. Breathing clean air? Think of the US Environmental Protection Agency. Watching a television set that does not explode (yet)? Give a nod to the Consumer Product Safety Commission. Looking forward to a nip of alcohol after work on Friday night? Your state's liquor authority will greatly influence your ability to do so. Throughout the book, we encourage you to observe the world around you with an eye to government agencies and policies. You may be surprised at how quickly your skill level grows at this game. Mastery takes a lifetime of applied work, but in truth, mastery never occurs in the government information world because governments are ever changing. Still, our goal is to define the contemporary fundamentals of government information for any nongovernment-documents librarian or student.

Government information should be considered a genre of public literature. Whether one is perusing a congressional hearing, a NASA technical document, a Food and Drug Administration (FDA) advisory, or a historic War Department pamphlet, this literature stands apart because of its provenance and official nature—concepts that become complicated in the era of easily modified online publications, as we will explore in chapter 1. Although government information exists at the state and local levels (city, county, and in some cases, neighborhood), this book focuses primarily on the US federal government. We intersperse examples from state and local governments, but we generally do not explore international or foreign government literature in depth, except for a few instances in which this content is essential to the information at hand. The US federal government is vast enough on its own and provides a good working model for other levels of government. One could argue that state and local governments do most of the actual governing, but the federal government certainly is the most prolific publisher. If one can appreciate the basic structure and function of the mammoth US federal government, other government models may be relatively easy to understand.

How the Book Is Structured

Fundamentals of Government Information is divided into two parts: part I, Overview of Key Government Information Resources, and part II, Government Information in Focus. As a result of feedback from those educating the future government information librarians, part I has been somewhat restructured from the first edition and now breaks out the law-related material into the following chapters: chapter 4, Introduction to Law; chapter 5, Public Laws and the *U.S. Code*; chapter 6, Regulations; chapter 7, Case Law and the Judicial Branch; and chapter 8, The President. Chapter 4 is a brief introduction that should help readers with the big concepts, and chapters 5 through 8 discuss the laws (and other publications) that are the result of the tripartite government of the United States.

Part II includes a new chapter called Patents, Trademarks, and Intellectual Property. In the first edition, patents were a part of the chapter on scientific and technical information, but reader responses let us know this important material needed its own chapter.

Throughout the text we try to focus on the processes of government and explain why the publications exist for the processes. Each chapter includes several exercises, allowing readers to assess their understanding of government information and think about real life situations involving government documents. These exercises are designed to (1) be useful in a library science classroom, (2) clarify some of the more challenging concepts in government information, and (3) give readers a chance to use a particular information resource to answer a question and evaluate its effectiveness step by step.

One note to the more informed readers of this book: with the December 16, 2014, change in the name of the Government Printing Office to the Government Publishing Office some readers may expect to find all references to the Government Printing

Office changed. We have tried to keep the name correct with the period of time referenced to enable further research. So when the reference is to the GPO *Style Manual* from 2008 or to the *Monthly Catalog,* the reference is, correctly, to the Government Printing Office.

Lastly, we welcome a band of new contributors to this second edition. As primary authors and editors we remain true to our *Fundamentals* vision, and we are pleased that this revised edition offers the expertise and perspective of more of our colleagues across the United States. We have also consulted with LIS faculty to ensure the best possible book for classroom use. This makes the book a true collaboration, even a conversation. And with government information, the conversation is always just beginning.

We hope all our readers find this journey through Congress, the courts, the president, federal agencies, statistics, regulations, and more to be a rewarding and memorable adventure.

Acknowledgments

CASS HARTNETT thanks the University of Washington Libraries for release time, her coworkers for covering extra hours, and Morag K. Stewart for editorial assistance.

ANDREA SEVETSON thanks her family and friends for their patience during the writing and editing process.

ERIC FORTE thanks Bonnie Grobar and Diana Houston of the Texas State Library and Archives for their inspiration.

PART I

Overview of Key Government Information Resources

CHAPTER 1

Introduction
The People's Information

ERIC FORTE

Government information provides a window and a mirror to current society and its history, documenting and informing the communities and citizens it governs. With the emergence of representative governments such as those of the United States, its states, cities, and counties, and many of the world's nations, government information is the people's information. The information a government produces—and the access to that information—often reflect the realities, debate, and discussion of the nation itself. Although sometimes considered a unique skill set requiring specialized knowledge and access tools, finding government information is a fundamental information competency. The ability to find and use government information ranges from necessity to responsibility, from inquiry to curiosity. And what one finds in government information is endlessly fascinating and often surprising.

Government information may cover nearly any topic, can be used by any citizen, and encompasses almost every type of information:

- tax forms
- voting records of senators and representatives
- educational standards laws that influence school curriculum
- the latest health, medicine, and science research
- information about the flu and other infectious diseases
- trade agreements affecting the import and export of consumer items
- pollution readings for your city
- weather records
- data on unemployment and prices
- brochures for national parks
- the personal papers of former presidents
- the wisdom of Smokey Bear, Woodsy Owl, and the lesser-known Sprocket Man (figure 1.1)

Government information comprises a broad array of types of material, such as

- historical documents
- legal treatises
- posters
- maps
- statistics and datasets
- scientific papers
- satellite imagery and aerial photographs
- databases and web services
- transcripts of press conferences and speeches by presidents, governors, members of Congress, and government officials
- Supreme Court decisions
- and much, much more

The closest thing to an official definition of a government publication is "informational matter which is published as an individual document at Government expense, or as required by law" (44 U.S.C. § 1901). This broad definition fits, as in the course of carrying out their missions, governments produce nearly every type of information product short of poetry and fiction, a diversity of output that fits the diversity of their populations. Yet as we shall soon see, this definition is in the context of publications generally *intended for public consumption*—what it does not necessarily cover is all of the internal records and raw data of various other informational, government-produced reports developed as part of the operational workings of government. The issues of what is government information (whether electronic or tangible), and what government information should be made public, have been subject to debate for the

FIGURE 1.1
Sprocket Man

entire lifetime of our nation—debates that have arguably intensified in recent years.

Relatively early in United States history, governments and libraries formed a special relationship to provide government information to citizens. This was especially true at the federal level, although it also applied generally to most states. Libraries became the repositories for government information, the conduits delivering government information to people. Citizens needing access to any of this information trekked to a local library designated, through agreement between the government and the library, to house government materials amongst its collections. Once there, citizens could not only access government information, but also be assisted by librarians who were experts in locating sometimes obscure, and frequently specialized and arcane, government information. These so-called depository libraries house the information of our democracy.

The information revolution of the last 20 years has sometimes altered the nature of government information, but has revolutionized access to that information—the Web is the preferred platform for publishing and accessing government information at all levels. Because government information is almost always without copyright, almost always free, and often specifically intended to be easily consumed by its population, it made a rapid and early transition to the Web as its preferred platform for both publication and access. No traditional library collection, not even scholarly journals, moved so rapidly and comprehensively online. While this rapid change has brought government information ever closer to the public and to reference librarians, government information still encompasses countless unique resources and characteristics requiring special expertise, information skills, and strategies (and some of it still exists in nonelectronic formats, whether print or microform). This book, coupled with a knowledge of civics and general reference skills, provides the foundations of utilizing government information.

Introduction

Government documents sometimes top the best-seller lists, such as the 9/11 Commission Report: The Official Report of the 9/11 Commission; Report of the Senate Select Committee on Intelligence Committee Study of the Central Intelligence Agency's Detention and Interrogation Program; the Warren Commission report (officially known as the *Report of the President's Commission on the Assassination of President John F. Kennedy*); and the Clinton impeachment era's Starr report (officially known as the *Referral from Independent Counsel Kenneth W. Starr in conformity with the requirements of Title 28, United States Code, section 595(c): communication from Kenneth W. Starr, independent counsel, transmitting a referral to the United States House of Representatives filed in conformity with the requirements of Title 28, United States Code, section 595(c))*.

Other government document gems don't sell any copies, but address very popular issues. The *Munson Report* famously assessed Japanese-American loyalty prior to Pearl Harbor (although these citizens were judged loyal, the report was suppressed after the attack and only resurfaced later as part of the mammoth set of congressional hearings about Pearl Harbor that took place after the war, and after Japanese-American citizens were detained in camps anyway). Another Munson, the famous 1970s-era New York Yankee baseball player Thurman Munson, who fatally crashed his private jet, is the subject of a report from the National Transportation Safety Board, *Thurman L. Munson, Cessna Citation 501, N15NY, near Canton, Ohio, August 2, 1979*. A plane crash into the Hudson River that had a happier ending thanks to pilot Chesley Sullenberger was the subject of *US Airways flight 1549 accident: hearing before the Subcommittee on Aviation of the Committee on Transportation and Infrastructure, House of Representatives, 111th Congress, first session, February 24, 2009*.

One of the most empowering aspects of understanding government information is the ability to conduct one's own fact-checking. Not sure what to make of a media or third-party account of a government event or report? Need to investigate an interesting tidbit forwarded to your e-mail, read on a blog, or heard on the radio? Want to find the actual reported statistics of a government agency, or check the veracity of an accusation from an angry political pundit—or a politically angry friend or relative? Want to get the real truth about a political attack ad? Depository libraries and government information librarians and specialists can lead people to the actual text of a piece of legislation, show details of the very budget a president proposed or Congress passed, find the actual words that an official said in a press conference, and produce the full text of the government report itself. Such primary, rather than secondary, access to government information is the whole reason government information exists, and government documents librarians thrive on empowering the public to understand and research the information and actions of their own governments.

Lest one think that government documents attempt to address just the facts, there's the *Roswell Report: Case Closed* from the US Air Force addressing fictitious (supposedly!) government encounters with aliens, and the aforementioned fictional character Smokey Bear, who stars in a whole series of US government documents. Yet the debate over government truth can be more serious: in the midst of national recessions that included significant corporate layoff activity, presidential administrations have twice attempted to stop their own reporting of mass layoffs, a statistic tracked in the course of duties by the Bureau of Labor Statistics (BLS). Such moves—both times reversed—were nonetheless often believed to be efforts to restrict government information for political gain. Similar concerns have also been aired over government science, such as disputed National Cancer Institute information discussing possible links between abortions and later incidents of breast cancer ("Abortion and Breast Cancer," 2003), and suppression of information in an Environmental Protection Agency report reiterating scientific evidence of human-induced causes of climate change (Revkin, 2003). And this doesn't even address the controversies around government information that, while never intended to be public, might nonetheless be hidden or obscured, such as reports of internal investigations, a government official's e-mails, internal reports of US diplomats based abroad, or information about mass government collection of citizen digital activity.

Government information, not surprisingly, covers many fascinating and useful historical topics. The massive, 130-volume set *War of the Rebellion* collects firsthand accounts, letters, maps, government reports, and more from both sides of the Civil War, providing a nearly endless source for historians, while World War II–era government posters (available online via Northwestern University at www.library.northwestern.edu/libraries -collections/evanston-campus/government-information/world-war-ii-poster -collection) illuminate many aspects of the American war effort. The storage of these government posters online at Northwestern is just one of many examples of government partnerships with libraries to preserve and give new life into government documents. Citizens come to depository libraries seeking official military histories for specific battles, geologic and archaeological reports on antiquities, demographic statistics of colonial America, or information about the specific ships they may have served on in the military as cataloged in the *Dictionary of American Naval Fighting Ships*.

Government information is by no means limited to the federal government, historical topics, or printed reports. One can search state court records to find business bankruptcies in one's town. Government information reveals that vanity license plates such as "ILVTOFU" and "DNASTY" have been rejected by state departments of motor vehicles, and the California Board of Registered Nursing allows the public to access the disciplinary records of nurses (figure 1.2). The Minnesota Department of Transportation provides access to inspection reports of the state's bridges, while Arizona's Maricopa County provides access to which of the county's speed cameras were activated by location, and how many citations were issued as a result. The media and citizens increasingly use government datasets; one popular application is using state property assessor data to map the sale price of homes in neighborhoods or beyond. The capabilities, possibilities, and increasingly, realities of e-government initiatives—providing government information *and* services online—are nearly limitless. And limitless is the imagination of the expert government documents professional who is adept at mastering the many opportunities for government services and information.

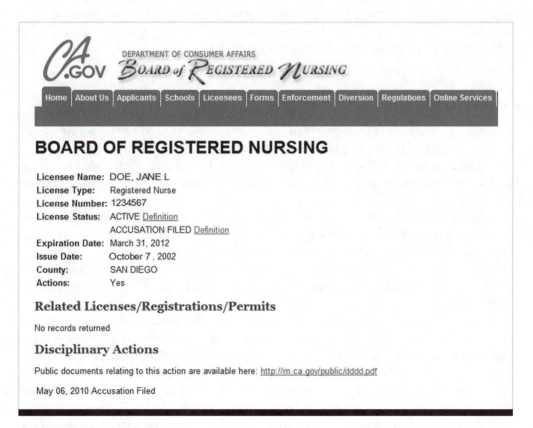

FIGURE 1.2

The California Database of Registered Nurses, One of Hundreds of Databases of Government Information

Issues in Government Information

This book, through its expert coverage of sources and strategies for finding and using government information, addresses in detail contemporary issues in government information. As mentioned, the ready Web availability of much government information potentially brings it much closer to citizens. Yet finding details such as the status of legislation, a statistic, an obscure technical report, or the location of local speed trap cameras requires specific knowledge, skills, and tools beyond a web search engine.

Also of vital importance in contemporary government information are issues related to access and preservation. While in some respects more government data are available than ever before, concerns about what and how much should be public information can—and have—placed limits on access. Meanwhile, the days of the Federal Depository Library Program (FDLP) handling permanent access through physical copies stored in the depository library program described below are largely over; born-digital government information suffers from incomplete and shifting efforts at preservation (though numerous excellent projects, both within the government information community and by GPO itself, are working hard on this issue), and the risk of certain government information disappearing before being archived is real.

Access to Government Information Post-9/11

As we'll see shortly, GPO has provided government information to depository libraries and the public for many years via the FDLP. While issues related to printing and fugitive documents have been real impediments to sharing government documents, it is access to government records in general that is the source of greater concerns about government openness.

Over the recent decades of the nation's history, public access to government records (as opposed to published government reports) has received increased attention. Until the Freedom of Information Act (FOIA) established procedures whereby government agencies must provide access to government records upon request, the federal government had wide authority to restrict access to perceived sensitive government information. FOIA, passed in 1966, immediately provided a mechanism for opening access to many unreleased government records. Since that time, further efforts to make government more open have frequently been balanced by concurrent efforts to restrict government information, a back-and-forth summarized well by McDermott (2007). The Nixon-era battle over the publication of the so-called Pentagon Papers—internal government reports that documented the Vietnam War operations in much more detail than previous public reports and communication—heightened debates over the openness of government information. Journalist Daniel Ellsberg came into possession of the Pentagon Papers and worked with several newspapers to publish them, but only after court battles that went all the way to the Supreme Court. The constitutional balance between information needed for an informed electorate, versus information needing to be kept from the public for security reasons, was played out two centuries after the debate begun in the Constitution (discussed in depth below).

And the debate continues. In the Obama era, both the documents released by Chelsea Manning to WikiLeaks, and the NSA documents released by Edward Snowden, led to further debate—one person's democratic openness is another person's treasonous disclosure. In both of these instances, just like with the Pentagon Papers, it wasn't FOIA—and certainly not FDLP or the National Archives—that led to release of government information. Rather, it was whistleblowers. The only sure thing moving forward would seem to be that the debate over where the line of secrecy and openness lies will continue.

Some sensitive government information is classified, and subject to declassification periods that can be many years long. Several sources for accessing previously classified documents are noted in chapter 8.

In recent years, even information long considered to be public has seen perceived erosion in access, with national security cited in the need to restrict public access to potentially harmful information. Fowler notes that "since 9/11 there have been many more restrictions on the documents that are being made available to the public," citing an 81 percent increase in classified documents (2007: 20–21). Such information included documents and databases relating to public water supplies, facilities with toxic or potentially toxic chemicals, and energy transmission, all efforts that Hernon (2004) discusses. Hernon generally concludes that any security gained through restricting access to such information is insufficient compared to the need for open government. Nonetheless, as Hogenboom (2008) asserts, agencies have been and will be more cautious. To government agencies, the negative implications in having their information potentially compromise national security outweigh the negative implications of withholding information from citizens.

A bigger issue, however, is the worry that it is not simply national security driving government secrecy. According to Gordon, "the original intent was to protect military secrets, but between 2000 and 2006 the program expanded to include anything embarrassing to the government" (2007). And in a far-reaching review of the history of government information policy, Jaeger (2007) traces the nearly uninterrupted trend of the federal government becoming increasingly open throughout the nation's history, only to have this trend seemingly reversed with the administration of George W. Bush, even before the 9/11 attacks spurred heightened concerns about enemy access to sensitive information. Website content was removed, and several very public battles about access and secrecy to government records began, with the administration seeking to limit or restrict access altogether. After 9/11, this trend accelerated. Yet as Jaeger continues, "much of the information being classified seems tenuously related to national security, such as information on auto and tire safety, the quality of drinking water supplies, safety violations by airlines, and the amount of money spent by the federal government on information technology" (847–848). Limitations on access to government correspondence with private corporations and contractors such as Halliburton occurred at the same time that the amount of government information collected about citizens increased. The administration was marked by wide-ranging and comprehensive actions to limit and influence information across the board. Jaeger ultimately concludes:

> The perspective of the administration appears based on a belief that access
> to information, in general, should be very limited and tightly controlled in

a centralized manner by the executive branch of the federal government.
It also appears to include the belief that information that is made available
for access should fit with the administration's opinions, as evidenced by the
attempts to influence scientific committees and research studies and reports.
Taken together, these policies have significant impacts on the amount and
types of information available for access as well as presenting serious questions about the long term impact on democracy in the United States and
internationally. (853)

The record of the Obama administration in this realm is famously mixed. On the one
hand, there is the administration's criminal investigation and potential prosecution in
the WikiLeaks/Manning and NSA/Snowden cases; on the other hand, the Obama
administration has publicly committed to more open government (see the Open Government Initiative at www.whitehouse.gov/open). This emphasis on increased transparency includes more open FOIA responses. And as we'll see in the next section, great
strides have been made to open up taxpayer-funded research and data to the taxpayers
themselves.

Open Access to Government-Funded Research

Another important contemporary issue in government information is the movement
toward greater access to federally funded scientific research. Each year, hundreds of millions
of dollars of federal money are distributed in the form of grants to scientists in order to
conduct research. Medical research may be the most prominent category of this support,
but scientists in all genres may receive funding from various federal funding agencies.

Historically, the results of this federally funded research generally have been written
up and find their final public form in scientific papers submitted to and published in
the key research journals in different disciplines, whereby they would be accessible to
other scientists, scholars, policymakers, and bureaucrats. These journals—published by
nonprofit scientific societies, private publishers, or a partnership between the two—
were accessible to most researchers in the United States, Europe, and the most developed nations because those who needed to read them either subscribed to the journals
themselves, or had access to a research library that subscribed. As most of these scientists were employed in universities and other research centers supported by libraries,
access to the results of the research wasn't really a problem, although one could easily
argue that access to taxpayer-funded research should be easily open to the taxpayers
themselves, and not require a library subscription (especially as most such libraries are
themselves funded largely by taxpayers).

However, recent decades have seen a well-documented accelerating and dramatic
inflationary pricing trend for many such journals. While the reasons for the inflation
are many, major factors are inelastic demand (a medical researcher cannot simply cancel
a subscription to a journal just because the price has risen, not if key findings are there)
along with a shift from nonprofit, society-published journals, to for-profit, privately
published journals whose incentive to publish is not simply to share knowledge, but
also to maximize profits and shareholder value. In many cases, journals that previously

cost hundreds of dollars per year quickly began to cost thousands of dollars per year, and both scientists and libraries began cancelling subscriptions. The effect of this rising cost barrier is simple: often scientists perform research using taxpayer dollars, and the results are given to private publishers, who manage the peer-review process and publishing and then sell the journals back to scientists and libraries at prices increasingly difficult to afford.

Scientists, libraries, Congress, and the president have begun to act to correct this situation. Librarian and scientist led efforts such as the Alliance for Taxpayer Access (www.taxpayeraccess.org) and the Scholarly Publishing and Academic Resources Coalition (SPARC, www.sparc.arl.org, an effort of the Association of Research Libraries) have taken action toward opening access to such research, with scientists and librarians around the world increasingly working to ensure that the results of taxpayer-supported research are accessible to the public they are meant to serve.

Most importantly, executive action has begun mandating that taxpayer-funded research be made available. The National Institutes of Health (NIH—see http://publicaccess.nih.gov) now requires that all scientific papers published with the support of NIH grants be deposited in the freely accessible public archive PubMed Central (www.ncbi.nlm.nih.gov/pmc) within 12 months of publication. Subsequent executive action requires open access provisions for all research supported by federal agencies with over $100 million in R&D spending (see www.whitehouse.gov/blog/2013/02/22/expanding-public-access-results-federally-funded-research). Proposed legislation could codify such requirements in law, but as of this writing, no legislation has been enacted. Open access to taxpayer-funded research will be mentioned in several later chapters, such as those on health, education, and scientific information.

Permanent Public Access to Government Information

The formats of government information have transitioned quickly in recent years. The print era evolved to the Web era; then HTML and PDF documents became blogs and wikis, which became videos, which became ever-evolving websites including social media aspects. Modern government documents may be in flux, each one changing continuously, with countless revisions and versions, making identifying a government document or a single distinct version of a government document—much less preserving it—increasingly complex. The government information professional can keep up with finding the information in changing formats. But figuring out how to catalog, archive, preserve, and access it in perpetuity is extremely difficult, and much is lost as agencies delete documents—sometimes on purpose but often simply because they lack a plan or mechanism for preservation (Pear, 2008).

GPO and the FDLP have made efforts to adapt. GPO's Federal Digital System (FDsys) strives to address these concerns by collecting and ingesting government information, verifying versions, providing authenticity, and preserving information in perpetually usable formats, an ambitious, if maddeningly difficult, set of tasks (Priebe et al., 2008). Numerous efforts, both private and nonprofit, aim to make at least some progress toward the idea of permanent public digital access, albeit in a limited and uncoordinated way. GPO maintains a Digitization Projects Registry (http://registry.fdlp.gov/), linking to some 100 valuable, but often very specific and somewhat limited, digitization projects. Broader organized projects include longtime open public information advocate Carl Malamud's Public.Resource.Org (http://public.resource.org), which is both an archive and an advocacy effort for open government information and addresses specific genres of government information, such as law, patents and trademarks, court cases and information, and National Technical Information Service and Government Accountability Office reports, although the organization is interested and involved in government information across the board. The Sunlight Foundation (www.sunlight foundation .com), "Making Government Transparent and Accountable," is a similar advocacy organization, as is OpenTheGovernment.org. These are only three of the most wide-ranging nongovernmental organizations aiming to protect access to our public government information.

The Internet Archive (www.archive.org) does mass-scale archiving and contains thousands of government documents. One looking for a known historical government document can frequently locate a copy in this archive. The largest scanning and digitization project (which includes large collections of government documents likely approaching GPO's vision of 2.2 million historical documents) is the Google Books Library Project. This project—of which the mass scanning of in-copyright works led to a multiyear legal battle—has scanned and stored a huge number of government documents. The library partners of the Google project took their copies of the scans from the projects and created the seminal HathiTrust archive. Recognizing the importance and scope of their digitized government materials, HathiTrust has begun a Registry of US Federal Government Documents project, which aims to catalog and point to a comprehensive collection of digitized historical federal government documents, which could easily become the single most significant archive of digitized government documents (www .hathitrust.org/usgovdocs_registry).

As revolutionary as this electronic migration has been for government information, many aspects of depository libraries and services are less changed. Just because federal regulations are freely available does not mean that many people know how to access them and understand what they mean. The same is true for many of the unique types of government information. Understanding these fundamentals of government information leads to exemplary service to citizens and is the goal of this book.

Background: History of Government Information

The unique nature of the United States' representative democracy gave government information an importance unprecedented in the history of information, knowledge, and libraries. To make informed decisions, people needed to know about the actions of their representatives in Congress and their nation. To this end, the United States Constitution contains the first mention of US government information, calling on Congress to keep and publish a journal of its proceedings:

> Each House shall keep a Journal of its Proceedings, and from time to time
> publish the same, excepting such Parts as may in their Judgment require
> Secrecy; and the Yeas and Nays of the Members of either House on any
> question shall, at the Desire of one fifth of those Present, be entered on the
> Journal. (US Const., art.1, sec.5)

This line from the Constitution, however, expresses the opposing forces in play in the early days of government information. While it calls for publication of a record of Congress, it also contains provisions to restrict government information, whether because of a need for secrecy or at the simple desire of a large majority.

Government information expert Charlie Seavey argues that "it seems fairly clear that the framers of the Constitution were very concerned that there be a free and easy flow of information in order to make democracy work" (2005: 42). To support this view, Seavey references not only the Constitution but the *Federalist Papers* and their underlying assumption of the need for an informed citizenry with access to government information. Seavey notes a Daniel Webster speech of 1825 in which Webster, discussing this informed citizenry, declares that "under the influence of this rapidly increasing knowledge, the people have begun, in all forms of government, to think, and to reason, on affairs of state . . . Regarding government as an institution for the public good, they demand a knowledge of its operations, and a participation in its exercise" (43).

President James Madison issued the most famous call for access to government information, writing in an August 4, 1822, letter to W. T. Barry:

> A popular Government, without popular information, or the means of
> acquiring it, is but a Prologue to a Farce or a Tragedy; or perhaps both.
> Knowledge will forever govern ignorance: And a people who mean to be
> their own Governors, must arm themselves with the power which knowl-
> edge gives. (Madison, 1822: 103)

This may be true, but a government that *did* little may be expected to have *produced* little government information: John Walters argues that for many decades after the nation's founding, the US federal government did not do much and produced a corresponding scarcity of official government information. Discussing the relative dearth of federal government, he writes,

> In its first 100 years, American political scientists revered a form of govern-
> ment Thomas Carlyle derisively described as "anarchy plus a street constable"
> . . . in accordance with these Jeffersonian tenets, the US government
> governed very little for much of the nineteenth century. Citizens generally
> demonstrated a corresponding indifference to politics. (Walters, 2002: 2–3)

As to the government information that did exist, its publishing was largely left to newspapers, which did not necessarily do a very accurate job. Walters quotes Alexis de

Tocqueville, who says that "the proceedings of American society leave fewer traces than do events in a private family. Nothing is written" (2002: 4). Indeed, Quinn notes that the "the idea of public information was a radical concept at the time of the American Revolution" (2003: 283). What the early leaders and political scientists thought about the nature of government information is subject to debate. What is not as open to debate was the relative lack of attention paid to accuracy, quality, or longevity when it came to actually printing government information.

Still, the idea of access to government information did exist and continued to evolve. Building on the mention in the Constitution, federal laws passed in 1795 (1 Stat. 443) and 1813 (Statute II, 13th Congress) further addressed distributing laws and printing government information for the benefit of the citizenry. The 1813 resolution (Statute II, 13th Congress) called for the printing of 200 extra copies of the journals, and sending a copy to each state legislature, college, and historical society. While this still constituted a small volume of printing—and, as Quinn notes, the quality of this outsourced printing was often poor (2003: 285)—the idea of printing extra copies of government documents and distributing them around the nation is a seminal one in the history of government information, hinting at fulfilling Madison's edict and inspiring the mature depository library system, an idea to which we'll return shortly.

During these early decades of the nation there was still a relatively small output of material to be printed. Beyond what appeared in newspapers, the output of the executive branch, scarce as it was, was often in the form of reports to Congress, and such material was published in a large catchall series called the United States *Congressional Serial Set*. Comprising a mix of congressional publications, executive agency reports, and messages and communications from the president, the *Serial Set* was the primary vehicle for all government information. Taken as a whole, it remains the single largest government publication and will occasionally be referred to later in this book.

The poor and inconsistent quality of government printing was addressed by the creation of the Government Printing Office (GPO) in 1860 (through the Joint Resolution in Relation to the Public Printing, 12 Stat. 117), which aimed to remove competing private printers from government publishing and bring such printing under the umbrella of the government itself. This act also marked the beginning of the printing of executive branch publications as separate, freestanding reports, although for another 40-plus years, they were also often printed as congressional documents in the *Serial Set*.

The years following saw growth in both government itself and government publications, driven largely by government science (specifically the study of agriculture, water, and geology, inspired by the Louisiana Purchase and lands on the frontier, beginning with the work of Lewis and Clark) and by slowly evolving ideas favoring a more active government role in the quality of life (Walters, 2002: 5–13). The federal government was starting to do more, publish more, and pay more attention to the quality of the publishing process.

Acts in the 1850s (11 Stat. 253, 11 Stat. 368, 11 Stat. 379) further advanced the idea of distributing these government documents via the central printing of extra copies and distributing those copies throughout the nation in what was the official creation of depository libraries. The 1813 act had called for copies to be sent to colleges, historical societies, and states. But now, each representative and senator was permitted to designate official depository libraries in his district. These libraries would then receive, at no cost, one of these extra copies of each government document that GPO printed. Depository libraries were spread across the lands of the governed, and they remain to this day.

In 1895, the General Printing Act advanced the idea of government publications much further: it compiled and updated all of these previous laws regarding the printing and distribution of government documents, streamlined federal printing and publishing, moved the FDLP from the Department of the Interior to the GPO, and mandated free public access in depository libraries (28 Stat. 601). The act also called for the creation of an ongoing bibliographic catalog of government documents (which became the *Monthly Catalog of United States Government Publications*). For the seeker of government documents, this act could scarcely be more important. It lay the foundation for 20th-century government information. In fact, the work of a depository library went essentially unchanged from the passage of this act in 1895 until the 1970s (Kessler, 1996: 371).

But it was another factor that truly led to the maturity of government information: Franklin Roosevelt and the New Deal. As Lee Shiflett explains, "the actual evolution of the GPO . . . is largely a product of the expansion of the executive department during the Great Depression and the response of the Roosevelt administration to the social problems that came to be considered in the domain of the federal government" (1982: 118–119). The federal government expanded quickly, and with it the quantity of government publications. As the quantity rose, so did the number of depository libraries. Issues remained, however. Sears (2008) discusses this period, describing how depository library designations did not change with geographic shifts in population (and congressional districts), how depository designations were sometimes political, and how some depositories were ill-equipped to either house or provide public service to their collections of government documents. The Depository Library Act of 1962 (76 Stat. 352) addressed these issues. It formally ingrained requirements for public service at depository libraries, and allowed more depository libraries to be designated, which quickly doubled their number from under 600 to 1,200 and truly leading to the modern era of government information and the depository library. Perhaps the most thorough and critical history of government publications is *U.S. Government Publication: Ideological Development and Institutional Politics from the Founding until 1970* (Walters, 2005).

Depository Libraries and 20th-Century Government Information before the Web

The expansion of government information continued for decades, only slowing some in the Carter and Reagan eras, which saw first the Paperwork Reduction Act of 1980 and then Reagan's decree to limit spending on information that did not truly serve the public interest (Richardson, 1982). Formats began to evolve as well, with the first government documents on microform shipping in 1977, the first CD-ROMs coming in the 1980s, and the first information served via the Web in the 1990s.

Depository libraries and services shared many characteristics in this mature period leading up to the Web era. Since the aforementioned Depository Library Act of 1962, federal depository libraries have come in two types: regionals and selectives. Of the 1,200 to 1,400 libraries that have been depositories in this modern era, some 50 of them are designated as regional depository libraries. These regionals have greater responsibilities: they serve selectives in their regions, providing interlibrary loan, reference, and support for government publication collection development. While regionals are required to receive all available government documents and to keep them forever, selectives are permitted to select particular classes of government documents to serve the educational and research interests of their primary clientele, and, after a period of time, are allowed to donate older government documents to other depositories, or to discard them, under the direction of their regional.

Selectives choose these classes of government documents for acquisition by working from the *List of Classes*. The *List of Classes* is a listing of over 10,000 categories (called classes) of government documents, and is available from the suite of tools available on the FDLP Desktop (www.fdlp.gov), the administrative home on the Web for the FDLP. A class may be a particular publication, a particular series, or a genre of publication within an agency. An official *List of Essential Titles* are recommended by the FDLP to be selected by all depository libraries and cover many popular and core topics, including laws and regulations; beyond that, a selective chooses some hundreds or thousands of these classes to best serve its local clientele. With so much government information freely online, these classes have been rendered less relevant, although they can still reflect a selective's area of expertise, and the class choices may still form the basis of bibliographic records (even for born-digital government publications that a library may choose to reflect in its local catalog(s)).

Depository libraries (whether regional or selective) do not, however, hold all federal government information that exists. As noted above, they hold largely what GPO has produced via its printing operations. It's no secret that historically a large number of executive agency publications were not printed by GPO and were not funneled through GPO. These so-called fugitive documents have often been collected by depository libraries, but only as a result of focused efforts to contact and procure copies directly from the issuing agencies. Walters (1996) offers a compelling review of the political tensions involved with the legislative branch's GPO overseeing functions of the executive branch (Congress's Joint Committee on Printing oversees GPO and federal printing), the result of which was sometimes executive agencies ignoring GPO and making their own arrangements to print documents. Nonetheless, GPO has a long history of working hard to ensure that important publications are part of the depository library program.

Note that basic records of government are not published or printed as government documents. Government information, in the context of both this book and the work of a librarian, is primarily focused of published government documents and information. Various records, correspondence, and more ephemeral items generated in the course of the government's business but not published and not intended for public usage may be found instead in the National Archives (covered in chapter 18). Further, some scientific and technical reports are not free of copyright and have not been distributed to depository libraries for various reasons (scientific reports will be covered in chapter 13). The chart in figure 1.3 demonstrates some of the key differences between GPO, NARA, and the Library of Congress (LC).

Meanwhile, as librarians built their government documents collections, service remained at the forefront. Depository libraries answered a myriad of questions and inquiries using the government documents in their collections. It is excellent service to these collections and their users that forms the basis of the remainder of the chapters in this book.

	GPO	NARA	LC
Purpose of Content Managed	"Keeping America Informed"—current and future access to all federal public documents.	Preserving essential evidence that documents the rights of American citizens, the actions of Federal officials, and the national experience.	Acts as the U.S. national library, and supports the information needs of the Congress.
Access	"Free public access" to FDLP content required by law	Limited public access permitted if conditions are met	Limited public access permitted if conditions are met
Time to Availability	Hours to days	Years (depends on records schedule)	Days to years
Cataloging/ Finding Aids	Cataloging and indexing required by law; done at the piece level	Finding aids generally at the collection level	Cataloging performed to manage very large collections; generally done at the piece level
Statutory View (digital products)	Specific mandate to manage digital content, create "directories," and manage a "storage facility" (44 USC 4101)	Digital content responsibility derived from definition of Federal records (44 USC Chap 29; 3301)	Appropriations and legislative oversight for digital projects (e.g., NDIIPP)
Format(s) of Content Managed (current state)	Tangible, including print, microfilm, CDs, and maps	Print, digital, image, sound, and manuscript	Print, digital, image, sound, and manuscript
Scope of Content Managed	Published information (i.e., public documents) of all three branches of the U.S. federal government.	Federal records and other historical materials relating to the U.S. national experience.	Collections are universal in scope, and include copyrighted material deposited by U.S. publishing firms.
Life-Cycle Stages of Content Managed	Assists agencies with content creation. Publishes final products, dissemination, cataloging, and preservation for permanent public access.	Manages preliminary records and final products, creates finding aids, and preservation.	Manages final products and rare objects, cataloging, and preservation.

FIGURE 1.3
Comparison of GPO, NARA, and LC. *Source: Government Printing Office*

State Depository Libraries and International Government Information

State governments, meanwhile, generally had and continue to have government documents depository programs bearing a resemblance to the federal program, although they have been less likely to have the concept of selecting certain classes (that is, a depository for a state typically receives all available publications for that state), and their publications and information may not be free of copyright. While states produce much less material than the federal government, they also usually lack quite so robust a system for distributing and managing state government documents.

These state depository programs feature a lot of variety. Early in their histories, a few states began systems of collecting government information, usually housed in libraries, universities, or museums. Most states, however, have state depository programs that date from the mid- to late-20th century. Smith et al. (2003) provide a state-by-state summary of documents programs.

Documents and information policies of foreign nations are much more varied. While some countries have government information distribution bearing some resemblance to the United States', most nations do not have a tradition of government information or its distribution. Some international organizations, such as the United Nations and the European Union, do have well-established depository systems. Morrison and Mann (2004) summarize programs and information from both foreign countries and international organizations.

Classification of Government Documents

Federal government documents in physical formats use a unique classification system called the Superintendent of Documents (SuDoc) system—indeed, this classification system also applies to much of web-based government information, as SuDoc is a useful classification tool beyond simple shelving arrangements. Like the call numbers derived from the Dewey Decimal and LC Classification Systems, SuDocs numbers are used to arranged items on shelves. Unlike Dewey and LC, whose classes are organized on the basis of subject, SuDocs classes are organized on the basis of issuing agency, subagency, and publication type. The system was developed in the late 19th century by Adelaide Hasse, a pioneering and strong-willed librarian who is a bit of a folk hero in government documents circles.

SuDoc Number Example
Health, United States, 2005
SuDoc HE 20.7042/6: 2005

HE: Department of Health and Human Services

HE 20: Centers for Disease Control

HE 20.7042/6: *Health, United States*

HE 20.7042/6: 2005: *Health, United States*, 2005

SuDoc numbers are devised and assigned by GPO. Some libraries classify and integrate their documents into their regular collections using LC or Dewey, but the SuDoc system is used in most depository libraries and in many standard bibliographies, such as the *Catalog of United States Government Publications.* Most states and some intergovernmental entities (notably the United Nations) and foreign governments also use their own classification systems.

Government Information in the Web Era

Government information quickly took advantage of the Internet era. For quite some time, GPO, at the urging of Congress, had been migrating a few items to electronic formats, usually on floppy disks. This continued through early online access projects such as the Federal Bulletin Board, which was a varied collection of selected government document files available via early Internet protocols such as WAIS, Telnet, and Gopher. But it was the wide adoption of the World Wide Web that led to the significant, profound, and lasting shift to electronic dissemination. Congress—in a visionary or perhaps luckily timed action—passed *The Government Printing Office Electronic Information Access Enhancement Act of 1993* (107 Stat. 112, the GPO Access Act) in January of 1993, mandating that GPO create an electronic public access system to important government publications such as the *Federal Register* and the *Congressional Record.* Just three months later, the first graphical web browser Mosaic was released, eventually leading to the explosion of the Web. The timing, if not the content itself, rendered the GPO Access Act the real kickoff of the era of widespread online government information for the public, as it created the GPO Access website, which included congressional, legal, regulatory, and other government documents. Soon thereafter, Congress (via its THOMAS website, in 1994) and executive agencies, such as early adopters the BLS and Bureau of the Census, led the rapid shift away from government documents printed and distributed via GPO, to agencies transforming and posting their government information directly on the Web. As Aldrich et al. wrote in 2000, "Strongly entrenched in print on paper since its origins in the 1890s, the FDLP has undergone a remarkably swift transition toward web-based information delivery, particularly after the launch of GPO Access in 1994" (274).

The transition has led to a situation where nearly all current federal government information is born digital and available online directly from the agencies. The process of this digital birth varies by agency, and sometimes resembles processes for creating and sharing earlier printed publications (e.g., producing PDF documents). Often, however, the Web era is a more decentralized information dissemination environment characterized by little central control (i.e., from Congress or the president) and inconsistent dissemination policies: one agency may have dozens of offices and individuals posting information from the agency with relatively little oversight, while other agencies have more rigid procedures for controlling website content (Mahler and Regan, 2007). Further, the public's discovery of government information takes place predominantly via popular search engines (e.g., Google) rather than via traditional government documents index and discovery tools (Shuler et al., 2010).

As Aldrich asserts, this fast, dramatic shift from a largely tangible paper collection to a ubiquitous web of government information has had many effects. Formerly distinct documents collections and services began to be a part of every librarian's realm, and the number of paper documents distributed to depository libraries plummeted. As government information moved rapidly and comprehensively online, the collections aspects of selectives and regionals began to blur in many ways. With the abundance of information online, it wasn't just that any library was now effectively a depository library in terms of its collection—any citizen held a depository library on his or her computer or mobile device. Access did not and does not equate to success, however, and expert knowledge of the many intricacies and nuances of government information remains as vital as ever.

GPO and the FDLP, which formerly spent much time in printing, distribution, and bibliographic control of government documents, have increasingly attempted to focus on service, preservation, and permanent public access, tasks made more difficult by the shifting distribution channels and formats of government information, as well as the concurrent political realities of a government responding to issues under the broad realm of security. And GPO's increasing emphasis in managing digital information led to a 2014 name change to the Government Publishing Office (P.L. 113-235 § 1301, 128 Stat. 2130, Dec. 16, 2014).

Sources Mentioned in This Chapter

Sources mentioned in this section do not duplicate the references that follow.

Famous Reports

9/11 Commission Report: The Official Report of the 9/11 Commission, http://purl.access.gpo.gov/GPO/
   LPS51934, SuDoc:Y3.2:T27/2/FINAL.
Dictionary of American Naval Fighting Ships. SuDoc: D 207.10:1/pt.A/991-.
Munson Report (Japanese on the West Coast) found in Joint Committee on Investigation of Pearl Harbor
   Attack. 1946. *Pearl Harbor Attack* pt 6, pp. 2682–2696, SuDoc:Y4.P31:P31/pt.6.
Referral from Independent Counsel Kenneth W. Starr in conformity with the requirements of Title 28, United States
   Code, section 595(c): communication from Kenneth W. Starr, independent counsel, transmitting a referral to the
   United States House of Representatives filed in conformity with the requirements of Title 28, United States
   Code, section 595(c), http://purl.access.gpo.gov/GPO/LPS1737, SuDoc:Y 1.1/7:105–310.
Report of the Senate Select Committee on Intelligence Committee Study of the Central Intelligence Agency's Deten-
   tion and Interrogation Program, www.intelligence.senate.gov/press/committee-releases-study-cias
   -detention-and-interrogation-program.
Roswell Report: Case Closed, SuDoc: D 301.2:R 73.
Thurman L. Munson, Cessna Citation 501, N15NY, near Canton, Ohio, August 2, 1979.
US Airways flight 1549 accident: hearing before the Subcommittee on Aviation of the Committee on Transportation
   and Infrastructure, House of Representatives, One Hundred Eleventh Congress, first session, February 24, 2009,
   http://purl.access.gpo.gov/GPO/FDLP455, SuDoc:Y 4.T 68/2:111–10.

War of the Rebellion (officially known as *The War of the Rebellion: A Compilation of the Official Records of the Union and Confederate Armies*) printed in the US *Congressional Serial Set* over some 20 years and available online in several locations.

Warren Commission report (officially known as the *Report of the President's Commission on the Assassination of President John F. Kennedy*), http://catalog.hathitrust.org/Record/000035711, SuDoc: Pr 36.8:K 38/R 29/report.

World War II–era government posters, www.library.northwestern.edu/govinfo/collections/wwii-posters/index.html.

GPO Sites

FDLP Desktop, www.fdlp.gov.

FDsys, www.gpo.gov/fdsys/.

List of Classes, http://purl.access.gpo.gov/GPO/LPS89650.

List of Essential Titles (*Essential Titles for Public Use in Paper or Other Tangible Format*), www.fdlp.gov/requirements-guidance-2/collections-and-databases/1443-essential-titles.

Monthly Catalog of United States Government Publications (1976–), http://catalog.gpo.gov.

Registry of US Government Publication Digitization Projects, http://registry.fdlp.gov.

SuDoc Classification System explanation, www.fdlp.gov/catalogingandclassification/cataloging-articles/1791-sudocs-classification.

Legislation (Chronological Order)

US Constitution, Art. 1, Sec. 5.

Promulgation of the Laws of the United States, 1 Stat. 443 Ch. 50 (1795).

Resolution for the Printing and Distribution of an Additional Number of the Journals of Congress, and of the Documents Published under Their Order, 3 Stat. 140 (1813).

Distribution of Public Documents, 11 Stat. 253 (1857).

Distribution of Certain Public Documents, 11 Stat. 368 (1858).

Keeping and Distribution of Public Documents, 11 Stat. 379 (1859).

Resolution in Relation to the Public Printing, 12 Stat. 117 (1860).

General Printing Act, 28 Stat. 601 (1895).

Depository Library Act of 1962, P.L. 87-579, 76 Stat. 352 (1962).

Freedom of Information Act (FOIA), P.L. 89-487, 80 Stat. 250 (1966).

Paperwork Reduction Act of 1980, P.L. 96-511, 94 Stat. 2812 (1980).

The Government Printing Office Electronic Information Access Enhancement Act of 1993, also known as the GPO Access Act, P.L. 103-40, 107 Stat. 112 (1993).

Consolidated and Further Continuing Appropriations Act, 2015, P.L. 113-235, 128 Stat. 2130 (2014).

Other

Alliance for Taxpayer Access, www.taxpayeraccess.org.

Committee on Institutional Cooperation (CIC), www.cic.net/home/projects/Library/BookSearch/GovDocs.aspx.

Congressional Record, http://purl.access.gpo.gov/GPO/LPS1671; SuDoc: X 1.1/A.

Federal Register, http://purl.access.gpo.gov/GPO/LPS1756, SuDoc: AE 2.106 (online), AE 2.7, or GS4.107.

Google Books Library Project, http://books.google.com.

HathiTrust Digital Library, www.hathitrust.org.

The Internet Archive, www.archive.org.

Open Government Initiative, www.whitehouse.gov/Open.

OpenTheGovernment.org, www.openthegovernment.org.

Public.Resource.Org, http://public.resource.org.

PubMed Central, www.ncbi.nlm.nih.gov/pmc.

Scholarly Publishing and Academic Resources Coalition (SPARC), www.sparc.arl.org.

The Sunlight Foundation, www.sunlightfoundation.com.

US *Congressional Serial Set,* http://purl.access.gpo.gov/GPO/LPS839, final bound version SuDoc:Y 1.1/2.

References

"Abortion and Breast Cancer." 2003. Editorial. *New York Times,* January 6. www.nytimes.com/2003/01/06/opinion/abortion-and-breast-cancer.html.

Aldrich, Duncan, Gary Cornwell, and Daniel Barkley. 2000. "Changing Partnerships? Government Documents Departments at the Turn of the Millennium." *Government Information Quarterly* 17, no. 3: 273–290.

Beck, Clare. 2006. *The New Woman as Librarian: The Career of Adelaide Hasse.* Lanham, MD: Scarecrow Press.

Fowler, Rhonda E. 2007. "I've Got a Secret: Government Information Availability and Secrecy." *DttP: Documents to the People* 35, no. 2: 18–23.

Gordon, Bennett. 2007. "For Their Eyes Only." *Utne Reader,* January/February. www.utne.com/2007–01–01/ForTheirEyesOnly.aspx.

Government Printing Office. 2004. *A Strategic Vision for the 21st Century.* Washington, DC: Government Printing Office.

Hernon, Edward. 2004. "A Post-September 11th Balancing Act: Public Access to U.S. Government Information Versus Protection of Sensitive Data." *Journal of Government Information* 30, no. 1: 42–65.

Hogenboom, Karen. 2008. "Lessons Learned about Access to Government Information after World War II Can Be Applied after September 11." *Government Information Quarterly* 25, no. 1: 90–103.

Jaeger, Paul T. 2007. "Information Policy, Information Access, and Democratic Participation: The National and International Implications of the Bush Administration's Information Politics." *Government Information Quarterly* 24, no. 4: 840–859.

Kessler, Ridley. 1996. "A Brief History of the Federal Depository Library Program: A Personal Perspective." *Journal of Government Information* 23, no. 4: 369–380.

Madison, James. 1910. *The Writings of James Madison, Volume IX, 1819–1836.* Edited by Gaillard Hunt. New York: G. P. Putnam's Sons.

Mahler, Julianne, and Priscilla Regan. 2007. "Crafting the Message: Controlling Content on Agency Web Sites." *Government Information Quarterly* 24, no. 3: 505–521.

McDermott, Patrice. 2007. "Current Government Information Policy and Secrecy." *DttP: Documents to the People* 35, no. 2: 24–29.

Morrison, Andrea M., and Barbara J. Mann. 2004. *International Government Information and Country Information: A Subject Guide.* Westport, CT: Greenwood Press.

Pear, Robert. 2008. "In Digital Age, Federal Files Blip into Oblivion." *New York Times,* September 13. www.nytimes.com/2008/09/13/us/13records .html.

Priebe, Ted, Amy Welch, and Marian MacGilvray. 2008. "The U.S. Government Printing Office's Initiatives for the Federal Depository Library Program to Set the Stage for the 21st Century." *Government Information Quarterly* 25, no. 1: 48–56.

Quinn, Aimee. 2003. "Keeping the Citizenry Informed: Early Congressional Printing and 21st Century Information Policy." *Government Information Quarterly* 20, no. 3: 281–293.

Revkin, Andrew, with Katharine Seelye. 2003. "Report by the E.P.A. Leaves Out Data on Climate Change." *New York Times,* June 19. www.nytimes.com/2003/06/19/politics/19CLIM.html.

Richardson, John. 1982. "The United States Government as Publisher Since the Roosevelt Administration." *Library Research* 4: 211–233.

Sears, Suzanne. 2008. "Connecting Constituents to Government Information: 150 Years of Congressionally Designated Libraries." *DttP: Documents to the People* 36, no. 3: 16–19.

Seavey, Charles. 2005. "Musings on the Past and Future of Government Information." *American Libraries* 36, no. 7: 42–44.

Shiflett, Orvin Lee. 1982. "The Government as Publisher: An Historical Review." *Library Research* 4: 115–135.

Shuler, John, Paul Jaeger, and John Bertot. 2010. "Implications of Harmonizing the Future of the Federal Depository Library Program within e-Government Principles and Policies." *Government Information Quarterly* 27, no. 1: 9–16.

Smith, Lori L., Daniel C. Barkley, Daniel D. Cornwall, Eric W. Johnson, and J. Louise Malcomb. 2003. *Tapping State Government Information Sources.* Westport, CT: Greenwood Press.

Walters, John Spencer. 1996. "The Presuperhighway Politics of U.S. Government Printing and Publishing, 1917–1960." *Journal of Government Information* 23, no. 2: 93–121.

Walters, John Spencer. 2002. "The Ideological Development of U.S. Government Publication, 1820–1920: From Jefferson to Croly." *Journal of Government Information* 29, no. 1: 1–15.

Walters, John Spencer. 2005. *U.S. Government Publication: Ideological Development and Institutional Politics from the Founding to 1970.* Lanham, MD: Scarecrow Press.

CHAPTER 2

How to Think Like a Government Documents Librarian

ANDREA SEVETSON

Introduction

Government information questions can be among the most challenging and rewarding queries that come to a librarian. Requests for infant mortality rates for South American countries or hearings from congressional committees come in as frequently as more involved questions like "I need census data from 1960 to 2010 with education information for my census tract" or "I need data comparing the economic recovery of the latest recession with that of the Great Depression." A patron may read about a recently released (and unsourced) US Census Bureau publication in the morning's paper or on a favorite website, or need to see FedBizOpps or the *Federal Register* to learn about a grant or business opportunity. Questions may require data or statistics from or about your city or county, the United States, or other countries. There may be a congressional hearing on torture, a proposed policy on school nutrition, or a controversial nomination for the Supreme Court in the news, and the patron wants to see who testified and what was said. Questions come from all directions and can reflect all kinds of needs, from a school project or term paper to community members researching data about the school age population for an upcoming bond measure.

Requests may not always make sense at the outset, but each represents a need. Developing your sense of the kinds of questions that get asked at your library will set you on a path of lifelong learning and success in your career.

Reference Interview Strategies

Documents librarians often think about where the information originated as a starting point for answering questions. This is partly because the Superintendent of Documents

(SuDocs) classification system uses agencies as the basis for its organization (both for print and for online publications and databases), but also because many finding tools created specifically for government information—indexes, abstracts, and publication lists—classify the information in that way. More government organizations than just the United States use an agency classification scheme to organize publications—different state governments and international organizations (IGOs) such as the United Nations and the European Union also use the authoring agency of the document to catalog publications. Because of this reliance on authoring agency for organization, librarians must consider where the document originated, and strategies for talking to library users revolve around this, as well. (See sidebar for more information on classification systems). Documents librarians often think of the authoring agency almost as a subject classification with environmental information coming from the Environmental Protection Agency (EPA), business information from the Department of Commerce, and international affairs information coming from the State Department, to name a few.

If the patron has asked a question and a government source springs to mind, generally only a bit of follow-up is needed to focus the question. For example, in response to the request for infant mortality rates for South American countries, the question "Do you need recent infant mortality rates or rates for a specific time period?" helps to narrow the scope of the question and decide whether to head for materials about or from those countries, or whether tables with international comparisons would suffice.

For experienced and novice users of government information, questions for which the right source doesn't come easily to mind can be more difficult. One old reference saw states that "the patron doesn't know what he wants, and if he did, he wouldn't tell you." While this may sometimes be true, often the patron knows more than he or she lets on initially. In fact, librarians have been known to think of patrons' initial questions as a hook because it seems as if some patrons believe that if they can interest you in their research, they'll get better assistance—and they may be right.

For the interactions where we find ourselves floundering, it's good to have a few stock questions to elicit additional information from the questioner. Consider asking about information already in hand (What information do you already have?) to see if there are any sources you might go back to for additional information. Another question (Who would be interested in producing this information?) goes to the mandate of the agency. Often researchers have some background or have done some research that can be helpful in directing you

The Government Documents Round Table (GODORT) Cataloging Committee hosts three toolboxes for Processing and Cataloging, one each for federal, international, and state and local documents. Each toolbox provides links to materials that are useful for more than just cataloging, including processing tools, lists of government organizations and depository libraries, megapages, e-mail discussion lists, library catalogs and agency publication lists.

In addition each contains items specific to the area of government. The *federal toolbox* has links to information on GPO item selection and classification information, processing, cataloging, and collections as well as information for verifying PURLs and Internet resources (including web search tools). The *international toolbox* includes map information and place names and IGO classification schemes. The *state and local toolbox* contains a list of state libraries, state depository systems, and the electronic sources for state publication lists.

to additional resources. When you know nothing about the request, a good strategy is to ask the patron to talk about his or her research. Good follow-ups include questions about sources already checked as well as the purpose of the research (Is it a short paper, a doctoral dissertation, or information for filing a business plan?). Each of these questions can draw out surprisingly useful information that will help steer you to the correct source. In addition, if you still know very little about the question, listening to the answers might give you a bit more time to think about how to proceed or to consult a knowledgeable colleague.

Some government information questions will go beyond the resources in your own library and even on the open Web. You'll find it extremely helpful to network (see Other Help: The Network later in this chapter) and to get to know the collection and people strengths of the libraries around you to help connect patrons to the needed material. How long have they been collecting government information? Are they depository libraries for the organization in question? Do they have collection strengths in the subject area under discussion? Are they considered research or subject specialty libraries? Do they have technical reports or patents? What other material do they have that you don't? Knowing the resources around you can help.

Today, most users look online first for information. This brings to light two important points. First, with libraries, Google, and others scanning and placing materials on the Internet, a growing amount of government information is available via the Web. Considering who would be interested in putting that information online can suggest where to look first (and second and third . . .). The second point is that not everything is available online yet, something difficult for many users to believe. Something harder still for librarians to accept is that the information simply may not exist (one of the hardest things for a librarian to do is to give up the search—to realize they have checked all of the likely places and the information isn't there). Having good search strategies can help you know if you've checked the likely sources.

Research Strategies

Different strategies abound for answering government information questions and for managing documents collections. A few to keep in mind include:

Strategy One: Learn Government Structure and Processes

Educate yourself on what the various government agencies do, and use that information to guide your searching. There is a knowledge base that will give you a head start on all of your reference questions. For the US government, that knowledge has its base in the organization of government (remember your civics class on how government works?) and can also be found, in part, in the *U.S. Government Manual*.

The *U.S. Government Manual* gives an outline of each agency and its functions. Information typically includes the following: a list of officials heading major operating units; a statement of the agency's purpose and role in the federal government; a brief history of the agency, including its legislative or executive authority; a description of its programs and activities; and information, addresses, and phone numbers to help users locate detailed information on consumer activities, contracts and grants, employment, publications, and other matters of public interest.

The initial discussion of an agency will tell you its scope of responsibilities. For example, "The Department of Agriculture develops agricultural markets, fights hunger and malnutrition, conserves natural resources, and ensures standards of food quality through safeguards and inspections" (National Archives and Records Administration, 2015: 97).

The agency's mission is followed by the statutory authority: "The Department of Agriculture (USDA) was created by act of May 15, 1862 (7 U.S.C. 2201)." The statutes (laws) that created the agency will have a wealth of additional material about specifics of the mandate and the responsibilities of the agency. For cabinet-level agencies, there is always a phone number, an organization chart, and a URL in the introductory information.

In addition to learning about the agency mandate, learn about government processes and what they are intended to do and how they work, and the publications that are generated. For instance, a bill is not just a bill: it represents part of the legislative process (chapter 3) and may go nowhere, be revised multiple times, or be incorporated into other legislation. There are also processes for rulemaking (chapter 6), environmental impact assessments (chapter 14), censuses and surveys (chapter 16), and more. Being familiar with the processes, which may include the questionnaires, strategies, or public input, will help you be aware of the agencies involved and potential sources for needed information.

Strategy Two: Note Oft-Used Sources

Look on the reference shelves to see the worn and rebound publications. Libraries will often have many of their favorite paper tools at their fingertips, though increasingly, reference collections have moved the older tools to the stacks. Most of the older textbooks will have good overviews of older indexes and finding aids (see texts in sidebar, especially chapter 3 in Boyd and Rips, for information on these classic indexes). Some libraries use these tools more than others, chiefly for budgetary reasons: they haven't cataloged older publications, or they don't have the resources to purchase online equivalents or other sources that might render these obsolete.

The online equivalent of seeing the most-loved print volumes is checking out librarian-created guides to resources. Librarians create lists of resources at almost every institution, so if you need a guide to California legislation or New York legislation, consult a guide from a library in that state. The guides should point you to online resources, as well as libraries with good collections of reference material if you need them (see the Guides section later in this chapter, as well as the GODORT cataloging toolboxes). Comparing lists created in different places will give you a good idea of what your colleagues find valuable.

Strategy Three: Review User Guides and Help

There is almost always a user guide. Some are better than others, but there is usually some help available when you go to a website or open an index. Given that most tools are created to fill a specific need, it can be worthwhile to look at the user information to see what information is provided.

Guides for print material generally include information about the organization of the publication, the abbreviation key, and how to read citations or abstracts. Online user guides should include information about the interface, the information in the website or database, any background needed to understand the material, and how to cite the information included.

A notable fact about government material: sometimes, useful information may not accompany the publication. For example, the questionnaire used for the 1880 census may not be in the census volumes themselves, but printed separately. Be prepared to do some research to find needed information.

Strategy Four: Consult the Statistical Abstract of the United States

Use what is on hand to identify resources and send you in the right direction—be it search engines such as USA.gov, or your library catalog. For statistics, a title that serves as both a reference source and an index to agency information is the *Statistical Abstract of the United States* (a key resource covered in detail in chapter 10 on statistical information). Organized by broad subject, the annually produced 1,400+ statistical tables represent all aspects of American life, and each table provides footnotes so that users can track the information back to the source for more information. For example, in the 2015 edition, table 149, "Personal Health Care Expenditures by Source of Funds: 2000 to 2012," includes the following in the metadata: "Centers for Medicare and Medicaid Services (http://cms.gov/nationalhealthexpenddata)." So if table 149 isn't detailed enough, the user can follow the footnote to go to the source and see if there is other information that will answer the question. (Note: While the Census Bureau produced the *Statistical Abstract* until 2012, in 2013 ProQuest began producing and selling the online version, and Bernan sells the print edition.)

Similar to the *Statistical Abstract* (which includes data from many agencies), other agencies have (or had) annual statistical reports on specific topics: *Agricultural Statistics, Business Statistics, Condition of Education, Highway Statistics, Sourcebook of Criminal Justice Statistics, Uniform Crime Reports* (also known as *Crime in the US*), *Public Land Statistics, Science and Engineering Indicators,* and the *World Military Expenditures and Arms Transfers,* to name a handful. Each title has certain kinds of information that make it valuable and some include information that may serve as an index of additional resources. For example, *Agricultural Statistics* provided international comparisons for production, imports, and exports, while *Uniform Crime Reports* and *Science and Engineering Indicators* have data users simply couldn't find elsewhere. Most of these compendia started much later than the *Statistical*

Abstract (1878), and, while the *Statistical Abstract* continues to this day, some of the other titles have completely changed their presentation as a result of being on the Internet, while others are no longer produced.

In addition to the United States, most states, governments, and international organizations also have (or had) statistical annuals. While many are as well organized and sourced as the *Statistical Abstract of the United States,* some are not as lengthy or do not provide as many links out to other agencies and many are not updated annually. (The *Statistical Abstract of the United States* provides a list of state and foreign statistical annuals in the appendixes if you need assistance identifying these.)

Strategy Five: Read about It

One of the best ways to learn about how governments actually work is to read books about different aspects of government. You may not agree with the political point of view, but getting the insider perspective can give you additional insight into the workings of specific parts of government.

You may choose to read a biography about each president, or about famous government figures like J. Edgar Hoover, or about past controversies and events like Wounded Knee, Watergate, and the Teapot Dome. Glenn Greenwald's *No Place to Hide: Edward Snowden, the NSA, and the U.S. Surveillance State* is a readable overview of the federal government security apparatus; Peggy Noonan, a former speech writer for Presidents Reagan and George H.W. Bush, wrote *What I Saw at the Revolution* that gives insight into the inner workings of the president's cabinet; *The Best and the Brightest* and *All the President's Men* can give insight into the White House of the 1960s and '70s; and *The Brethren* (by Bob Woodward and Scott Armstrong) covers the inner workings of the Supreme Court. There are many more, with the book reviews in the *Washington Post* providing a good resource of what Washington insiders may be reading.

Strategy Six: Consult Government Information Textbooks

Looking at a current or historical textbook for information on government agencies and publishing patterns may be useful, and when working with intergovernmental organizations (IGOs) or state publications, there may be books written that detail publishing patterns, key documents, and legislative or parliamentary processes and the publications.

Many documents librarians have their favorite textbooks at their desks or cataloged as part of the reference collection to ensure quick and easy access. Names like Schmeckebier and Eastin, Morehead, Robinson, and Boyd and Rips are common in discussions among documents librarians, as the actual titles of the texts are somewhat interchangeable.

Older, Treasured Texts

The first and second editions (1931 and 1941) of *United States Government Publications* were written by Anne Morris Boyd, an associate professor of library science at the University of Illinois. For the 1949 third edition, Boyd was joined by Rae Elizabeth Rips of the Detroit Public Library to create a classic text popularly known as Boyd and Rips. This 1949 edition has extensive indexes and is almost encyclopedic in its approach, covering the history, organization, duties, and major publications of each agency.

Government Publications and Their Use had four editions. The 1936 and 1939 editions were written by Laurence F. Schmeckebier, with the 1961 and 1969 editions coauthored by Roy B. Eastin, Superintendent of Documents (1949–53). Schmeckebier was a member of the Brookings Institution's Institute for Government Research and wrote a number of monographs on different government agencies. The Schmeckebier texts are shorter than Boyd and Rips, however, the later editions bring readers into the 1960s and capture changes in the evolving government information environment and the depository library program.

One of Schmeckebier's early works was the seminal *The Statistical Work of the National Government.* Divided into 36 chapters by subject, this 1925 text is the best explanation and listing of federal government statistics up to the 1920s. He goes into detail about the differing methods of data collection and the resulting impact on the statistics.

More recently, Joe Morehead has written *Introduction to United States Government Information Sources.* The first edition was printed in 1975; updates followed in 1978, 1983, 1992, 1996, and 1999. The 1992 edition, coauthored by Mary Fetzer, may be considered an update to the 1949 Boyd and Rips text, as the executive branch publications are covered more extensively than in the other editions. Morehead uses lots of examples of documents but doesn't discuss processes (legislation, rulemaking, etc.) in as much depth as Boyd and Rips.

The three editions (1988, 1993, and 1998) of *Tapping the Government Grapevine,* by Judith Schiek Robinson, are known for their engaging reading and for relative brevity. Robinson is Professor Emeriti at the Graduate School of Education, State University of New York at Buffalo.

In their three editions of *Using Government Information Sources* (1985–1986, 1994, 2001), Sears and Moody approached government information very differently than all of the other texts to date, organizing the material around the most effective kinds of searches: subject searches, agency searches, statistical searches, and special techniques. Jean Sears, now retired, was the head of the Government Documents Department at Miami University Libraries in Oxford, Ohio. Marilyn Moody is currently dean of the University Library and professor at Portland State University.

Strategy Seven: Keep Up-to-Date

Look for news and journal articles that supplement your knowledge of frequently used materials. For instance, when looking for materials on Congress, in addition to chapter 3 of this book, check your local news sources, and the *Washington Post,* or the *New York Times* for discussion of current, topical legislation and how it proceeds through Congress. Good examples will both inform your use of the materials and allow you to create engaging presentations.

With journals, the Internet, and web-based training, it's easier than ever to keep up on issues and to both renew skills and acquire new ones. Online training is a boon for those who don't have the time, or whose libraries don't have the budget to support attendance at conferences or other training events.

One of the cheapest and easiest things to do is join the relevant electronic discussion lists. They can be invaluable for getting the latest information. Open discussion lists such as GOVDOC-L and INTL-DOC are valuable not only for bringing information to you, but also for allowing you to query your colleagues when you get a tough question. Some government agencies or programs—including the Federal Depository Library Program (FDLP)—also have lists to which they post information. GODORT's wiki contains a long list of these!

For those with government information as part of their responsibilities, there are a few more tips for staying in the know. First, check out the professional literature. *DttP: Documents to the People* is the quarterly journal of GODORT of the ALA. If you're not an ALA member, you can subscribe to the journal for $35 per year; however, ALA members can join GODORT for $20 per year and receive *DttP* as a membership benefit. The journal is written for practitioners and has relatively short articles, columns, reviews, and conference wrap-ups.

Government Information Quarterly is written at a more scholarly level and describes itself as "an international journal that examines the intersection of policy, information technology, government, and the public" (Elsevier, 2015). The subscription price, currently $213 per year, is steep; however, the journal's website allows you to view tables of contents for each issue, read abstracts of many articles, and purchase individual articles.

Another journal to subscribe to includes *Government Computer News* (*GCN*), available free in print or online. Articles from *GCN* are often noted in blogs such as Free Government Information (FGI). Several free e-mail newsletters, including the "*GCN* Daily" update, help you to stay on top of the issues.

Web-based training is now offered by professional associations, vendors, and GPO. GPO's FDLP Academy started in 2014 and pulls together online training about the FDLP, Federal Digital System (FDsys), federal agency information, and other information of interest to government information librarians. The North Carolina Library Association Government Resources Section has a very active online training program coordinated by Lynda Kellam: "Help! I'm an Accidental Government Information Librarian" has as its goal "a series of webinars designed to help us all do better reference work by increasing our familiarity with government information resources, and by discovering the best strategies for navigating them." Both the FDLP Academy and the Help! series are recorded for future viewing. In addition, be sure to ask your library vendors about training sessions, or other material, for their products.

Don't forget publications, blogs, and social networking sites from your favorite agencies, which can be an easy way to keep up-to-date, especially if your job is focused in specific areas.

Search Engines

While an Internet search will often bring up the desired results, it may just as easily bring an avalanche of information that doesn't answer the question. Before turning to the Internet, it is important to understand what will and won't show up from a search engine. When you use general search engines, take the time to learn about any advanced search features to help craft a better search, and to learn about the limitations.

Search engines don't always makes these apparent, so a quick search of the literature, as well as guides librarians have written, will be useful.

To obtain results more focused on government entities, there are a few government-specific search tools that help you focus searches. USA.gov, founded on September 22, 2000, and initially called Firstgov.gov, is administered by the Federal Citizen Information Center (part of the General Services Administration—see www.usa.gov/About .shtml) and focuses on searching government information. In addition to the search box, there are links to popular services and, the A to Z list of government agencies, and more. Search engines such as Google and DuckDuckGo allow users to limit results to .gov or .mil domains; GODORT's Federal Toolbox includes a list of other search engines that may be useful.

Many government agencies have databases on their sites, such as FDsys (GPO) and American FactFinder (Census Bureau). FDsys contains bills, laws, and congressional and agency publications on it (FDsys is covered in chapter 3 on congressional publications and chapter 5 on public laws and the *U.S. Code*). American FactFinder, meanwhile, has census information including population statistics for each state, county, and place in the United States (and is covered in detail in chapter 16 on the census). But note that popular search engines may not search into the databases, often known as the deep Web—hence the content of these rich resources can go uncovered unless you are aware of these databases. For example, you will often find census information posted on a city or county website, but it may not provide the needed detail; likewise, you may find a purported bill or a government report located on another site, but will need to check the official database for an authenticated version.

Catalogs and Collections

The *Monthly Catalog of U.S. Government Publications,* or *MoCat,* is the granddaddy of government documents indexes. Starting in 1895, it was organized by SuDocs classification (agency). The quality of the indexing has increased greatly since it began. July 1976 was a watershed time for *MoCat,* marking the date when catalogers at the Government Printing Office (which in 2014 was renamed the Government Publishing Office) started using LC subject headings and the records were accepted by OCLC. Because of the standardization of the catalog records, July 1976 also marks the start of the online version (http://catalog.gpo.gov), called the *Catalog of Government Publications,* or *CGP.* Be aware that *CGP/MoCat* does *not* catalog technical reports, which are indexed elsewhere (discussed in chapter 13, Scientific and Technical Information). While you may find some technical reports in the *CGP,* they would be an incremental percentage of what is available. (For a more in-depth treatment of the *MoCat* and its history and use, see Morehead, pages 89–90, 92–101.)

A vendor, Paratext, offers the Public Documents Masterfile, which includes not only the historical *MoCat,* but a variety of other government documents. OCLC's WorldCat (www.worldcat.org) includes *CGP* as part of the free WorldCat.org database. *CGP* is also available as a separate database in OCLC's fee-based offerings (note: SuDocs numbers may not be part of the WorldCat default display). ProQuest is in the process of updating the content in their online *Monthly Catalog 1895–1976* offering and will be rereleas-

874

P18. SUPPLIES DIVISION

[Act approved June 8, 1872, authorized the establishment of a blank agency for Post-Office Department which afterward became Division of Post-Office Supplies, the work being carried on by a superintendent under control of 1st assistant Postmaster-General.
Placed under supervision of 4th assistant Postmaster-General, Dec. 1, 1905, since when it has been known as Supplies Division.]

Classification
no.

P18.1:	**Annual reports**
(date)	[None issued.]
P18.2:	**General publications**
P84[1]	Postal supplies. List of postal supplies furnished presidential offices, post-office inspectors, and Railway Mail Service by 4th assistant Postmaster-General. July 1, 1909.
P84[2]	Postal supplies. List of postal supplies furnished post-offices of 4th class by 4th assistant Postmaster-General. July 1, 1909.
P18.3:	**Bulletins**
(nos.)	[None issued.]
P18.4:	**Circulars**
(nos.)	[None issued.]

Pr. PRESIDENT OF UNITED STATES
(Apr. 30, 1789–Dec. 31, 1909)

[As complete lists can not be made of all original prints of official papers of the Presidents, references are given below to such compilations of presidential papers as are public documents. The most complete collection is Richardson's Compilation of messages and papers of Presidents, 1789–1897, in 10 volumes (Y4.P93[1]:3[1-10]). This set also appears as a Congressional document of the 53d Congress, serial no. 3265[1-10]. It contains all the presidential papers through Cleveland's 2d administration, ending Mar. 4, 1897. For later administrations these papers are generally accessible in separate form. The 10th volume of Richardson's set includes, besides the index containing "a large number of encyclopedic articles," the papers of President McKinley relating to War with Spain, and many papers of the earlier Presidents which had been omitted from their proper places.

The separate issues of the Presidents' papers from Washington through Madison are listed under Early Congress papers (Z4.1:). The list of Early Congress papers will appear later in separate form.

Annual messages, besides being found in the publications as indicated under the name of each President (Pr1.1:–Pr27.1:), are also found in the Senate and House journals; 1848–92, in Messages and documents (Y8.); 1859–1909, in Abridgment of messages and documents (Y4.P93[1]:2); and in Congressional record and its predecessors as tabulated below, in every case being in that part which contains the proceedings at the opening of each regular session of Congress:

> 1790–1823, in Annals of Congress (X1.–X42.)
> 1824–1836, in Register of debates in Congress (X43.–X71.)
> 1833–1872, in Congressional globe (X72.–X180.)
> 1873–1909, in Congressional record (X181.–X439.)

It may be mentioned here that until the removal of the seat of Government to Washington, the annual messages are referred to as "speeches" because those of George Washington and John Adams were delivered orally before the two legislative branches in general assembly. Thomas Jefferson established the custom, which has ever since been followed, of sending his annual statement in the form of a message.

Executive orders prior to Oct. 1905, were sometimes printed as presidential papers, but were more frequently issued in printed form only by those Departments immediately concerned in their promulgation. Since Oct. 1905, it has been customary for the President to send all Executive orders to the Bureau of Rolls and Library, State Dept., to be printed on foolscap paper for limited distribution on demand.

Inaugural addresses, besides being issued separately, are found in the Senate journals and in the Congressional record.]

FIGURE 2.1
1909 *Checklist* Detail

ing it for sale in the near future. For pre-1976 publications, there is a growing body of libraries that have cataloged their older documents in WorldCat, so WorldCat covers a good portion of historical documents as well.

For those who need listings of older materials, another resource is the *Checklist of United States Public Documents, 1789–1909,* Third Edition Revised and Enlarged, Volume 1, Lists of Congressional and Departmental Publications, better known as the 1909 *Checklist.* While the subject index was never produced, this is a well-worn reference tool for many, listing all congressional and executive branch publications up to 1909. The 1909 *Checklist* is notable because it provides not just the SuDocs classification number for a publication, but also background information on various series (see figure 2.1). A number of scanned copies are available online, including the University of North Texas (UNT Digital Library), which has a searchable and browsable version at http://digital.library.unt.edu/ark:/67531/metadc1029.

Also remember that, up until the early 1900s, many important agency publications were also included in the US *Congressional Serial Set* (see chapters 3 and 9 for a discussion) that was distributed to libraries. The Public Printing and Binding Act (Mar. 1, 1907, P.L. 59-153) changed the distribution to allow certain libraries (for example, the libraries of the House and the Senate, sometimes referred to as posterity libraries) to continue to receive the more complete *Serial Set* with the executive branch materials. As a cost-cutting measure, Public Law (Pub. L. or P.L.) 59-153 changed the rules so that depository libraries received a version of the *Serial Set* that did not include much of that material, since they may have received an agency (or departmental) version of the publication printed outside of the *Serial Set* (Sevetson, 2013). The 1909 *Checklist* notes if materials are included in the *Serial Set.*

While the overlap between the *Serial Set* and the agency publications may have decreased with P.L. 59-153, it is still possible that a library may have two or more copies of the major reports—one in the *Serial Set* and one that was issued separately. Wooster College has a wonderful website, the US *Congressional Serial Set* Finding List, highlighting executive branch material in the *Serial Set.* Both ProQuest and Readex have produced commercial versions of the Serial Set.

The biggest collection of publications across agencies is FDsys (www.fdsys.gov/). The legislation enabling FDsys is discussed in chapter 1. Its initial focus was on providing electronic access to congressional publications, and it later expanded to host publications from the Supreme Court and other, generally smaller, agency websites. GPO Access began in the mid-1990s and, in 2010, content was rebranded as FDsys, the largest cross-agency effort to provide and maintain access to federal government information.

Outside of government, several large scale scanning projects are notable for their wide inclusion of government publications: the HathiTrust (www.hathitrust.org), the Internet Archive (www.archive.org), and the Google Books Library Project (see chapter 1 for more background on each of these projects). Each includes thousands, if not hundreds of thousands, of government documents. For more government-focused digitization projects, look at the GPO Digitization Projects Registry (http://registry.fdlp.gov/).

Commercially Produced Collections

Several vendors have digitized collections of government publications, and offer these collections for sale to libraries. While most of the ProQuest collections were originally released in microfiche with print indexes, ProQuest has created a comprehensive collection (online) of congressional materials including the *Congressional Serial Set, American State Papers,* hearings, committee prints, CRS reports, the *Congressional Record,* and bills and resolutions. In 2014 they released the *Executive Orders and Presidential Proclamations,* and they have a growing collection of documents from the executive branch. The *Executive Branch Documents* collection serves as the index and full text of the materials listed in the 1909 *Checklist.* (This was originally released in microfiche as the *CIS Index to U.S. Executive Branch Documents, 1789–1909,* and there was an add-on module that took the collection to 1932.) Now available online, this collection includes the indexing and full text for approximately 400,000 documents included up through 1932, and ProQuest is adding additional years to this collection.

Another collection found in many libraries is the Readex non-depository collection. For many decades thousands of titles per year were identified by GPO and listed in the *MoCat* but not actually distributed to libraries. (Beginning in the 1950s, GPO identified the items sent to depository libraries by inserting a "bullet mark" or black dot in the bibliographic entry.) Starting in 1953, Readex began harvesting these non-depository documents, reproducing them in microform, and selling them to interested libraries. This collection was of particular use to regionals and other libraries wanting to create comprehensive collections of government documents, helping them complement their depository collections. Readex began selling depository materials this same way (in a microfiche set). Over the years, GPO steadily included more government publications in its depository distribution, and Readex ceased the non-depository collection in 2008. Readex online collections include the *Serial Set* and *American State Papers* and the more recent *Joint Publications Research Service (JPRS) Reports, 1957–1995,* and the *Foreign Broadcast Information Service (FBIS) Daily Reports, 1941–1996* but do not include full-text or scanned versions of the non-depository documents.

The legal publisher HeinOnline also offers several series including *Congressional Record* bound volumes, US Reports, US Treaties, the *Federal Register* and the *Code of Federal Regulations,* and more.

Agency Websites and Publication Lists

Many agencies have issued their own publication catalogs that are useful in identifying older publications (search the *CGP* using the phrase "list of publications" for a sampling). These may have been published annually, or compiled to cover longer time periods. Research libraries and regional depository libraries will often have these in their collections. Though they are used less and less, they are still of value to verify the existence of a document. Note: a list of publications from, for example, the US Department of Commerce will not usually include all of the subagencies, so you may want to start at the bottom of the organization chart, rather than at the top.

Almost all federal agencies have large and well-developed websites. To find the URL for an agency or subagency, USA.gov (which also provides lines to federal and state agencies by agency name or government structure) or your favorite search engine should quickly locate it.

Tips for Navigating Agency Websites

Because of their sheer size, some agency websites can be confusing. To get started, here are a few tips. Look for:

- **A site map.** This will provide a good overview of information available at the site.
- **An index.** This can be much more effective than searching the site unless you know exactly what you are looking for.
- **Topic or issue pages.** Similar to an index, fact sheets and other introductory material are sometimes grouped under headings such as Information for Citizens or Just for Teens. Many sites include an Education section with information designed to educate the general public at various levels, including primary and secondary school students, and college undergraduates.
- **About pages**. To provide an overview of the agency's mission.
- **A Publications or Library menu.** Many agencies have an extensive array of publications online. These may be centrally located or divided by topic.
- **An Ask Us or Contact Us link.** Most agencies are eager to provide information about their services.

Depository Library Programs

Before the Internet there was ... paper. Lots of paper. Libraries received these paper publications, along with microfiche and CD/DVDs and a score of other formats, and endeavored to make the material available. These are the government publications that arrive through various acquisitions channels including gifts, exchanges, or purchases or other means. Governments at all levels want to get their publications to people and, therefore, have arrangements to deposit their publications with libraries, where the documents are freely available to the public at large. Depository programs exist for US states, the federal government, foreign governments, and many international organizations (the United Nations, the European Union, and more). The US version is the FDLP (see sidebar earlier in this chapter for the GODORT cataloging toolbox discussion of each of these lists).

The FDLP provides a way to distribute federal government publications to the public through libraries. While the law has been amended many times (see chapter 1 for an overview), currently some 1,200 state, academic, public, law, agency, and other types of libraries participate. Since the passage of P.L. 87-579 on August 9, 1962, the program has been divided into selective and regional libraries. Selective libraries can select items they would like from the program, and regional libraries must take, and keep, a copy of everything. Selective depository libraries may withdraw publications using guidelines set up by their regionals. The FDLP home page (www.fdlp.gov) provides information on the program from initial deposit to deselection of materials. This site should be consulted (frequently!) by those with responsibility for depository library operations. Regional libraries are also great resources for new librarians as they have programmatic responsibility for libraries in their region. Librarians with responsibilities for (US) depository collections should make it a point to find out who these folks are and consult as necessary.

Few other depository library organizations provide the same descriptive information about their programs as does the FDLP about the US depository program. Often headquarters libraries serve as the program managers for state and international organization depository programs. For example, the UN headquarters library, the Dag Hammarskjöld, is the program manager for the United Nations Depository Program, and the California State Library manages the California depository library program. These libraries often provide a high level of assistance for reference inquiries as well as operational questions related to the depository program.

Other Help

In addition to the resources already listed here, there are several other ways to ask for and receive help with reference or operational questions.

Guides

The largest repository of library guides is Springshare's LibGuides. As of March 2015, Libguides.com hosted upwards of 436,000 guides from more than 4,800 libraries around the world. Guides are searchable by content and author; best of all—they are publicly available. A smaller effort is the GODORT online handout exchange (http://wikis.ala .org/godort/index.php/Exchange). While there might be many guides on local census resources or federal legislation, for example, there may be only a few on subjects such as the Americans with Disabilities Act or the Organization of American States. Ask for permission before copying, but guides in either collection may be used to assist in creating your own guide.

Data Providers

Many federal agencies have phone and e-mail listings for contacting individuals within the agency for help on topics specific to that agency. Agencies such as the Departments of Labor and Agriculture and the Census Bureau are data providers and have employees who are experts in how the data was created. These employees are often wonderful resources for those with very specific questions about the data. While contacting the agency should not necessarily be your first step, it should always be an option if other methods for finding the answer don't pan out.

The Network: Professional Organizations, Conferences, and Vendors

Don't forget your colleagues: Government information specialists, government documents librarians—whatever the name is, there are librarians who may be able to help you.

At the national level, the ALA has GODORT, started in 1972. This is a group for any librarian interested in government information, and its membership is librarians who work with all levels of government information—local, regional, state, federal, and international. GODORT has many useful resources on their wiki. Its mission is "(a) to provide a forum for the discussion of problems and concerns and for the exchange of ideas by librarians working with government documents; (b) to provide a nexus for initiating and supporting programs to increase the availability, use and bibliographic control of documents; (c) to increase communication between documents librarians and the larger community of information professionals; (d) to contribute to the education and training of documents librarians" (ALA/GODORT Bylaws, 2012). GODORT often has all-day pre-conferences at the ALA Annual Conference.

The American Association of Law Libraries, or AALL, has a Government Relations Committee which represents, promotes, and advocates the information policy interests of the Association regarding policies, laws, regulations, and other developments that may affect the Association, law librarianship, law libraries, or the dissemination of information.

The Special Libraries Association (SLA) has a Government Information Division or DGI which acts as a conduit for SLA librarians to exchange ideas on the value and use of government information (at all levels of government) and government libraries. The DGI website features conference reports, a frequently updated blog, and the Government Information Division News Feed. There is also an electronic discussion list and a Facebook group

The FDLP also hosts conferences. Watch the FDLP website for news of conferences in the spring and fall. These conferences have been held in person, and, more recently, there have been some virtual conferences. Either way, this is a great continuing education opportunity. Unlike most conferences, there is no registration fee.

Most state library associations have groups that discuss government information issues, and larger metropolitan areas also often have these groups. State or local groups help you get to know about the libraries around you and personnel and collection strengths. Even if you aren't in the area, a regional group worth investigating is the Law Librarians' Society of Washington, DC (LLSDC). Established in 1939, many members work in federal libraries and thus have expert working knowledge of publications and resources within their agencies. The LLSDC website includes a very useful sourcebook for those needing detailed knowledge of federal legislation, rulemaking, and other resources vetted by LLSDC.

Because government publishes on all topics, other organizations within the American Library Association are interested in government information, such as the Association of College and Research Libraries (ACRL), the Maps and Geospatial Information Round Table (MAGIRT), and the Federal and Armed Forces Libraries Round Table (FAFLRT). Other organizations include the Medical Library Association (MLA) and the International Federation of Library Associations and Institutions Government Information and Official Publications Section (IFLA-GIOPS). For almost any group of librarians, there is a tie-in with government information.

Finally, a group worth knowing is the vendor community. Getting to know the folks selling resources, and getting to know the resources available (through reviewing website information or trialing products) is part of the job of any librarian or information professional. Most libraries have processes whereby librarians recommend resources for purchase, so knowing what is available and having a wish-list can be quite useful at the end of the fiscal year when there may be some extra dollars left to spend in the collections budget. In addition to knowing the products available, sales representatives and trainers can funnel information back to product managers to make products more usable. On a more personal level, vendors can also be a useful source of information if you are job hunting, as they will have contacts in many libraries.

Wherever you have your network, this is a group of people who not only will assist you with reference inquiries, but will be colleagues throughout your career. They're the people you'll get together with at conferences and often write letters of recommendations for your next job hunt or your promotion. Treat them with care!

Citation and Style Manuals

One of the hardest moments for many scholars isn't actually writing the paper, it's the time when they have to put their bibliographies or endnotes together. Did they remember to make notes of everything they needed, or do they need to go back and find something typed on a computer or jotted on paper? While faculty select manuals such as MLA, APA, Chicago, Turabian, the *Bluebook*, and more, most of these manuals leave room for improvement in providing decent examples of how to cite government documents.

What Is Version Control (and Why Should I Care)?

In the paper world, documents almost always had a publication date, giving readers the knowledge that they could refer to a text from a specific date. Congressional bills have versions (see Definitions of Common Versions of Bills at FDsys) both to indicate which stage of the legislative process the bill has reached, and also to facilitate discussion of a particular edition of a bill. Unfortunately, not all publications (in print or online) are delineated as specifically. And web publications can disappear in the blink of an eye as with the speeches of Britain's Tory party which were scrubbed from the website and the Wayback Machine in 2013 (Lepore, 2015).

Insert the phrase *version control for government information* in a search engine and you'll see discussions about why this is such an important concept: first so that you can see when and by whom changes were made (if we're talking about a process, such as creating legislation or making regulations), but also to have the assurance that, if you're looking at a document or a web page, you're looking at the edition from the relevant time—be it the most current, or, in the case of a lawsuit, the edition of the document that was available at a particular point in time relating to the litigation.

With electronic/online documents becoming the norm, having version control will become ever more important—not just for determining the status of bills, laws, and regulations, but also for something as simple as knowing which version of a web page is being reviewed.

This cannot be overemphasized: the golden rule of citations is that *a citation must include enough information for readers to find their way back to the item cited*. Librarians often have researchers coming to the desk to assist in figuring out incomplete or inaccurate citations, as well as helping users create good citations. The goal here is good scholarship.

Before starting to write—ideally, when the research is started—it is quite helpful to find the style manual required. Different faculty and different disciplines demand different citation styles, and they don't appreciate it (and may even downgrade the work!) when writers don't follow this. If the work is being done with publication in mind, manuscripts may be rejected if the citations are not done correctly. Check what is required and do it right the first time.

Next, while style manuals are on the whole correct, they don't always make all of the most sensible decisions regarding government information sources. For example, section 17.309 of *The Chicago Manual of Style* (15th edition) seems to indicate that when citing a congressional bill, one should cite the *Congressional Record*. This creates extra work for the student to see if the bill was read into the *Record,* and a small crisis if the bill isn't found there (as many are not). Often, erroneously, writers will try to force material into one style and create problems for readers trying to look at the cited material. It is incumbent upon the writer to be aware of errors and omissions in the style manuals so that editors or faculty can be consulted about problems.

> **Websites on Citing Government Information**
>
> ---
>
> **American Memory, Library of Congress**
> http://memory.loc.gov/ammem/amlaw/lwcite.html
> *This website provides sample citations to the legislative information in the American Memory Project.*
>
> **Citing US Government Publications, Indiana University, Bloomington**
> http://libraries.iub.edu/guide-citing-us-government-publications
> *This guide has good discussions of access points and elements to consider in creating correct citations.*
>
> **DocsCite, Arizona State University**
> www.asu.edu/lib/hayden/govdocs/docscite/docscite.htm
> *This website creates citations using APA and MLA.*
>
> **Introduction to Basic Legal Citation, Legal Information Institute, Cornell University Law School**
> www.law.cornell.edu/citation
> *This was revised in fall 2014 and contains a PDF version and tutorials.*

While the 16th edition of *The Chicago Manual of Style* has fixed the problem with the congressional bills (see section 14.295) the important take-away is that you need to get the reader back to the item you are looking at. When in doubt, consult!

Citing Government Documents

The only manual specifically about citing government information is Debora Cheney's *The Complete Guide to Citing Government Information Resources,* though there are other citation manuals that cover government information in addition to other types of material. In addition to this book, many websites discuss citing government information and compare different style manuals (see sidebar). More than just the differences in how government information may be cited, there are specific challenges facing users of government information. These challenges are outlined in this section.

Citing Online Materials

Online government information is the norm now, and so of course URLs are to be included in citations. Some of the challenges facing citations to online government information include:

- Often the most current issue of a government journal has a URL ending in something like "current issue." When the next issue is loaded, it becomes the current issue, rendering the citation inaccurate.
- When using a database, a URL may be session-specific. Using the URL at a later time results in a 404 Not Found error message.
- A newer version of a cited resource may exist in the same location. For numeric data, numbers may be updated or completely refreshed; for text, a new version of a publication may be loaded or a corrected version may overwrite the previous one.
- After the change in presidential administrations, the whitehouse.gov website is moved to the National Archives and has a new domain created (like http://georgewbush-whitehouse.archives.gov). In addition to the presidential websites moving, agency websites may also be overhauled at this point, resulting in new organization and perhaps new policies and other content. Users end up with dead links to even well-referenced publications. Congressional websites may also change with each Congress.
- It's important to cite the publisher of the material, not the database it came from. For example, both Congress.gov (a freely available resource) and ProQuest Congressional may include the same material. Be sure to provide the name of the database where you found the material and enough information to find the resource within that database.
- Some style manuals require an accessed date, so that if something changes, users may be able to find routes to the version that was posted on a specific date.

Citing Laws: P.L., S.A.L., or U.S.C.?

Probably the most challenging citation issue for writers is when to cite the public law (P.L.), the *Statutes at Large* (S.A.L.) or the *U.S. Code* (see chapter 5 for a description of each). The P.L.s and S.A.L.s may be considered equivalent citations; however, the S.A.L. has page number as part of the citation, so it is used differently. The *U.S. Code,* however, is very different. While the public laws and *Statutes at Large* may be thought of as more static (the text doesn't change, though a new law may revoke or amend all or part of an older one), the *U.S. Code* changes with each new law. In paper form, there is a new version of the *Code* every six years, with annual amendments, so users may be citing the 2001 amendment, for instance, because they are looking at the body of law that has been accumulated to that date.

Here are a few rules to follow:

- Cite the public law when noting the actual piece of legislation passed, such as the GI Bill (P.L. 78-346), the Voting Rights Act of 1965 (P.L. 89-110), or the Whaling Treaty of 1936 (P.L. 74-525).

- Cite the public law if the name is the actual name of the law. If the Detainee Treatment Act of 2005 is part of a law with a different name, then let the reader know that: for example, the Detainee Treatment Act of 2005 (Title X of P.L. 109-148).
- Cite the statute (Stat.) when writing about a provision of the legislation, for example, the Detainee Treatment Act, Title X of P.L. 109-148 (119 Stat. 2739). The page number here, 2739, takes the user to the particular page under consideration.
- Cite the U.S. Code (U.S.C.) when discussing the body of law—8 U.S.C. § 1101 (1988)—at a point in time. For example, part 314 of the Immigration Reform and Control Act of 1986 (100 Stat. 3439, 8 U.S.C. § 1152, 1153) regarding specific visas, was amended with P.L. 100-658 in 1988 and several times after that. If you were talking about the 1988 amendments specifically, you could reference the public law or the statute; when discussing the body of immigration law, citations need to reference the U.S. Code, including the year, as at different points in time, the law will have changed. (Refer to chapter 5 to learn how laws fit into the S.A.L. and the U.S. Code.)
- When citing the print U.S. Code, the year must be included. Then the reader will know that, for example, the writer was citing the 1997 version of 8 U.S.C. § 1153, as opposed to the 2002 edition. Dates for online sources will vary, so be sure to check the source for hints about currency and editions.

Versions

Draft environmental impact statements, an engrossed bill, a proposed rule . . . all of these things are versions of a work and must be cited as such. A common misunderstanding might be that one version is more important than another, and this might be true in terms of the weight each document is given in decision making; however, the important thing in the world of citations is that the writer identifies the version used so that others can consult the same material.

When citing congressional bills, the FDsys.gov Help lists more than 50 versions of bills—each with its own abbreviation (for some examples, refer to chapter 3). Members of Congress must be specific about which version they are referencing so as to avoid confusion, and writers must do the same thing. For online versions of bills, the text format and the PDF format will note the version differently. Currently the text versions note the version at the top of the document, for example, CONSIDERED AND PASSED IN THE HOUSE, Job Creation and Unemployment Relief Act of 2008, H.R. 7110, while PDF versions currently note the version at the bottom of the pages, as in H.R. 7110 CPH. Of course, like all things congressional, formatting has changed over time, so it is important to understand that versions exist, and to note appropriately.

State legislation may also have multiple versions of bills, as will legislation and rules from intergovernmental organizations.

Citing the date an online version is accessed may also be vital to referencing the correct version. Then if a newer version of a database or PDF overwrites the version cited, it is easy to note that there may be differences. If a citation doesn't note the accessed date, consult the date the article or book was published and use that to approximate the accessed date.

Beyond Citations: Elements of Style

As discussed above, when writing for publication it is necessary to know the citation style used by a journal or a book publisher. In addition to citations, it is important to pay attention to the other elements of style demanded through these resources.

The *GPO Style Manual* capitalizes the word *Federal,* and government publications and agency websites follow that rule (GPO, 2008: 58). Writers in social science journals using *The Chicago Manual of Style,* however, will use the lowercase *federal* unless it is part of a name, as in the Federal Bureau of Investigation or the *Federal Register* (*Chicago Manual of Style*, 2010: 414). The GPO's manual has an uppercase bias; *Chicago* has a lowercase bias.

Style manuals control what gets capitalized, when and if numbers are written out, spelling, punctuation, and more. They don't exist to torment writers (though that may be an added benefit); they exist to ensure consistency across the publication. A good way to figure out what material is included in a particular style manual is to consult the table of contents.

Conclusion

Being a government documents librarian, government information specialist, or information professional who occasionally works with government content will bring you in contact with a group of uniquely committed colleagues. These colleagues are interested not just in the publications themselves, but also in the processes of government. Information professionals who work with government publications appreciate, as perhaps no other group of librarians can, the tidbits of arcane knowledge that can assist in helping patrons and colleagues alike—not just by producing the answer, but by teaching how to find it, and being able to explain it all. Learning the basics and staying up-to-date can both start you out and keep you going in a successful career working with government information.

Exercises

1. Read the front page of your daily newspaper or news site and note when state or federal government (or international organizations) are mentioned. Then try to figure out, as specifically as possible, which part of each organization is being mentioned.

2. When a catastrophic event takes place, such as a train or plane crash, hurricane, oil spill, volcanic eruption, or tsunami, make a list of which parts of government or international organizations have lead roles or subordinate roles.

3. You read that the federal government prepared a new report on terrorism; you have no further information. Discuss the strategies and tools you would use to locate the report.

4. Does the library that you regularly use have a government information collection? How is it organized and noted in the catalog? Is there a print or online version of the *Serial Set?* What is considered to be the best collection near you? What criteria did you use to figure out the "best"?

Sources Mentioned in This Chapter

Sources mentioned in this section do not duplicate the references that follow.

GPO Websites

Digitization Projects Registry, http://registry.fdlp.gov/.
FDLP Academy, www.fdlp.gov/about-the-fdlp/fdlp-academy.
FDsys, www.gpo.gov/fdsys/.
FDsys Help on Versions of Congressional Bills, www.gpo.gov/help/index.html#about_congressional _bills.htm.
Federal Depository Library Program home, www.fdlp.gov.
SuDocs classification system, www.fdlp.gov/catalogingandclassification/ cataloging-articles/1791-sudocs-classification.

Electronic Discussion Lists, Journals, and News

DttP: Documents to the People, http://wikis.ala.org/godort/index.php/DttP.
Free Government Information (FGI), www.freegovinfo.info.
GODORT's list of LISTSERVs (including GOVDOC-L, INTL-DOC, and more), http://wikis.ala.org/ godort/index.php/GODORT_Listservs#%20INTL-DOC.
Government Computer News (GCN), www.gcn.com.
Government Information Quarterly (GIQ), www.journals.elsevier.com/government-information-quarterly.

Sources for the Monthly Catalog of U.S. Government Publications

Catalog US Government Publications or CGP (1976–), http://catalog.gpo.gov.
Monthly Catalog of United States Government Publications, SuDocs: G.P. 3.8 (various titles) 1895- .
OCLC, GPO Monthly Catalog, www.oclc.org/support/services/firstsearch/documentation/dbdetails/ details/GPO.en.html.
Paratext Public Documents Masterfile, described by Indiana University—Bloomington (2015), http:// libraries.iub.edu/public-documents-masterfile.

Other Resources

American FactFinder, http://factfinder.census.gov.
Bureau of the Census, www.census.gov.

Checklist of United States Public Documents, 1789–1909, http://digital.library.unt.edu/ark:/67531/
    metadc1029.

Cheney, Debora, ed. 2002. *The Complete Guide to Citing Government Information Resources*, 3rd ed.
    Bethesda, MD: LexisNexis.

Google Books Library Project, http://books.google.com.

HathiTrust, www.hathitrust.org.

Internet Archive, www.archive.org.

LibGuides, www.libguides.com.

Non-Depository Government Publications, 1953–2008. Chester, VT: Readex.

North Carolina Library Association Government Resources Section, Help! I'm an Accidental Govern-
    ment Information Librarian, www.nclaonline.org/government-resources/help-im-accidental
    -government-information-librarian-webinars.

State Depository Library Programs listing, http://wikis.ala.org/godort/index.php/State_Depository
    _Library_Systems.

Statistical Abstract of the United States, www.census.gov/compendia/statab.

U.S. Government Manual, http://purl.access.gpo.gov/GPO/LPS2410 or www.usgovernmentmanual
    .gov, SuDoc: AE 2.108/2 (online) or GS 4.109.

USA.gov, www.usa.gov.

Wooster College, US *Congressional Serial Set* Finding List, http://libguides.wooster.edu/
    congressionalserialsetfindinglist.

WorldCat, www.worldcat.org.

Professional Associations

American Association of Law Libraries (AALL) Government Relations Committee, www.aallnet.org/
    mm/Leadership-Governance/committee/activecmtes/government.html.

American Library Association, www.ala.org, also provides links to the divisions and round tables.

American Library Association Government Documents Round Table (GODORT):
    Handout Exchange, http://wikis.ala.org/godort/index.php/Exchange;
    Toolboxes for Processing and Cataloging, http://wikis.ala.org/godort/index.php/Cataloging#
        GODORT_Cataloging_Committee.27s_Toolbox_for_Processing_and_Cataloging;
    Wiki, http://wikis.ala.org/godort.

International Federation of Library Associations and Institutions Government Information and Official
    Publications Section (IFLA-GIOPS), www.ifla.org/en/giops.

Law Librarians' Society of Washington, DC (LLSDC), www.llsdc.org.

LLSDC Legislative Sourcebook, www.llsdc.org/sourcebook.

Medical Library Association, www.mlanet.org.

Special Libraries Association Government Information Division (SLA-DGI), http://units.sla.org/
    division/dgi/.

Readings

Bernstein, Carl, and Bob Woodward. 1973. *All the President's Men*. New York: Simon and Schuster.

Greenwald, Glenn. *No Place to Hide: Edward Snowden, the NSA, and the U.S. Surveillance State*. 2014. New
    York: Henry Holt and Co.

Halberstam, David. 1972. *The Best and the Brightest*. New York: Random House.

Noonan, Peggy, 1990. *What I Saw at the Revolution: A Political Life in the Reagan Era*. New York: Random
    House.

Woodward, Bob, and Scott Armstrong. 1979. *The Brethren: Inside the Supreme Court*. New York: Simon and Schuster.

Texts

Boyd, Anne Morris, and Rae Elizabeth Rips. 1949. *United States Government Publications*. 3rd ed. New York: H. W. Wilson.

Morehead, Joe, and Mary K. Fetzer. 1992. *Introduction to United States Government Information Sources*. 4th ed. Englewood, CO: Libraries Unlimited.

Robinson, Judith Schiek. 1998. *Tapping the Government Grapevine*. 3rd ed. Phoenix: Greenwood.

Schmeckebier, Laurence F. 1925. *The Statistical Work of the National Government*. Baltimore: Johns Hopkins.

Schmeckebier, Laurence F., and Roy B. Eastin. 1969. *Government Publications and Their Use*. 4th ed. Washington, DC: Brookings Institution.

Sears, Jean L., and Marilyn K. Moody. 2001. *Using Government Information Sources: Electronic and Print*. 3rd ed. Phoenix: Greenwood.

References

ALA Government Documents Round Table. 2012. "Bylaws." American Library Association. http://wikis.ala.org/godort/images/c/cf/GODORT_Bylaws_2012.pdf.

The Chicago Manual of Style. 2010. 16th ed. Chicago: University of Chicago Press.

Elsevier. 2015. "Government Information Quarterly." Accessed January 2015. www.journals.elsevier.com/government-information-quarterly/.

Government Printing Office. 2008. *Style Manual: An Official Guide to the Form and Style of Federal Government Printing*. Washington, DC: Government Printing Office. http://purl.access.gpo.gov/GPO/FDLP510.

Lepore, Jill. "The Cobweb: Can the Internet Be Archived?" *New Yorker*, January 26, 2015, pg 34–41. www.newyorker.com/magazine/2015/01/26/cobweb Volume 90, issue 45.

National Archives and Records Administration. 2015. "U.S. Government Manual: Browse." Washington, DC: Government Publishing Office. http://purl.access.gpo.gov/GPO/LPS2410.

Sevetson, Andrea L., et al. 2013. *The Serial Set: Its Make-up and Content*. Bethesda, MD: ProQuest.

CHAPTER 3

Congressional Publications

CASSANDRA HARTNETT

Introduction

A health sciences librarian consults a congressional hearing on recalls of unsafe food. A public librarian traces a congressional bill on climate change. How did each become proficient in researching congressional activity? Both recognize that congressional literature is one of the great hidden collections in our nation's libraries and on the open Internet. Think looking at Congress will bring you into a dry, inexplicable vortex of lawmaking? Think again: congressional publications provide a picture of almost every aspect of American culture and life, including topics as far flung as animal abuse, art, credit card debt, high school debate topics, cemetery desecration, gun control, vaccines, vaping, and all aspects of defense and veterans affairs. As the voice of the people, Congress looks at problems. Where a problem cannot be solved at the state government level, via existing federal laws and regulations, or through other institutions, interested parties can bring forth their concerns for Congress to address via legislation, the writing of new laws. The United States Constitution calls for Congress to make "all Laws ... necessary and proper" (Constitution, art. I, sec. 3).

Congress also has oversight authority for the executive branch of government, which means that Congress must authorize every agency, and the agency's leadership must go before Congress at regular intervals for funding, known as the appropriations process. Congress must pass 13 appropriations bills by October 1 of each year so that adequate funds may be expended from the US Treasury to give the federal government the money to operate. As each agency defends its spending needs to Congress, the appropriations process becomes an overview of our national priorities. Vice President Al Gore was once taken to task for making a comment that sounded like he invented the Internet while serving as a US senator (Hillman, 2000). Despite Mr. Gore's overstatement, Congress does fund Big Science. Without the willingness of Congress to commit US research funds to all kinds of scientific, medical, and computing endeavors, progress in these areas would be dramatically slowed or nearly halted. Congress has been called the most influential legislature in the world, with good reason (Oppenheimer, 1983).

Political activists, trade and industry members, and lobbyists have their own interests in Congress; celebrity watchers may have another; historians, journalists, archivists, or political scientists yet another. Librarians are interested in the literature of Congress, the published output, what Congress did and what it produces. We work to collect and preserve that literature and make it more accessible to all. If you spend time with government documents librarians, you will notice that they are enthusiastic about congressional information. They tend to wax rhapsodic about the first time they really "got" the US *Congressional Serial Set* or picked up a hearing that they just could not stop reading.

To catch some of that enthusiasm, start by learning about some typical congressional publications:

- Bills, resolutions, and aids for tracking their progress
- Committee hearings
- Research reports and other committee literature
- The US *Congressional Serial* Set
- Main floor transcription (the *Congressional Record*)
- Video proceedings
- Calendars and journals

These official government sources may be consulted directly, but they can be accessed more efficiently, with increased navigation and discovery abilities, by using commercially published summaries, indexes, and digital resources, as well as community-created online resources, covered in the Guides and Indexes section of this chapter. Archival information on Congress (office records, members' papers, constituent mail, and so on) is addressed in chapter 18.

Congress and Its Structure

Congress is bicameral, meaning it has two chambers: the House of Representatives, with 435 members apportioned according to each state's population; and the Senate, with two senators from each state for a total of 100. Combine the two and the result is an ever-fascinating, complex example of representative government.

A congress (or term of congress) spans two years starting January 3 of the odd-numbered years, with each session generally lasting one year. Researchers refer to congressional time in terms of congress and session, as in the year 2016 is the 114th Congress, second session, or 114–2.

Trivia Time

After the 20th Amendment's passage in 1933, all new congresses start on January 3; prior to that, the opening day of Congress varied. Many congresses have included a third session, but in the post–World War II era, there has been a consistent pattern of two-session congresses. See www .senate.gov/reference/Sessions/session Dates.htm for list of session dates.

A vast majority of the work of Congress occurs in committee and subcommittee, not on the floor of the House or Senate. When picturing Congress at work, actively fight the familiar images of impassioned speeches on the "main floor" of the House or

Senate, even though both bodies convene in that manner when Congress is in session. Instead, try to imagine smaller gatherings, in much less spectacular rooms—this is the bread and butter of Congress: committee work. Tracking down a tidbit of congressional information means figuring out the context: did the information come about because of floor action or committee work, and for what purpose? The PBS NewsHour, in its online site @theCapitol, notes that committees

> have been called "scattered nodes of power," fiefdoms and laboratories, and committees are all of these. According to Congress watcher Norman Ornstein, the committee system is the "natural form of division of labor in such a large and complex body as the Congress." (Public Broadcasting Service, 2009)

There are about 20 committees in each chamber, as well as five joint committees, and a handful of select or special committees convened to address specific one-time or recurrent concerns. One may recognize committee names from the daily news. Each is further divided into numerous subcommittees. Some subcommittees are so well established that their websites are more developed and useful than those of their parent committees.

Newcomers should be fearless and humble in learning about congressional structure, and look everywhere for answers. Librarians may acquire resources like Robert G. Kaiser's *Act of Congress: How America's Essential Institution Works, and How it Doesn't* or CQ Press's *Congress, Reconsidered* to supplement more traditional reference works, such as CQ's *Guide to Congress* or the used-for-decades congressional publication *How Our Laws Are Made*. Whenever using an online system, whether Congress.gov or something flashier, make sure to use the Help pages, which will also help explain congressional vocabulary and conventions.

For Starters: Congress.gov

Congress.gov, the LC's main site for Congress, is a basic starting place for the novice searcher. Congress.gov makes it simple to browse for bills, calendars, hot topics, congressional committees, laws, and congressional history. The United States Government Publishing Office (GPO), the longtime official publisher for Congress, supplies the published bills, laws, and other documents available on Congress.gov; one can also search GPO's holdings directly using the Federal Digital System (FDsys, www.FDsys.gov). A new congressional researcher would go far simply by setting aside time to learn Congress.gov's organization and content.

Legislative Process and Publications

Many Americans born in the 1960s or later enjoyed *Schoolhouse Rock!* cartoons (Dorough et al., 2002), now ubiquitous in the YouTube era. *America Rock* is a subset of catchy civics lessons. "Just a Bill" conveys in four marvelous minutes one bill's basic path from conception of the idea ("there oughta be a law!") to the struggle to get the introduced bill out of committee. "Just a Bill" depicts the so-called dance of legislation, a term made more popular by Seattle-based author and attorney Eric Redman. In his 1973 book of that title, Redman describes his internship for Senator Warren Magnuson, trying to get a particular piece of health care legislation passed.

The dance of legislation is an overwhelming topic to most Americans. People rightfully suspect that all kinds of factors—timing, politics, and priorities—go into making legislation succeed or fail. With a very low success rate for individual bills, it is hard to feel optimistic, much less in command of all the various steps. Bills have to pass both houses and be signed by the chief executive (president) to become law. If the president vetoes a bill, it returns to Congress, where it must be passed by a two-thirds majority of both chambers. A bill must be passed by the adjournment of the Congress in which it was introduced or it automatically dies, and most bills die.

Walking through the Legislative Process

Let us walk through the basic legislative process now. Don't worry; this will only hurt a little.

1. Prior to its introduction, each bill must find a champion or advocate within Congress. Bills can originate in either house, except for revenue or appropriations bills, which, per the Constitution, must start in the House. The bill is introduced by one or more sponsoring and cosponsoring members of Congress and is immediately referred to a committee, subcommittee, or multiple committees, sometimes without any comment or debate. All of this is chronicled in the *Congressional Record,* discussed below.

2. If the committee decides to further consider the measure, it may hold *hearings* (see Records of Committee Meetings: Hearings), calling in expert witnesses to testify on the matter at hand, much like a court of law. It may also commission a research report (known as a *Committee Print*) to gain more direct information about the general question. Committee staff or the Congressional Research Service (CRS, elite researchers within the LC) are most often responsible for producing committee prints. Most measures, however, never get to this point.

Bill Introductions from the
Congressional Record
Measures Referred

The following bills and joint resolutions were introduced, read the first and second times by unanimous consent, and referred as indicated:

By Mrs. SHAHEEN (for herself, Ms. COLLINS, Mr. WHITEHOUSE, and Mrs. MURRAY): S. 447. A bill to amend title 28, United States Code, to prohibit the exclusion of individuals from service on a Federal jury on account of sexual orientation or gender identity; *to the Committee on the Judiciary.*

By Mr. KAINE (for himself and Mr. WARNER): S. 465. A bill to extend Federal recognition to the Chickahominy Indian Tribe, the Chickahominy Indian Tribe-Eastern Division, the Upper Mattaponi Tribe, the Rappahannock Tribe, Inc., the Monacan Indian Nation, and the Nansemond Indian Tribe; *to the Committee on Indian Affairs.*

Source: Cong. Rec., Feb. 11, 2015, p. S926; emphasis added.

3. The committee may vote to change the text of the bill before sending it back to the main floor for further consideration. This revision process is referred to as *markup.*

4. If the committee members can mostly agree (dissenting views are valued, but a majority must agree), then and only then is the measure reported out of committee. This means that a *committee report* is issued, often providing the revised text and the arguments in support. Reports generally recommend the bill for passage, and minority dissenting views are sometimes included as well (note that there are other kinds of committee reports published, but this is the primary type). The bill then returns to the floor of the House or the Senate for reconsideration, debate, and vote by the entire chamber. Most bills do not make it back to the floor.

5. Amendments to a bill may be offered on the floor and voted on. Votes can occur in three ways: by voice (with the presiding officer determining if the ayes or nays have it); by division or standing vote (members literally stand and are counted); or by record vote, also called roll call voting. Since 1973, the House has conducted roll call votes via electronic means, in which both the vote and the voter's identity are recorded. The Senate continues the age-old process of verbally calling out each Senator's name and recording his or her vote.

6. In the House, the bill may also be sent back (recommitted) to committee for further consideration. This can be a stalling mechanism to either encourage or discourage support of the bill.

7. If the bill passes on the floor of one chamber, it is then referred to the other chamber, where it undergoes an identical process. It is also possible to have an identical or nearly identical bill making its way through the other chamber concurrently. If the bill passes the second chamber but that chamber changes language or offers amendments, or if it passes a different bill, a conference committee is appointed with members from each chamber. (If the two chambers have passed identical bills, a conference committee is not needed.) The conference committee meets to reconcile editorial and substantive differences between the two versions of the bill. Often a conference report is issued with changes noting which chamber's (House or Senate) bill language was used—and in some cases there is a true mix, borrowing from both texts, or a significant rewriting. Aside from the bill language, conference reports also contain a joint explanatory statement explaining the committee's decisions.

8. Once the bill clears the conference committee, this compromise version must be voted on in both chambers (this step is needed only if there were changes from both chambers during the conference).

9. After it has passed both chambers, the bill goes to the president's desk where it is either signed or vetoed within 10 days, not counting Sundays. The president can issue a written veto or simply not sign the bill; an unsigned bill amounts to a veto (a pocket veto) if Congress is out of session but becomes law if Congress is in session. A two-thirds majority of both houses of Congress can overturn a veto (see chapter 8 for more about finding veto messages).

10. The bill, now a law, is assigned a public law (P.L. or Pub. L.) number, published first in paperback or "slip" form, then more formally in *United States Statutes at Large*. For more detail on this and subsequent steps, see chapter 5, Public Laws and the *U.S. Code*.

Bills and Resolutions

One could think of an introduced bill or resolution as the first draft of a proposed new law. Bills and resolutions, which we will refer to generically as bills, or measures, vary in length from one short page to more than 2,000 pages. Who writes the text of bills? Bills have to be introduced by a member of Congress but technically can be written by anyone. Most bills are likely written by congressional staff (oftentimes attorneys) and typically are the result of requests from or consultations with private industry, non–governmental organizations, private citizens, the president, or staff within the executive

TABLE 3.1
Types of Legislation

Types of measure	Noted as	Special notes
Bills	H.R. 1 S. 1	Bills and other measures are numbered sequentially in the order that they are introduced. Bills may be private (affecting only specific individuals or parties) or public; omnibus (on many topics) or target (single topic). Must pass both houses.
Joint Resolutions	H.J.Res. 1 S.J.Res. 1	Tend to have a limited focus or be related to money measures or technical corrections. Constitutional amendments must be introduced as Joint Resolutions and are forwarded to the 50 states for approval (rather than the president). Must pass both houses.
Concurrent Resolutions	H.Con.Res. 1 S.Con. Res. 1	Internal measures of Congress. Tend to express facts or principles jointly. Used to set time of adjournment, appoint members to joint committees, send congratulatory messages to foreign leaders. Published in *Statutes at Large*.
Resolutions, sometimes referred to as *Simple Resolutions*	H.Res. 1 S.Res. 1	Considered only by one chamber, usually refer to procedural matters. Can also express the sentiment of the House or Senate on something over which it has no jurisdiction (e.g., 111-1 S. Res. 23, honoring the life of Andrew Wyeth).
Public Law	P.L. 1	All measures that become law are assigned a P.L. number in the order in which they are passed. P.L.s are published first in a "slip" or paperback edition and later produced in a bound official edition, *U.S. Statutes at Large*. Can be public or private laws. *See chapter 5, Public Laws and the U.S. Code, for next steps after a bill becomes law.*

Note: For further information about bills, see www.gpo.gov/fdsys/browse/collection.action?collectionCode=BILLS. To learn all of the types of legislation and versions, see www.gpo.gov/help/index.html#about_congressional_bills.htm.

branch. After a bill is introduced in either the House or Senate, it embarks on its journey toward becoming (or not) an official law. Once passed by either chamber, the bill
may be referred to as an act. Resolutions are just like bills but come in a few different
types: joint, concurrent, and simple; see table 3.1 for a full listing.

One of the standard requests by users of government documents is some variation
of "I'm following a bill in Congress and I need to know how far it has gotten in the
process." This is the grand practice of bill tracking or bill status. Users are essentially
asking for the last official action taken on a piece of legislation. When you are viewing a bill summary via an online resource such as Congress.gov, the tracking history
can usually be found under a heading like Actions. In most databases, users can choose
between Major Congressional Actions (a list of just the big steps of the process) or All
Congressional Actions (much more detail, including the dates of significant meetings
related to the bill, comments made on the floor, etc.) or simply Last Action. Frequently,
the person asking the question will need to be convinced that a particular bill died
in committee because it is hard to translate lack of action as a kind of action or outcome. No one wants to think that a favorite piece of legislation has died a quiet and
unceremonious death. For more information about bill tracking, see the Bill Tracking,
Legislative Histories, and Other Resources section near the end of this chapter.

Many landmark pieces of legislation (e.g., the Brady Bill) are reintroduced in several
congresses before ultimately succeeding. In each subsequent congress, such bills' numbers
and titles will likely change, but they still are considered part of an act's legislative history.
They may be known by a popular name that varies from their actual title. In law librarian
Mary Whisner's humorous essay "What's in a Statute Name?" she cites everything from
the Chain Store Act to the CAN–SPAM Act, noting that "the Sherman Antitrust Act was
not always called that, does not use the word 'antitrust,' and was not even written by Senator Sherman" (Whisner, 2005: 174). Frequently, bills or laws are known by an acronym.

As the bill works its way through the legislative process, it may have amendments to
the original text, resulting in different versions of the bill. There are approximately 52
different version types—luckily this count includes many parallel processes from the House
and Senate. Examples of versions include Introduced in House or Senate, Engrossed in
House or Senate, Received in House or Senate, Enrolled Bill and many (many) more.
For a complete list of all bill versions, along with an explanation of each, see: www.gpo
.gov/help/index.html#about_congressional_bills.htm.

More Notes on Bills

New laws often update existing laws. The full title of many bills begins, "[A Bill] to
Amend . . ." and involves striking out existing legal text and inserting new phrases. On
the other hand, every once in a while a piece of legislation does break new ground
and may come to be considered a landmark law. See the Air Quality Act of 1967 (P.L.
90-148, 81 Stat. 485 (1967)) for one example, or how about the Servicemen's Readjustment Act of 1944 (P.L. 78-346, 58 Stat. 284 (1944))—did you guess that this was
really the GI Bill? Bills and laws can be on a single topic (target legislation) or on many
different topics (omnibus bills). Unusual phrasing, such as "a bill to do X, and for other
purposes," is a telltale sign of an omnibus bill.

Congress passes both public and private laws. Public laws apply to the entire population; private laws are for the benefit of specific individuals or organizations. For example, consider the plight of a widow whose home sat within the boundaries of the Rocky Mountain National Park. Upon her husband's death, she might have been forced to move, if not for the Betty Dick Residence Protection Act of 2006 (Private Law 109-1, 120 Stat. 3705 (2006)), "to permit the continued occupancy and use of the property . . . by Betty Dick for the remainder of her natural life." Or what about the plight of Nguyen Quy An, a Vietnamese man who risked his life to save American soldiers during the Vietnam War? Thanks to Private Law 104-4 (110 Stat. 4288 (1996)), certain naturalization requirements were waived for An, making it simpler for him to become an American citizen.

Most Bills Die

The percentage of bills that never find their way out of committee is quite high and has varied over the decades, sometimes reaching as high as 96 percent. From 2003–2014, depending on the year, 85 to 94 percent of House bills simply went nowhere. For the corresponding years in the Senate the range was 75 to 96 percent (Brookings Institution and American Enterprise Institute, 2013).

Despite their centrality to this process, *physical* copies of bills have not been widely distributed outside of Congress, probably due to their high volume (in some sessions more than 10,000 have been introduced in the House alone) and the number of iterations in each congress. GPO produced bills for library users on diazo microfiche, distributed through the depository program, 1979 to 2000. Librarians can purchase historical runs of bills in preservation quality microform from the LC Duplication Services (microfilm) or ProQuest (microfiche).

Online access to historic bills continues to improve. The earliest bills may be found through the American Memory Project (1799–1875 for the House, 1819–1875 for the Senate; see figure 3.1 for an example of a bill), then from 1993 on via Congress .gov and FDsys. ProQuest leads the commercial market with its Digital US Bills and Resolutions. This product contains full-text searchable bills in PDF format along with basic indexing, back to 1789. A few other commercial or nonprofit publishers offer online access to bills, but only from 1989 on, or later; see the Law Librarians' Society of Washington DC's *Sources for the Text of Congressional Bills and Resolutions,* www.llsdc .org/sources-for-congressional-bills-resolutions.

Records of Committee Meetings: Hearings

A bill, once introduced and referred to committee or subcommittee, has an uncertain fate. If it rises in a committee's highest priority, the committee will schedule a hearing (step 2 in the steps of legislation, above) and call witnesses to testify. Hearings are fact-finding investigations and provide an unparalleled glimpse at what Congress—and presumably the nation—deems to be important at the time. Hearings are generally held in Washington, DC, but may be conducted elsewhere as well, as field hearings. The testimony of witnesses makes hearings invaluable primary resources for high school level research and beyond. Hearings are a little bit like the *Congressional Record* in their theatrical, read-aloud aspect, but the critical difference is that hearings

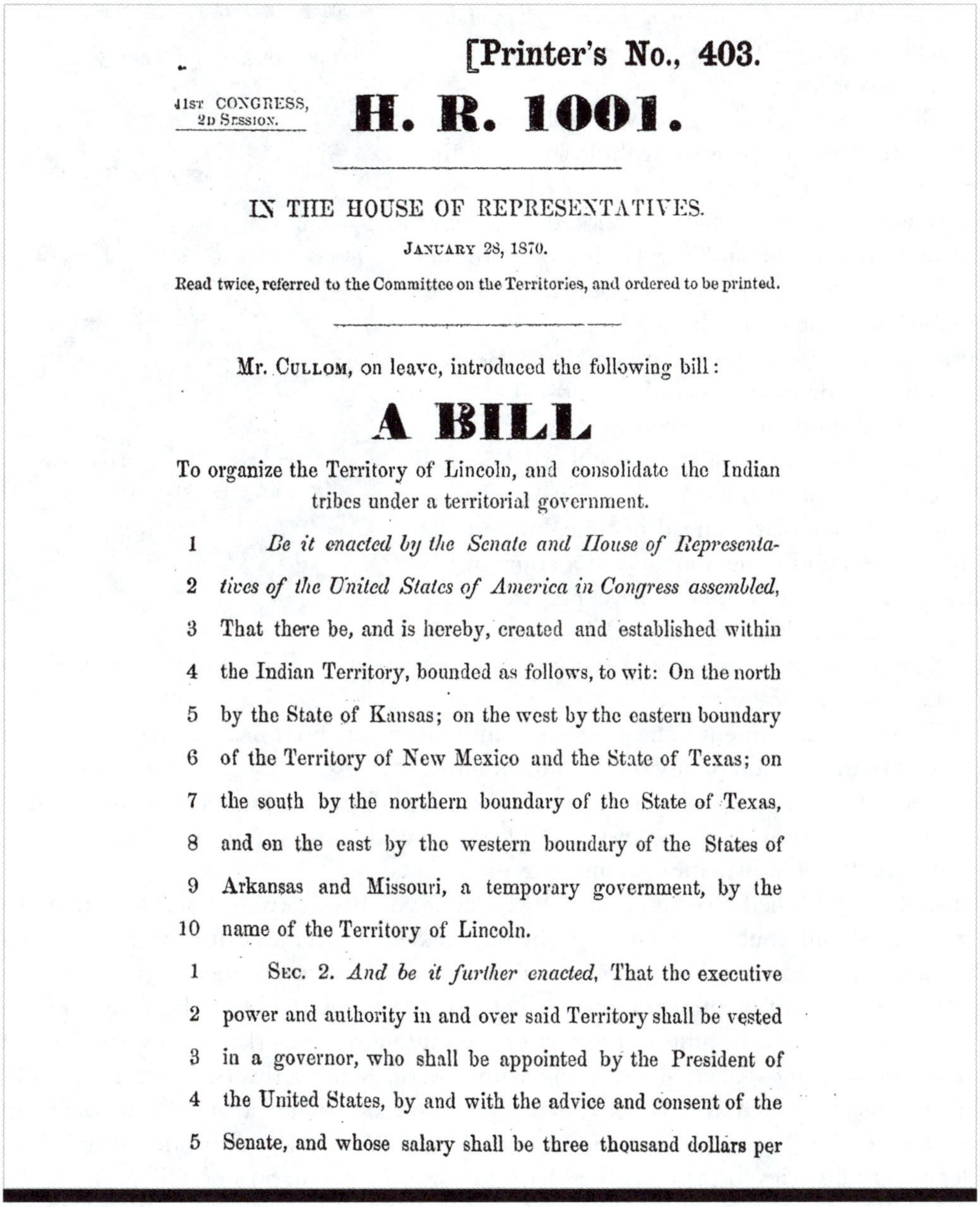

[Printer's No., 403.

41st CONGRESS,
2D SESSION.

H. R. 1001.

IN THE HOUSE OF REPRESENTATIVES.

JANUARY 28, 1870.

Read twice, referred to the Committee on the Territories, and ordered to be printed.

Mr. CULLOM, on leave, introduced the following bill :

A BILL

To organize the Territory of Lincoln, and consolidate the Indian
tribes under a territorial government.

1   *Be it enacted by the Senate and House of Representa-*

2   *tives of the United States of America in Congress assembled,*

3   That there be, and is hereby, created and established within

4   the Indian Territory, bounded as follows, to wit: On the north

5   by the State of Kansas; on the west by the eastern boundary

6   of the Territory of New Mexico and the State of Texas; on

7   the south by the northern boundary of the State of Texas,

8   and on the east by the western boundary of the States of

9   Arkansas and Missouri, a temporary government, by the

10   name of the Territory of Lincoln.

1   SEC. 2. *And be it further enacted,* That the executive

2   power and authority in and over said Territory shall be vested

3   in a governor, who shall be appointed by the President of

4   the United States, by and with the advice and consent of the

5   Senate, and whose salary shall be three thousand dollars per

FIGURE 3.1
A Sample Bill from "A Century of Lawmaking for a New Nation," Part of the Larger American Memory Project from the Library of Congress

take place in committee while the *Record* content comes from speeches on the floors of the House and Senate (see the section "The *Congressional Record*" later in this chapter). Ask librarians to list the top five types of government documents most useful for contemporary and historical research, and hearings will undoubtedly make most people's lists. Recent hearings include titles as diverse as *The Benefits of Promoting Soil*

Health in Agriculture and Rural America, Astrobiology and the Search for Life in the Universe, and *Labor Issues in Bangladesh.*

All aspects of a hearing are vulnerable to political influence: the decision to hold it in the first place, its scheduling and location, to what degree it is widely advertised or promoted, the tenor of questions asked, and the choice of witnesses called. Sevetson (2015) notes that witnesses tend to fall into four overarching groups: political figures (such as Lima, Ohio, mayor David Berger), famous personalities (recording artist LL Cool J), affected individuals (pancreatic cancer patient and author Randy Pausch), and experts (Cornell astronomer Joseph Burns). Witnesses are asked to prepare their remarks ahead of time, but are also subject to questioning, much as in a court of law. Even though the witnesses have prepared statements—which they deposit with the committee clerk, typically two days before testifying—there are also court reporters on hand to make a true transcription.

> **This Site Ain't Big Enough for the Both of Us**
>
> The discouragingly partisan tenor of some member and committee websites makes the sites risky to consult for verifiable, bias-free content. Senate committees now clearly label majority and minority sections on their sites; typically House committees provide the minority with completely separate official sites, see http://democrats.smallbusiness.house.gov or http://democrats.agriculture.house.gov. For individual member's pages likely to contain a hint of partisan slant, try http://clay.house.gov or http://issa.house.gov.

Getting at the content of hearings or even finding out about hearings has never been easier, but there is still plenty of room for improved access. Every committee and many subcommittees have websites, most with (uncorrected) transcripts, social media, a video channel, RSS feeds or other notification features. With a minimum of effort, the committee can push information to interested individuals.

Consult published hearings from GPO, even if you have to wait months for them to be released: fully published hearings include evidence submitted for the record, correspondence, and other relevant material provided to the committee, all of which can make up over half of the content of a published volume. Published hearings include both versions of the testimony: the version submitted to the clerk, and the transcript of what was actually spoken aloud, along with questions and answers. Frequently, copyrighted material such as newspaper articles is inserted into a hearing; this has been an impediment for hearings digitization projects on the Web. GPO distributes hearings to depository libraries in print (as they have for over 75 years), on microfiche (from the 1970s on), and digitally (from 1994 on). The House or Senate may withhold release of some hearings, known as unpublished hearings. These may not be public for years due to concerns of confidentiality, national security, trade secrets, and other factors (see chapter 18, Historical and Archival Information, for additional notes). ProQuest offers comprehensive indexing and digital access to current and historic hearings back to 1824 through the Congressional Hearings Digital Collection.

Hall et al. (2014) cite Costello and others who note gaps in the committee release or publication of full hearings, especially in electronic form, meaning some that should be included in FDsys are not deposited there; a GPO working group is striving to improve this situation. Independent special projects for digitized hearings have emerged online; two examples: the University of New Orleans's Earl K. Long Library offers its own interface to selected digitized hearings and publications at http://louisdl.louislibraries.org/cdm/landing page/collection/p120701c01125, and the Stanford University Libraries offers digitized hearings from the Joint Committee on Atomic Energy 1946–1977 at http://collections.stanford.edu/atomicenergy. Broad keyword searching for hearings in a library's online catalog can be as simple as combining a search term with "hearing" (uranium AND hearing). More sophisticated searching (by factors such as witness and bill number) requires special tools (see the Indexes section of this chapter).

Consider a specific hearing from 2007: the issue at hand was mental health care for veterans, particularly those returning from Iraq and Afghanistan. One particular bill (S.2162) had been introduced and referred to the Senate Committee on Veterans Affairs on October 15, 2007. Nine days later (very quickly in congressional terms), a formal hearing was convened on this bill, along with four other bills on veterans' health, with the nondescript title *Hearing on Pending Legislation* (see sidebar). The ultimate fate of this particular bill? It became P.L. 110–387, 122 Stat. 4110 (that's the number of the Congress, the 110th, followed by the designation for the 387th public law passed in that Congress), known as the Veterans' Mental Health and Other Care Improvement Act of 2008.

Example of the Question and Answer Period of a Congressional Hearing

---

SENATOR MURRAY: OK. Can you give us today what the wait times are?

DR. KUSSMAN: For?

SENATOR MURRAY: For all veterans. Can you tell us what the wait time is?

DR. KUSSMAN: As I reported, we believe on the basis of the data that we have, 95 percent of the 39 million appointments that we see every year are done within the 30-day expectation. These are not urgent or emergency appointments, but routine appointments and things for veterans within 30 days of when they ask for it.

SENATOR MURRAY: Can you give me a reason why the *Charlotte Observer's* information is so different?

DR. KUSSMAN: I will have to get back to you on that.

Source: Hearing on Pending Legislation, 2007: 25–26.

Research Reports

The legislative branch documents most likely to be read by a broad audience are research reports. There are at least four different kinds of legislatively relevant government research reports:

1. **Committee Prints:** Committee prints are information briefings or research reports requested by a committee member as part of a deliberative process or simply to investigate an issue. Prints are frequently quite short in length. Most members of Congress are not scientists, but still their job requires them to make decisions about complex technical matters. Sometimes they need a crash course.

For this purpose, they rely on expert witnesses at hearings, but they may also need to read a book on the subject at hand. Committee prints are concise, factual reports compiled by committee staff, the CRS, or other scholars. Committee prints can also be of great use to generalist researchers. Some prints are more helpful than others; the less exciting ones are simply compilations of readings, much like a course pack, or gathering of facts to support a certain viewpoint. An example of a recent print is the Senate Committee on Finance's 340-page Staff report on comprehensive tax reform for 2015 and beyond (S. Prt. 113-31). Committee prints were not distributed through the depository program until the mid-1970s.

2. **Government Accountability Office Reports:** The Government Accountability Office (GAO), a legislative branch agency, is frequently referred to as a watchdog or auditing agency for the entire federal government. GAO has been churning out slim, well-researched reports for decades, initially under its former name, the General Accounting Office. GAO reports tend to be 30 pages or less in length and focus specifically on government efficiency, with a special eye to government waste. Recent titles here include *Drug-Impaired Driving: Additional Support Needed for Public Awareness Initiatives* (GAO-15-293, February 2015); *Air Force: Actions Needed to Strengthen Management of Unmanned Aerial System Pilots* (GAO-14-316, April 2014); and *Food Safety: Additional Actions Needed to Help FDA's Foreign Offices Ensure Safety of Imported Food* (GAO-15-183, January 2015).

3. **Congressional Budget Office Reports:** Congressional Budget Office (CBO) reports are highly valued as dispassionate cost estimates. As legislation is drafted, particularly at the point when it is reported out of committee, CBO estimates are required so that Congress will know the actual price tag of a proposed new law. This is another office that is held up as a standard for nonpartisan assessments.

4. **CRS Reports:** CRS reports are the most famous of this genre. They tend to be under 30 pages and can be requested by members of Congress for any reason at all: to satisfy constituent or member needs; to offer background material or a literature review before a bill is drafted; or to perform specialized, frequently investigative, research. They are broader in scope than committee prints because prints reflect a specific committee's needs. Recent CRS reports include *Hospital-Based Emergency Departments: Background and Policy Considerations* and *The "Islamic State" Crisis and U.S. Policy*. The CRS is a bureau within the LC employing about 700 staff, including many librarians.

Some have argued that Congress's confidential relationship with CRS would be at risk were all reports to be instantly released to the public. Legislation introduced to mandate the reports' wider distribution has not yet succeeded, although an introduced bipartisan measure, *The Congressional Research Service Electronic Accessibility Resolution of 2015* (114 H. Res. 34), directs the clerk of the House to provide the public with Internet access to certain (not all) CRS reports. An archive of OpenCongress.org's wiki provides a history of this decades-long story at https://web.archive.org/web/20150321015306/https://

www.opencongress.org/wiki/Congressional_Research_Service_Reports. Because these reports were historically excluded from the Federal Depository Library Program, several notable efforts have taken place to ensure their wider distribution. On the open Web, the Federation of American Scientists has been collecting CRS reports and putting them online for years. And the University of North Texas has added historic runs of reports to its well-curated digital holdings at http://digital.library.unt.edu/govdocs/crs. The search functionality and completeness of these free resources varies. On the commercial side, Penny Hill Press of Damascus, Maryland, sells the reports directly at www .pennyhill.com. ProQuest offers online CRS reports, together with committee prints in the Congressional Research Digital Collection.

Committee Reports

As previously discussed, when a bill makes it through the committee phase and moves back to the House or Senate floor, one says that it is *reported* out of committee (step 4 in the steps of legislation, above). The committee releases a report, almost always recommending passage (the releasing of reports has been the practice for some decades but was not always consistently done in earlier years). Committee reports tend to contain a general statement of the committee's rationale for supporting the bill, a copy of the marked-up bill, a CBO cost estimate, and a brief legislative history (longer form legislative histories include an annotated list of all committee publications, bills, and debate associated with a law). They may also include a tally of how many committee members voted yea and nay on various clauses of the bill, and minority and additional views. Other types of committee reports include findings of congressional investigations, and a wide range of administrative and miscellaneous publications, including reports requested by the House or Senate. Committee reports are included in the US *Congressional Serial Set.* One type of report, Senate executive reports, concerns treaties or nominations of individuals. Courts and legislative historians use committee reports, typically many years later, to help determine legislative intent (for example to indicate what Congress really intended in passing P.L. 108-173, 117 Stat. 2066 (2003), the Medicare Prescription Drug, Improvement, and Modernization Act).

Congressional Documents

Another form of congressional literature is simply referred to as documents. Documents can include a wide variety of materials ordered printed by both (or either) chamber, including reports of executive departments, agencies, and independent organizations; reports of special investigations made for Congress; and annual reports of nongovernmental organizations (Government Publishing Office, 2015). Senate executive (or "lettered") documents (so called because they were assigned alphabetically arranged letters instead of numbers) contain the text of treaties as presented to the Senate for ratification by the president of the United States. In 1981, Congress started using the more descriptive term *Senate treaty documents,* and these materials are now numbered instead of lettered (Sevetson, 2013).

The US *Congressional Serial Set*:
Reports, Documents, and So Much More

Hundreds of libraries across the United States consider the US *Congressional Serial Set* to be part of their most valued holdings. An earlier sister publication, the *American State Papers,* consists of the papers and reports of Congress from colonial times to approximately 1838. The *Serial Set,* as it is known, is a specially bound set of House and Senate reports and documents from 1817 onward. The collation as a printed set was important for many years. (Today's online users, who can navigate directly to specific reports or documents, have little reason to care about which report is bound with which.)

In the 19th century especially, the *Serial Set* included all kinds of special reports *to* Congress, such as those of various expeditions and explorations, communications from the president, reports from executive branch agencies, as well as the House and Senate Journals (discussed later in this chapter) from 1817 to 1952. Its official binding was once sheepskin, so it was known as the Sheep Set, and the materials were, for many years, clustered together for binding based on their size (not the most intuitive method for efficient retrieval). This practice stopped with the 96th Congress (1979), as printers instituted measures to control the format of the set and bound the reports and documents in numerical order. Users who have a House or Senate report or document number and would like to locate the material in the *Serial Set* will need a conversion table to identify the proper *Serial Set* volume number. See the *Schedule of Volumes of the US Congressional Serial Set* supplied by the Law Librarians' Society of Washington, DC, at www.llsdc .org/serial-set-volumes-guide for one example of a lookup tool. The set is numbered continuously, with the first volume starting at 1. Volumes now number well over 15,000.

The *Serial Set* continues on today, though selective depository libraries stopped receiving the bound volumes in the 1990s, along with the bound version of the *Congressional Record*—the printing for both was prohibitively expensive. The *Serial Set* is also available, both on deposit and commercially, in microform, for those collections that desire a tangible copy of this historic gem. The University of North Texas hosts an inventory of *Serial Set* volumes from the volume 1 to 13219–3 held in American libraries at http:// digital.library.unt.edu/govdocs/ssi.

The early 2000s saw the emergence of two commercial online editions of the *Serial Set* by ProQuest (formerly a part of LexisNexis) and Readex. For researchers, it is worthwhile to seek out an institution subscribing to either. The dawn of these digital editions ushered in a grand new era of congressional research, making possible full-text searching, individual or geographic name searching, the linking of related documents, the viewing of beautiful full-color digitized maps and illustrations, and immeasurably improved subject access. It is as if the earlier surges forward in access, like the blossoming of advanced government documents indexing and MARC cataloging in the 1970s, have been replicated in the early-21st-century context with a digital flourish. Figure 3.2 shows a sample record from the Readex edition. For a highly readable, visually appealing collection of essays highlighting the *Set's* most notorious treasures and tawdry scandals read *The Serial Set: Its Make-up and Content* (Sevetson, 2013); it is recommended reading for anyone who wants to learn more about the *Serial Set* and have fun along the way.

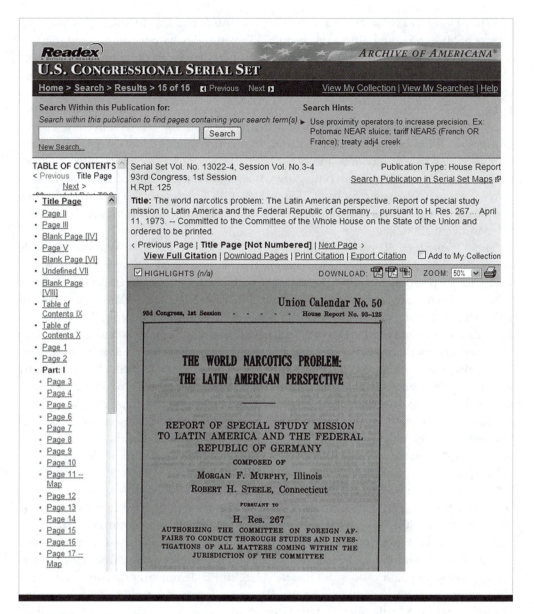

FIGURE 3.2
A Sample Page of the Readex US *Congressional Serial Set, Digital Edition*

The *Congressional Record*

Next, we consider a transcript of floor activity—an edited, inexact transcript with a checkered past, the *Congressional Record*. When the House or Senate convenes as a whole, there is a need to record what transpired. How often does Congress meet? In the latter half of the 20th century, Congress has been open for business anywhere from 224 to 375 days per session (American Enterprise Institute, 2002).

What a long and colorful history the *Congressional Record* has! In 1802, *National Intelligencer* publisher Samuel Smith successfully lobbied the Senate to allow stenographers to take notes at its meetings, a practice the House already allowed. Smith eventually sold his thrice-weekly Washington newspaper to a firm that would become a famous capital area publisher, Gales and Seaton. Gales and Seaton published a *Register of Debates* (1824–1837) which was a first- and third-person accounting of congressional activity. After losing their government contract to cover ongoing legislation, they secured congressional funding to essentially compile a prequel: the *Annals of Congress,* in which they used newspaper accounts and other sources to create a "reconstructive" account of the years 1789–1824. Their competitors, Blair and Rives, produced the *Congressional Globe* starting in 1833, and by law (17 Stat. 510), GPO took over the production of the congressional gazette starting on March 4, 1873, for reasons of efficiency and economy (Hernon et al., 2002).

The *Congressional Record* is published each day Congress is in session, as a quickly printed paperback form (the daily edition), then later as a bound version. The *Record* makes for surprisingly interesting reading. As with any transcript, it can become a bit of a theatrical play, and the arena of congressional discourse has been called "great theatre" (Weisberg and Patterson, 1998). On the main floor of either house, each day usually includes a prayer and the Pledge of Allegiance. There will likely be introduction of bills and resolutions with immediate referral to committee, along with the inevitable suspension of the rules in order to accomplish some task. There may be debates of bills currently under consideration, speeches, or voting. In many cases, ceremonial proclamations follow, such as National Polycystic Kidney Disease Awareness Week (154 *Cong. Rec.* S8142).

How usable is the *Congressional Record*? The two different editions of this serial may confuse users. The red, hardbound *Congressional Record* is considered the official edition, and its pagination varies from the daily (newsprint, paperback) edition. So when considering a citation to the *Congressional Record,* verify that the reference is to the bound edition, *not* the daily. The bound, official edition is considered the default, especially for legal contexts. The daily edition is divided into four distinct sections: House (the H pages), Senate (the S pages), the Daily Digest (the D pages, a summary of that day's actions), and the Extension of Remarks (the E pages). The official edition uses continuous pagination for each session, so the numbers can get to be quite high (into the tens of thousands), and it does not use the H, S, and E designation that are used in the daily edition, integrating and repaginating those sections and offering a separate bound compilation of the Daily Digests. The daily edition is indexed biweekly and the official edition at the end of each session, or annually. Also appearing in the sessional index (from 1873 on) is a list of yea and nay votes, showing which way members of Congress voted on a particular measure. Although it is enjoyable to read in its bound edition, the physical books have been hard to come by since 1990 and may be printed and indexed 10 or more years after the discourse has occurred. To save money, GPO limits the distribution to regional federal depository libraries, approximately one library per state. All other depository libraries receive the paperback daily edition and microfiche official version.

Users can access the full text of the Internet-era (1993–present) *Congressional Record* via *Congress.gov* (daily edition only) and FDsys (both *Congressional Record* editions available), and commercial editions via ProQuest, Westlaw, *CQ.com,* and others. ProQuest and William S. Hein are two vendors currently supplying a full-text online *Congressional Record* (official edition) back to its earliest years.

There is another interesting wrinkle to the *Congressional Record:* it is not a verbatim record. Practices have varied over the years, but there has been lenience (curtailed in recent decades) in letting members edit their own remarks before the publishing of the official edition (one of the reasons for the delayed publication of the final official version). The establishment of an Extension of Remarks section helped clarify those words actually spoken on the floor and those simply added to the record after the fact. In the official version, the Extension of Remarks section is integrated into the main *Record.* Even today, remarks not made on the floor are indicated in a different font or with a bullet, depending on the chamber.

Other Resources

A Century of Lawmaking

A Century of Lawmaking for a New Nation was an early effort by the LC to digitize congressional material for the first century of the republic. An online collection within the larger American Memory Project, it includes bills, laws, the *Congressional Record* and all its predecessors, the House and Senate Journals, and selected volumes of the US *Congressional Serial Set.* Although the optical character recognition system is not equivalent to today's standards, and the search function has fewer advanced options than most of today's electronic texts, the project was a very important step for the LC and it is still quite usable and navigable. As its title implies, *A Century of Lawmaking* covers only 100 years, 1774–1875, and it is not comprehensive even for those years.

C-SPAN and Video Proceedings

Public perception of Congress changed irrevocably with the dawn of C-SPAN, a television station and website dedicated to video coverage of congressional proceedings, covering both houses since 1986. C-SPAN is a private, nonprofit company financed by the cable television industry as a public service. In its current incarnation, C-SPAN covers the House; C-SPAN2 the Senate (along with Book TV programming all weekend, librarians will note). Its video archive in West Lafayette, Indiana, includes all aired programs back to 1987. C-SPAN's backfile is now free online, streaming from 1993 and earlier, a tremendous public benefit, at www.c-span.org. Advanced search allows users to search by date, tag, format (e.g., debate, forum, interview, moot court, remarks, etc.), program title, program summary, person name or title, geographic location, organization, and closed captioning program text. Digital video recording and web archiving of public meetings has nearly become standard practice even in many local governments, and one can now find many video proceedings of congressional activity directly from www.House.gov, www.Senate.gov, and www.Congress.gov.

Calendars, Journals, and Statistics

The official calendars for Congress are the *Calendars of the U.S. House of Representatives and History of Legislation* (a wordy title, basically the House calendar and a list of measures under consideration) and the *Senate Calendar of Business* (a similar resource, but with more emphasis on committee activity). Both are issued daily when Congress is in session and list the official days of the session and recess, and the expected business for the day. Senate committees also publish their own distinct legislative calendars. The House calendars started in around 1900 (though early issues may be difficult to locate); the Monday issues and the final issue cumulate information, providing an excellent way to track legislation in both the House and Senate. The concise calendars are organized into different chapters around the legislation and are fairly simple to look through, consisting of maybe 150 pages for each session. Today, calendar information is available on House and Senate websites, as well as Congress.gov, although official calendars and journals are also still produced.

The Constitution called for a journal of proceedings of Congress (US Constitution, Article I, Section 5). Thus the House *Journal* and the Senate *Journal* were born. The *Journals* are summations of actual actions, in outline (not narrative) form. These resources are helpful for historic research and determining the sequence in which congressional actions took place as they are organized chronologically. The *Journals,* starting in 1789, provide an excellent way to track legislation back to the origins of the country. Earlier legislative processes did not include hearings or even reports to leave a tracking trail. The *Journals* were published as part of the *Serial Set* from 1817 to 1952, as stand-alone series with the SuDoc classification stems XJH and XJS (1953–2010), and most recently via FDsys (House only, 1992–present). The *Journals* allow users to see where a bill went and what happened during the process. They have long included roll call votes (under "Yea and Nay," more recently under "Votes in House" and "Votes in Senate"). Today, the *Journals* still save researchers valuable time. *Journals* include bill number, name, title, and subject indexes as part of a history of bills feature.

For cumulative year-to-date metrics on Congress's volume of work, such as numbers of measures introduced, bills reported on, bills passed, quorum calls, minutes in session, pages of proceedings, and executive branch nominations (military and civilian), consult the *Resume of Congressional Activity,* published as part of the *CR Daily Digest.*

Guides and Indexes

Guides

A college professor was recently overheard to remark, "There's got to be something between the two-second sound bite you hear on the news and some 900-page congressional report." There is, and it is up to librarians to make these intermediate tools more accessible and widespread. For decades, selected publishers have been invaluable to librarians as we try to make Congress and its daily actions understandable to our patrons and to policy makers themselves. The publications of Congressional Quarterly

(CQ, part of the larger CQ RollCall, some content of which is now accumulated and synthesized in CQ.com) and CQ Press (an imprint of SAGE Publications) are perhaps the best example of translating congressional action into plain English. What makes CQ publications especially useful? Articles are written at a high school English level, and congressional action is summarized, frequently in the form of box scores telling the reader the ultimate outcome on a certain issue.

For decades, reference librarians kept current with Congress by reading the *CQ Weekly Report,* newspapers, and possibly the Daily Digest section of the *Congressional Record* daily edition. One could argue that the *CQ Weekly Report* is still a better approach than the newspaper because CQ cites actual bills, hearings, or reports with full identifying information, whereas newspaper articles continue to be notoriously poor in that regard. This has improved in the digital age, when articles and especially blogs can include hyperlinks to real congressional documents. The *CQ Almanac* is available as an online subscription back to 1945, and many CQ monographs are available as e-books. One can learn an entire year's congressional highlights by consulting the *CQ Almanac,* and several years via *Congress and the Nation.* This approach is still very useful and CQ has greatly increased accessibility and searchability with CQ.com, a subscription service especially valued by lobbyists for its congressional news updates throughout the day, archive of *CQ Weekly,* and other useful features.

Congressional Digest is another worthwhile publication, a monthly magazine devoted to congressional affairs, known for its pro/con format and guest columns written by legislators and congressional analysts. It began publication in 1921, when publisher Alice Gram Robinson sought to educate newly franchised voters (i.e., women) on controversial topics of the day. Each issue has a single theme (credit card reform, compulsory national service, biofuels expansion, etc.). It is available online via aggregator services, including EBSCOhost. There are also long-standing newspapers (now online as well)

Community-Created Online Guides to Congressional Research

There are many ways to discover congressional guides authored by librarians and other information specialists (see chapter 2 for professional associations and the GODORT Handout Exchange, which includes resources on Congress). Guides built using Springshare's LibGuides platform are easy to find by entering *libguides congress* into any search engine. Independent groups as diverse as the Sunlight Foundation (via www.opencongress.org) and Project Vote Smart (www.votesmart .org) supply congressionally oriented information in line with their advocacy positions, offering valuable "remixed" content not found elsewhere. The Law Librarians' Society of Washington, DC, founded in 1939, has a particularly useful set of guides grouped together as LLSDC's Legislative Source Book (www.llsdc.org/sourcebook). Other notable collections include the following:

University of California, Berkeley, http://sunsite3.berkeley.edu/wikis/congresearch

Indiana University, http://congress.indiana.edu

Policy Agendas Project, www.policyagendas.org

focusing on Congress: *The Hill, Roll Call,* and The Fed Page section of the Politics tab on the online *Washington Post.*

Indexes

The CIS Index and ProQuest Congressional

The CIS, now a division of ProQuest, was founded by Jim and Esthy Adler in 1969 (see sidebar). The Adlers' vision was to make the riches of congressional publishing more accessible to the general public, and they started a minor revolution. They started with a print index and abstract (the *CIS Index*) along with a microfiche collection, all now available online.

Both the print and online products provide subject, title, witness, SuDoc number, bill number, and report number access to material that can be difficult to find, or lacking altogether, in library online catalogs. When the products debuted, they shed a bright light of access on the vast congressional committee publications in federal depository collections. First included were hearings, reports, documents, and committee prints; now modules are available for the *Congressional Record,* bills and resolutions, and executive branch materials. Beginning in 1983, there is a separate volume featuring fully researched legislative histories, pointing users to all the congressional publications associated with a particular piece of legislation (prior to 1983, the legislative histories were more bare-bones).

ProQuest Congressional (the online interface) includes a basic subscription with add-on modules for the full text of the *Serial Set,* Hearings, CRS reports and Committee Prints, the *Congressional Record,* bills and resolutions, Executive Branch Documents, and Executive Orders and Presidential Proclamations. As one academic reviewer noted, the CIS division of ProQuest "has long been noted for quality productions, including finding aids and microfiche collections. Their publications are part of a core reference collection that any government documents collection should consider" (Lamont, 1997).

> ### Names and Abbreviations Might Be Confusing
>
> Those new to the world of government documents sometimes confess that they get lost in the abbreviations and names of various publishers. The publishers wisely choose authoritative, governmental-sounding names for their companies. Here are the ones most apt to be confusing. CQ/Roll Call (Congressional Quarterly/Roll Call) publishes a myriad of reference products including almanacs, guides to government, *CQ Researcher,* CQ.com, and much more. Congressional Information Service (CIS) is a division of ProQuest, and its *CIS Index* forms the backbone of ProQuest Congressional. CIS is not to be confused with the CRS, a division of the LC.

Bill Tracking, Legislative Histories, and Other Resources

All along the dance of legislation, GPO publishes congressional literature (see figure 3.3). Most current publications (mid-1990s to present) are available through FDsys, with print-on-paper and microfiche copies of some types of publications still freely distributed through the Federal Depository Library Program (FDLP). The research to pull together the publications associated with the creation of a law is referred to as creating a legislative history. ProQuest Congressional and Legislative Insight, HeinOnline, and many legal publishers sell published legislative histories to libraries. Having a legislative history available for laws in which your patrons are interested, and having this published in online form including all of the related publications, can be miraculously time-saving for users—especially when you consider larger or more complex pieces of legislation such as the USA PATRIOT Act (P.L. 107-56, 115 Stat. 272 (2001)) with more than 170 publications associated with it: 70 bills and resolutions, 8 reports, 39 hearings, *Congressional Record* citations and more! Legislative histories are sometimes confused with bill tracking: a legislative history is the list of the publications that were created as the bill became a law; bill tracking includes information about where a bill went as it made its way through the process to become a law (or not). And of course, bill tracking tools can be extremely helpful when creating a legislative history, so one can easily understand the confusion between the two concepts.

Bill tracking is a common research task. Bill tracking is available on *Congress.gov* only back to 1973. What if one needed to track a bill from a previous time period? The *Congressional Record*'s official edition includes a History of Bills section for each year

TABLE 3.2
Frequently Requested Materials and Recommended Sources

Type of information needed	Suggested resource
Plain English explanation of congressional activity	**Daily:** CQ.com, Daily Digest section of the *Congressional Record (Daily Ed.)*, newspapers, blogs **Weekly:** *Roll Call, The Hill*, The Fed Page section of Politics tab *(Washington Post)*, *CQ Weekly* **Monthly:** *Congressional Digest* **Annually:** *CQ Almanac* **Span of years:** *Congress and the Nation*, scholarly published books
Bill summary, status	Congress.gov, FDsys, CQ.com, ProQuest Congressional, House and Senate *Journals*
Legislative history	Congress.gov, FDsys, CQ.com, ProQuest Congressional, ProQuest Legislative Insight, Hein-Online's US Federal Legislative History Library
Information about members of Congress	*Congressional Directory*, members' own websites, Congress.gov, CQ.com, ProQuest Congressional, *Biographical Directory of the United States Congress*, *CQ's Politics in America*, OpenCongress.org
Historical sources (selected)	*Congressional Record* and its predecessors, US *Congressional Serial Set*, House & Senate *Journals*, published and unpublished hearings
Voting (tally of members' votes on bills, etc.)	"Yea and Nay Votes" section of the *Congressional Record Index*, ProQuest Congressional, *CQ Almanac, Congressional Index*
Rise and fall of different topics before Congress; movement of bills through Congress	www.policyagendas.org; legex.org

Displayed is an outline of the many steps in our Federal lawmaking process from the introduction of a bill by any Member through passage by the U.S. House of Representatives and U.S. Senate and approval by the President of the United States. Since the large majority of laws originate in the House, the example shown below starts with that body.

The **U.S. GOVERNMENT PUBLISHING OFFICE (GPO)** was established to provide essential printing and binding for the Congress and there is a close relationship between Congress and GPO. This relationship is demonstrated here by the many instances when GPO's electronic dissemination and printing services are required in the lawmaking process.

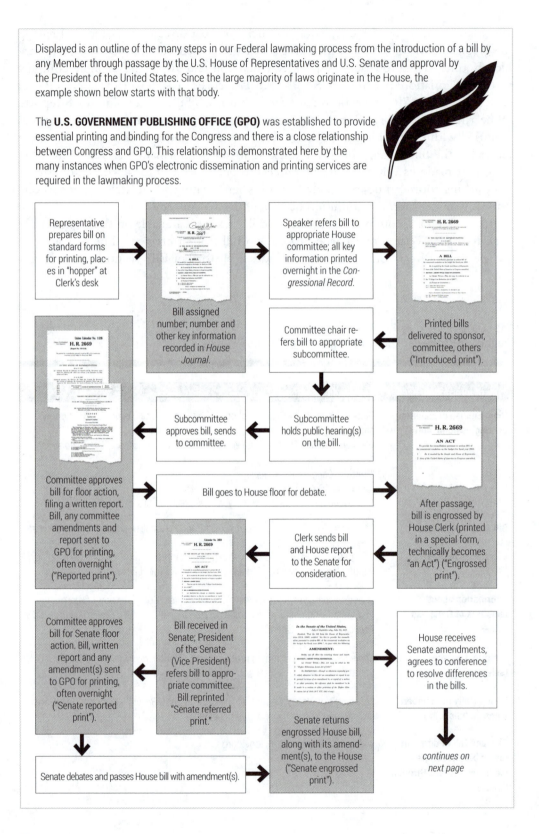

Representative prepares bill on standard forms for printing, places in "hopper" at Clerk's desk

Bill assigned number; number and other key information recorded in *House Journal*.

Speaker refers bill to appropriate House committee; all key information printed overnight in the *Congressional Record*.

Printed bills delivered to sponsor, committee, others ("Introduced print").

Committee chair refers bill to appropriate subcommittee.

Subcommittee holds public hearing(s) on the bill.

Subcommittee approves bill, sends to committee.

Committee approves bill for floor action, filing a written report. Bill, any committee amendments and report sent to GPO for printing, often overnight ("Reported print").

Bill goes to House floor for debate.

After passage, bill is engrossed by House Clerk (printed in a special form, technically becomes "an Act") ("Engrossed print").

Clerk sends bill and House report to the Senate for consideration.

Committee approves bill for Senate floor action. Bill, written report and any amendment(s) sent to GPO for printing, often overnight ("Senate reported print").

Bill received in Senate; President of the Senate (Vice President) refers bill to appropriate committee. Bill reprinted "Senate referred print."

Senate returns engrossed House bill, along with its amendment(s), to the House ("Senate engrossed print").

House receives Senate amendments, agrees to conference to resolve differences in the bills.

Senate debates and passes House bill with amendment(s).

continues on next page

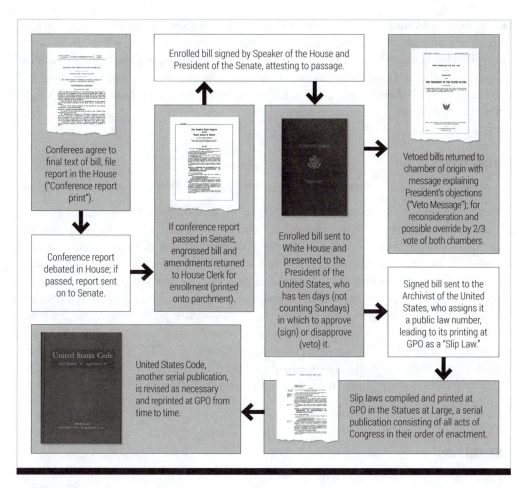

FIGURE 3.3
A Simplified View of the Legislative Process, Emphasizing GPO's Printing of Bills:
How a Bill Becomes Law

that provides references to actions taken on a given bill with the corresponding page numbers in the *Record* where those actions are recorded. The House and Senate *Journals,* referred to above, also contain an index to bills. For further information on bill tracking as a part of legislative history, consult Joe Morehead's detailed discussion of legislative history (Morehead, 1999: 159–164). For many years librarians relied on the *Digest of Public General Bills and Resolutions,* an annual volume printed by the GPO from 1937 to 1990, and a privately produced resource, Commerce Clearing House's *Congressional Index,* a loose-leaf publication that included status tables arranged by bill number.

Today's generation of government information specialists are unlikely to know about loose-leaf services, but apt to know about powerful data visualizations such as Legislative Explorer, http://legex.org, which lets users follow the literal movement of bills (appearing like points of light in a Congressional Milky Way) from 1973 forward, with the option to filter them by topic, type of legislation, chamber, party, or specific bill. FollowtheMoney.org, tracks donations to congressional campaigns. Govtrack.us adds statistical analyses to openly available congressional data; its user-friendly widgets are embedded on many Congress members' pages. CongressionalData.org is a coalition of many activist groups calling for open and reusable congressional data. Beyond bill tracking, table 3.2 shows the type of questions government documents librarians field every day, and some of the sources they consult.

Conclusion

This chapter explored the rich, complex literature of Congress. Knowing the context of any particular piece of congressional information—where it falls in the legislative process—is critical. Learning about Congress is manageable if done incrementally, and is easier for those who can tolerate the messiness of the legislative process. Although the sheer volume of congressional output is staggering, there are plain English summaries from specialized news organizations and publishers like CQ, indexing services (both commercial and governmental), and boiled-down reports (like those from the CRS). If one were limited to using only five free websites for congressional research, the best bets might be Congress.gov; House.gov; Senate.gov; FDsys; and the nonprofit, nongovernmental c-span.org. Congress, like every other sector of our government and our lives, is opening up rapidly with the help of new technology; perhaps even the most profound changes are yet to come.

Exercises

1. Watch C-SPAN or any video coverage of congressional activity for 15 minutes, with the aim of sharpening your skills. Pay particular attention to the kind of information exchanged and the technical knowledge of the speaker or witness. Can you identify the convener of the proceedings? Keep a tally of how many times the following kinds of congressional literature or actions are mentioned:

Bill	Calendar
Amendment	Congressional Record
Vote	Conference
Hearing	House or Senate Journal
Report	

2. Find out the following for your home address:

   Your congressional district:
   Your representative:
   Your senators:
   Sources consulted:

3. Try your skill at tracking legislation. Use Congress.gov, FDsys, House.gov, or Senate.gov to select current legislation that interests you. Commit to following this legislation: devise a mechanism that works for you to check its status monthly until the end of the current congress (could be as long as two years). Even if you do not follow through and check on your legislation, what system would you have set in place to do so?

4. Follow a medical issue or concern through Congress. Using secondary sources (CQ publications, newspapers, journal articles, books), identify congressional literature concerning a specific medical topic (diabetes, stem cell research, smoking cessation, and multiple sclerosis are but a few examples). What kind of attention has Congress paid to this topic over the years or decades?

5. One more angle on congressional attention: choose an NGO (nongovernmental organization) or nonprofit of your choice. Explore this group's website, and determine how well you can learn about relevant legislation via their resources. Possibilities include the following organizations:

   The Tea Party Patriots (www.teapartypatriots.org)
   Celiac Disease Foundation (Celiac.org)
   United Association (www.ua.org)

6. Find an example of a member or committee website showing significant bias and one that seems more balanced. What language do you see that indicates the bias?

7. Can you find the Congressional Budget Office estimate for S. 952, the Harmful Algal Blooms and Hypoxia Research and Control Amendments Act of 2009? According to the estimate, what would be the estimated outlay of spending under S. 952 for the year 2014?

Sources Mentioned in This Chapter

Sources mentioned in this section do not duplicate the references that follow.

American Enterprise Institute for Public Policy Research and Brookings Institution. 2002. *Vital Statistics on Congress, 2001–2002.* Washington, DC: American Enterprise Institute. Tables 6-1 & 6-2: 146–147.
Bill Versions, www.gpo.gov/help/index.html#about_congressional_bills.htm.
C-SPAN, www.c-span.org (Links to C-SPAN2).
Calendars of the U.S. House of Representatives and History of Legislation. 1935–. Washington, DC: Government Publishing Office.
Century of Lawmaking for a New Nation, http://memory.loc.gov/ammem/amlaw/. Includes *American State Papers, Annals of Congress,* Bills and Resolution, *Congressional Globe, Congressional Record,* Journals (of Congress and the Continental Congress), *Register of Debates, U.S. Serial Set* and *Statutes at Large.*
CIS Index Annual. 1971–. Ann Arbor, MI: ProQuest.
Congress and the Nation. 1964–. Washington, DC: Congressional Quarterly, Inc. and CQ Press.
Congress.gov, Congress.gov/.
Congressional Digest. 1921–. Washington, DC: Congressional Digest.
Congressional Index. 1938–. Chicago: Commerce Clearinghouse.

Congressional Record (daily). 1873–. Washington, DC: Government Publishing Office. Available online
 (1994–), www.gpo.gov/fdsys/browse/collection.action?collectionCode=CREC.

Congressional Record (bound). 1873–. Washington, DC: Government Printing Office. Available online
 (1999–), www.gpo.gov/fdsys/browse/collection.action?collectionCode=CRECB.

Congressional Research Service Reports, University of North Texas Digital Library, http://digital
 .library.unt.edu/explore/collections/CRSR/browse/.

CQ Almanac. 1945–. Washington, DC: CQ Press.

CQ Researcher. 1991–. Washington, DC: Congressional Quarterly and EBSCO.

CQ Weekly (title varies). 1956–. Washington, DC: CQ Press.

CQ.com. 2000–. Washington, DC: Congressional Quarterly.

CQ's Politics in America. 1999–. Washington, DC: CQ Press.

Digest of Public General Bills and Resolutions. 1937–1990. Washington, DC: Library of Congress. http://
 catalog.hathitrust.org/Record/000520678.

Dorough, Bob, et al. 2002. *Schoolhouse Rock!* Burbank, CA: Buena Vista Home Entertainment.

FDsys, www.gpo.gov/fdsys/.

Federation of American Scientists, Congressional Research Service Reports, www.fas.org/sgp/crs/.

Follow The Money, www.followthemoney.org.

Govtrack, Govtrack.us.

Guide to Congress (6th ed.) 2008. Washington, DC: CQ Press.

HeinOnline. 2000–. Buffalo, NY: William S. Hein.

The Hill, www.thehill.com.

House.gov.

How Our Laws Are Made, (H.doc 110-49) www.gpo.gov/fdsys/pkg/CDOC-110hdoc49/pdf/
 CDOC-110hdoc49.pdf.

Joint Committee on Atomic Energy Digital Library, http://collections.stanford.edu/atomicenergy.

Lamont, Melissa. 1997. "CIS Index to Unpublished US Senate Committee Hearings (review)." *Journal of
 Government Information* 24, no. 6: 607.

Law Librarians' Society of Washington, DC, www.llsdc.org.

Legislative Explorer, Legex.org.

LibGuides, http://springshare.com/libguides.

OpenCongress.org https://web.archive.org/web/20150321015306/https://www.opencongress.org/
 wiki/Congressional_Research_Service_Reports.

Penny Hill Press, www.pennyhill.com.

Policy Agendas Project, www.policyagendas.org.

Project Vote Smart, http://votesmart.org.

ProQuest Congressional, www.proquest.com/libraries/academic/databases/proquest-congressional.html
 (description only).

Redman, Eric. 1973. *The Dance of Legislation.* New York: Simon and Schuster.

Resume of Congressional Activity, www.senate.gov/pagelayout/reference/two_column_table/Resumes.htm.

Roll Call, Washington, DC: CQ Roll Call, Inc. www.rollcall.com.

Schedule of Volumes of the U.S. Congressional Serial Set, www.llsdc.org/serial-set-volumes-guide.

Senate Calendar of Business, www.collectionCode=CCAL/.

Senate.gov.

Sources for the Text of Congressional Bills and Resolutions, www.llsdc.org/sources-for-congressional-bills-resolutions.

Sunlight Foundation, http://sunlightfoundation.com.

United States House and Senate Committee Hearings and Publications, http://louisdl.louislibraries.org/cdm/
 landingpage/collection/p120701c01125.

United States Statutes at Large. 1789–. Washington, DC: Government Publishing Office.

US *Congressional Serial Set.* 1817–. Washington, DC: Government Publishing Office.

US *Congressional Serial Set* Inventory, University of North Texas Digital Library, http://digital.library.unt.edu/govdocs/ssi/.

Westlaw, www.westlaw.com.

References

Brookings Institution and American Enterprise Institute for Public Policy Research. 2013. *Vital Statistics on Congress, 2013.* Washington, DC: Brookings Institution. Tables 6–1 & 6–2. http://brookings.edu/vitalstats.

Dodd, Lawrence C. 2013. *Congress Reconsidered.* 10th edition. Thousand Oaks, CA: CQ Press.

Government Publishing Office. 2015. "About Congressional Documents." www.gpo.gov/fdsys/browse/collection.action?collectionCode=CDOC.

Hall, Laurie, Heidi Ramos, Suzanne Ebanues. 2014. "Online Congressional Hearings Project and Open Forum with DLC." (Recorded conference presentation.) http://login.icohere.com/fdlpmeetings?pnum=EJW40691.

Hearing on Pending Legislation: Hearing Before the Committee on Veterans' Affairs. 2007. Washington: Government Printing Office. October 24, 2007. http://purl.access.gpo.gov/GPO/LPS93891, Errata: http://purl.access.gpo.gov/GPO/LPS99778.

Hernon, Peter, Harold C. Relyea, Joan F. Cheverie, and Robert E. Dugan. 2002. *United States Government Information: Policies and Sources.* Westport, CT: Libraries Unlimited.

Hillman, G. Robert. 2000. "Exaggerating the Exaggeration? Gore's Internet Quote, Other Remarks Keep GOP's Spin Machine Humming." *Dallas Morning News,* April 6: 1A.

Holtz-Eakin, Douglas. "The President's (Former) Economy Guru." By Terry Gross. *Fresh Air,* January 26, 2006, www.npr.org/templates/story/story.php?storyId=5173072.

Kaiser, Robert G. 2013. *Act of Congress: How America's Essential Institution Works, and How It Doesn't.* New York: Alfred A. Knopf.

Morehead, Joe. 1999. *Introduction to United States Government Information Sources.* Englewood, CO: Libraries Unlimited.

Oppenheimer, Bruce I. 1983. "How Legislatures Shape Policy and Budgets." *Legislative Studies Quarterly* 8, no. 4 (Nov.): 551–597.

Panangala, Sidath Viranga. 2007. *Veterans' Health Care Issues.* Washington, DC: Congressional Research Service, Domestic Social Policy Division. Nov. 30, 2007.

Public Broadcasting Service. 2009. @THE CAPITOL: Overview: The Committee System in the US Congress. Washington, DC: PBS. http://web.archive.org/web/20120603131545/www.pbs.org/newshour/@capitol/committees/committees_overview.html.

Sevetson, Andrea, ed. 2013. *The Serial Set: Its Make-up and Content.* Bethesda, MD: ProQuest.

Sevetson, Andrea. 2015. "Hearings and the ProQuest Congressional Hearings Digital Collection." Bethesda, MD: ProQuest. http://proquest.libguides.com/ld.php?content_id=5140490.

Weisberg, Herbert F., and Samuel C. Patterson. 1998. *Great theatre: the American Congress in the 1990s.* Cambridge, England: Cambridge University Press.

Whisner, Mary. 2005. "Practicing Reference . . . What's in a Statute Name?" *Law Library Journal* 2005–09: 169–183. www.aallnet.org/products/pub_llj_v97n01/2005–09.pdf.

CHAPTER 4

Introduction to Law

ERIC FORTE AND PEGGY ROEBUCK JARRETT

Introduction

Law is the foundation of government information. Every agency, every source, and every concept in this book has its origins in law. The Constitution is the founding law of the United States, and as discussed in chapter 1, the Constitution contains the origins of not just our federal government, but of government information as well. The Constitution created the overall structure of government and the responsibilities of the different branches of government, which in turn create and govern the operation of the government through all of its agencies, as well as the publications and information the agencies produce. This means that an understanding of law and the different kinds of law is essential for one working with government information.

Still, there is a difference between the knowledge needed by a lawyer practicing law and by a librarian working with legal government information. Lawyers go through specialized schooling. State courts have rules about admission to the bar, including passing a bar exam, in order to represent clients and give legal advice. But as a reference or government information librarian who understands the basic sources and strategies for *finding* the law, it can be very empowering—not to mention a lot of fun—to connect patrons with legal resources and the law itself. While most librarians can easily and quickly navigate their way around almost any bibliographic database or discovery tool, it takes some special knowledge to understand how to find the law, making the librarian who is comfortable doing so ever valuable. Finding the law is a skill that can be learned. Start with an understanding of the basic nature of law, add a knowledge of the sources of law, top it off with the searching and organizational skills learned in other areas of librarianship, and the result is that finding the law, and helping people do the same, can be accomplished.

The next several chapters will introduce the primary sources of law (whose origins in Congress were covered in the previous chapter) and strategies for using them. And always remember: you may lead someone to the law, but after that, step back. Librarians can help people identify, find, and use legal resources, but interpreting and applying the law is up to them, or their lawyer, as often

> patrons in search of legal information are also looking for someone to vali-
> date their argument or assure them that they have a "good case." A librarian's
> responsibility ends after providing assistance in finding information and
> stops short of providing validation or an opinion; patrons then need to be
> told to consult with an attorney licensed to practice law in their state. Telling
> patrons how to interpret the details of a law or how a law applies to them,
> or dispensing any kind of legal advice, are all acts that can be construed as
> the unlicensed practice of law, which is illegal. (Knapp, 2009: 1439).

In fact, the term *legal research* often denotes the research that lawyers do for their clients. But legal research is also done by law students, paralegals, and self-represented (*pro se*) litigants. Scholars and students in a variety of disciplines may want to do legal research, as well as journalists and authors. These chapters focus on basic aspects of legal research—finding the text of laws and cases—not the deeper work of analyzing and synthesizing legal information to reach a legal conclusion. Further, we will focus on the free law resources available from governments. A full-fledged law library uses these resources along with commercial resources. For instance, the *United States Code* (discussed in chapter 5) is a standard source of statutory law, and the government's version of it is available in depository libraries and free online. A law library serving people engaged in frequent and in-depth research, however, will use not only these free versions, but also the value-added versions available for purchase from various legal information publishers and vendors.

Chapters 5–8: The Kinds of Law

There are four types of federal law. The first and simplest is the US Constitution and its amendments. It is easily found online and in the standard sets of statutory law discussed in chapter 5.

The second type of law is statutory law. The Constitution states that Congress shall make the laws. The laws that Congress makes (through the process described in chapter 3) are collectively known as statutory law. These laws are referred to as statutes. Statutory law is covered in chapter 5 on Public Laws and the *U.S. Code*.

Next is administrative law, also referred to as regulatory law, covered in chapter 6 on Regulations. This is the law that is found in rules and regulations from executive departments and agencies. These rules largely detail how the executive branch will per-form its role of enforcing the laws of Congress. To a lesser extent, administrative law also refers to the works and actions of the president's office, through executive orders and proclamations, legal decisions, and orders from the Office of Management and Bud-get (covered in chapter 9).

Finally there is case law, or opinions written by a judge or judges in the course of resolving disputes. The body of law created by these opinions is also called common law and often referred to as precedent. Case law is the type of law most difficult to locate using only government information sources. Historically, only US Supreme Court decisions were generally available, since they were printed by GPO and distributed through the Federal Depository Library Program, while lower federal court decisions were published in commercial legal sets often outside the scope and access of depository libraries lacking large, purchased legal reference collections. The simplest explanation for how it came to be that private, commercial publishers controlled such an important government publication as federal case law is a combination of tradition and opportunity. Our legal system is based on English common law, which was privately published. There was no tradition of courts disseminating their own opinions or governments publishing them. American publishers saw a market opportunity and began to collect and publish these important, precedent-setting cases, adding value with indexes and digests, and thus creating a case reporting system unique to the United States. In recent years, technology has made case law easier to access via freely available websites, but private publishers remain important in case law publishing. Chapter 7, Case Law and the Judicial Branch includes discussion of the publication of opinions and finding free case law online.

One could classify a fifth kind of law, treaties—agreements between two or many sovereign nations. As treaties are negotiated by the president (though ratified by the Senate), they will be covered in chapter 8 on the presidency.

Law of States and Other Jurisdictions

While this brief summary of the types of law is from a federal perspective, states and local governments produce most of the actual laws that govern society. For instance, read the Constitution; it doesn't say anything about murder. Does that mean that murder was not officially illegal unless an early Congress passed a law preventing it? Not quite. For many years after the founding of the nation, the federal government and its lawmaking were generally limited to affairs of the running of the federal government itself. States and local governments did (and still do) most of the lawmaking that governed the lives of the citizenry. So at the time of the US Constitution's adoption, the state constitutions, statutes, and case law addressed basics such as preventing murder and theft, and even these early state constitutions often in part simply adopted English common law.

States generally have the same four sources of law. Each state has its own constitution; its own statutory law consisting of the laws passed by its legislative branch; its own administrative law comprising the rules made by state executive agencies; and its own case law, the law derived from opinions of state courts. Further, counties and cities promulgate law via local codes and ordinances that deal with local issues. Accessibility of the law varies from state to state, but as with federal law sources, access is usually through a combination of government and commercial, print and online, free and fee-based sources. Each of the subsequent three law chapters will address the respective state versions of that type of law.

Primary versus Secondary Legal Resources

The laws—constitutions, statutes, regulations, and cases—are considered primary sources. Secondary sources is a term applied to materials about the law, for example law review articles, hornbooks, casebooks, treatises, digests, and practitioner-oriented publications that explain, annotate, and give context to some aspect or topic of the law, while citing to the appropriate primary source. Legal researchers often turn to secondary sources first as a way to aid access to primary sources. Governments, however, are generally not in the habit of producing secondary legal sources. (A rare but notable exception: Congress, with the help of the CRS, prepares a weighty secondary source, *The Constitution of the United States of America: Analysis and Interpretation*. This resource, updated with biennial supplements, summarizes significant Supreme Court interpretations of every clause of the US Constitution, and is available to federal depository libraries.) It should also be noted that governments do produce other law-related materials that are neither primary nor traditional legal secondary sources. Legislative materials (discussed in chapter 3) and agency publications (discussed in chapter 9 and throughout the book), for example, may be useful in many legal contexts.

Although law libraries purchase and legal researchers use commercial secondary sources, most academic and public libraries do not acquire them in print or online beyond what may be available in broader electronic packages. Freely available secondary sources like Google Scholar and the Social Sciences Research Network (SSRN) offer access to articles by legal scholars and Wikipedia sometimes provides a useful roadmap to a major legal subject or case, with appropriate citations. Sources like HathiTrust and Google Books have some free full-text out of copyright, historical law volumes.

Because most secondary legal sources are not government information, the following chapters focus on primary government information sources. However, when diving into legal research, it's always a good strategy to first look for a reliable secondary source that provides context and explanation.

Law Libraries

Although government information librarians can help the public with many legal reference questions, particularly those involving laws and regulations, there are times when referral to a law library is necessary or a consultation with a law librarian is helpful. There are close to 200 law libraries participating in the Federal Depository Library Program. Of those, 152 are law school libraries, and 36 are state court libraries. The rest are federal government or public law libraries. Public law libraries, which tend to be situated in large urban areas and may or may not be federal depositories, are especially experienced with assisting the non-lawyer doing their own legal research or involved in a court action without a lawyer (a *pro se* or self-represented litigant).

The American Association of Law Libraries (AALL) has a government relations policy that supports broad, permanent public access to and preservation of official government information, www.aallnet.org/mm/Leadership-Governance/policies/Public Policies/policy-government.html. AALL also has a Government Documents Special Interest Section, that although much smaller than ALA's GODORT, is similarly populated with librarians working with and interested in government publications.

For Further Reading, see the Public Library Toolkit from the American Association of Law Libraries, www.aallnet.org/sections/lisp/Public-Library-Toolkit.

Reference

Knapp, Jeffrey. 2009. "Legal Research: An Introduction to Key Online and Print Sources." *Choice* 46, no. 8: 1439–1449.

CHAPTER 5

Public Laws and the *U.S. Code*

PEGGY ROEBUCK JARRETT

Introduction

"I'm looking for a law." People often approach public service desks saying just that. Are they looking for state law on medical marijuana, divorce, or living wills, perhaps? Or the federal law on health insurance, special education, oil spills, voting rights, or food safety? All of these are examples of statutory law, that is, law created by a legislative body as opposed to a court or constitution. Chapter 3 described the process of legislation, from bill introduction to enactment, and discussed the congressional publications available at each stage. This chapter focuses on what happens next, after a bill becomes law at the federal level. The short explanation is that once a bill is enacted, it is assigned a public law number and published as a slip law. The public laws are compiled chronologically in the *United States Statutes at Large*. These laws are then codified—arranged by subject—and incorporated into the *United States Code*. But as with most specialized research involving multiple publications and formats, and over 200 years' worth of content, the devil is in the details. Paying attention to these details and, at the same time, seeing the big picture of how laws are organized and published are excellent strategies for success in finding laws and helping other people with their research.

Public Laws

Slip laws, the first official form of enacted legislation, are exactly what they sound like. Each law is issued individually. It can be a single sheet (a slip of paper), or hundreds of pages long (more like a pamphlet), prepared by the Office of the Federal Register (OFR) of the National Archives, and published by the Government Publishing Office (GPO). Some large depository libraries, particularly law libraries, still receive these print slip laws from GPO, and keep them for a few years until the hardbound *Statutes at Large* volumes, discussed later in this chapter, are issued and received. GPO's Federal Digital

System (FDsys) has all the public laws, digitally authenticated, from the 104th Congress, 1st session, 1995 to date. Note that in some sessions, Congress may pass a small number of private laws that affect a single person or small group. These private laws are available on FDsys, and will be published in the *Statutes at Large,* but our concern here is public laws.

Public law (Pub. L. or P.L.) numbers are assigned by the OFR. The system is straightforward: numbers are assigned first by the session of Congress and then in the order they were passed. The first law enacted during the 113th Congress is designated as Public Law 113-1; the second, Public Law 113-2. This chronological arrangement is irrespective of subject matter—for example, the Patient Protection and Affordable Care Act, passed during the 111th Congress, is Pub. L. No. 111-148. It is followed by Pub. L. No. 111-149, which concerns wetlands. It is also helpful to remember that, in modern times, each Congress spans two years, or two sessions (the 111th Congress, for example, took place in 2009 and 2010).

Along with assigning public law numbers, OFR prepares the laws for publication by providing pagination of the laws in the *Statutes at Large,* even though those permanent volumes are usually issued several years later. Researchers can find a wealth of other information by looking at a public law. In the margin notes and header of the public laws, you can find the date of enactment, bill number, *United States Code* citation, and popular name, if one exists. At the bottom is a brief legislative history section, giving citations to major congressional actions taken, such as a committee report and dates of debate found in the *Congressional Record.* These notes are not part of the law, but useful aids for researchers. And whether in print from GPO or online on FDsys, the new public laws look the same and have the same citation as they will when published in the *Statutes at Large.*

Public law numbers first appeared in the margins of *Statutes at Large* volumes in the early 1900s and later, in 1957, they moved to the header. The standard legal citation manual, *The Bluebook: A Uniform System of Citation,* requires that legal citations use P.L. numbers along with the *Statutes at Large* volume and page number. For example, a legal resource would cite the major health law as Patient Protection and Affordable Care Act, Pub. L. No. 111-148, 124 Stat. 119 (2010). A citation to an older law, before P.L. numbers appeared, would include the chapter number, for example, Panama Canal Act, ch. 1302, 32 Stat. 481 (1902). If the year is in the name of the act, omit the parentheses, as in The Homestead Act of 1862, ch. 75, 12 Stat. 392. Although the rules of legal citation may seem intimidating, all these examples provide helpful information to people looking for a law: a name, a year, a number (chapter or public law), and a page.

Compilation of Statutory Law: *United States Statutes at Large*

The *Statutes at Large* is the authoritative source of federal statutory law (the body of law passed by the US Congress). A statute is simply a law or act enacted by a legislature. Slip laws are the first official form of enacted law, but the *Statutes at Large* are the permanent form of laws passed in a particular session of Congress. Once the *Statutes at Large* volumes are issued, they supersede the individual slip laws. The generic name for *Statutes*

PUBLIC LAW 113–187—NOV. 26, 2014   128 STAT. 2003

Public Law 113–187
113th Congress

An Act

To amend chapter 22 of title 44, United States Code, popularly known as the
Presidential Records Act, to establish procedures for the consideration of claims
of constitutionally based privilege against disclosure of Presidential records, and
for other purposes.

Nov. 26, 2014
[H.R. 1233]

*Be it enacted by the Senate and House of Representatives of
the United States of America in Congress assembled,*

Presidential and
Federal Records
Act Amendments
of 2014.
44 USC 101 note.

SECTION 1. SHORT TITLE; TABLE OF CONTENTS.

(a) SHORT TITLE.—This Act may be cited as the "Presidential
and Federal Records Act Amendments of 2014".

(b) TABLE OF CONTENTS.—The table of contents for this Act
is as follows:

Sec. 1. Short title; table of contents.
Sec. 2. Presidential records.
Sec. 3. National Archives and Records Administration.
Sec. 4. Records management by Federal agencies.
Sec. 5. Disposal of records.
Sec. 6. Procedures to prevent unauthorized removal of classified records from Na-
        tional Archives.
Sec. 7. Repeal of provisions related to the National Study Commission on Records
        and Documents of Federal Officials.
Sec. 8. Pronoun amendments.
Sec. 9. Records management by the Archivist.
Sec. 10. Disclosure requirement for official business conducted using non-official
         electronic messaging account.

SEC. 2. PRESIDENTIAL RECORDS.

(a) PROCEDURES FOR CONSIDERATION OF CLAIMS OF CONSTITU-
TIONALLY BASED PRIVILEGE AGAINST DISCLOSURE.—

(1) AMENDMENT.—Chapter 22 of title 44, United States
Code, is amended by adding at the end the following:

**"§ 2208. Claims of constitutionally based privilege against
disclosure**

Determinations.
Public
information.
Notifications.
Time periods.
44 USC 2208.

"(a)(1) When the Archivist determines under this chapter to
make available to the public any Presidential record that has not
previously been made available to the public, the Archivist shall—
    "(A) promptly provide notice of such determination to—
        "(i) the former President during whose term of office
the record was created; and
        "(ii) the incumbent President; and
    "(B) make the notice available to the public.
"(2) The notice under paragraph (1)—
    "(A) shall be in writing; and
    "(B) shall include such information as may be prescribed
in regulations issued by the Archivist.

Regulations.

FIGURE 5.1
Public Law/Statutes at Large, Pub. L. No. 113-187, 128 Stat. 2003 Presidential and
Federal Records Act Amendments of 2014

at Large is session laws—the laws of a particular session of a legislative body. The most
important concept is that session laws are chronological. They include the laws passed
by a particular legislative body, in order. They are not arranged by subject, nor are they
incorporated with relevant laws from earlier sessions to form the law in force (at that
time). That arrangement is a code, discussed later in this chapter.

History of the *United States Statutes at Large*

Why start a discussion of the *Statutes at Large* with its history? Like many federal legal publications, it has a long history involving multiple editions prepared and published by both the government and the private sector. Publishing legacies affect how legal titles are organized and arranged today, so a bit of history can be helpful in understanding the body of laws. The idea of making the laws passed by Congress available to the public began with the very first Congress. An Act to provide for safekeeping of the Acts, Records and Seal of the United States, mandated that new laws be delivered to the Secretary of State, who in turn was to deliver copies to all senators, representatives, and state executives, and to publish each law in at least three public newspapers (1 Stat. 68 (1789)). Just six years later, Congress ordered "to be printed and collated at public expense, a complete edition of the laws of the United States," with 4,500 copies of these compilations distributed around the states and territories of the young nation (1 Stat. 443 (1795)). This edition, *Laws of the United States,* is known as the Folwell edition (named for the printer, as is often the case with older legal publications) and covers 1789–1814. The next authorized edition is the Bioren and Duane edition, also called *Laws of the United States,* which was published until 1845.

In 1845, Congress authorized a new edition, printed by Little & Brown, which was called for the first time *United States Statutes at Large.* It was to contain "the articles of Confederation, the Constitution, all the public and all the private laws and resolves, whether obsolete, repealed, or in force, and whether temporary or permanent . . . and all treaties with foreign nations and Indian tribes" (5 Stat. 798 (1845)). This was an important turning point—not only did Little & Brown publish the laws retrospectively, but its contract was extended over the years, creating an ongoing publication of statutory law. In 1874, responsibility was shifted from the private publisher to GPO, first under the authority of the Department of State, and currently under the direction of the Archivist of the United States, through the OFR.

Large libraries and most law libraries either have the Little & Brown edition or reprints of it, labeled and shelved as one continuous set titled *United States Statutes at Large.* The publication pattern of the early volumes is not straightforward. For example, volumes 1–5 contain public laws, volume 6 contains private laws, and volumes 7–8 contain treaties. Early volumes also cover more than one congressional session. Volumes 13–49 cover a single Congress each. The current practice of one volume per annual congressional session began in 1937. As time went on, and the nation grew, each Congress passed more and more laws, so recent volumes are divided into multiple books, which are labeled part 1, part 2, and so on. Volume 121, for example, is in two parts, and volume 124 is in four parts. The page numbers included in each part are printed on the book's spine, which is helpful since citations are to volume and page number. (For more on the history see Conklin and Aclund, 1992).

It is also worth noting that, along with public and private laws, the *Statutes at Large* include concurrent resolutions, presidential proclamations, reorganization plans, constitutional amendments, and, until 1948, treaties and international agreements. When using the print set—even if you have a good citation—careful reading of the spine, and a willingness to pull a volume off the shelf and look at the information on the title page is an excellent strategy for figuring out how to find the law being sought!

Using the *United States Statutes at Large*

As discussed in the previous section, the *Statutes at Large* is available in print at some depository and most law libraries. It is also available online, for free to the public, but researchers need to navigate to both GPO's FDsys and the Law Library of Congress. The authenticated collection on FDsys starts with 1951, the 82nd Congress, 1st Session (Volume 65). The Law Library of Congress collection covers 1789 to 1950 (volumes 1–64). A scan of the Little and Brown edition, 1789 to 1875, is also available in the LC American Memory Project, *A Century of Lawmaking for a New Nation.* HeinOnline, if available, is a good commercial choice, since it has a complete, searchable collection in one place, volume 1, 1789 to the present.

Despite the inconvenience of needing to use both FDsys and the Law Library of Congress website to access all the volumes of the *Statutes at Large,* a complete historical collection, freely available to the public, is a recent development. In 2011, GPO and LC announced a collaborative project to "digitize some of our nation's most important legal and legislative documents," including the *Statutes at Large* (GPO, 2011). This project was strongly supported by the library community, including the American Library Association and the American Association of Law Libraries. The LC had digitized the volumes covering 1951 to 2002, but adding this collection to what was then GPO Access (the predecessor of FDsys) required approval by the Joint Committee on Printing (JCP), the congressional committee that oversees GPO's operation. After JCP approval, the collection was ingested by GPO and in 2013, descriptive metadata was added. Subsequent volumes have been added, so the digital collection is as current as the print.

Public availability is important to law librarians because the print edition of the *Statutes at Large* is "legal evidence of the laws," 1 U.S.C. § 112, which means it is admissible as evidence. But because the most important feature of the *Statutes at Large* is the chronological presentation of laws as they are passed, it can be argued that the collection is most useful for historical research, including but not limited to historical legal research. Legislation may do several things. It may add new law, amend existing law, or repeal existing law in whole or in part. To study the development of a particular area of law, researchers might want to look at all relevant legislation passed by Congress over a period of years. For example, a student exploring federal gun control law might immediately think of the Brady bill, the Brady Handgun Violence Protection Act, P.L. 103-159, 107 Stat. 1536 (1993). It was major gun control legislation, but it was neither the first, nor the latest, gun control law passed. To find a complete picture of federal gun control legislation, the student might want to look at all the public laws on the topic passed over the years, which would mean looking through many volumes of the *Statutes at Large* (this question might also spark a conversation with the librarian about the purpose of the research and how much time can be allotted!) Another example is water pollution. Researchers studying the history of clean water laws would look to the Federal Water Pollution Control Act of 1948, the Federal Water Pollution Control Act Amendments of 1972 (also known as the Clean Water Act of 1972), the Clean Water Act of 1977, and the Water Quality Act of 1987. In both of these cases—gun control and water pollution—researchers might first look for a secondary source (a book, article, encyclopedia) that discusses and gives citations to major legislation on the topic. Keep in mind that a historical picture does not present the law in force—either currently in force or in force during a particular moment in time. To find the federal water laws in force today, researchers need a source that organizes and incorporates new and amended sections, and removes repealed sections. This is a code, which will be discussed later.

Finding laws in the print *Statutes at Large* is best done with some known information, in particular the date or Congress (the session number). Each volume contains a subject index (later volumes include a title index as well), but researchers do need a willingness to check more than one term, and perhaps flip a few pages. Using the landmark water pollution laws as an example, the terms changed over the years. In 1948, *water* is a fruitful term but *pollution* is not. In 1972, *pollution* is better and *clean* does not work at all. In some cases, the index term might point to a page in the middle of the law. Laws often have popular titles, referred to as short titles as part of the act—section 2 of the 1977 amendments to the Federal Water Pollution Control Act says the act may be "commonly referred to as the Clean Water Act." Sometimes the popular name is just that—the popular name. If a researcher is looking for the text of the large welfare reform law of 1996, the subject index in the 1996 *Statutes at Large* under *welfare* leads to the Personal Responsibility and Work Opportunity Reconciliation Act of 1996. Note that the subject and title indexes are repeated within each volume part.

Browsing online is another option, and also best done with as much information as possible. In FDsys, the *United States Statutes at Large* is included in the longer, browse all, alphabetical list, not in the short list on the front screen. Once there, it is easy enough to click through to the correct year and browse the chronological list of laws. To search, use the FDsys advanced search feature, www.gpo.gov/fdsys/search/advanced/advsearchpage .action. Users can search the full text and/or the metadata. Additional fields include session, subject, or popular name. GPO offers a series of helpful FDsys tutorials on advanced search, retrieve by citation, using metadata, and more, at www.gpo.gov/fdsysinfo/instructional _video.htm. For the volumes prior to 1951, available at the Law Library of Congress website, researchers need to use searchable PDFs of entire volumes. Just a few years are organized by chapter, but this is an ongoing project.

Popular name tables, in print or online, can be incredibly useful tools for finding citations when all you know is the name of law, such as the Endangered Species Act or No Child Left Behind. The official table of popular and statutory names is a part of the *United States Code,* and it gives both the public law and *Statutes at Large* citations. The Office of the Law Revision Council offers an online version, http://uscode.house.gov/ popularnames/popularnames.htm and an alternative source is available from Cornell's Legal Information Institute, www.law.cornell.edu/topn/0. Using popular name tables and annual indexes, or even searching FDsys or a commercial source such as HeinOnline, is best done with as much information as possible. Even the popular name tables are generally limited to official names, not for names the public and media may use informally after the fact. To fill the knowledge gap, secondary sources—books, articles, encyclopedias—are helpful. For major legislation, a quick web search will yield the correct name, and perhaps even the citation. The Personal Responsibility and Work Opportunity Reconciliation Act of 1996 (welfare reform) and the Servicemen's Readjustment Act of 1944 (G.I. bill) are two such examples. If the legislation sought is more obscure, a search of scholarly literature, perhaps Google Scholar, may be necessary to find an official name, a date, or best of all, a citation.

Codification of Statutory Law: *The United States Code*

The *Statutes at Large* are the source of all the public and private laws enacted by Congress, but researchers who seek the law as it is currently in force, or was in force at a particular point in time, look to the codified statutes—the *United States Code* (figure 5.2). Codification is an arrangement by subject (classification) with all the related material together and all the pieces of legislation that affect a particular part incorporated—that is, the additions, amendments, and repeals passed over the years are incorporated to update the laws. Along with all the changes Congress enacts, it most often passes legislation that touches on more than one topic (recall the complex process described in chapter 3). Codification takes new legislation apart and puts the pieces together with existing legislation on the same subject. If a researcher wanted to read the immigration, environmental, or food safety laws currently in force, the *U.S. Code* is the place to start, rather than combing through the volumes of session laws.

Not every enacted law is in the *U.S. Code*. Only public laws of a "general and permanent nature" are codified. General means widely applicable. So the public law naming the William Kenzo Nakamura United States Courthouse in Seattle (P.L. 106–478) is in the *Statutes at Large* (114 Stat. 2183), but not in the *U.S. Code*. Permanent is self-explanatory; the best examples of temporary laws not codified are appropriations as they cover the allocation of funds for one specific fiscal year.

Positive Law

Researchers may run across the term *positive law*, referring to the results of work that cleans up and restates the language of statutory law. As part of an ongoing project that will eventually include the entire *U.S. Code*, 27 titles have been enacted into positive law. The process starts when the Office of the Law Revision Counsel prepares a positive law codification bill for an entire title. Nothing new is added, but the organization is improved, obsolete provisions are removed, and technical errors are corrected. Congress then considers and enacts the entire title into positive law. Why is this necessary? Because laws constantly change and as sections are added, removed, and amended by Congress, small codification inconsistencies develop over time.

Why is it important? In a nutshell, this is about authority. Like the *Statutes at Large*, positive law titles are legal evidence of the law on a given date. Non-positive law titles are only considered prima facie (accepted on its face) evidence of the law. (See 1 U.S.C. § 204(a) and 1 U.S.C. § 112 for the legal explanation, and go to http://uscode.house.gov/codification/legislation.shtml for OLRC's explanation and list of current positive law codification projects.) It is unlikely to happen, but if there is a discrepancy in language between the *Statutes at Large* and the *U.S. Code* in one of the titles enacted into positive law, the *U.S. Code* is authoritative. If the discrepancy is in one of the titles not enacted into positive law, the *Statutes at Large* is authoritative. Why do librarians need to know all this? Title 26, the Internal Revenue Code, has not been enacted into positive law, so we occasionally encounter people who heard a rumor suggesting the Internal Revenue Code is not binding. Despite the rumor, the I.R.C. is the law. (For more discussion, see Whisner, 2009.)

Subsec. (f)(2)(B), (C). Pub. L. 95–632, §11(4)(B), (C), added subpar. (B), redesignated former subpar. (B) as (C), and as so redesignated, substituted "Neither subparagraph (A) or (B)" for "Neither subparagraph (A)".

Subsec. (f)(3). Pub. L. 95–632, §13, substituted "a summary by the Secretary of the data on which such regulation is based and shall show the relationship of such data to such regulations" for "a statement by the Secretary of the facts on which such regulation is based and the relationship of such facts to such regulation".

Subsec. (f)(4), (5). Pub. L. 95–632, §11(4)(D), added pars. (4) and (5).

Subsec. (g). Pub. L. 95–632, §11(5), added subsec. (g).

1976—Subsec. (f)(2)(B)(ii). Pub. L. 94–359 substituted "subsection (b)(1)(A)" for "subsection (b)(A), (B), and (C)".

EFFECTIVE DATE OF 1982 AMENDMENT

Pub. L. 97–304, §2(b), Oct. 13, 1982, 96 Stat. 1416, provided that:

"(1) Any petition filed under section 4(c)(2) of the Endangered Species Act of 1973 [subsec. (c)(2) of this section] (as in effect on the day before the date of the enactment of this Act [Oct. 13, 1982]) and any regulation proposed under section 4(f) of such Act of 1973 [subsec. (f) of this section] (as in effect on such day) that is pending on such date of enactment [Oct. 13, 1982] shall be treated as having been filed or proposed on such date of enactment under section 4(b) of such Act of 1973 [subsec. (b) of this section] (as amended by subsection (a)); and the procedural requirements specified in such section 4(b) [subsec. (b) of this section] (as so amended) regarding such petition or proposed regulation shall be deemed to be complied with to the extent that like requirements under such section 4 [this section] (as in effect before the date of the enactment of this Act) were complied with before such date of enactment.

"(2) Any regulation proposed after, or pending on, the date of the enactment of this Act [Oct. 13, 1982] to designate critical habitat for a species that was determined before such date of enactment to be endangered or threatened shall be subject to the procedures set forth in section 4 of such Act of 1973 [this section] (as amended by subsection (a)) for regulations proposing revisions to critical habitat instead of those for regulations proposing the designation of critical habitat.

"(3) Any list of endangered species or threatened species (as in effect under section 4(c) of such Act of 1973 [subsec. (c) of this section] on the day before the date of the enactment of this Act [Oct. 13, 1982]) shall remain in effect unless and until determinations regarding species and designations and revisions of critical habitats that require changes to such list are made in accordance with subsection (b)(5) of such Act of 1973 [subsec. (b)(5) of this section] (as added by subsection (a)).

"(4) Section 4(a)(3)(A) of such Act of 1973 [subsec. (a)(3)(A) of this section] (as added by subsection (a)) shall not apply with respect to any species which was listed as an endangered species or a threatened species before November 10, 1978."

ABOLITION OF HOUSE COMMITTEE ON MERCHANT MARINE AND FISHERIES

Committee on Merchant Marine and Fisheries of House of Representatives abolished and its jurisdiction transferred by House Resolution No. 6, One Hundred Fourth Congress, Jan. 4, 1995. Committee on Merchant Marine and Fisheries of House of Representatives treated as referring to Committee on Resources of House of Representatives in case of provisions relating to fisheries, wildlife, international fishing agreements, marine affairs (including coastal zone management) except for measures relating to oil and other pollution of navigable waters, or oceanography by section 1(b)(3) of Pub. L. 104–14, set out as a note preceding section 21 of Title 2, The Congress. Committee on Resources of House of Representatives changed to Committee on Natural Resources of House of Representatives by

House Resolution No. 6, One Hundred Tenth Congress, Jan. 5, 2007.

§ 1534. Land acquisition

(a) Implementation of conservation program; authorization of Secretary and Secretary of Agriculture

The Secretary, and the Secretary of Agriculture with respect to the National Forest System, shall establish and implement a program to conserve fish, wildlife, and plants, including those which are listed as endangered species or threatened species pursuant to section 1533 of this title. To carry out such a program, the appropriate Secretary—

(1) shall utilize the land acquisition and other authority under the Fish and Wildlife Act of 1956, as amended [16 U.S.C. 742a et seq.], the Fish and Wildlife Coordination Act, as amended [16 U.S.C. 661 et seq.], and the Migratory Bird Conservation Act [16 U.S.C. 715 et seq.], as appropriate; and

(2) is authorized to acquire by purchase, donation, or otherwise, lands, waters, or interest therein, and such authority shall be in addition to any other land acquisition authority vested in him.

(b) Availability of funds for acquisition of lands, waters, etc.

Funds made available pursuant to the Land and Water Conservation Fund Act of 1965, as amended [16 U.S.C. 460*l*–4 et seq.], may be used for the purpose of acquiring lands, waters, or interests therein under subsection (a) of this section.

(Pub. L. 93–205, §5, Dec. 28, 1973, 87 Stat. 889; Pub. L. 95–632, §12, Nov. 10, 1978, 92 Stat. 3766.)

REFERENCES IN TEXT

The Fish and Wildlife Act of 1956, as amended, referred to in subsec. (a)(1), is act Aug. 8, 1956, ch. 1036, 70 Stat. 119, as amended, which is classified generally to sections 742a to 742d and 742e to 742j–2 of this title. For complete classification of this Act to the Code, see Short Title note set out under section 742a of this title and Tables.

The Fish and Wildlife Coordination Act, as amended, referred to in subsec. (a)(1), is act Mar. 10, 1934, ch. 55, 48 Stat. 401, as amended, which is classified generally to sections 661 to 666c of this title. For complete classification of this Act to the Code, see Short Title note set out under section 661 of this title and Tables.

The Migratory Bird Conservation Act, referred to in subsec. (a)(1), is act Feb. 18, 1929, ch. 257, 45 Stat. 1222, as amended, which is classified generally to subchapter III (§715 et seq.) of chapter 7 of this title. For complete classification of this Act to the Code, see section 715 of this title and Tables.

The Land and Water Conservation Fund Act of 1965, as amended, referred to in subsec. (b), is Pub. L. 88–578, Sept. 3, 1964, 78 Stat. 897, as amended, which is classified generally to part B (§460*l*–4 et seq.) of subchapter LXIX of chapter 1 of this title. For complete classification of this Act to the Code, see Short Title note set out under section 460*l*–4 of this title and Tables.

AMENDMENTS

1978—Subsec. (a). Pub. L. 95–632, among other changes in text preceding par. (1), inserted reference to the Secretary of Agriculture with respect to the National Forest System and substituted the establishment and implementation of a plan to conserve plants for the establishment and implementation of a plan to conserve

FIGURE 5.2
United States Code

History of the *United States Code*

Like the *Statutes at Large,* the *U.S. Code* has a long publication history that is worth discussing. Codification of federal laws, a way to solve the challenge of figuring out the current law as more and more laws were passed, was first addressed in 1866. Congress directed that "three persons, learned in the law . . . revise, simplify, arrange, and consolidate all statutes of the United States, general and permanent in nature" (14 Stat. 74). The result was the first official codification, the *Revised Statutes of the United States.* It was published in 1875 as volume 18 of the *Statutes at Large* and is divided in 70 titles (subjects). Despite all the work, there were enough errors that a replacement volume that both corrected and updated the law was published in 1878. After that, more time passed, more laws were passed, and still, the problem of efficiently finding current law had not been solved. A few commercial legal publishers worked on arrangement schemes, as did House and Senate committees tasked with law revision, but it was not until 1926 that the first *U.S. Code* was published, with the assistance of the now experienced commercial publishers. The new code had 50 titles. Not long after, Congress directed the publication of supplements and new editions. New editions have been published every six years, the most recent being 2012. Annual cumulative supplements, labeled I through V, are also published. Libraries that keep older editions typically keep the volumes that make up the edition (1994, 2000, 2006, etc.) plus the cumulative Supplement V for each edition.

Using the *United States Code*

GPO publishes the *U.S. Code,* but the responsibility for preparing the new editions and supplements falls to the Office of the Law Revision Counsel (OLRC) of the US House of Representatives. The attorneys who work for the OLRC examine every public law to see what should go in the code (laws of a general and permanent nature) and where (classification). Remember that a single law passed by Congress can be hundreds of pages long and include provisions on a variety of topics. Some pieces of a single law may be general and permanent while others may be temporary, like those voluminous appropriations bills or an omnibus bill. The complicated and detailed organizational work of the OLRC benefits all citizens who need to find the law.

The current *U.S. Code* comprises 54 titles, each covering a particular topic. For instance, Title 6 is Domestic Security; Title 21 is Food and Drugs; Title 26 is the Internal Revenue Code; and Title 43 is Public Lands. Some titles are quite specific, like Title 35 (Patents), and others are broader, like Title 33 (Navigation and Navigable Waters). Title 42 (Public Health and Welfare) can even be described as a kitchen sink, since it includes social security, housing, school lunches, civil rights, employment discrimination, atomic energy, domestic violence, health insurance, flood insurance, hazardous waste cleanup, and more. Physically, Title 42 spans more volumes than any other title by far. Each title is further divided into chapters. For example, Title 43 (Public Lands) includes chapters on the Bureau of Land Management, the United States Geological Survey, grazing, easements, drainage, and the sale and disposal of public lands. Each chapter is divided further and may have subtitles, subchapters, or parts. Although the chapters are useful for browsing, the basic unit of each title is the *section*. Legal citations, according to *The Bluebook,* are to the title and section. For example, the authority to establish grazing districts is cited as 43 U.S.C. § 315, even though within the hierarchy of Title 43, grazing is in chapter 8A.

For 85 years, starting in 1926, the *U.S. Code* had a 50-title arrangement. Recently, in 2011, Title 51, National and Commercial Space Programs, was added. In 2014, Title 52, Voting and Elections, was added. As of this writing, Title 54, National Park Service and Related Programs, has been enacted as positive law but not yet published. What about Title 53? It is reserved for future content. The OLRC is also working on a new Title 55, Environment. It was submitted in a previous Congress to the House Committee on the Judiciary to enact as positive law. The purpose of these new titles is not to change the meaning of the law, nor to create new law, but to organize existing law in a more useful way, and to correct technical errors. Environmental law is a good example. A substantial body of environmental law has been enacted since 1970, but it has been classified to several different titles throughout the code. Having one source of environmental policy, air, water, land, and hazardous substances law makes sense, at least from the perspective of users (including librarians). More information on current codification projects is available at the OLRC website, http://uscode.house.gov/codification/legislation.shtml#current_plaw.

The text of the code is available in print and online, from a variety of sources. In choosing a format and source, keep in mind two concepts: organizational context and currency of information. First, context matters. The point of codification is to put like topics together in a classification scheme. Sections of the code do not exist in a vacuum; they relate to the surrounding sections. Language in a section before or after, or a few section numbers away, might be incredibly important. And a term used in one section might be defined in another. So researchers need to look at these surrounding sections, and with print, it is much easier to flip the pages and *see* surrounding sections, or, to put it another way, *visualize* the context. That is, of course, possible to do with digital sources, but it can be easier to lose one's place in the scheme of the information. Second, currency matters. Researchers using the code are usually looking for the current, applicable law. As mentioned earlier, new editions of the official *U.S. Code* are published every six years, with annual cumulative supplements published during the intervening years. Unfortunately, the volumes run behind. Researchers requiring the current law will need to update the print as well as the digital version

> **Federal statutory law citations, according to *The Bluebook: A Uniform System of Citation:***
>
> ---
>
> • ***United States Statutes at Large:*** Endangered Species Act of 1973, Pub. L. No. 93–205, 87 Stat. 884 (name of act, P.L. number, followed by volume-publication-page of session laws—year would follow if not in the name)
> • ***United States Code:*** Endangered Species Act of 1973, 16 U.S.C. § 1531–1544 (2012) (name of act, code title-publication-section or sections, followed by year of edition in parentheses)

on GPO's FDsys, which mirrors the print. At this writing (early 2015), the 2012 edition is complete and Supplement I, covering January 3, 2013, to January 16, 2014, has been published. The editor's note in the 2012 edition states efforts are being made to update the code in a more timely manner. In the past, the print publication of the editions and supplements was generally two or more years out-of-date, so one year is indeed an improvement.

Like the *Statutes at Large,* the official *U.S. Code* from GPO is available in print at some depository and most law libraries. The set has a good general index that is quite detailed (the 2012 edition index is in four volumes). Index references are to the title and section of the code, section being the basic unit. It has a popular name table, "Acts Cited by Popular Name," which references the *Statutes at Large* citation and not necessarily the code citation. Code citations are given for acts classified to discrete sections, and for short titles (at the beginning of a law, when Congress states the name by which the law can be cited, such as the Clean Water Act of 1977, or the Patient Protection and Affordable Care Act). What if a researcher is looking for a particular section of an act and wants to know where it is codified? The *U.S. Code* has tables just for that. Table II is a list of sections of the *Revised Statutes of 1878* and where they were classified to the *U.S. Code.* Table III is an extensive list that includes all public laws which have been classified, at any time since 1789, to the *U.S. Code.* What about titles that have been revised during a positive law codification? See Table I, which maps former to new sections.

The two online governmental sources for the *U.S. Code* are FDsys and the OLRC website. Each offers free public access to editions from 1994 on. Editions from 1925 to 1988 (content to 1993) are available for free from the Law Library of Congress Guide to Law Online, www.loc.gov/law/help/guide/federal/uscode.php. These historical editions are accessed via HeinOnline, through an agreement with William S. Hein & Co., Inc.

The editions on FDsys are obtained from the OLRC and updated each year. In FDsys, researchers can browse the *U.S. Code,* search, or retrieve by citation. It is important to pay attention to the date since more than one year is available. To find the most current year available select it from the browse menu, or click on "show only recent editions" from the search results. Another option is to limit by date using the facets on the left. No matter, searchers should make a note of the year in order to update the code section. Updating can be done either by searching within the Public Laws database, or navigating back out to the *U.S. Code* page and clicking on United States Code Classification Tables (figure 5.3). Updating is important because researchers need to make sure the law they are relying upon has not been recently amended or repealed. That said, some researchers might be seeking the law as it was in force in a specific prior year. Just as print users can look at earlier editions on the shelf, FDsys users can look at earlier editions online. GPO has provided extensive metadata for each code section. Whether the desired section is found through search or browse, the More link leads to the metadata. Scroll down to find the document in context—an excellent feature to help users see the context in an online environment.

The *U.S. Code* on the OLRC site was enhanced in 2013. Researchers can search and browse. For each code section, currency is noted by giving the most recent public law number incorporated into the text. As of this writing, in early 2015 at the very start of the 114th Congress, the OLRC website is up-to-date; all the public laws (of a general and permanent nature) from the 113th Congress have been codified and incorporated by the OLRC. It is more current, by a year, than the *U.S. Code* on FDsys because GPO

Page 2251 TABLE III—STATUTES AT LARGE

110 Stat.	Pub. L.	Section	Page	Title	Section	Status
1996—Aug. 22 104–193		110(t)	2175	42	9835	
		110(u)	2175	25	639	Rep.
		110(v)	2175	20	6143	Elim.
		110(w)	2175	5	552a	
		111	2176	42	405 nt	
		112	2176	42	9926	
		114(a)(1)	2177	42	1396v	
		114(a)(2)	2177	42	1396u–1	
		114(b), (c)	2180	42	1396a	
		114(c)	2180	42	1396r–6	
		114(d)(1)	2180	42	1396a	
		114(d)(2)	2180	42	1396b	
		115	2180	21	862a	
		116	2181	42	601 nt	
		201(a)	2185	42	1382	
		201(b)	2185	42	1382 nt	
		202(a), (b)	2185, 2186	42	1382	
		202(c)	2186	42	1382 nt	
		203(a)(1)	2186	42	1382	
		203(a)(2)	2187	42	1382 nt	
		203(b)	2187	42	1382 nt	
		203(c)	2187	42	1382 nt	
		204(a)	2187	42	1382	
		204(b)	2188	42	1383	
		204(c)(1)	2188	42	1382c	
		204(c)(2)	2188	42	1383	
		204(d)	2188	42	1382 nt	
		211(a), (c)	2188, 2189	42	1382c	
		211(d)	2190	42	1382c nt	
		211(d)(5)(B)	2191	2	901	
		211(d)(5)(C)	2192	2	665e	Rep.
		211(d)(5)(D)	2192	42	401 nt	
		212(a), (b)(1)	2192, 2193	42	1382c	
		212(b)(2)	2193	42	1382 nt	Rep.
		212(c)	2193	42	1382c	
		212(d)	2194	42	1382c nt	
		213(a)	2194	42	1383	
		213(b)	2195	42	1382b	
		213(c)	2195	42	1382a	
		213(d)	2195	42	1382a nt	
		214(a)	2195	42	1382	
		214(b)	2196	42	1382 nt	
		215	2196	42	1382 nt	
		221(a), (b)	2196, 2197	42	1383	
		221(c)	2197	42	1383 nt	
		222	2197	42	1383 nt	
		231	2197	42	1383f	
		232	2198	42	1382 nt	Elim.
		301(a), (b)	2199	42	654	
		301(c)(1), (2)	2200	42	652	
		301(c)(3), (4)	2200	42	666	
		302(a)	2200	42	657	
		302(b)(1)	2204	42	664	
		302(b)(2)	2204	42	654	
		302(c)	2204	42	657 nt	
		303(a)	2204	42	654	
		303(b)	2205	42	654 nt	
		304(a)	2205	42	654	
		304(b)	2205	42	654 nt	
		311	2205	42	654a	
		312(a)	2207	42	654	
		312(b)	2207	42	654b	
		312(c)	2208	42	654a	
		312(d)	2209	42	654b nt	
		313(a)	2209	42	654	
		313(b)	2209	42	653a	
		313(c)	2212	42	1320b–7	
		313(d)	2212	42	503	
		314, 315	2212, 2214	42	666	
		316(a)–(d)	2214, 2215	42	653	
		316(e)(1)	2215	42	652	
		316(e)(1)	2215	42	653	
		316(e)(1)	2215	42	663	
		316(e)(2), (f)	2216	42	653	
		316(g)(1)	2218	42	654	
		316(g)(2)	2218	26	3304	
		316(g)(3)	2219	42	503	
		316(g)(4)	2219	26	6103	
		316(h)	2220	42	653 nt	
		317, 321	2220, 2221	42	666	
		322	2221	28	1738B	
		323	2222	42	666	
		324(a)	2223	42	652	
		324(b)	2223	42	654	
		325(a)	2224	42	666	
		325(b)	2226	42	654a	

FIGURE 5.3

U.S. Code Classification Table

uses the same data from which it publishes the print volumes, and that data takes longer to prepare. OLRC staff updates the code sections during congressional sessions and notes pending updates. Updating can also be done, of course, through the classification tables provided or searching public laws on FDsys.

One drawback of both the OLRC site and FDsys is the lack of online versions of the print indexes. Their inclusion in the online versions would be welcome, since legislative language can be difficult and keywords can be common, appearing throughout the code, making keyword searching inefficient. Indexes help users—particularly users who know a bit about what they are looking for—more easily locate relevant code sections. Besides the indexes, why seek out the print editions of the *U.S. Code?* In the law library setting, it happens because *The Bluebook* prefers citations to the *U.S. Code,* rather than the commercially published versions or any online sources. Another reason is stated on the About section of FDsys: "While every effort has been made to ensure that the *U.S. Code* database on FDsys is accurate, those using it for legal research should verify their results

> **Tips to Find the Correct Code Section**
>
> Whether using online or print, free or commercial, some basic tips will help you find the correct code section. Begin with a basic understanding of how the material is organized (titles and sections); perhaps start with a secondary source (a law review article or book); use the index; use the tables (if you have a public law and want to know where it is codified); and be flexible about combining sources as well as formats (print index plus online updating).
>
> Another option is to consult or refer to a law or government information librarian. Government information librarians should be familiar with the workings of the *U.S. Code* in print and on FDsys, and law librarians may have knowledge of alternate sources and suggestions for more obscure research questions.

against the printed version of the *U.S. Code* available through the Government Printing Office" (GPO, 2015). In other words, print still matters. It is the authoritative format for researchers relying on the language of the law.

Other good options for free online access to the *U.S. Code* are Cornell's Legal Information Institute, www.law.cornell.edu/uscode/text, a not-for-profit open access site, and Findlaw, www.findlaw.com/casecode/uscodes, a commercial but free site (now owned by Thomson Reuters, also the parent company of Westlaw). On the commercial fee-based side, the two largest commercial legal publishers produce excellent print and electronic editions. Law libraries may have one or more of the print editions: *United States Code Annotated* (U.S.C.A), published by Thomson West, and *United States Code Service* (U.S.C.S), published by LexisNexis. Both are annotated sets, meaning they include summaries of judicial decisions that interpreted the code section. Both also include other research aids, such as citations to law reviews, historical notes, extensive indexes, and tables. They are updated with supplementary pamphlets but because of the print format, are not as up-to-date as their online counterparts, which also offer commercial enhancements. *U.S.C.A.* is available on WestlawNext and WestlawNext Campus Research; *U.S.C.S.* is on Lexis Advance and LexisNexis Academic.

Once the sought after code section is identified and retrieved, researchers can not only read the law as it existed at the time of publication, but can also trace the history of that particular section. At the end of each section, in parentheses, are source credits—

the citations to all the parts of all the public laws that have gone into the creation of that particular section of the code. The credits start with the initial public law and give the citations for all the subsequent amendments that make up the current law. These are sometimes followed by historical and revision notes, and then by details of the changes made by the amendments over the years. These source credits are also called the statutory history, meaning a focused look at changes in enacted language over time (not to be confused with legislative history, discussed in chapter 3). They are also part of the FDsys metadata.

State Laws and Codes

States follow similar publication patterns for laws passed by the legislative body. Session laws are issued, then a codification of the acts of a general and permanent nature. But the publication *practice* varies widely. First, the language varies, for example *The Acts of Assembly of Virginia, Statutes of California,* and *Laws of Pennsylvania* are all session laws, whether called acts, statutes, or laws, and the *General Laws of the Commonwealth of Massachusetts, Colorado Revised Statutes,* and *Code of Iowa* are all statutory compilations, or codes, whether they are called laws, statutes, or a code.

Another variation is publisher. In Washington, the official state code is the *Revised Code of Washington,* but two commercial publishers produce sets with editorial additions, *West's Revised Code of Washington Annotated* (Thompson West) and the *Annotated Revised Code of Washington* (LexisNexis). What should a librarian do? Check to see if another librarian has created a research guide, of course! State law libraries (often the library of the highest appellate court in the state), county law libraries, and law school libraries usually have guides to their particular jurisdiction on their websites. Also, members of the American Association of Law Libraries (AALL) Government Documents Special Interest Section have produced bibliographies, now published by William S. Hein & Co., Inc., and available on HeinOnline.

Online availability and coverage vary as well. Good starting points for free public access include the Law Library of Congress Guide to Law Online, US States and Territories, www.loc.gov/law/help/guide/states.php, Cornell's Legal Information Institute listing by jurisdiction, www.law.cornell.edu/states/listing, and the National Conference of State Legislatures' State Legislative Websites Directory, www.ncsl.org/aboutus/ncslservice/state-legislative-websites-directory.aspx. On the commercial side, coverage is excellent, of course, for researchers with access to the WestlawNext or LexisNexis products with sophisticated tools. For historical state session laws and codes, HeinOnline is the most comprehensive source.

Digital Authentication

For primary legal sources, if there is a discrepancy between the print and online version, the print is authoritative. But the reality is that information, including legal information, is moving from print to digital and some libraries are choosing to limit print collections and allocate scarce resources to electronic collections. In the case of federal statutory law, publication is both print and digital. GPO, as a provider of official information, recognizes that digital authentication is a necessary part of preservation and permanent public access. Digital documents can be altered, and it is particularly important that legal information—*the law*—is reliable and can be trusted. GPO uses digital signatures, which they describe as serving the same purpose as "handwritten signatures or traditional wax seals on printed documents." GPO provides a great deal of information about their program and the technology used here, www.gpo.gov/authentication/. In addition, to further the goal of digital preservation, in the fall of 2014, GPO announced they will seek certification for FDsys as a Trustworthy Digital Repository (GPO 2014).

Digital authentication is an issue for the states as well as for the federal government. Several states have adopted the Uniform Electronic Legal Material Act (UELMA), which offers a framework for providing trustworthy primary legal material online. Links to the text of UELMA, plus a FAQ and history, are available in the advocacy section of the AALL website, www.aallnet.org/Documents/Government-Relations/UELMA.

Conclusion

Government information librarians, no matter the type of library they work in, need to be familiar with federal statutory law—the public laws, *Statutes at Large,* and the *U.S. Code*—in print and online. It also makes sense to be familiar with their state statutory law—session laws and codes, in print and online, commercial and official. And while we are at it, it is a good idea to know how the local government (the city council, for instance) publishes legislative enactments. A person might walk in to a library and say, "I'm looking for a law," and then ask for the federal Freedom of Information Act, the state marijuana law, *and* the number of household pets allowed by the city zoning code. And the best answer is "let me help you find all that."

Further Research

The Law Librarians' Society of Washington, DC's *Legislative Sourcebook* includes many detailed research guides, lists, and tables, www.llsdc.org/sourcebook.

For an in-depth legal research textbook, see Barkan, Steven M., Barbara A. Bintliff, and Mary Whisner. 2015. *Fundamentals of Legal Research,* 10th ed. St. Paul, MN: West Academic.

Exercises

1. What is the most recent public law enacted?

2. A researcher is writing about hazardous waste cleanup and asks for the Super-fund law. What is the official title? What is the public law number? *Statutes at Large* citation? Where is it codified?

3. A newspaper story on food safety states the Food and Drug Administration has mandatory recall authority under the Food Safety Modernization Act. Find the act and the section of the *United States Code* dealing with mandatory recall authority. Cite both the act and the code.

4. 20 U.S.C. § 1401(9) defines "free appropriate public education" for special educa-tion. What is the statutory history of this section? What is the short title of the act?

5. Pick a state. Using a source of state codes online, find out the age of consent for marriage in that state.

Sources Mentioned in This Chapter

American Association of Law Libraries. UELMA Resources. www.aallnet.org/Documents/Government-Relations/UELMA.

American Association of Law Libraries Government Documents Special Interest Section. State Bibliog-raphies. www.aallnet.org/sections/gd/Bibliographies.

The Bluebook: A Uniform System of Citation, 19th ed. 2010. Cambridge, MA: The Harvard Law Review Association.

Cornell Law School, Cornell Legal Information Institute, www.law.cornell.edu.

FDsys, www.gpo.gov/fdsys/.

Findlaw, www.findlaw.com/casecode/uscodes.

Google Scholar, http://scholar.google.com.

HeinOnline, www.heinonline.org.

Law Library of Congress, Guide to Law Online, www.loc.gov/law/help/guide.php.

Law Library of Congress, *United States Statutes at Large,* 1789–1950, www.loc.gov/law/help/statutes-at-large/index.php.

Lexis Advance, www.lexisnexis.com/en-us/products/lexis-advance.page.

LexisNexis Academic, www.lexisnexis.com/hottopics/lnacademic.

Library of Congress. *A Century of Lawmaking for a New Nation: Statutes at Large.* http://memory.loc.gov/ammem/amlaw/lwsl.html.

National Conference of State Legislatures State Legislative Websites Directory. www.ncsl.org/aboutus/ncslservice/state-legislative-websites-directory.aspx.

United States. 1789. *The Public Statutes at Large of the United States of America from the Organization of the Government in 1789, to March 3, 1845.* Boston. MA: Charles C. Little and James Brown. http://purl.access.gpo.gov/GPO/LPS52578.

United States. 1799. *Laws of the United States.* Washington, DC: Folwell.

United States. 1845. *Laws of the United States of America.* Philadelphia, PA: John Bioren and W. John Duane.

United States Code. Washington, DC: Government Publishing Office. Available at www.gpo.gov/fdsys and http://uscode.house.gov.

United States Code Annotated. Eagan, MN: Thomson Reuters.

United States Code Service. Charlottesville, VA: LexisNexis.

United States House of Representatives, Office of Law Revision Council, http://uscode.house.gov.

United States Statutes at Large. Washington, DC: Government Printing Office. (1789–1874 published by
    Little & Brown). 1951–date available at www.gpo.gov/fdsys; 1789–1950 available at www.loc.gov/
    law/help/statutes-at-large/index.php.
WestlawNext, http://legalsolutions.thomsonreuters.com/law-products/westlaw-legal-research.
WestlawNext Campus Research. http://campus.westlaw.com.

References

Conklin, Curt E., and Francis Aclund. 1992. *An Historical and Bibliographic Introduction to the United States
    Statutes at Large.* Provo, UT: Government Publications Press.
GPO (Government Publishing Office). 2011. Press release, *GPO and Library of Congress to Digitize His-
    toric Documents,* February 16, 2011. www.gpo.gov/pdfs/news-media/press/11news13.pdf.
GPO (Government Publishing Office). 2014. News release, *GPO Prepares to Become First Federal Agency
    Named as Trustworthy Digital Repository for Government Information,* December 18, 2014. www.gpo.gov/
    pdfs/news-media/press/14news28.pdf.
GPO (Government Publishing Office). 2015. "About United States Code." www.gpo.gov/help/index
    .html#about_united_states_code.htm.
Whisner, Mary. 2009. "The United States Code, Prima Facie Evidence, and Positive Law." *Law Library
    Journal* 101, no. 4 (Fall): 545–56. www.aallnet.org/products/pub_llj_v101n04/2009–30.pdf.

CHAPTER 6

Regulations

CASSANDRA HARTNETT

Introduction

Americans in the know read nutritional labels. The list of food ingredients is rank-ordered, with the most prevalent ingredient listed first—a point of common public awareness. It is also widely understood that when the nutritional content is expressed in percent daily values, or %DV, this is based on the recommended dietary guidelines of the United States Department of Agriculture (USDA). If you notice these simple details from everyday life, you already have a baseline appreciation of federal regulations. The labeling of food for nutritional content and allergens is an example of regulations in action.

We learned in chapter 4 that all three branches of government (legislative, executive, judicial) produce materials that carry the force of law: legislation, regulation, and case law, respectively. The legislative branch *passes* laws, the executive branch *enforces* laws, and the judicial branch *interprets* laws. In passing laws (also known as statutes or statutory law), Congress authorizes or "empowers" the executive branch agencies to put forth regulations, and regulations thus become "the last step in the legislative process" (Arrigo, 2003: 99). Regulations are also referred to as administrative or bureaucratic law. Rules are synonymous with regulations.

Regulations are the agency-based enforcement of the laws mandated by the legislature. Congress passes laws—49 U.S.C. § 106 (2012) authorizes a Federal Aviation Authority to operate within the Department of Transportation, for example—but it falls to the agencies to carry out Congress's statutes (in this case, enforce federal laws about aviation). Statutory law is the authorization; regulations are the nitty gritty details developed by the agencies. Agencies can modify existing regulations or develop new ones, as long as they are operating within their legal authority. See the sidebar for one example of federal aviation regulations, in this case a listing of standard symbols and terms used in aviation. Think we don't need regulations? Better hope that the pilot of your next flight knows how to land when there's a poor RVV.

An Excerpt from the *Code of Federal Regulations*
(Explanations and editorial comments are added in *italics*.)

Title 14—Aeronautics and space *(This is the "Title" or broad, overarching topic.) (The Title is further subdivided into increasingly specific areas.)*

CHAPTER I—FEDERAL AVIATION ADMINISTRATION, DEPARTMENT OF TRANSPORTATION

(Within Titles, each Chapter is reserved for a federal agency.) SUBCHAPTER F—AIR TRAFFIC AND GENERAL OPERATING RULES PART 97—STANDARD INSTRUMENT PROCEDURES

§ 97.3 Symbols and terms used in procedures

(The part number is the lowest unit of citation. Not all regulations are overly technical, as the following illustrates.)

RA means radio altimeter setting height.

RVV means runway visibility value.

SIAP means standard instrument approach procedure.

65 knots or less means an aircraft that has a stalling speed of 65 knots or less (as established in an approved flight manual) at maximum certificated landing weight with full flaps, landing gear extended, and power off.

T means nonstandard takeoff minimums or specified departure routes/procedures or both.

TDZ means touchdown zone.

(The CFR is cited by Title, Part, and Year of Publication. The above excerpt is properly cited 14 CFR 97.3, 2014.)

Many people cringe at the thought of learning more about federal executive agencies and their regulations. Sometimes (not always) regulations can be dry and dense reading. People may also experience a fundamental conflict in thinking about regulations (tax rules may seem overly restrictive, safety regulations crucial). Americans may not be inclined to think of stewarding the nation's regulations as part of the good citizen role, but one study concluded that

> Federal regulations are among the most important and widely used tools for
> implementing the laws of the land—affecting the food we eat, the air we
> breathe, the safety of consumer products, the quality of the workplace, the
> soundness of our financial institutions, the smooth operation of our busi-
> nesses, and much more. Despite the central role of rulemaking in executing
> public policy, both regulated entities (especially small businesses) and the
> general public find it extremely difficult to follow the regulatory process;

> actively participating in it is even harder. (Committee on the Status and
> Future of Federal E-Rulemaking, 2008: 1)

In this chapter, we offer a brief overview of the process and literature of federal regulations. We explore the *Code of Federal Regulations (CFR)*, a topical arrangement (called a codified version) of all current regulations, along with its companion sources the *Unified Agenda,* the *Federal Register,* the *List of CFR Sections Affected* (known as the *LSA*), and the *e-CFR.* We consider the ongoing development of e-rulemaking; three core online resources, FederalRegister.gov, Regulations.gov, and Reginfo.gov; and one simplified diagram making regulations much more understandable, the Reg Map. Our discussion begins with publications, and the first publication comes as part of the planning process, before agency officials start actually drafting new rules.

Unified Regulatory Agenda and Reginfo.gov

Regulatory agency officials are constantly looking ahead, anticipating their next regulatory moves. They don't do this in isolation: they work with the Regulatory Information Service Center (RISC), a help center within the US General Services Administration (GSA) (figure 6.1). RISC compiles the *Unified Agenda of Federal Regulatory and Deregulatory Actions* (known as the *Unified Agenda*) as well as Reginfo.gov, probably the best source for understanding all things regulatory. According to Reginfo.gov, RISC gathers and publishes information on federal regulations and their effects on society, and reports its findings with an aim of improving understanding and management of the rulemaking process. Since 1978, federal agencies haven't had a choice: they're required to publish agendas of regulatory and deregulatory activities. The Center publishes the *Unified Agenda* in the spring and fall of each year. The *Regulatory Plan,* part of the fall edition, lists regulatory priorities, giving extra details about the most significant regulatory actions anticipated in the coming year. (Regulatory Information Service Center, 2015)

The *Unified Agenda* and the *Regulatory Plan* are online at Reginfo.gov, current versions along with historical volumes back to 1995. The *Agenda* lists specific regulatory actions organized by agency, while the *Plan* compiles narrative essays from each agency stating general regulatory priorities or themes. RISC assigns a Regulation Identifier Number, or RIN, to each entry in the *Unified Agenda.* The RIN can help track a currently proposed regulation. It can also be used years after the fact to identify earlier regulatory efforts, link to related RINs, and trace success/failure rates.

The *Unified Agenda* provides a first-time user of rules a picture of the nation's enormous, diverse, 12-month regulatory plans. What kinds of problems are the agencies trying to fix? In browsing the fall 2014 *Unified Agenda,* we see the finalizing of rules to "explicitly ban the smoking of electronic cigarettes on air carrier and foreign air carrier flights in scheduled intrastate, interstate, and foreign air transportation" (Department of Transportation, 2014) along with a government proposal for "more complete and consistent information about the nutrient content and ingredient composition of pet food products" (Food and Drug Administration, 2014). No subject, grand or small, escapes the possibility of regulation.

The Regulatory Process

To learn the steps of the regulatory process, use a helpful chart known as the Reg Map (figure 6.2). The Reg Map was created by ICF, Incorporated (a policy consulting company), and was last revised in 2003 with the cooperation of RISC. Do not be skeptical due to the revision date. Disclaimers state that the map is not endorsed by the GSA as a legal document, yet it has still proven to be one of the most relied upon informal guides to the regulatory process.

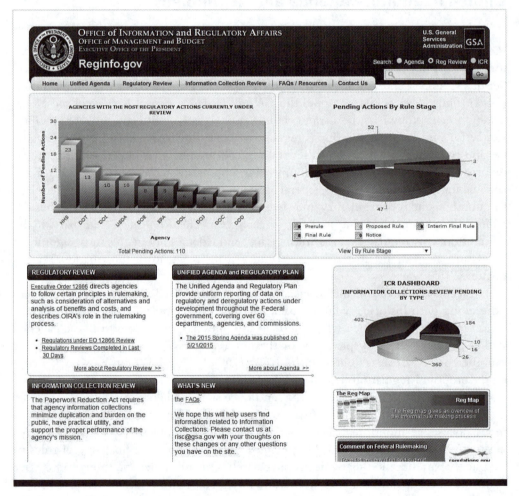

FIGURE 6.1
The Regulatory Information Service Center's Reginfo.gov

To start the rulemaking process, there needs to be an *initiating event,* a compelling need for new regulations (see *Step One* in figure 6.2). The push to regulate may come from a legal requirement, a lawsuit or petition, a regularly scheduled review, or sources outside the agency: Congress, the president, other agencies, state governments, advisory committees, the public, the commercial sector (if companies feel that they cannot conduct business properly), and advocacy groups (perceiving a wrong that could be righted through regulation). Initiating events can also come from within the agency, based on reaction to new scientific information that would impel new rules, or even a current event, accident, or tragedy. Even though there may be passion for the cause, concerned parties must first *determine that rulemaking is an appropriate response* to their need (see *Step Two* in figure 6.2). To do so, they review relevant sections of the Federal Administrative Procedure Act (5 U.S.C. § 553, 2012).

The Administrative Procedure Act (APA), passed in 1946 as P.L. 79-404, is the law that delineates the rulemaking process. The APA, like the *Federal Register* itself, came in the wake of embarrassing moments in the mid-1930s when federal government officials could not determine which federal regulations were in force (Office of the Federal Register, 2006). The APA underwent a major revision on September 6, 1966, with the passage of P.L. 89-554, which further elaborated the steps one sees in the Reg Map today.

If the action under consideration has met the criteria of the APA as noted in Step Two (see figure 6.2), agency officials must *publish a notice of proposed rulemaking and call for public input* (see *Step Three* in figure 6.2). This process is referred to by regulators as notice and comment. As one becomes more experienced in moving around the *Federal Register* or Regulations.gov, one learns to look for notices of proposed rulemaking (NPRMs), frequently listed in an Action category or column. An NPRM is the first widely published indicator, subsequent to the agency's published regulatory agenda, that specific rulemaking is under way. At this stage, there is also the possibility of a process called negotiated rulemaking, wherein stakeholders actively negotiate aspects of a proposed rule. The Office of Management and Budget (OMB), specifically its Office of Information and Regulatory Affairs (OIRA) must review (prepublication) all proposed rules deemed "significant" (see *Step Four* in figure 6.2). OIRA plays a major coordinative role in the regulatory process and is a pivotal agency to know about (see sidebar under "Recommended Sources of Additional Information").

Suppose the agency has published its NPRM and asked for public comment (usually for a period of at least 60 days). Officials now take the time to consider the input they have received. All comments, whether received via Regulations.gov, e-mail, fax, or print-on-paper letter, are considered part of the official record, could be published online for public review, and should therefore not contain sensitive, personal, or confidential material. Note that although many agencies publish comments directly on Regulations.gov, more than 100 agencies do not publish their comments on Regulations .gov. The list of nonparticipants is diverse, including the Central Intelligence Agency, the Federal Communications Commission, the LC, and many others (Regulations.gov, 2015b). Published or not, agency regulators must address the concerns voiced during the comment period somewhere in the proposed rule. Like a congressional bill that dies in committee, some initiating events do not result in regulations. Instead, many attempts see parties going back to the drawing board—back to the initiating event stage

The Reg Map

Informal Rulemaking

Step One
Initiating Events

Agency Initiatives

Agency initiatives for rulemaking originate from such things as:
- Agency priorities and plans
- New scientific data
- New technologies
- Accidents

Required Reviews

Statutory Mandates

Recommendations from Other Agencies/External Groups/States/Federal Advisory Committees

Lawsuits

Petitions

OMB Prompt Letters

Step Two
Determination Whether a Rule Is Needed

Administrative Procedure Act Provisions

Under the Administrative Procedure Act provisions that are included as part of the Freedom of Information Act at 5 U.S.C. 552, agencies are required to publish in the *Federal Register*:
- Substantive rules of general applicability
- Interpretive rules
- Statements of general policy
- Rules of procedure
- Information about forms
- Information concerning agency organization and methods of operation

Step Three
Preparation of Proposed Rule

Proposed Rule

A notice of proposed rulemaking proposes to add, change, or delete regulatory text and contains a request for public comments.

Administrative Procedure Act Provisions

Under the Administrative Procedure Act provisions at 5 U.S.C. 553, rules may be established only after proposed rulemaking procedures (steps three through six) have been followed, unless an exemption applies. The following are exempted:
- Rules concerning military or foreign affairs functions
- Rules concerning agency management or personnel
- Rules concerning public property, loans, grants, benefits, or contracts
- Interpretive rules
- General statements of policy
- Rules of agency organization, procedure, or practice
- Nonsignificant rules for which the agency determines that public input is not warranted
- Rules published on an emergency basis

Note: Even if an exemption applies under the Administrative Procedure Act provisions, other statutory authority or agency policy may require that proposed rulemaking procedures be followed.

Optional Supplementary Procedures to Help Prepare a Proposed Rule

Advance Notice of Proposed Rulemaking
An advance notice of proposed rulemaking requests information needed for developing a proposed rule.

Using The Reg Map

The Reg Map is based on general requirements. In some cases, more stringent or less stringent requirements are imposed by statutory provisions that are agency specific or subject matter specific. Also, in some cases more stringent requirements are imposed by agency policy.

FIGURE 6.2
The Reg Map™

Step Four

OMB Review of Proposed Rule

OMB Review Under Executive Order 12866

OMB reviews only those rulemaking actions determined to be "significant."

Independent agencies are exempt from OMB review.

Step Five

Publication of Proposed Rule

Administrative Procedure Act Provisions

The Administrative Procedure Act provisions at 5 U.S.C. 553 require proposed rules to be published in the *Federal Register*.

Step Six

Public Comments

Comments

Under the Administrative Procedure Act provisions of 5 U.S.C. 553, an agency must provide the public the opportunity to submit written comments for consideration by the agency.

As required by Public Law No. 107-347, agencies must provide for submission of comments by electronic means and must make available online the comments and other materials included in the rulemaking docket under 5 U.S.C. 553 (c).

Executive Order 12866 established 60 days as the standard for the comment period.

The holding of a public hearing is discretionary unless required by statute or agency policy.

Specific Analyses for Steps Three and Seven

Regulatory Planning and Review (E.O. 12866)

Would the rule have a $100 million annual impact, raise novel issues, and/or have other significant impacts? → **If yes**   Prepare economic impact analysis.

Regulatory Flexibility Act (5 U.S.C. 601–612)

Is a notice of proposed rulemaking required by law? → **If yes**

Would the rule "have a significant economic impact on a substantial number of small entities"? → **and yes**   Prepare regulatory flexibility analysis.

Note: Under limited circumstances analyses also are required for certain interpretive rules involving internal revenue laws (5 U.S.C. 603, 604).

Paperwork Reduction Act (44 U.S.C. 3501–3520)

Does the rule contain a "collection of information" (reporting, disclosure, or recordkeeping)? → **If yes**   Prepare information collection clearance package for OMB review and approval, and prepare request for public comments.

Unfunded Mandates Reform Act (2 U.S.C. Chs. 17A, 25)

Does the rulemaking process include a proposed rule? → **If yes**

Does the rule include any Federal mandate that may result in the expenditure (direct costs minus direct savings) by State, local, and tribal governments, in the aggregate, or by the private sector, of $100 million in any one year (adjusted annually)? → **and yes**   Prepare unfunded mandates analysis (unless an exclusion applies).

FIGURE 6.2 (continued from previous page)

Step Seven

Preparation of Final Rule, Interim Final Rule, or Direct Final Rule

Final Rule

A final rule adds, changes, deletes, or affirms regulatory text.

Special Types of Final Rules

Interim Final Rule
An interim final rule adds, changes, or deletes regulatory text and contains a request for comments. The subsequent final rule may make changes to the text of the interim final rule.

Direct Final Rule
A direct final rule adds, changes, or deletes regulatory text at a specified future time, with a duty to withdraw the rule if the agency receives adverse comments within the period specified by the agency.

Step Eight

OMB Review of Final Rule, Interim Final Rule, or Direct Final Rule

OMB Review Under Executive Order 12866

OMB reviews only those rulemaking actions determined to be "significant."

Independent agencies are exempt from OMB review.

Step Nine

Publication of Final Rule, Interim Final Rule, or Direct Final Rule

Congressional Review Act (5 U.S.C. 801-808)

An agency must submit most final rules, interim final rules, and direct final rules, along with supporting information, to both houses of Congress and the General Accounting Office before they can take effect.

Major rules are subject to a delayed effective date (with certain exceptions).

Action by Congress and the President could have an impact on the rule.

Administrative Procedure Act Provisions

Under the Administrative Procedure Act provisions that are included as part of the Freedom of Information Act at 5 U.S.C. 552, agencies are required to publish final rules, interim final rules, and direct final rules in the *Federal Register*.

Federal Register Act (44 U.S.C. 1501-1511)

The Federal Register Act at 44 U.S.C. 1510 (implemented at 1 CFR 8.1) requires rules that have general applicability and legal effect to be published in the *Code of Federal Regulations*.

Drafting Requirements for Rulemaking Documents

Agendas for Rules Under Development or Review

FIGURE 6.2

(continued from previous page)

to start over. For the purposes of this discussion, a positive outcome is assumed at every stage.

After review by OMB, the regulation-in-the-making can be *published as a proposed rule* (PR) in the *Federal Register* and Regulations.gov (see *Step Five* in figure 6.2). At this point, stakeholders have something definite to which they can react and on which they can comment. The PR must be accompanied by *another call for comments* (see *Step Six* in figure 6.2). A proposed rule includes a *preamble,* background about the action under consideration written in plain language. In preambles, agencies must address issues arising in the first public comment cycle. Collections of preambles are sometimes reprinted as separate publications. *Radiological Health: March 1936–March 1978,* a compilation of *Federal Register* preambles on radiological health (Food and Drug Administration, 1980) is one example. Each proposed rule is assigned a *docket number,* like a case or tracking number. The docket number stays with the regulation all the way through its process. Comments received and anything related to the regulation that the agency releases must reference this number.

Assuming that the agency receives comments on the PR, it works to respond to the concerns in its writing of the final rule. The *final rule is prepared* (see *Step Seven* in figure 6.2), and *again OIRA reviews it* (see *Step Eight* in figure 6.2), since it may have changed significantly since its proposed stage. In *Step Nine* (see figure 6.2), *Congress and the Government Accountability Office may review* the final rule.

Along its path, experts from multiple agencies review a proposed regulation. If a reviewing agency finds that something in the proposal under review violates existing laws or regulations (or doesn't meet criteria established thereby), the action has no chance of making it all the way to a final regulation. (This happened in 2007 when the Sierra Club and other groups petitioned the EPA to develop warning labels for carcinogens in air fresheners. The EPA published a notice in the *Federal Register* that they received the petition, but agency experts determined it failed to meet the criteria of Section 2 of the Toxic Substances Control Act, so the EPA would pursue no further action (Environmental Protection Agency, 2007).) Assuming a proposed regulation passes through all of these steps, it becomes a final rule and is published in the *Federal Register* and Regulations.gov. It will be integrated into the next edition of the printed *CFR,* and its presence will be duly noted in the *List of CFR Sections Affected.* Final rules become effective no sooner than 30 days after they are printed in the *Federal Register* (Office of the Federal Register, 2011).

The *Federal Register* and Regulations.gov

Proposed regulations are first published in the *Federal Register,* a Monday to Friday daily newspaper of the federal government that has been published since 1936, thanks to P.L. 74-220, the Federal Register Act, passed July 26, 1935. The *Federal Register* is considered an official publishing outlet of the executive branch of government, so in addition to proposed regulations, it contains presidential executive orders, proclamations, and decision directives; announcements of public agency hearings (known as Sunshine Act notices); alerts about federal grant opportunities; notices about future rulemaking; and more. The National Archives and Records Administration produces a readable 10-page history of the *Federal Register* that provides easy background on this publication so pivotal to the daily functioning of the government (Office of the Federal Register, 2006), as well as a practical guide to its use (Office of the Federal Register, 2009). The Law Librarians' Society of Washington DC (LLSDC) also offers the valuable *Research Guide to the Federal Register and Code of Federal Regulations.*

The official online *Federal Register* is available via FDsys at www.gpo.gov/fdsys/browse/collection.action?collectionCode=FR, back to 1994. Using the advanced search feature, one can perform complex fielded searching, limiting the search to just the *Federal Register,* or browse an entire issue or its table of contents. As with many GPO products, it is delivered in PDF (bearing a digital signature of authenticity), XML, or text.

The *Federal Register* in its printed form is not the easiest source to navigate; each issue is organized by agency, and the table of contents lists the agencies and their proposed actions—there is no daily index. The *Federal Register* is continuously paginated, so page numbers reach into the tens of thousands each year, and it is cited by volume number, page number, and date. A twice-monthly index, searchable by agency and broad subject, is cumulated in an annual index volume. A commercially published index, the *CIS Federal Register Index,* was published from 1984 to 1999 only. Starting in 1994, with widespread searchable online access to the current *Federal Register* through GPO and numerous private publishers, use of printed indexes declined, although the Law Library Microform Consortium (LLMC) has digitized the historic run of (GPO-produced) annual printed indexes. Today's users of the free online versions from GPO and the Office of the Federal Register can choose to peruse an online table of contents or a cumulative index for each year as navigation aids, in addition to the general and advanced search capabilities. HeinOnline's *Federal Register Library*, a commercial subscription, offers full text of the resource and its indexes, back to 1936. The same database (1936 to 1993 only) is available for free from the Law Library of Congress Guide to United States Executive Law Online, www.loc.gov/law/help/guide/federal/uscode.php, through a special arrangement with publisher William S. Hein.

Significantly, GPO and the Office of the Federal Register collaborated on a completely new approach to the *Federal Register,* released July 2010 at www.federalregister.gov. This much more visually appealing, truly interactive (XML-based) edition invites the user to browse, search, follow eye-catching headlines, or view brief videos. The broad categories are Money, Environment, World, Science and Technology, Business and Industry, and Health and Public Welfare. A thin banner across the top of the page quantifies that day's content (e.g., 108 Notices, 6 Proposed Rules, 6 Rules, and 2 Significant Regulations, in 221 pages). As XML, its content can easily be used by other online applications. A disclaimer clarifies that this is a prototype. As of the publication of this book, the site still does not serve as a legal substitute for the FDsys digital edition or print-on-paper GPO edition.

While www.federalregister.gov is essentially the online rendition of a daily newspaper, Regulations.gov is a more far-reaching portal, debuting in 2003. It too is updated daily (figure 6.3) and is the principal place for the public to read and comment on proposed regulations. Administered by an executive committee of representatives from 39 federal departments and agencies, it is truly a collaborative project, "your voice in federal decision-making." Users can search, comment, and read others' comments about proposed rules, final rules, and other agency matters from hundreds of federal government entities. Comments submitted here are as official as those submitted via fax, e-mail, or US mail. A system of docket folders is used to group related materials. One can limit a search by keyword, agency, date, comment period, docket number, title of document, and document type, and one can sort results by any of these dimensions as well. In recent years, more and more supporting and related regulatory materials have been contributed by agencies. For example, the Food and Nutrition Service filed a 55-page proposed regulation involving changes to the Child and Adult Care Food Program (CACFP), and in the same docket folder they uploaded a 67-page regulatory impact statement providing a cost-benefit analysis of the action. The interface is simple and intuitive. For those wishing to improve their regulatory research skills, visiting Regulations.gov every now and then and perusing regulations up for comment is an educational practice—seeing what is trending or what new regulatory apps are available is interesting, even entertaining. The Learn tab shows an even more simplified regulatory picture. The Federal Docket Management System (www.fdms .gov), a system closed to the public but used by authorized federal employees, helps manage electronic documents related to rulemaking.

FIGURE 6.3
Regulations.gov Screenshot

The *Code of Federal Regulations*

All federal government regulations currently in force are published in the *CFR* in a codified, or topical, arrangement. A basic working understanding of the *CFR* and the *Federal Register* is a relevant skill for any public service librarian, educator, or public official. Many veteran librarians will be familiar with the look and feel of the printed *CFR,* approximately eight shelves of brightly colored paperbacks in most of the print-on-paper reference collections in the country.

TABLE 6.1
CFR Titles

1: General Provisions	**27:** Alcohol, Tobacco Products and Firearms
2: Grants and Agreements	**28:** Judicial Administration
3: The President	**29:** Labor
4: Accounts	**30:** Mineral Resources
5: Administrative Personnel	**31:** Money and Finance: Treasury
6: Domestic Security	**32:** National Defense
7: Agriculture	**33:** Navigation and Navigable Waters
8: Aliens and Nationality	**34:** Education
9: Animals and Animal Products	**35:** Panama Canal
10: Energy	**36:** Parks, Forests, and Public Property
11: Federal Elections	**37:** Patents, Trademarks and Copyrights
12: Banks and Banking	**38:** Pensions, Bonuses and Veterans' Relief
13: Business Credit and Assistance	**39:** Postal Service
14: Aeronautics and Space	**40:** Protection of the Environment
15: Commerce and Foreign Trade	**41:** Public Contracts and Property Management
16: Commercial Practices	**42:** Public Health
17: Commodity and Securities Exchanges	**43:** Public Lands: Interior
18: Conservation of Power and Water Resources	**44:** Emergency Management and Assistance
19: Customs Duties	**45:** Public Welfare
20: Employees' Benefits	**46:** Shipping
21: Food and Drugs	**47:** Telecommunications
22: Foreign Relations	**48:** Federal Acquisition Regulations System
23: Highways	**49:** Transportation
24: Housing and Urban Development	**50:** Wildlife and Fisheries
25: Indians	INDEX
26: Internal Revenue	

The *CFR*'s 50 titles, or topical areas, range from Protection of the Environment (Title 40) to Internal Revenue (Title 26) to Public Health (Title 42); see the full listing in table 6.1. These numbers have no numeric correlation to the titles of the *U.S. Code*—a common misperception—and, depending on context, either resource could be referred to as "The Code"—though generally that term is used for the *U.S. Code*. The *CFR* is compiled by the Office of the Federal Register and published in online, print, and microfiche by GPO, and sold by many commercial publishers as well. Since the *CFR* is used as a current tool—to determine whether a rule is in force—most libraries retain only the most current edition, relying on law libraries and online vendors to supply older, superseded volumes (FDsys has them back to 1994). *CFR* editions from 1938 to 1995 are available for free from the Law Library of Congress Guide to United States Executive Law Online, www.loc.gov/law/help/guide/federal/uscode.php, through an agreement with William S. Hein & Co., Inc. Specialized legal research sometimes requires understanding prior regulations. The printed *CFR* comes with an annual index volume, allowing the user to search the *CFR* by agency or broad topic area. Commercially produced indexes, providing more fine-grained subject access, have been published over the years, notably the *CIS Index to the Code of Federal Regulations* (annually, 1977–2001) and *West's Code of Federal Regulations: General Index* (annually, 2006–present).

The printed *CFR* is published annually in rolling updates, with the total set divided into quarters: titles 1–16 are published to be current as of January 1; titles 17–27 to be current as of April 1; titles 28–41 to be current as of July 1; titles 42–50 to be current as of October 1. If there are no regulatory changes in a particular volume for an entire year, libraries or individual subscribers still receive a new cover to place over the previous year's volume. New regulations may strike out, amend, or update older ones, and the entire *CFR* is updated over the course of one year. Watching the (printed) *CFR* covers change color is a marker of a year's passage for many documents and law librarians. One title, Title 3 (*The President, Compilation & Reports*) should not be replaced when the new edition arrives; all of its volumes must be retained for historic purposes. Title 3 contains materials such as executive orders and proclamations not codified with the rest of the *CFR* (see chapter 8 on the presidency). When you visit a library, the *CFR* shelves should include all the old Title 3 volumes back to 1938 (Hartnett, 2006).

> **Quantifying Regulations**
>
> Massive quantities of regulations (not quite as thrilling as a jellybean jar at the county fair) are worth measuring for their sheer volume. Download annual page counts of the *CFR* and *Federal Register* back to the 1930s in Excel or PDF tables from www .federalregister.gov/learn/tutorials/. See how one professor at George Mason University's Mercatus Center visualizes the growth in regulations at http://mercatus.org/video/visualizing -growth-federal-regulation-1950 (McLaughlin, 2014).

e-CFR

GPO and the Office of the Federal Register have teamed up to create an *e-CFR,* updated *daily,* a big change from the quarterly edition. The result, not considered a legal version of the *CFR* at the time of this writing, is online at www.ecfr.gov/cgi-bin/ECFR?page=browse. This differs from the FDsys version (referred to as the *CFR Annual Edition*), which matches the updating pattern of the printed set.

The *List of CFR Sections Affected, or LSA*

For regulatory devotees who live, breathe, and die by the printed *CFR,* a recurrent task is determining which sections of the *CFR* are affected by new rules published daily in the *Federal Register* and on Regulations.gov. Assume that an agency (e.g., the FAA) is busy throughout the year: proposing rulemaking, announcing public hearings, and filing proposed and final rules. If one were restricted to using printed sources (as some courts still require), then aside from reading the daily *Federal Register,* how would one keep up with this, since the print-on-paper *CFR* is only revised annually? The answer lies in a slim monthly publication (print and online), the *List of CFR Sections Affected* (*LSA*). Specialists in industry, healthcare, environmental safety, business, and many other fields, are typically required to monitor the regulations in their fields. They know the *CFR* title, chapter, and part they need to follow. The *LSA* section shown in the sidebar includes the *part number* (of Title 14, *CFR*) on the left side, and the *page numbers* of that year's *Federal Register* (still the preferred legal method of citing) on the right margin. Even our FAA section, 14 CFR 97, has been updated with some new developments since its last annual *CFR* compilation. The print-on-paper *LSA* includes only those updates occurring in one month, and the online version includes daily updates of revisions occurring that month.

Luckily for today's researchers, there are easier ways to track changes to a section of the *CFR*. Regulations.gov is searchable by agency and type of action, and www.federalregister.gov has an advanced search letting users query a specific *CFR* citation and subscribe to the search results as an RSS feed. With minimal effort, one could do much the same with FDsys and commercial versions of regulatory resources as well. And, as mentioned above, the *e-CFR* takes all the changes and automatically updates the *CFR* on a daily basis (although not considered a legal version as yet).

**TRIVIA TIME:
What Happened to Title 35?**

Feel like there's something missing? Title 35 of the *CFR* was last published in 2000; that's because Panamanian control of the canal commenced on January 1, 2000.

List of CFR Sections Affected
(November 2014)
Changes January 2, 2014, through November 28, 2014

14 *CFR*—Aeronautics & space

CFR Part	*Federal Register* page number
73	51076, 53649
91	53643
93	52132, 52134
95	50920
97	50696, 50698, 54457, 54460, 55451, 55453
97.21–97.37	11705, 12379, 13535, 16178, 21605, 24321, 24325, 29665, 33422, 33427, 39964, 40620, 46666, 46675, 51889, 57433, 63525, 63532, 68354, 68357

E-rulemaking: The Perennial Hope for Efficiency and Transparency

Rulemaking was born in the New Deal era and thus reflects its roots in print-on-paper governance. The *Federal Register,* printed daily, was the primary public forum for the rulemaking activities. Print-on-paper letters via US mail or in-person remarks at public hearings were the normal means of comment. Over the years, newer electronic technologies (e.g., fax and e-mail) were accepted as means for receiving public comments, but they merely fed into the established rulemaking structure that was still predominantly print-based.

Given the tremendous diversity of federal agencies, the rulemaking system also was quite decentralized. Then, during the Reagan years, the regulatory process changed with Executive Order 12291, which gave the OMB extensive powers over the regulatory apparatus—perhaps the single most important reform of the rulemaking process since the APA in 1946. The order empowered the OMB to identify duplication, overlap, and conflict in rules, which federal agencies then were required to rectify, and to review existing and new rules for consistency with administrative policies. The order required the use of cost-benefit analysis and established a "net benefit" criterion for rulemaking (CQ Press, 2008: 7).

This more centralized oversight and consistent administration of the federal rulemaking process set the stage for further improvements in efficiency and transparency as modern technologies advanced. In the George W. Bush era, an electronic government (e-government) initiative emerged, with e-rulemaking its major component, using digital technologies to develop and implement regulations (Executive Office of the President, 2003). The Obama administration focused on using empirical, systematic review of all regulations, furthering international regulatory cooperation, and reducing burdens. Regardless of ongoing changes, it makes sense that each step in the regulatory process taken by agencies be done in a uniform, consistent manner, handled by evolving technology. There should be agreed-upon elements in the records kept across agencies and in the compatibility of systems used to manage the records.

Exploring Agency Websites for Regulatory Content

Out of the universe of federal departments, agencies, commissions, and quasi-official establishments, between 60 and 300 (depending on criteria used) have significant regulatory functions. The Federal Motor Carrier Safety Administration makes a good case study of a regulatory agency at www.fmcsa.dot.gov. On its website, a Regulations section covers drivers, vehicles, and company policies. Clicking on any of the topics allows the user to read the regulations exactly as they are printed in the *CFR.* For most topics, a guidance or interpretation is also available in FAQ style. Other notable regulatory sites include the Food and Drug Administration (www.fda.gov/RegulatoryInformation/default.htm), the Nuclear Regulatory Commission (www.nrc.gov/reading-rm/doc

-collections/reg-guides), and the EPA (www.epa.gov/lawsregs/). One can imagine that much of the regulatory content found by casual users of the Web comes through such federal agency sites; what they find will be specifically scoped to the agency's purview and they don't need to understand the *Federal Register* or *CFR*. Well-curated agency sites can offer invaluable insight into the context and intent of regulations, the kind of content not found elsewhere.

Users can find another kind of information on many agency sites: guidance documents. These nonlegally binding writings represent an agency's most current thinking on a topic, its best practices. Guidances are an agency's way of explaining (to industry, for example) possible techniques for adhering to its regulations. The FDA has used Guidances (or "Good Guidance Practices") for years; see www.fda.gov/AboutFDA/Transparency/TransparencyInitiative/ucm285282.htm.

Regulatory agencies also contain adjudicative bodies similar to courts of law; they hear cases regarding regulations and publish decisions, directives, opinions, orders, and reports. These agency actions are subject to judicial review (Hernon et al., 2002). To read more about this process, consult the *Dictionary of American History* (Goostree and Greenfield, 2003). The University of Virginia Library offers a list (by agency) of "Administrative Decisions and Other Actions" (http://guides.lib.virginia.edu/administrative_decisions).

State and Local Codes

Just as states have their own constitutions, legislatures, and court systems, all states have executive agencies whose rulemaking parallels that of the federal government. These agencies announce their rulemaking activities in publishing outlets similar to the *Federal Register* (the *Washington State Register,* the *Colorado Register,* and the *Pennsylvania Bulletin,* for example). After a notice and comment period, the agencies publish their final rules in these same publications. Next, the final rules are integrated into the state equivalents of the *CFR;* these compiled, codified regulations are generally called administrative codes (e.g., the *Washington Administrative Code,* the *Colorado Code of Regulations,* the *Pennsylvania Code*)—your state's title may vary. You can find all 50 states' administrative codes linked to from many different online guides, two of the most notable being the National Association of Secretaries of State, which has an Administrative Codes and Registers Section (www.administrativerules.org) and the Public Library of Law (www.plol.org) under the Regulations tab.

The pattern is replicated at the county and municipal levels as well. Your local government has a municipal or county code or both (depending on the governance structure), with sections covering topical areas such as safety, parking violations, and parks and recreation. Most people are aware of their local county health departments, but do not have any idea where to find the county health code or how they might work to change it. It is also common for smaller jurisdictions to adopt wholesale already established codes from industry or safety organizations. The practice of adopting an external set of rules or standards into one's own code is called incorporation by reference, a common practice with building and fire safety regulations, and it can take place at the federal level as well. The major legal publishers (e.g., West, LexisNexis) provide subscription services aggregating state and local codes. The Law Librarians' Society of Washington, DC, maintains a helpful list of state legislatures, state laws, and state regulations (www.llsdc.org/state-legislation), as does the Law Library of Congress (www.loc .gov/law/help/guide/states.php). In many cases, these state links lead to city and county regulatory sources (codes) within two or three clicks.

Recommended Sources of Additional Information

The Office of Management and Budget's Office of Information and Regulatory Affairs (OIRA), an oversight office established in 1980, is a pivotal regulatory entity. The public web page at www .whitehouse.gov/omb/inforeg_default describes OIRA's exact role in everything from analyzing the quality of information going into the regulatory process, to monitoring privacy and confidentiality concerns within the federal government sphere, to coordinating certain aspects of federal statistics. The introductory chapter of CQ Press's *Federal Regulatory Directory* provides a readable, in-depth, plain English guide to the regulatory process and the history of regulation, including OIRA's role.

The regulatory arena draws many advocacy groups and watchdogs. The Center for Regulatory Effectiveness (www.thecre.com) monitors access to regulations and access to quality data, and shares its independent analyses with Congress. The Center for Effective Government (www.foreffectivegov .org) formerly OMBWatch changed its name in 2013 to indicate both its expanded role over the years and its overall goal: effective government reflecting the American people's needs and priorities. The organization promotes transparency, sound government processes, and citizen involvement.

> **Cass Sunstein and the Office of Information and Regulatory Affairs (OIRA)**
>
> One of the most prolific contemporary writers and thinkers on government and the regulatory state is Cass R. Sunstein, Harvard Law School, who served as OIRA Administrator from 2009–2012. An academic turned government insider, Professor Sunstein possesses a sweeping view of the regulatory terrain, and writes about it in a popular, accessible way. Chapter One of *Valuing Life: Humanizing the Regulatory State* (Sunstein, 2014) is his personal account of the forty-five person OIRA staff and its work making the regulatory gears turn. He describes the internal RISC and OIRA Consolidated Information Service (ROCIS), what factors cause proposed regulations to be labeled economically significant, and regulation as an example of "government by discussion."

Regulatory Awareness Projects

A variety of online projects aim to increase public awareness of the regulatory process. Regulation Room (www.regulationroom.org), with the motto "people talking to people talking to government," is a project of the Cornell e-Rulemaking Initiative (CeRI), hosted by the Legal Information Institute (LII). Instead of just filing comments, respondents have the opportunity to discuss regulations with each other. CeRI faculty and students moderate the discussions, and the project has research, teaching, and learning goals as well as a civic purpose. George Mason University's RegData.org project measures the size and scope of federal regulations by industry back to 1997.

TABLE 6.2
Frequently requested regulatory materials and recommended sources

User Needs	Suggested Resource
Plain English explanation and map of the regulatory process	Reginfo.gov, Regulations.gov
The *Federal Register* (Notices; proposed, interim, and final rules; presidential documents; other significant executive documents)	FederalRegister.gov, FDsys, Regulations.gov (*Federal Register* in a disaggregated form) HeinOnline, Lexis-Nexis Academic, Westlaw
The *Code of Federal Regulations* (final rules currently in force) and *List of CFR Sections Affected*	FDsys, www.e-CFR.gov HeinOnline, Lexis-Nexis Academic, Westlaw
Federal agency regulatory plans and past accomplishments (*Unified Agenda & Regulatory Plans*)	Reginfo.gov, FDsys (for Unified Agendas & Regulatory Plans that have been printed in the *Federal Register*)

Conclusion

One can expect continued reform of the federal regulatory system and increased public awareness due to tools like www.federalregister.gov, online advocacy groups, and new online projects. Some lawmakers have recently called for the discontinuation of the printed *Federal Register* (113th Cong., H.R. 4195, *Federal Register Modernization Act*), which seems like a reasonable possibility for the not-so-distant future so long as there are sufficient processes and safeguards in place to ensure that regulatory information in digital form is permanently available for public access. Regardless of format, the purposeful work of improving our regulatory system, creating tools that make regulating simpler to accomplish, understand, and discover, must continue. It is an effort in which librarians can play a critical role, encouraging users to try a variety of pathways, tapping our own knowledge networks, and keeping current with sources.

Exercises

1. Experiment with Regulations.gov to see if your favorite corporation has commented on proposed regulations. What did you find?

2. According to the latest Unified Agenda, which three agencies have the most rulemaking planned for the next six months?
3. Find a federal regulation currently in force regarding the safe handling of human blood. Can you cite the resource properly?
4. What is The Seafood List maintained by the FDA? Is it guidance or a regulation?
5. Do any recent regulatory actions published by the federal government affect an area close to your home zip code? How did you find out?

Sources Mentioned in This Chapter

Sources mentioned in this section do not duplicate the references that follow.

Legislation

Federal Register Act, P.L. 74–220, 49 Stat. 500 Chapter 417 (1935).
Administrative Procedure Act (APA), P.L. 79–404, 60 Stat. 237, Chap. 324 (1946).
Government Organization and Employees, P.L. 89–554, 80 Stat. 378 (1966).

Other Sources

Administrative Decisions and Other Actions, guides.lib.virginia.edu/administrative_decisions.
Administrative Procedure Act, www.archives.gov/federal-register/laws/ administrative-procedure/.
Center for Effective Government, www.foreffectivegov.org/rulemaking/.
Center for Regulatory Effectiveness, www.thecre.com.
CIS Federal Register Index, 1984. Bethesda, MD: Congressional Information Service.
CIS Index to the Code of Federal Regulations, 1978. Bethesda, MD: Congressional Information Service.
Code of Federal Regulations, www.gpo.gov/fdsys/.
e-CFR, www.ecfr.gov/cgi-bin/ECFR?page=browse.
Federal Register, www.gpo.gov/fdsys/browse/collection.action?collectionCode=FR.
FederalRegister.gov, www.federalregister.gov.
HeinOnline. 2015. *Federal Register Library.*
Law Librarians' Society of Washington, DC: State Legislatures, State Laws, and StateRegulations, www.llsdc.org/state-leg.
Law Library of Congress, www.loc.gov/law/help/guide/states.php.
List of CFR Sections Affected, www.gpo.gov/fdsys/browse/collection.action?collectionCode=LSA.
National Association of Secretaries of State, Administrative Codes and Registers Section, www.administrativerules.org.
Office of Management and Budget's Office of Information and Regulatory Affairs (OIRA), www.whitehouse.gov/omb/oira/.
Public Library of Law, www.plol.org.
Reg Map, www.reginfo.gov/public/reginfo/Regmap/index.jsp.
RegData.org: a product of the Mercatus Center, George Mason University, http://regdata.org.
Reginfo.gov, www.reginfo.gov.
Regulation Room, www.regulationroom.org.

Regulations.gov, www.regulations.gov.

Research Guide to the *Federal Register* and Code of Federal Regulations, www.llsdc.org/fr-cfr
-research-guide.

Unified Agenda of Federal Regulatory and Deregulatory Actions, www.reginfo.gov/public/do/
eAgendaMain/, www.gpo.gov/fdsys/.

West's Code of Federal Regulations General Index, www.worldcat.org/oclc/64195650/.

References

Arrigo, Paul. 2003. "Federal Rules and Regulations: What are They, Where Did They Come From,
and How Do I Find Them?" In *Government Publications Unmasked: Teaching Government Information
Resources in the 21st Century,* edited by Wendy Mann and Theresa R. McDevitt, 73–84. Pittsburgh, PA:
Library Instruction Publications.

Center for Effective Government. 2014. "About Us." www.foreffectivegov.org/about-us.

Chu, Vivian S. and Todd Garvey. 2014. *Executive Orders: Issuance, Modification, and Revocation.* Washington
DC: Library of Congress, Congressional Research Service. April 16. www.fas.org/sgp/crs/misc/
RS20846.pdf.

Committee on the Status and Future of Federal e-Rulemaking and American Bar Association Section
of Administrative Law and Regulatory Practice. 2008. *Achieving the Potential: The Future of Federal
e-Rulemaking: A Report to Congress and the President (Executive Summary).* http://ceri.law.cornell.edu/
documents/executive-summary.pdf.

CQ Press. 2008. *Federal Regulatory Directory.* Washington, DC: CQ Press.

Department of State. 2015. "Rulemaking." www.state.gov/m/a/dir/rulemaking/c42660.htm.

Department of Transportation, 2014. "Smoking of Electronic Cigarettes on Commercial Aircraft." RIN:
2105–AE06. www.reginfo.gov/public/do/eAgendaViewRule?pubId=201410&RIN=2105-AE06.

Environmental Protection Agency. 2007. "Air Fresheners; TSCA Section 21 Petition."

Executive Office of the President. 2003. *E-Government Strategy Implementing the President's Management
Agenda for e-Government.* http://permanent.access.gpo.gov/lps36050/2003egov_strat.pdf.

Federal Register 72 (245), December 21. www.gpo.gov/fdsys/pkg/FR-2007-12-21/pdf/07-6176.pdf.

Federal Motor Carrier Safety Administration. "Regulations." 2015. www.fmcsa.dot.gov/regulations.

Food and Drug Administration. 1980. *Radiological Health: March 1936–March 1978.* Rockville, MD:
Dept. of Health, Education, and Welfare, Public Health Service, Food and Drug Administration.

Food and Drug Administration. 2014. "Updated Standards for Labeling of Pet Food." RIN: 0910-AG09.
www.reginfo.gov/public/do/eAgendaViewRule?pubId=201410&RIN=0910-AG09.

Goostree, Robert S., and Kent Greenfield. 2003. "Administrative Justice." *Dictionary of American History.*
Ed. Stanley I. Kutler. 3rd ed. Vol. 1. New York: Charles Scribner's Sons, 2003. 22–23. *Gale Virtual
Reference Library.*

Hartnett, Cass. 2006. "Government Regulations: Protective, Restrictive, and Influenced by the Public."
DttP: Documents to the People 32, no. 2 (Spring): 29.

Hernon, Peter, Harold C. Relyea, Joan F. Cheverie, and Robert E. Dugan. 2002. *United States Government
Information: Policies and Sources.* Westport, CT: Libraries Unlimited.

McLaughlin, Patrick. 2014. Visualizing the Growth of Federal Regulation since 1950.
Mercatus Center, George Washington University, http://mercatus.org/video/
visualizing-growth-federal-regulation-1950.

Office of the Federal Register. 2006. *The Office of the Federal Register: A Brief History Commemorating the 70th Anniversary of the Publication of the First Issue of the Federal Register March 14, 1936*. Washington, DC: Office of the Federal Register, National Archives and Records Administration. www.archives .gov/federal-register/the-federal-register/history.pdf.

Office of the Federal Register. 2009. "About the Federal Register." www.archives.gov/federal-register/ the-federal-register/about.html.

Office of the Federal Register. 2011. "A Guide to the Rulemaking Process." www.federalregister.gov/ uploads/2011/01/the_rulemaking_process.pdf.

Office of the Federal Register. 2015. "Tutorials, History, and Statistics." https://www.federalregister.gov/ learn/tutorials. Includes "Federal Register Document Pages, Annual Percentage Change" and "Code of Federal Regulations: Total Pages Published."

Regulations.gov. 2015. "Frequently Asked Questions: Rulemaking Process." www.regulations.gov/#!faqs.

Regulations.gov. 2015b. "Non-Participatory Agencies." www.regulations.gov/docs/Non_Participating _Agencies.pdf.

Regulatory Information Service Center. 2014. "Introduction to the 2014 Regulatory Plan." www .reginfo.gov/public/jsp/eAgenda/StaticContent/201410/VPStatement.html.

Regulatory Information Service Center. 2015. "Current Regulatory Plan and the Unified Agenda of Regulatory and Deregulatory Actions." www.reginfo.gov/public/do/eAgendaMain.

CHAPTER 7

Case Law and the Judicial Branch

PEGGY ROEBUCK JARRETT

Introduction

Judicial branch publications are sometimes perceived by government documents librarians as more mysterious or challenging than publications from the legislative or executive branch. The explanation for this perception may be that few judicial publications are distributed through the Federal Depository Library Program (FDLP) and case law created by the judiciary has a long history of commercial publication. This chapter will discuss case law and its finding aids, and the relatively recent free official and unofficial online sources that have brightened the landscape of case law research for government information librarians and the people they help. This chapter will also discuss the court system and other court documents and judicial branch publications.

As discussed in chapter 4, Congress creates law by passing legislation, the executive branch enforces the law by promulgating regulations, and the judicial branch interprets the law and determines if it is constitutional. The courts apply law to individual situations and through this process produce case law. It is a bit more complex than that, but it is definitely worth understanding—and is even understandable!

The place to start is the Constitution, which states the "judicial power of the United States, shall be vested in one Supreme Court, and in such inferior courts as the Congress may from time to time ordain and establish" (US Const. art. III § 1). The framers wanted the judicial branch of the federal government to be independent, ensuring fairness and impartiality. Federal judges serve for life and can only be removed by impeachment. And judicial salaries cannot be reduced by the president or Congress. Independence does not mean an absence of a relationship, however, since the framers set up checks and balances among the branches of government. The president appoints federal judges, and the Senate confirms them. Congress also creates inferior courts, which are the federal courts below the Supreme Court. Congress decides the jurisdiction and number of judges for each federal court, and appropriates money for judicial operations.

What is case law? It is law, created by a federal or state judge or a panel of judges in the course of resolving disputes, and comprises written resolutions of the legal issues. The written resolution is in the form of an opinion. (Note, not all opinions are published, and not all courts issue opinions.) Opinions are primarily, but not exclusively, issued by appellate courts (the exception is federal trial courts) and deal with issues of law, not fact. Juries, in trial court proceedings, decide facts (guilty or not guilty of a crime, responsible for medical malpractice or not). Opinions with precedential value are published, online or in print. A print collection of opinions is called *reports* or a *reporter.* Precedents are the legal principles or rules higher courts decide and then determine should be applied in other cases with similar issues and facts. This system allows similarly situated people to be treated the same.

The body of law created by all these judicial opinions is the common law. Here in the United States, because of our early ties with England, we adopted the English common law system. The other Western legal tradition, flowing from Roman law, is civil law. Civil law is a comprehensive body of law in the form of a code. To complicate matters a bit, Louisiana, because of its French and Spanish legal heritage, is a mixed jurisdiction and has both civil and common law. And, as discussed in previous chapters, we have codified law—the *United States Code* and the *Code of Federal Regulations.* But the United States is a common law country—our codes are arrangement schemes, not attempts to create a unified, comprehensive body of law.

It is helpful to understand the relationship between case law and statutory law. Congress can enact or amend statutes to address a Supreme Court decision. For example, Lilly Ledbetter worked for almost 20 years for Goodyear Tire & Rubber at much less pay than her male counterparts. She did not discover the pay disparity for quite some time. Although initially successful in her lawsuit, the Supreme Court ruled that she did not have a valid claim because she did not file suit within 180 days of her very first Goodyear paycheck, *Ledbetter v. Goodyear Tire & Rubber Co.,* 550 U.S. 618 (2007). Congress (with the president who prioritized this issue) was able to correct this by the Lilly Ledbetter Fair Pay Act of 2009, Pub. L. No. 111–2, 123 Stat. 5, which says the date for determining pay discrimination claims can be the receipt of any paycheck, not just the first instance of discrimination. Congress made the law retroactive, to the day before the Supreme Court ruling that denied Ledbetter's claim. In the *Ledbetter* opinion, the Supreme Court interpreted the law in a way Congress did not like, so Congress changed the law. That cannot happen, of course, if the issue is one of constitutional interpretation. In the case *Citizens United v. F.E.C.,* 558 U.S. 310 (2010), the court declared that limits on corporate and union expenditures for independent communications (like television ads) violate the right of free speech. To change the law set down by *Citizens United* now requires a constitutional amendment or the Supreme Court to revisit the issue and overturn its own ruling.

It is also helpful to understand some vocabulary. A case is the entire legal proceeding—all the events from initiation to the final resolution. The word *case* is also used interchangeably with *decision* and *opinion*—in this instance the word is shorthand for case law, the subject of this chapter. This brings us to the reference interview. If people state they are "looking for a case," ask what they know about it. Is it a state or federal case? Might they have names and dates? Do they have a citation? Where did they hear about it? They may not be looking for case law (an opinion), but for information about a celebrity murder trial, which would mean a referral to contemporaneous media accounts or to the court itself.

The Court System

The United States judicial system has two parts: state courts and federal courts. All 50 states have a judiciary established by their state constitutions and legislatures. Whether a case is heard in state court or federal court depends on the nature of the dispute and the parties involved. Questions involving the US Constitution or a law passed by the US Congress, or cases in which the United States is a party, are heard in federal court. The Constitution gives federal courts jurisdiction (meaning the authority to hear a case) in a few topical areas—bankruptcy, admiralty, and intellectual property—but leaves a great deal to the states. As a result, most of the legal issues citizens encounter in their personal lives are the jurisdiction of state courts—for example, marriage and divorce, inheritance, landlord and tenant, traffic violations, and crimes under state law.

Each state is different but court systems, both state and federal, share similarities, including a hierarchical structure (see figures 7.1 and 7.2). The structure is often, but not always, a three-tiered system: trial courts, intermediate courts of appeals, and an appellate court of last resort. Cases flow from the lower (trial) courts up to the higher (appellate) courts. Washington State's judicial system is a good example. The trial courts are organized by county and called superior courts. They are general jurisdiction courts, meaning they hear a broad range of civil and criminal cases. Civil cases are disputes between individuals, businesses, governmental organizations, and nongovernmental organizations. An example of a civil case is when a person slips and falls and then sues the landowner for monetary damages. Other examples include a landlord-tenant dispute, a marital dissolution, or a contract dispute between companies, or between an individual and a company. Below the superior courts is another set of trial courts, called courts of limited jurisdiction, which are narrowly focused. In Washington, they are called municipal courts if created by a city (Seattle Municipal Court) and district courts if created by a county (King County District Court). These courts handle criminal misdemeanors, traffic offenses, including driving under the influence, requests for no-contact orders in domestic violence cases, small claims, and other civil disputes. Civil cases are limited by how much money is involved and criminal cases by the seriousness of the offense. Superior, municipal, and district courts are all trial courts, so there is not a written opinion (meaning no case law produced). These trial courts decide facts—guilty or not guilty, liable or not liable.

Cases from Washington State trial courts are appealed, if a party believes there is a legal error, to the Court of Appeals, which has three geographic divisions. Above the Court of Appeals is the Supreme Court, Washington State's court of last resort. Almost all states use the term Supreme Court. One notable exception is New York, which calls its court of last resort the Court of Appeals and has some trial courts called Supreme Courts (this is a well-known fact for watchers of the television show Law & Order, but may be confusing to others just trying to do legal research!). Rules for making an appeal, what court it goes to, and whether or not a case has to be accepted, vary from state to state. The important point is that state appellate courts issue opinions which resolve legal issues, thus creating case law.

The federal courts also have three levels: trial, intermediate appellate, and a court of last resort, which, as noted earlier, is the only court established by the Constitution. The trial courts are the federal district courts. There are 94 judicial districts and each state has at least one. Bankruptcy courts are separate courts within each district. There are also two federal trial courts with national jurisdiction: the US Court of International Trade and the US Court of Federal Claims. With the exception of the specialized courts, the federal trial courts are general jurisdiction courts, handling both civil and criminal cases.

The intermediate level is the courts of appeals. The 94 judicial districts are organized into 12 regional circuits which hear appeals from that jurisdiction. For a visual of the states in each circuit, see the Federal Court Locator map, www.uscourts .gov/court_locator.aspx. There is also a Court of

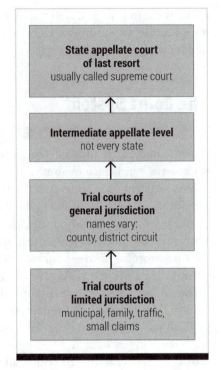

FIGURE 7.1
State Court Organization

Appeals for the Federal Circuit, which handles specialized cases, such as patent cases, plus appeals from international trade and federal claims courts. And there are a few other courts of special jurisdiction such as the US Tax Court and the US Court of Appeals for Veterans Claims.

The highest level, and the court with the highest profile, is the United States Supreme Court. The Supreme Court can hear appeals from the federal circuit courts of appeals and the state courts of last resort. It also has original jurisdiction, meaning it can hear a case from beginning to end if the dispute is between two states or between states and the federal government. A party that wants to appeal to the Supreme Court files a writ of certiorari, which is a request that the Supreme Court direct the lower court to send up the record of the case for review. The court grants or rejects the writ, and then reviews the merits of the case before deciding to put the case on the docket (its list of current cases). Only a very small number of cases—less than one percent of those filed—is heard and decided each year. Supreme Court Rule 10 states "review on a writ of certiorari is not a matter of right, but of judicial discretion. A petition for a writ of certiorari will be granted only for compelling reasons," and the definition of compelling is up to the justices. In the 2013 term, 7,376 cases were filed. Of those, only 79 were argued and the Court issued 67 signed and six per curiam (unsigned) opinions. (Roberts, 2014). (Per curiam opinions are usually, but not always, issued in noncontroversial cases with well-settled law.) Although the number of opinions issued is quite small, the subjects of those opinions are newsworthy (and even compelling): voting rights, campaign finance, same-sex marriage, religious freedom, capital punishment, cell phone searches, and affirmative action in higher education. An excellent source for court watchers is the well-regarded SCOTUSblog, www .scotusblog.com, which provides ongoing comprehensive coverage and analysis.

Publication of Opinions

As noted at the start of this chapter, case law is written in the form of a published opinion. Opinions are collected in sets of books called case reports, or reporters. The organization of a reporter is sequential; opinions are published in chronological order. Official reports have been designated as official by a legislative or judicial body (the mechanism varies from state to state—it might be by a procedural rule, for example). Official reports can be produced by the government or a commercial entity under the direction of the government, or be commercial products designated as official. Official versus unofficial is important to determine the reliability of the opinion (if there is a discrepancy, the official version governs). And as more states move to digital publication of opinions, it is also a concern of librarians and other advocates who believe official government information should be authentic and permanently preserved for public access, no matter the format.

FIGURE 7.2
Federal Court Organization

Published versus unpublished, however, is the important distinction to researchers, whether or not they are lawyers, who are trying to identify case law in order to build a legal argument. When an opinion is issued, the judge or panel of judges decides if it has precedential value or not. Opinions deemed to set precedent—which are a fraction of the total number of opinions—are published. Those lacking precedential value are labeled, for example, as *unpublished, not for publication,* or *not precedent.* Some confusion arises here because unpublished opinions became available with the advent of online legal research systems. This led to the need for courts to decide if counsel could cite an unpublished opinion in a brief (the legal and factual arguments submitted to the court). Court rules on this topic vary and anyone working on a brief needs to be familiar with the rules of the particular court.

Print Reporters

US Supreme Court opinions are published in three print reporters. The official edition, *United States Reports,* is published by GPO and distributed through the FDLP. The two unofficial editions are *West's Supreme Court Reporter* from Thomson West and *United*

States Supreme Court Reports, Lawyers' Edition from LexisNexis. Both unofficial reporters have many editorial additions and research aids.

The lower levels of federal courts lack official reports, with a few specialized exceptions such as the GPO published *Reports of the United States Tax Court.* Published opinions from the circuit courts of appeals are found in the *Federal Reporter,* published by Thomson West. Published opinions from the district courts are found in the *Federal Supplement,* also published by Thomson West. Although commercially published, these opinions are law. How can this be? Early American case law was privately published, just as English case law was privately published. The word *reporter* originally meant the person who recorded, compiled, and edited court opinions. In fact, the first volumes of the *United States Reports* are nominative reports, named for their original publisher (e.g., Dallas, Cranch, Howard, Wallace, etc.).

The dominant player in print is West Publishing, acquired by Thomson Reuters in 1996. Founded by two Minnesota brothers in 1872, West developed an organized system of reporting state appellate court opinions by dividing the country up into regions, and creating sets called regional reporters. They started with their own geographical region, which in the 19th century was the Northwest. Thus the *North Western Reporter* includes appellate court opinions from Minnesota, Wisconsin, and Michigan, while the *Pacific Reporter* includes a huge swath of the country—not just the Pacific Coast states, but Kansas, Colorado, and Utah. These regional reporters along with West's federal reporters make up what is called the National Reporter System. Many states rely on the National Reporter System for their case law publication and no longer publish their own reports. For example, Indiana designates West's *Northeastern Reporter* and Pennsylvania designates West's *Atlantic Reporter* as official. It is worth noting that some states still have their own official reports, but contract out to a commercial publisher. Washington State's official reports, *Washington Reports* (Supreme Court) and *Washington Appellate Reports,* are contracted out for publication to LexisNexis, under the guidance of the Washington Courts' Office of the Reporter of Decisions. Thus they are deemed official. A good source for identifying reporter coverage for individual states is Table T1.3, States and the District of Columbia, in *The Bluebook: A Uniform System of Citation.*

Case Citations

There are many rules governing case citations, including *The Bluebook* and local rules of state courts. In general, case citations follow a pattern of party names, volume number, reporter abbreviation, page number, court (if not clear from the reporter), and year. For example, the US Supreme Court opinion, *PGA Tour Inc. v. Martin,* 532 U.S. 661 (2001), can be found starting on page 661 of volume 532 of the *United States Reports.* Opinions found in more than one report (an official state report and also a regional reporter from Thomson West) may have parallel citations, meaning two citations to the same opinion. For example, the opinion cited as *Goodridge v. Dep't of Pub. Health,* 440 Mass. 309, 798 N.E.2d 941 (2003), can be found both in volume 440 of the *Massachusetts Reports* and volume 798 of the *North Eastern Reporter 2d.* These examples are print-based and tied to a particular publisher, whether commercial or government. With the flourishing of electronic publication, some, including law librarians, have argued that a vendor- and medium-neutral citation form needs to be developed, particularly to support broader public access to legal material. (For more on neutral citations, see Coggins et al., 2012 and Martin, 2007).

Elements of a Case

Opinions, whether in print or online, have several elements (see figure 7.3). The party names, reporter citation, docket number, and date are at the beginning. The docket number is assigned by the court and is useful when looking for briefs and other documents briefly discussed later in this chapter. The names of counsel are also listed, a prefatory statement gives the disposition (affirmed or reversed, for example), and a headnote or syllabus summarizes the points of law. These summaries, which can be a page or longer, are helpful in understanding the issues and determinations, and in finding other similar opinions, but they are not law. Neither are the dissenting and concurring opinions. Only the majority opinion is law.

Updating

It is important to note that once an opinion is published, if it is overturned by a higher court, it is not removed from the reporters or databases. It remains published. Attorneys, law students, and anyone requiring the current, applicable law absolutely need to update the opinion—meaning verify its validity by making sure it was not later reversed or overruled—using the commercially produced Shepard's Citation Service (available on LexisNexis) or KeyCite (on WestlawNext). This process is often referred to as making sure the opinion is still *good law.* By typing the case citation into either of these online citators, researchers can find prior and subsequent history (is it still good?) as well as find citations to other cases which can help with further research.

Finding Case Law

Finding an opinion with a known citation can be fairly straightforward. Equipped with knowledge of available sources—free and commercial—and bits of information such as a party name, jurisdiction, court, and date (which can sometimes be identified from news sources), librarians and researchers can find a particular published opinion. On the other hand, finding case law on a particular topic can be more challenging and is often best done with preliminary research using secondary sources, which will be discussed later in this chapter.

The relative ease or difficulty of searching and retrieving may depend on the resources a librarian or researcher can access. The online commercial sources are the most comprehensive, and offer sophisticated interfaces, but access is not universal, and familiarity with the search system is often helpful. Some colleges and universities provide campus-wide access to LexisNexis Academic or WestlawNext Campus Research. Those

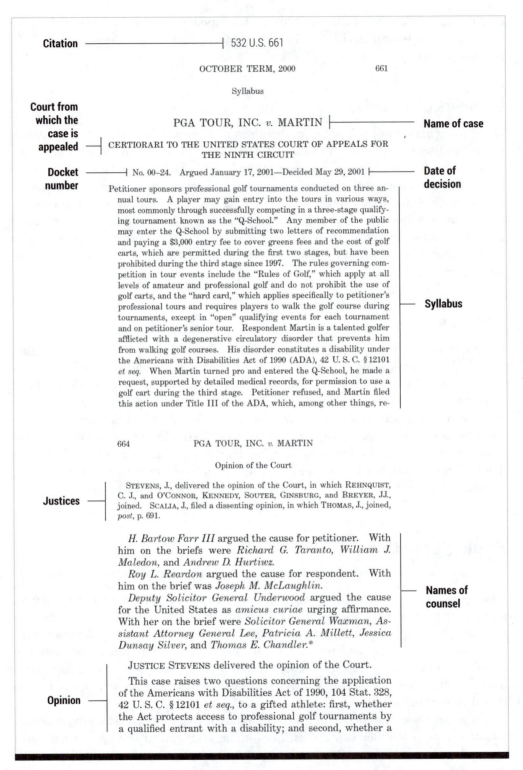

Citation — 532 U.S. 661

OCTOBER TERM, 2000   661

Syllabus

Court from which the case is appealed —

Name of case —

PGA TOUR, INC. *v.* MARTIN

CERTIORARI TO THE UNITED STATES COURT OF APPEALS FOR THE NINTH CIRCUIT

Docket number — No. 00–24. Argued January 17, 2001—Decided May 29, 2001 — **Date of decision**

Petitioner sponsors professional golf tournaments conducted on three annual tours. A player may gain entry into the tours in various ways, most commonly through successfully competing in a three-stage qualifying tournament known as the "Q-School." Any member of the public may enter the Q-School by submitting two letters of recommendation and paying a $3,000 entry fee to cover greens fees and the cost of golf carts, which are permitted during the first two stages, but have been prohibited during the third stage since 1997. The rules governing competition in tour events include the "Rules of Golf," which apply at all levels of amateur and professional golf and do not prohibit the use of golf carts, and the "hard card," which applies specifically to petitioner's professional tours and requires players to walk the golf course during tournaments, except in "open" qualifying events for each tournament and on petitioner's senior tour. Respondent Martin is a talented golfer afflicted with a degenerative circulatory disorder that prevents him from walking golf courses. His disorder constitutes a disability under the Americans with Disabilities Act of 1990 (ADA), 42 U. S. C. § 12101 *et seq.* When Martin turned pro and entered the Q-School, he made a request, supported by detailed medical records, for permission to use a golf cart during the third stage. Petitioner refused, and Martin filed this action under Title III of the ADA, which, among other things, re- **Syllabus**

664   PGA TOUR, INC. *v.* MARTIN

Opinion of the Court

Justices — STEVENS, J., delivered the opinion of the Court, in which REHNQUIST, C. J., and O'CONNOR, KENNEDY, SOUTER, GINSBURG, and BREYER, JJ., joined. SCALIA, J., filed a dissenting opinion, in which THOMAS, J., joined, *post*, p. 691.

Names of counsel —

H. Bartow Farr III argued the cause for petitioner. With him on the briefs were *Richard G. Taranto, William J. Maledon,* and *Andrew D. Hurtivz.*

Roy L. Reardon argued the cause for respondent. With him on the brief was *Joseph M. McLaughlin.*

Deputy Solicitor General Underwood argued the cause for the United States as *amicus curiae* urging affirmance. With her on the brief were *Solicitor General Waxman, Assistant Attorney General Lee, Patricia A. Millett, Jessica Dunsay Silver,* and *Thomas E. Chandler.**

Opinion — JUSTICE STEVENS delivered the opinion of the Court.

This case raises two questions concerning the application of the Americans with Disabilities Act of 1990, 104 Stat. 328, 42 U. S. C. § 12101 *et seq.*, to a gifted athlete: first, whether the Act protects access to professional golf tournaments by a qualified entrant with a disability; and second, whether a

FIGURE 7.3
Elements of a U.S. Supreme Court Opinion

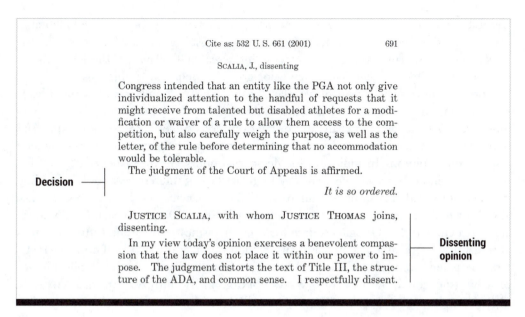

Cite as: 532 U. S. 661 (2001)   691

SCALIA, J., dissenting

Congress intended that an entity like the PGA not only give individualized attention to the handful of requests that it might receive from talented but disabled athletes for a modification or waiver of a rule to allow them access to the competition, but also carefully weigh the purpose, as well as the letter, of the rule before determining that no accommodation would be tolerable.

The judgment of the Court of Appeals is affirmed.

Decision

It is so ordered.

JUSTICE SCALIA, with whom JUSTICE THOMAS joins, dissenting.

In my view today's opinion exercises a benevolent compassion that the law does not place it within our power to impose. The judgment distorts the text of Title III, the structure of the ADA, and common sense. I respectfully dissent.

Dissenting opinion

FIGURE 7.3   (continued from previous page)

systems, if available, are the best first choice for general academic researchers. Law school contracts limit access to versions with more content and features—Lexis Advance and WestlawNext, along with Bloomberg Law—to law school students and faculty. There are also lower-cost commercial sources such as Casemaker, Fastcase, and VersusLaw, which are aimed at practicing attorneys. County, or public, law libraries may subscribe to one of these online services, or a slice of an online service, for use by public patrons. Print resources may be an excellent option for researchers who are in geographic proximity to a law school, county law library, or state law library.

Free Case Law Online

What if the commercial online or print sources are not available? Some courts offer recent opinions on their websites. Start with the federal court locator, www.uscourts .gov/Court_Locator/CourtWebsites.aspx, the National Center for State Courts' directory, www.ncsc.org/Information-and-Resources/Browse-by-State/State-Court-Websites .aspx, or the Law Library of Congress Guide to Law Online: US Judiciary, www.loc .gov/law/help/guide/federal/usjudic.php and the states, www.loc.gov/law/help/guide/ states.php. If the opinion is not available from the court, try one of the collections of free, unofficial federal and state case law, or if appropriate, the growing United States Courts Opinions collection on GPO's FDsys. Coverage in these collections varies, and most free sites do not offer sophisticated finding aids and search tools, but instead rely on keyword searching and browsing. A few sites will be discussed here, but the landscape is rapidly changing, so a good strategy is to start with an online guide, particularly one that is regularly updated. Many law libraries offer guides such as Georgetown

Law Library's *Free and Low Cost Legal Research Guide,* www.law.georgetown.edu/library/research/guides/freelowcost.cfm, the University of Washington Law Library's *Free Law Online,* https://lib.law.washington.edu/content/research/freelaw, and the Law Library of Congress's *Guide to Law Online,* www.loc.gov/law/help/guide.php.

Google Scholar's collection of case law, http://scholar.google.com, has the advantages of a familiar look and feel, and broad coverage: all the US Supreme Court opinions since 1791, federal appellate and district opinions since 1923, and state appellate opinions since 1950. At this writing, it is the most comprehensive free source of federal district court opinions. In addition, Google Scholar offers a feature, labelled *cited by,* that helps users find other opinions that may be related or of interest (as a tool for finding more cases to read, it is similar to Shepard's Citation Service and Keycite, but it is not a tool for making sure a particular case is still good law). One drawback for librarians and researchers is that Google's source for opinions is not transparent. Other free sites with a mix of federal and state case law include Findlaw (owned by Thomson Reuters, the parent company of Westlaw), http://caselaw.findlaw.com, the Public Library of Law (sponsored by Fastcase), www.plol.org, Justia, http://law.justia.com/cases, OpenJurist, http://openjurist.org, and Cornell's Legal Information Institute, www.law.cornell.edu.

USCOURTS on FDsys

One of the most interesting developments in the past several years is the addition of the United States Courts Opinions (USCOURTS) collection on FDsys. USCOURTS is a collaborative venture between GPO and the Administrative Office of the United States Courts (AOUSC). The AOUSC provides a wide range of support to the judicial branch and is supervised by the Judicial Conference of the United States, the policy-making body of the judicial branch. In 2011, the Judicial Conference approved a pilot program to provide district and appellate court opinions from 29 courts to GPO. In 2013, the Judicial Conference opened the program to any interested federal court. As of this writing, in the spring of 2015, all 12 courts of appeals have chosen to participate, plus 40 district courts, 47 bankruptcy courts, and the US Court of International Trade. The collection includes opinions starting in 2004, but the earlier years are incomplete. Files are securely transferred to GPO, which allows GPO to digitally authenticate them. The opinions are arranged by court and can be browsed by year. To search the full text or metadata, use advanced search, www.gpo.gov/fdsys/search/advanced/advsearchpage.action. Metadata fields include circuit, court name, party names, and nature of suit. The metadata also has a Document in Context feature which lists other opinions associated with that particular case (for example, an earlier order in the same case, if it is also on FDsys). The metadata, the ability to search across courts, and digitally authenticated content are all advantages of USCOURTS. The disadvantage is that approximately half the federal courts are not yet participating. Significant progress has been made since the pilot started, but much still needs to be done to accomplish the goal of providing the public comprehensive access to federal court opinions.

The United States Supreme Court Online

US Supreme Court opinions are the most widely available court opinions, although they are not part of the USCOURTS collection on FDsys. The Supreme Court's website makes slip opinions—opinions not yet printed in the bound volumes—available the same day an opinion is issued, at www.supremecourt.gov/opinions/opinions .aspx. The Supreme Court also offers PDFs of the bound volumes from 1991 on, www .supremecourt.gov/opinions/boundvolumes.aspx. Unlike many of the files available from GPO's FDsys, the Supreme Court's PDFs are not digitally authenticated, and the website cautions that "only the printed bound volumes of the *United States Reports* contain the final, official opinions of the Supreme Court of the United States. In case of discrepancies between a bound volume and the materials included here—or any other version of the same materials, whether print or electronic, official or unofficial—the printed bound volume controls." *United States Reports* from 1754 to 2004 are also available in PDF from the Law Library of Congress, through an agreement with William S. Hein & Co., Inc., http://loc.heinonline.org/loc/LOC?index=usreportsloc (the same agreement that allows the LC to offer free public access to historical editions of the *United States Code* and other resources). Opinions from 1937 to 1975 are available as ASCII text files from FLITE (Federal Legal Information Through Electronics), a US Air Force database, now hosted by NTIS, http://supcourt.ntis.gov. This same collection is available as bulk data on FDsys, www.gpo.gov/fdsys/bulkdata/SCD, but is not authenticated.

Finding Case Law by Subject

Finding relevant case law on a particular topic can be more difficult than retrieving a known opinion because choosing the right search terms and taking full advantage of the commercial databases' finding aids requires some knowledge of the subject. A good option is to start with secondary sources, instead of jumping into a case law database. Secondary sources are materials about the law—they include articles, treatises, encyclopedias, and materials aimed at practicing lawyers. Secondary sources are distinguished from primary sources—meaning the law (cases, statutes, administrative law). They provide helpful context, explanations, and citations to the law, including case law. Law libraries and commercial databases are the best options to access secondary sources. Both LexisNexis Academic and WestlawNext Campus Research offer legal encyclopedias, journals, and law reviews (journals published by law schools). HeinOnline has an excellent collection of academic law reviews, including older issues. Free options include the American Bar Association's search engine for open access law journals, www .americanbar.org/groups/departments_offices/legal_technology_resources/resources/ free_journal_search.html; Wex, the Legal Information Institute's collaborative legal dictionary and encyclopedia, https://www.law.cornell.edu/wex; and Google Scholar's collection of articles, http://scholar.google.com. As with free case law, when looking for free secondary sources, a smart strategy is to start with an updated research guide.

Briefs, Oral Arguments, and PACER

Briefs are the written legal and factual arguments that advocates submit to the court in a particular case. Researchers sometimes want these so they can read the legal reasoning from both sides, possibly to uncover strategies or find citations to other cases. The Supreme Court lists sources for and ways to obtain its briefs, including the handful of libraries that serve as depositories for the print briefs. Large law libraries may also have collections of Supreme Court briefs in microfiche. Briefs from state or federal appellate courts are best looked for at law libraries within the geographic region, but may only be available from the court. It is always wise to check the website of the court in question.

Oral arguments—the advocates' oral presentations and questions by the judges—may also be of interest. The Supreme Court website has audio from 2010, www.supremecourt.gov/oral_arguments/argument_audio.aspx, and Oyez, a project at ITT Chicago-Kent College of Law, has audio from 1955, www.oyez.org (oyez, which means *hear ye,* is traditionally said at the opening of a court session). For lower federal courts, check the court's website. Most federal and state appellate courts offer audio or video of recent arguments. The Court of Appeals for the Ninth Circuit has a YouTube channel, www.youtube.com/user/9thcirc/videos.

Dockets are another resource legal researchers may seek. Docket numbers are unique numbers assigned by courts at the start of a case. The docket refers to the cases before a court: for example, a person asking if the Supreme Court "put a case on its docket" is asking if the Supreme Court decided to hear the case. A docket is also the record of the activities, including legal papers filed by the parties and directives of the court, in a particular case. This record is sometimes referred to as the docket sheet. Why would a researcher be interested in the docket sheet and the underlying documents? Some may want to delve behind the scenes and read the documents submitted to and produced by the court because they are following the case quite closely and want to read all the arguments and strategies. If the case is newsworthy, media outlets, public interest groups, or other organizations may post some documents online—so a general web search is a sensible first step, followed by looking for a library guide on docket research and a referral to a law library.

PACER (Public Access to Court Electronic Records), https://www.pacer.gov, provides the docket sheets and many associated documents from federal appellate, district, and bankruptcy courts, and is managed by the AOUSC, with policies set by the Judicial Conference. PACER does not include Supreme Court dockets or documents, and most important, PACER is not free to the public. When the judiciary asked for funding for a public electronic court record system, Congress did not appropriate money, but directed that the program be funded by fees, Pub. L. No. 101-515, § 404(a), 104 Stat. 2101, 2132 (1990). Users need to register and create an account. If the fees do not exceed $15 in a quarterly billing cycle, the fee is waived; this allows minimal occasional use at no cost. Federal courthouses offer public access terminals to on-site users and individual academic researchers may apply for fee waivers for scholarly research. That said, many in the government documents community, particularly law librarians, would like PACER to be more fully part of the FDLP. At the same time, some information activists would like PACER to be open to all, while privacy advocates are concerned about the personal data in court records.

In 2007, a pilot program offering unrestricted access to PACER was opened to a small number of depository libraries. Less than a year later, the pilot was shut down due to a massive download of documents (Lyons 2009). In 2010, the Judicial Conference approved another pilot, this time for a training and education program in partnership with GPO and the American Association of Law Libraries (AALL). In 2012, the program was opened to any interested depository library, public law library (such as a county law library), or public library that agrees to provide PACER training materials to the public. Public patrons still need to create their own PACER accounts and incur charges. In return for providing training assistance, participating libraries' institutional accounts are exempt from the first $50 of usage charges per quarter.

Another notable project to open up PACER is RECAP the Law: "turning PACER around," which was developed by the Center for Information Technology Policy at Princeton University and is now jointly run with the Free Law Project, https://www .recapthelaw.org. RECAP is a Firefox and Chrome extension that automatically downloads PACER documents into a public archive. Anyone can search and retrieve documents from the archive, although users should be aware that the authenticity of the documents is not guaranteed and documents may contain private information that was not, but should have been, redacted.

Statistics, Sentencing, and More

Criminal justice, political science, and history researchers are among those who might search for judicial workload statistics. How many cases were filed? How many per judge? How many immigration, civil rights, or bankruptcy cases commenced in federal district court? How many in the circuit courts of appeals? How many criminal defendants in drug, firearms, or fraud cases? Detailed statistical tables are released annually in *Judicial Business of the U.S. Courts*. The reports are archived from 1997 to date, http:// purl.access.gpo.gov/GPO/LPS2715. Additional historical information is available from the Federal Judicial Center, www.fjc.gov/history/home.nsf/page/courts.html. Another government source is the Bureau of Justice Statistics, which has a variety of court-related publications, www.bjs.gov. Syracuse University's Transactional Records Access Clearinghouse (TRAC) uses the Freedom of Information Act to obtain data on federal enforcement, including immigration courts, http://trac.syr.edu. TRAC's judge information center has a tool that filters federal district court caseload data by judge name, type of suit, and geographic district. For the states, the Court Statistics Project, a joint project of the National Center for State Courts and the Conference of State Court Administrators publishes workload statistics for all 50 states plus the District of Columbia and Puerto Rico, www.courtstatistics.org. The data is provided by each state. For individual state workload statistics, which may be more detailed than what is reported to the Court Statistics Project, look for a resource on the state court's web page.

The Federal Judicial Center (FJC) is the research and education arm of the judicial branch. Although the intended audience of the reports and publications produced is judges and court employees, FJC publications, many of which are available through the FDLP, can be useful to a wide-range of library users. Topics include national security, bankruptcy, copyright, voter registration, and judicial ethics, www.fjc.gov/public/home.nsf. The FJC site also has a history section with a biographical directory of judges and a research guide.

The United States Sentencing Commission, www.ussc.gov, is an independent agency within the judicial branch. Its role is to establish criminal sentencing policies and practices for the federal courts, to advise Congress, and to gather, analyze, and distribute data and information. The Commission's noteworthy publications are the annual *Guidelines Manual,* http://purl.access.gpo.gov/GPO/LPS5528, which provides nonbinding sentencing ranges for federal crimes, and the *Sourcebook of Federal Sentencing Statistics,* http://purl.access.gpo.gov/GPO/LPS56837. The legal primers and congressional reports may also be of interest to people researching federal crime and punishment.

Conclusion

The work of the judicial branch will always be a source of reference questions. The courts produce a tremendous amount of work, and although a fraction of that work becomes law, and a fraction of the law is in the news, those newsworthy cases are about some of our country's most hotly debated issues. They are about life, death, sex, drugs, and rock and roll. They are about how we speak, vote, work, do business, treat our environment, and practice our religions. These issues, whether current or historical, can be research topics in a variety of disciplines beyond the confines of law. A government information librarian in a public or academic library may be a resource to ask "about a case," since courts are part of government. These questions can be challenging, and referring to or checking with a law librarian might be appropriate, but government information librarians can delve deeply into these research topics. The judicial branch may not be as familiar as the executive or legislative branches, but it is not completely shrouded in mystery. After all, the federal judiciary even has its own YouTube channel, https://www.youtube.com/user/uscourts! Use your reference skills, be curious, be creative, look at a research guide, ask a colleague, and take advantage of the increasing availability of free law sources.

Further Research

For an in-depth legal research textbook, see Barkan, Steven M., Barbara A. Bintliff, and Mary Whisner. 2015. *Fundamentals of Legal Research,* 10th ed. St. Paul, MN: West Academic.

Exercises

1. What is the most recent United States Supreme Court opinion?
2. In 2014, the United States Supreme Court ruled that a for-profit company could seek a religious exemption to the contraceptive coverage mandate in the Affordable Care Act. What is the name of the case? The citation? Which justice wrote the majority opinion? Which justices dissented?
3. What federal circuits include Colorado, Illinois, and Florida? How many federal districts are there in California?
4. Identify a Ninth Circuit Court of Appeals opinion in FDsys USCOURTS. Can you find that same opinion in another source such as Google Scholar or Findlaw? Is the opinion on the website of the Ninth Circuit?
5. Pick a state. Find the website of the state's court system. Are opinions from the highest appellate court available online? Are any audio or video of oral arguments?

Sources Mentioned in This Chapter

American Bar Association, Free Full-Text Online Law Review/Journal Search, www.americanbar.org/groups/departments_offices/legal_technology_resources/resources/free_journal_search.html.

Bloomberg Law, www.bna.com/bloomberglaw.

The Bluebook: A Uniform System of Citation, 19th ed. 2010. Cambridge, MA: The Harvard Law Review Association.

Bureau of Justice Statistics, www.bjs.gov.

Casemaker, www.casemakerlegal.com.

Cornell Law School, Cornell Legal Information Institute, www.law.cornell.edu. Wex, https://www.law.cornell.edu/wex.

Court Statistics Project, www.courtstatistics.org.

Fastcase, www.fastcase.com.

Federal Court Locator, www.uscourts.gov/court_locator.aspx.

Federal Judicial Center, www.fjc.gov.

Federal Judiciary Channel, https://www.youtube.com/user/uscourts.

Federal Legal Information Through Electronics (FLITE), http://supcourt.ntis.gov. Bulk data at www.gpo.gov/fdsys/bulkdata/SCD.

Federal Reporter. Eagan, MN: Thomson Reuters.

Federal Supplement. Eagan, MN: Thomson Reuters.

Georgetown Law Library, Free and Low Cost Legal Research Guide, www.law.georgetown.edu/library/research/guides/freelowcost.cfm.

Google Scholar, http://scholar.google.com.

Government Publishing Office. Federal Digital System (FDsys). United States Court Opinions (USCOURTS), www.gpo.gov/fdsys/browse/collection.action?collectionCode=USCOURTS.

HeinOnline, www.heinonline.org.

Judicial Business of the U.S. Courts, http://purl.access.gpo.gov/GPO/LPS2715.

Justia, https://law.justica.com/cases.

Law Library of Congress, Guide to Law Online: US Judiciary, www.loc.gov/law/help/guide/federal/usjudic.php.

Law Library of Congress, Guide to Law Online: US States & Territories, www.loc.gov/law/help/guide/states.php.

Lexis Advance, www.lexisnexis.com/en-us/products/lexis-advance.page.

LexisNexis Academic, www.lexisnexis.com/hottopics/lnacademic.

National Center for State Courts, State Court websites, www.ncsc.org/Information-and-Resources/Browse-by-State/State-Court-Websites.aspx.

OpenJurist, http://openjurist.org.

Oyez, www.oyez.org.

PACER (Public Access to Court Electronic Records), www.pacer.gov.

Public Library of Law, www.plol.org.

RECAP the Law, www.recapthelaw.org.

SCOTUSblog, www.scotusblog.com.

Syracuse University, Transactional Records Access Clearinghouse (TRAC), http://trac.syr.edu.

Thomson Reuters. Findlaw, www.findlaw.com/casecode/uscodes.

United States Court of Appeals for the Ninth Circuit YouTube channel, www.youtube.com/user/9thcirc/videos.

United States Reports. Washington, DC: US Supreme Court. 1991–date available at www.supremecourt .gov/opinions/boundvolumes.aspx. 1754–2004 available at http://loc.heinonline.org/loc/LOC?index=usreportsloc.

United States Sentencing Commission, www.ussc.gov. *Guidelines Manual,* http://purl.access.gpo.gov/GPO/LPS5528. *Sourcebook of Federal Sentencing Statistics,* http://purl.access.gpo.gov/GPO/LPS56837.

United States Supreme Court, www.supremecourt.gov. Slip opinions, www.supremecourt.gov/opinions/slipopinions.aspx. Oral argument audio, www.supremecourt.gov/oral_arguments/argument _audio.aspx. Court rules, www.supremecourt.gov/ctrules/ctrules.aspx.

United States Supreme Court Reports, Lawyers' Edition. Charlottesville, VA: LexisNexis.

United States Tax Court, *Reports of the United States Tax Court.* Washington, DC: Government Printing Office.

University of Washington School of Law, Gallagher Law Library, Free Law Online, https://lib.law .washington.edu/content/research/freelaw.

VersusLaw, www.versuslaw.com.

WestlawNext, http://legalsolutions.thomsonreuters.com/law-products/westlaw-legal-research.

WestlawNext Campus Research. http://campus.westlaw.com.

West's Supreme Court Reporter. Eagan, MN: Thomson Reuters.

References

Coggins, Timothy L., John Cannan, & Jennifer Laws, eds. 2012. "Universal Citation and the American Association of Law Libraries: A White Paper," *Law Library Journal* 103, no. 3 (Summer): 331–357. www.aallnet.org/mm/Publications/llj/LLJ-Archives/Vol-103/2011–03/2011–22.pdf.

Lyons, Susan. 2009. "Free PACER: Balancing Access and Privacy." *AALL Spectrum* 13, no. 9 (July): 30–33. www.aallnet.org/mm/Publications/spectrum/Archives/Vol-13/July-2009/pub-sp0907-pacer.pdf.

Martin. Peter W. 2007. "Neutral Citation, Court Web Sites, and Access to Authoritative Case Law." *Law Library Journal* 99, no. 2 (Spring): 329–364. www.aallnet.org/mm/Publications/llj/LLJ-Archives/Vol-99/pub_llj_v99n02/2007–19.pdf.

Roberts, Chief Justice John, *2014 Year-End Report on the Federal Judiciary,* www.supremecourt.gov/publicinfo/year-end/2014year-endreport.pdf.

CHAPTER 8

The President

ANDREA SEVETSON

We owe it, therefore . . . to declare that we should consider any attempt on their part to extend their system to any portion of this hemisphere as dangerous to our peace and safety.

Four score and seven years ago our fathers brought forth, upon this continent, a new nation . . .

Let me assert my firm belief that the only thing we have to fear is fear itself, nameless, unreasoning, unjustified terror . . .

I believe that this nation should commit itself to achieving the goal, before this decade is out, of landing a man on the moon and returning him safely to the earth.

—*Presidential speeches*

Introduction

These are wonderful, famous quotes from speeches given by United States presidents. Are they easy to locate? What about the other speeches and writings from the presidents, such as memos to generals, cabinet secretaries, and more? What about orders that may be signed by the president dealing with issues of national security? What about letters to family members? And what about 100, 200, years ago? Can we get all of the documentation from the Wilson administration?

Think about the daily activities of the president. The president gets up; eats breakfast; works out or goes for a run; goes into the Oval Office and writes or signs letters, laws, or other documents; meets with cabinet secretaries; lunches with someone, maybe the vice president or legislative leaders; reviews drafts of policies and upcoming speeches; meets with more people, maybe even the National Security Council or foreign dignitaries; goes out to a dinner and makes a speech; and goes home and works some more. Every minute is scheduled and every day produces letters, papers, speeches, memoranda, and more (see sidebar on page 143). In fact, the *Compilation of Presidential Documents* lists more than 120 different items coming from the White House in June 2010 alone. This includes letters to Congress, remarks at different events, notices, messages, memoranda, and more—a remarkable output for one person.

Now consider events that call for action (disasters, press conferences, shootings, military actions) and how each of these requires a statement or action from the president. The presidency is a big job, and has gotten bigger and bigger through the years as demands on the president's time have increased. The first administration of President Truman had fewer than 75 public activities annually, while President Obama, in his first term of office (2009–12), averaged 287 (Ragsdale, 2014: table 4–12). And these are just the documented public events; that figure doesn't include all of the meetings, phone calls, and other items of business that make up a president's day.

Where does it all start—what exactly is the president's job and from where does presidential authority stem? It starts with the powers invested in the president by the Constitution, which are heavily intertwined in the checks and balances between the branches of government. For instance, the president can propose laws (though not actually introduce them in Congress) while Congress makes the law, the president may veto legislation; the president appoints judges and high-ranking executive branch officials, but the Senate confirms the appointments; the president is the commander in chief of the armed forces, while Congress has the power to declare war and to appropriate defense funding; the president can negotiate treaties, but the Senate must ratify any treaties before they take force; the president oversees the executive branch, but Congress passes laws to create and govern the executive branch, as well as to authorize and appropriate funds, a power that cannot be underestimated (CQ Press, 2008: vii).

Presidential power has grown over the years, as reflected in books such as *The Growth of Presidential Power: A Documented History* by William Goldsmith (1974), and the *Powers of the Presidency* (2008), both of which discuss presidential power using the same types of divisions: unilateral powers of the presidency, chief of state, chief administrator, legislative leader, chief diplomat, commander in chief, and chief economist. Reviewing those constitutional powers really helps understand the president's daily activities.

So how is all of this activity documented? There is now a well-established White House press corps to document presidential activities for the news world, whether via television, newspapers, blogs, or other online outlets. Internally, documentation such as personal diaries, letters, memos, and records of all of the activities of office, are collected and organized for posterity by White House staff assisted by staff from the National Archives and Records Administration (NARA). Presidential records are deposited with NARA at the conclusion of the presidential term of office.

Historically, presidents may not have thought in terms of saving papers and correspondence for posterity, but the passage of the Presidential Records Act (PRA) of 1978 (see below, Ownership of Presidential Documents) changed the ownership of the materials from private, belonging to the president, to public, belonging to the nation. Under 36 CFR 1270.30, the president must first consult the archivist of the United States before disposing of papers.

Presidential Documents

In 1974, librarian Arnold Hirshon wrote that presidential documents could be divided into four categories: *public, executively controlled, official,* and *personal.* Looking for papers,

Daily Schedule of President Kennedy

October 22, 1962	John F. Kennedy
9:15 am	President arrived in the office
10:30–11:00 am	Hon. George McGhee, Department of State
11:00–11:46 am	Hon. Dean Rusk, Hon. George Ball, Hon Martin Hillenbrand, Hon. Michael Forrestal, Hon. McGeorge Bundy (Off the record, Political Track)
11:47–12:30	The above 11:00 am group plus Hon. Paul Nitze, Colonel Armstrong (Off the Record re: Berlin contingency)
3:00–4:00 pm	National Security Council Meeting
4:03–4:45 pm	Hon. A. Milton Cbote, Prime Minister of Uganda; Mr. James Simpson, Minister of Economics of Uganda; Hon. Grace Ibingira, Minister of Justice of Uganda; Hon. Apolo Kironde, Uganda's Representative-designate to the United Nations; Mr. John Kakonge, Secretary General, Uganda People's Congress; Hon. G. Menned Williams; Hon. A.G. Matthews; Hon Edmond Hutchinson, AID
4:45–5:30 pm	Cabinet Meeting
5:30–6:30 pm	Bipartisan Legislative Leaders Meeting
7:00–7:17 pm	Address by the President to the Nation concerning the developments in Cuba
7:20 pm	The President went to the Mansion
7:44 pm	Returned to the office
8:01 pm	To the Mansion

Source: ProQuest History Vault, 1961–1963.

speeches, and other documents, it is easy to see that the presidents have done a rather haphazard job of collecting this information for posterity prior to the PRA. Martin Van Buren burned correspondence he deemed of little value, while Millard Fillmore directed his executor to burn all family correspondence (Hirshon, 1974: 380, 382). Teddy Roosevelt was the first president to present his papers to the LC in 1917. Prior to that, the LC had simply purchased most of the papers from former presidents or their heirs.

Speeches such as the State of the Union and inaugural addresses have always been easy to find, and there are many privately printed compilations of these as well as those produced by the US government. Other materials have proven more challenging. Reviewing Hirshon's division of types of documentation makes it easier to ascertain which papers will be easy to find, which may take more digging, and which may be close to impossible (1974). Those divisions are examined in more detail here.

Public Papers and Speeches

These documents relate to the public role of the president—speeches such as the State of the Union message, news conferences, press releases, executive orders and proclamations, and other materials released by the White House. All of these are considered in the public domain and are relatively easy to find.

Executive orders and proclamations belong to a broader grouping of documents known as presidential directives—that is, the president directing some action. Executive orders and proclamations are not defined in law. Historically there has been little difference between them, but recently most executive orders relate to how the government works, while most proclamations announce something.

It might seem that most executive orders, as they may be considered inward facing, wouldn't affect the general population; however, in reality this isn't true. Executive orders may have a broader significance as, for example, E.O. 9066, issued by President Franklin Roosevelt on February 19, 1942, that directed the "Secretary of War, and the Military Commanders to prescribe military areas in such places and of such extent as he or the appropriate Military Commanders may determine, from which any or all persons may be excluded." This was the executive order that was used to round up those of Japanese ancestry living on the West Coast for internment (Roosevelt, 1942).

Proclamations tend to be more celebratory in nature and may be used to announce holidays, commemorative months, and other occasions. The sidebar shows examples of some presidential proclamations and executive orders.

Executive orders, compilations, speeches, and other communications may appear in one (or more) of four established outlets: the White House website, Whitehouse.gov; the *Public Papers of the Presidents of the United States* (a bound compilation of presidential papers and records); the *Compilation of Presidential Documents* (formerly weekly, now daily); and the *Federal Register* (for executive orders, proclamations, and directives only). Depending on the import of a speech or appearance, it may also appear in newspapers such as the *New York Times* and the *Washington Post*. All public papers are, and remain, in the public domain.

Proclamations and Executive Orders from January 2015

Executive Order 13687-Imposing Additional Sanctions With Respect to North Korea

Proclamation 9227-Religious Freedom Day, 2015

Proclamation 9228-Martin Luther King, Jr., Federal Holiday, 2015

Executive Order 13688-Federal Support for Local Law Enforcement Equipment Acquisition

Executive Order 13689-Enhancing Coordination of National Efforts in the Arctic

Proclamation 9229-American Heart Month, 2015

Proclamation 9230-National African American History Month, 2015

Proclamation 9231-National Teen Dating Violence Awareness and Prevention Month, 2015

Executive Order 13690-Establishing a Federal Flood Risk Management Standard and a Process for Further Soliciting and Considering Stakeholder Input

Source: FDsys.gov, Compilation of Presidential Documents, January 2015.

Executively Controlled Documents

Executively controlled documents are those created by other agencies in the executive branch, but over which the president, as chief executive, has authority. Documents in this category include daily briefings, memos, and other materials routed to the White House from various executive branch agencies.

There is no clear channel by which these executively controlled documents move into the public domain, as they are not strictly controlled by the president and don't fit into the sources used for public papers. Some may be unclassified or released by the agency through normal procedures, and others may be produced when a sitting or former president releases them. Probably the biggest concern for researchers needing this material is that, like the other document categories that follow (Official Papers and Personal Papers), there is no single place to locate these documents, once released.

The daily briefing, the first meeting of the president's day, is a national security update on foreign intelligence and domestic terrorism. It is now noted on the schedule and first came to light ". . . with the disclosure that President Bush was informed by the August 6 (2001) version that terrorists associated with Osama bin Laden might try to hijack an airplane" (Pincus, 2002: A33). While the presidential daily briefings, or PDB, have apparently been going on for years, very little is known of the briefings and what they contain. There are, however, several websites containing unattributed content providing background on the PDB. Pincus points out that "one irony about the public flap over the Aug. 6 PDB item is that it has highlighted a long-standing argument about the CIA's determination to keep all PDBs from being turned over to anyone not on its distribution list."

Another example of executively controlled material is the March 14, 2003, opinion on interrogation from John Yoo while serving in the George W. Bush administration's Office of Legal Counsel in the Department of Justice. The Yoo memo (Yoo, 2003), "Military Interrogation of Alien Unlawful Combatants Held Outside the United States," is referenced in many congressional hearings, but actually finding a copy on government websites is difficult, if not impossible. After the 2008 declassification of the memo, it is much easier to find on nongovernmental websites. Many reasons why this memo is considered controversial were expressed in the press, on blogs, and by Congress. Principal among these was the claim in the memo that the president was above the law (*Los Angeles Times,* 2008). With claims like these, it's no wonder the president wanted to keep this memo classified and that Congress (and the press) wanted to examine it.

A president may claim executive privilege to withhold information, a trend prevalent in the George W. Bush administration. For more detail, as well as its overall effect on government, check the Secrecy News site, a service of the Federation of American Scientists (www.fas.org/blog/secrecy/). In 2007, Pulitzer Prize–winning newspaper reporter Charlie Savage published a book on this topic, and presidential power in general, *Takeover: The Return of the Imperial Presidency and the Subversion of American Democracy* (Savage, 2007).

Unlike the executive orders and proclamations discussed earlier, some presidential directives fall into the category of executively controlled documents, as they are "cloaked in official secrecy" (Relyea, 2008: 2). Over the years, depending on the president and the purpose, these directives from the president have been referred to by different titles such as National Security Directives, National Security Action Memoranda, Presidential Review Directives, and Presidential Decision Directives. Some of these may not see the light of day for 25 years or longer. A CRS report describes such activities for each administration, starting with Eisenhower, and gives some details about the nature and number of directives and what they are called, making it easier for the reader to infer whether or not the directives are public or classified (Relyea, 2008: 9–12). An example from the Nixon administration demonstrates the kinds of material gathered and usage of that material by the president:

> When Richard Nixon became President, he appointed Henry Kissinger as his national security advisor. Kissinger recruited a substantial and influential NSC staff, and they produced national security position papers which were designated National Security Study Memoranda (NSSM). They were developed through the use of various interdepartmental working groups composed of high level representatives from pertinent agencies. Beginning with a study answering 26 questions on Vietnam, multiple NSSMs were immediately assigned. . . . The NSSMs were among the resources used by the President when determining national security policy, which he would express in National Security Decision Memoranda (NSDM). (Relyea, 2008: 10)

Another group of presidential directives stems from the president's National Security Council (NSC). The NSC was created by the National Security Act of 1947 and has been revised many times. The NSC advises the president "with respect to the integration of domestic, foreign, and military policies relating to the national security so as to enable the military services and the other departments and agencies of the Government to cooperate more effectively in matters involving the national security" (50 U.S.C. § 402).

One thing the NSC does is to direct intelligence, and these directives are particularly hard to come by in a timely fashion. For example, a top-secret memo dated December 9, 1947 (declassified March 30, 1983), "instructs the CIA director to initiate and conduct covert psychological operations designed to counteract Soviet and Soviet-inspired activities that threaten world peace" (ProQuest History Vault, 1960–1975).

In trying to review the NSC directives, a report from the General Accounting Office states:

> Because NSC did not give us access to the directives we could not analyze NSDs [national security directives] issued by the [George H.W.] Bush administration. We do not know how many NSDs have been issued by the Bush administration, but we do know that 51 were issued through the fall of 1990. We examined unclassified NSC summaries of five NSDs issued by the administration and concluded that four of the five NSDs make U.S. policy. (General Accounting Office, 1992: 1)

The report goes on to note that most directives issued during the Truman and Eisenhower administrations have been declassified while most directives written since 1961 remain classified. Further, there was a report in 1988 on the use of presidential directives released 1961–88 to make and implement US policy that found that at least 1,042 presidential directives had been issued, and 247 had been publicly released. It also noted that 116 of the directives served three functions; they established policy, directed the implementation of policy, and/or authorized the commitment of government resources. (General Accounting Office, 1992: 2)

Some unclassified national security directives may be found at the Federation of American Scientists' website (www.fas.org). Several Homeland Security Directives of the George W. Bush and Barack H. Obama administrations are found in the (*Weekly*) *Compilation of Presidential Documents* and on the White House website (and the archived website from the Bush administration). Finally, University Press of America has a microfilm collection titled *Documents of the National Security Council* that contains many of the documents created for the NSC. This is included online in the ProQuest History Vault module *Vietnam and American Foreign Policy, 1960–1975*.

Official Papers

Papers in this category are also referred to as private papers or White House files. Papers may contain draft proposals, personal notes, memoranda, personal correspondence, and other documents that circulate behind the scenes and are directly related to the particular president's work. Hirshon further divides these into two categories: working papers and records of office. Working papers are stuff that surrounds office life—drafts of speeches, interoffice communications, and memoranda. The records of office are the historical files that Hirshon claims "do not bear directly upon the actions of the president, but which provide a chronicle of those actions" (Hirshon, 1974: 368). Examples include audio recordings, diaries, and notes of meetings.

Official papers are of great interest to those trying to see just where a particular thought or phrase entered a policy, or who actually said what in a meeting, as recollections months or years later often prove fuzzy. Famously, it was the release of the tapes from the Nixon White House during the Watergate investigation that hastened the resignation of President Nixon. Official papers are deposited in presidential libraries; materials (memos, documents, etc.) forwarded to the president from executive branch employees are held by NARA.

Personal Papers

Finally, we have personal papers. Hirshon quotes Chief Justice Marshall: "Letters to the president in his private character, are often written to him in consequence of his public character, and may relate to public concerns" (1974: 371). Certainly there are types of documents that are personal in nature—notes between spouses, love letters, and some correspondence and e-mail. Hirshon notes in his appendix that "in 1964 there was a dispute over 'love letters' which President Harding had sent to Carrie Phillips. These letters cannot be disclosed until 2014 due to a court order" (1974: 387). [Note: The correspondence took place before Harding was president and can now be found at the LC; www.loc.gov/collections/warren-harding-carrie-fulton-phillips-correspondence.]

Often controversy surrounds these documents because they give a view of the president and his character unseen by the public. In the 21st century we have new concepts of privacy because of what may be shared on social networking sites and via texts and tweets from cell phones, but these discussions are not new to the White House, where it seems that everything the president says and does may be considered of interest.

Controversies

The first edition of this text discussed three controversies—ownership of presidential documents, issues around the (*Weekly*) *Compilation of Presidential Documents,* and signing statements. This second edition retains the discussion of the first two controversies, but in place of the discussion of signing statements (which can be said to be more noteworthy in regards to the George W. Bush presidency), includes a discussion on presidential powers as illustrated through the recent immigration debate.

Ownership of Presidential Documents

Often heirs of presidents have controlled their papers, resulting in cases like an heir to George Washington cutting up fragments of documents to give to requestors for anything "that bears the impress of his venerated hand," (Hirshon, 1974: 372) and Martha Washington burning almost all of her correspondence with her husband.

While Theodore Roosevelt was the first president to give his papers to the LC, his was not the first set of papers collected there. In fact, with a few exceptions, the LC has been relatively successful in collecting papers of the presidents. (For background on the disposal of presidential papers, see Hirshon, 1974: 377–389.) Online guides to holdings of presidential papers include the following:

- Miller Center of Public Affairs at the University of Virginia, http://millercenter .org/president/papers/
- Library of Congress (see the LC Archival Finding Aids by name of president), www.loc.gov/rr/mss/f-aids/mssfa.html

Prior to 1974, the materials from a term of office were considered the president's property. In the wake of the impeachment investigation of Richard Nixon, Congress passed the Presidential Records and Materials Preservation Act (P.L. 93-526) on December 19, 1974, some four months after Nixon's resignation. Papers that had been impounded as evidence in the Watergate hearings were transferred to the General Services Administration (GSA). The law also abrogated an agreement giving Nixon ownership of his papers, and established the National Study Commission on Records and Documents of Federal Officials. The commission explored issues of ownership, control, disposition, and preservation of historical materials (Schick et al., 1989: 16). President Nixon challenged this law, but lost in the case of *Nixon v. Administrator of General Services* 433 U.S.

425 (1977). Under the provisions of the Presidential Records and Materials Preservation Act, the Nixon papers were transferred from GSA to the National Archives.

The Presidential Records Act (PRA) of 1978, P.L. 95-591, based on the work of the commission, was amended by the National Archives and Records Administration Act of 1984, P.L. 98-497 (44 U.S.C. § 2201–2207) and governs the official records of presidents and vice presidents created or received after January 20, 1981—everything from Ronald Reagan forward. In essence, the PRA changed the legal ownership of the official records of the president from private to public, and established a new statutory structure under which presidents must manage their records.

Specifically, the Presidential Records Act:

- Defines and states public ownership of the records.
- Places the responsibility for the custody and management of incumbent Presidential records with the President.
- Allows the incumbent President to dispose of records that no longer have administrative, historical, informational, or evidentiary value, once he has obtained the views of the Archivist of the United States on the proposed disposal.
- Requires that the President and his staff take all practical steps to file personal records separately from Presidential records.
- Establishes a process for restriction and public access to these records. Specifically, the PRA allows for public access to Presidential records through the Freedom of Information Act (FOIA) beginning five years after the end of the Administration, but allows the President to invoke as many as six specific restrictions to public access for up to twelve years. The PRA also establishes procedures for Congress, courts, and subsequent Administrations to obtain special access to records that remain closed to the public, following a thirty-day notice period to the former and current Presidents.
- Requires that Vice-Presidential records are to be treated in the same way as Presidential records. (National Archives and Records Administration, 2015a)

As we saw in previous chapters, Congress passes the law and the president (or executive branch) carries out the law. The PRA is a stark example of how different interpretations of the law by different administrations can lead to vastly different outcomes. Three separate executive orders interpreting the PRA have been issued to date, each revoking the previous one: E.O. 12667 (54 Fed. Reg. 3403); E.O. 13233 (66 Fed. Reg. 56025); and E.O. 13489 (74 Fed. Reg. 4669). E.O. 12667 and E.O. 13489, issued by Presidents Reagan and Obama, respectively, appear relatively straightforward and are similar in general policy. The middle executive order, E.O. 13233, issued by President George W. Bush, differs from the executive orders in the other two by, among other things, citing *Nixon v. Administrator of General Services* in establishing precedent for requiring a "demonstrated, specific need" for access to particular records, as well as detailing the procedures by which former presidents could invoke presidential privilege to withhold records. Bush also added the final item in the above list, bringing vice presidential records in line with those of incumbent or former presidents (Bush, 2001).

Where ownership issues get really interesting (and discussed in the press) is with the disclosure of records for nominations. Two examples from nominees to the US Supreme Court serve to illustrate the issues. Associate Justice Elena Kagan worked first for President Clinton as associate counsel to the president (1995–1996) and then as deputy assistant to the president for domestic policy and deputy director of the Domestic Policy Council (1997–1999). An earlier nominee to the Supreme Court, Harriet Miers, served as White House counsel for George W. Bush before he nominated her to the court.

Why does it get interesting? Members of the Senate get to confirm presidential appointments, and, as part of the confirmation process, the Senate can ask to review documentation that was generated under the current or previous administrations and has been attributed to the nominee. Presidents can be generous, or stingy, in allowing the memos and other material to be a part of that confirmation process. For the nomination of Elena Kagan, Presidents Obama and Clinton allowed the release of the thousands of documents from the Clinton administration. During the failed nomination of Harriet Miers, however, when the Senate called for release of documents related to her service, incumbent President George W. Bush declined, "deeming it an infringement of executive privilege" (Baker and Murray, 2005: A01) to a great hue and cry in the press. The documents were never released.

(Weekly) Compilation of Presidential Documents

See description under Compilations on page 156.

The lack of official editorial standards has come into play at least once in determining what is printed in the *Weekly Compilation*. Donald Smith detailed a controversy in the Reagan administration when Deputy Press Secretary Larry Speakes admitted to fabricating presidential comments that were then included in the series. Smith writes, "not all off–the-cuff remarks are included—or are they? Moreover, readers do not know who officially makes, and thereby has responsibility for, decisions concerning what

FIGURE 8.1
Compilation of Presidential Documents—President Obama's Speech on Immigration Reform

is released" (Smith, 1989: 215). An off-quoted gaffe is that of President Reagan, who, during a microphone test, said, "My fellow Americans, I'm pleased to tell you I just signed legislation which outlaws Russia forever. The bombing begins in five minutes."

This was covered heavily in the press, and yet doesn't appear in any compilations of his papers—perhaps because, as noted by Doder in the *Washington Post,* "White House spokesman Larry Speakes continued to insist that the remark was off the record and as such would not be acknowledged by the White House. 'I have not commented on it and I don't intend to,' he said, according to United Press International" (1984: A26). Another quote, President Clinton's response to the question of "boxers or briefs," was included in the *Weekly Compilation,* as it was a question asked during an appearance on MTV (Clinton, 1994: 848).

Today's scholars can take some comfort in resources such as C-SPAN to replay and preserve important speeches. Recordings may be used to check official transcripts. Whether or not more such documented instances occur, the ability to rewrite history is certainly worth keeping in mind as users and librarians alike look for what was actually reported in the *Weekly Compilation of Presidential Documents.*

Immigration

On November 20, 2014, President Obama announced an Immigration Accountability Executive Action (yet another type of directive) that revised some immigration policies and initiated several programs (see figure 8.1). "According to the President, the action was taken in response to the absence of legislation addressing major problems within the immigration system. The President has stated that his executive action is temporary, and that his successor can rescind some or all of its provisions. Those opposed to the executive action argue that it was taken largely for political purposes. They contend that once granted, the temporary measures it encompasses would be difficult to revoke. Separately, a debate has arisen as to whether the President has the legal authority to take such action, with the administration and others arguing the President's action falls within his authority, and many in Congress arguing the President has overstepped it" (Kandel et al., 2015).

Defenders of the president note that other presidents had issued executive orders regarding immigration, but detractors called him "Emperor Obama" and, even before his changes were announced, "Republicans in Congress denounced them as reaching far beyond his constitutional powers" (Nakamura, et al. 2014). In his address to the nation, Obama noted, "The actions I'm taking are not only lawful, they're the kinds of actions taken by every single Republican president and every single Democratic president for the past half century. And to those members of Congress who question my authority to make our immigration system work better or question the wisdom of me acting where Congress has failed, I have one answer: Pass a bill" (Obama, 2014).

So what gives the president the authority to act in this way? The November 20, 2014, memo, actually issued by Secretary of Homeland Security Jeh Johnson, notes that its intention is to "reflect new policies for the use of deferred action." Through the title of the memo, "Exercising Prosecutorial Discretion with Respect to Individuals Who Came to the United States as Children and with Respect to Certain Individuals Who Are the Parents of U.S. Citizens or Permanent Residents," we can learn that this is being done through the use of prosecutorial discretion (figure 8.2). Footnotes 1 and 3 in the memo note that "deferred action, in one form or another, dates back to at least the

1960s. 'Deferred action' per se dates back at least as far as 1975." George W. Bush used deferred action in August 2001, issuing "guidance providing deferred action to individuals who were eligible for the recently created U and T visas" (Johnson, 2014).

One of the arguments against this type of prosecutorial discretion is that Obama's actions go beyond nonenforcement of deportation laws and grant affirmative benefits to illegal immigrants (Ruger, 2015). Other criticisms include states' rights issues (the right of states to determine immigration policy) and the position that all illegal immigrants, who have broken the law, are getting blanket amnesty.

Secretary
U.S. Department of Homeland Security
Washington, DC 20528

Homeland Security

November 20, 2014

MEMORANDUM FOR: León Rodríguez
Director
U.S. Citizenship and Immigration Services

Thomas S. Winkowski
Acting Director
U.S. Immigration and Customs Enforcement

R. Gil Kerlikowske
Commissioner
U.S. Customs and Border Protection

FROM: Jeh Charles Johnson
Secretary

SUBJECT: **Exercising Prosecutorial Discretion with Respect to Individuals Who Came to the United States as Children and with Respect to Certain Individuals Who Are the Parents of U.S. Citizens or Permanent Residents**

This memorandum is intended to reflect new policies for the use of deferred action. By memorandum dated June 15, 2012, Secretary Napolitano issued guidance entitled *Exercising Prosecutorial Discretion with Respect to Individuals Who Came to the United States as Children*. The following supplements and amends that guidance.

The Department of Homeland Security (DHS) and its immigration components are responsible for enforcing the Nation's immigration laws. Due to limited resources, DHS and its Components cannot respond to all immigration violations or remove all persons illegally in the United States. As is true of virtually every other law enforcement agency, DHS must exercise prosecutorial discretion in the enforcement of the law. Secretary Napolitano noted two years ago, when she issued her prosecutorial discretion guidance regarding children, that "[o]ur Nation's immigration laws must be enforced in a strong and sensible manner. They are not designed to be blindly enforced without consideration given to the individual circumstances of each case."

FIGURE 8.2
Secretary Johnson's Memo Announcing New Policies for Deferred Action in Immigration

Presidential Libraries

While many politicians have donated or sold their papers to archives, since the 1950s there has been a system of presidential libraries. As noted earlier, especially prior to the PRA, handling of presidential papers of all kinds had been haphazard. Franklin Roosevelt thought that presidential papers were an important part of the national heritage and should be accessible to the public (National Archives, 2015b). Roosevelt used the Rutherford B. Hayes library as a model for his idea, and developed the concept of presidential libraries constructed and equipped with private funds and administered by the National Archives (Schick et al., 1989: 6). President Truman asked archivist Wayne Grover to "insert a clause into the draft of the proposed Federal Records Act that would make it possible for presidents and high government officials to deposit their papers in the National Archives" (Schick et al., 1989: 10–11).

The passage of the Presidential Libraries Act in 1955 (P.L. 84–373, 69 Stat. 695) allowed ... presidents to create libraries for their papers, and set up the libraries as field branches of the National Archives. These field branches were built with private funds, but are federally maintained. Prior to 1955 there were seven presidents with papers in historical libraries or other special libraries, and since that date, 13 presidential libraries have been established, as President Hoover also established a library after passage of the act (in addition to the Hoover Institution at Stanford University).

It wasn't until the Presidential Records Act (PRA) of 1978 that the government took legal ownership of the papers; the Presidential Libraries Act allowed for deposit of the papers, not ownership. A subsequent law, the Presidential Libraries Act of 1986 (P.L. 99-323, 100 Stat. 495), required endowments for each library, and made some attempt at limiting the size of the libraries so as to control costs. The 1986 legislation created the interesting situation of placing the president in the role of fund-raiser. It also allows the archivist of the United States to solicit funds for these libraries.

The libraries (which also serve as museums) often reflect the interests of the president. Each of the libraries now has a website hosted by the National Archives; see www .archives.gov/presidential-libraries for a complete listing. The George W. Bush library website features some tough trivia questions, the Franklin D. Roosevelt library website has a virtual tour featuring images and quotes about the Great Depression and World War II, and the Kennedy library website has an interactive section on the "dynamic history of the Kennedy Administration."

Sources for Speeches and Publications from the Executive Office

Listing every possible source for presidential speeches and publications, from *Vital Speeches of the Day* to one's local hometown newspaper, would be an overwhelming prospect. With a few exceptions, the list below will focus on official (free) sources for these publications, as they are widely available at depository libraries; many larger libraries commonly purchase or subscribe to the commercial products included here. Notes indicating online availability are included in the List of Sources at the end of the chapter.

Meta Sites

The *American Presidency Project* (www.presidency.ucsb.edu), located at the University of California, Santa Barbara, was established in 1999 and currently contains more than 109,000 documents related to the presidency. While this is the best gathering of materials available online, it focuses on the public papers (speeches, executive orders, and so on) gathered from the various compilations, so it generally will not have the type of material outlined in the other categories: the executively controlled, official, or personal papers.

Declassified Documents Reference System (DDRS), a commercial product from the Gale Group, is a growing collection of more than 116,000 declassified documents from presidential libraries. Many of the documents in this file fall into the executively controlled category and contain White House confidential files as well as material from the CIA, FBI, the National Security Council, and more. Database coverage is shown as 1945–2006.

Executive Orders and Presidential Proclamations (ProQuest) is a commercial product based on the 1983 *CIS Index to Presidential Executive Orders.* The online version contains the indexing and full text of executive orders and presidential proclamations found covering 1789–2014. The collection also includes selected directives, memoranda, and correspondence from *Public Papers of the President* and the *Weekly Compilation of Presidential Documents,* public land orders, statements of administration policy (1997–2015), presidential pardons, signing statements (1931–2010), and national security and homeland security directives (1989-forward).

United States Presidential Library (HeinOnline) is a commercial product that contains an assortment of presidential materials including the full text of presidential proclamations, executive orders, and certain other presidential documents promulgated during 1936–2001 (from Title 3 of the Code of Federal Regulations), the *Messages and Papers of the Presidents,* the *Public Papers of the President,* and the *Daily* and *Weekly Compilation of Presidential Documents.* Also included are the *Economic Report of the President, Hearings before the President's Commission on the Assassination of President Kennedy, Public Papers and Addresses of Franklin Delano Roosevelt, U.S. Wickersham Commission Reports,* and the *U.S. National Commission on Law Observance and Enforcement.*

A somewhat different addition to the collection of meta sites is *WhiteHouse.gov,* the official website of the president, which is something of a mixed blessing. It is a great resource for materials on the sitting president, including speeches, press releases, featured legislation, photos, and the president's schedule. Unfortunately, once a president leaves office, no resources, other than biographical material of previous presidents and first ladies and related material, stays on the site—it is essentially wiped clean with each new administration. At precisely 12:01 P.M. EST on January 20, 2009, the White House website announced that not only had change come to America (Barack Obama's campaign slogan), but that change had come to Whitehouse.gov as well. Content from the Bush administration was moved to the presidential library operated under the National Archives (www.archives.gov/presidential-libraries) where it may not be available for the first five years after the end of the administration. The website at George W. Bush library had the following statement posted in 2010: "The George W. Bush Presidential records are governed by the Presidential Records Act (PRA). Under the provisions of the PRA, George W. Bush Presidential records are not available to public access requests for the first five years after the end of the Administration. George W. Bush Presidential records will become subject to Freedom of Information Act requests on January 20, 2014" (National Archives and Records Administration, 2010). When President Obama leaves office, staff at the National Archives will harvest the content of Whitehouse.gov (as they did with George W. Bush), and once again we'll have a clean slate as a new president begins.

Compilations

The *Code of Federal Regulations,* or *CFR* (Title 3, The President), contains presidential proclamations and executive orders from 1936 forward. The first executive order included in Title 3 is #7316 (March 13, 1936). The first proclamation included in Title 3 is #2161 (March 19, 1936). Title 3 of the *CFR* (and remember, the *CFR* was covered in depth in chapter 6, Regulations) is the only title of the set that does not get replaced annually—proclamations and executive orders are published chronologically, and so are not codified like the rest of the *CFR*. As with all of the other materials in the *CFR,* these documents are posted initially in the *Federal Register* and then printed in the *CFR*.

There is also a codification of presidential proclamation and executive orders at the National Archives website (www.archives.gov/federal-register/codification/index.html) spanning 1945–1989; the printed publication was distributed to depository libraries under the SuDocs number AE 2.13. Note that when searching by date in the *Federal Register* one should be sure to search for dates beyond the date of issuance as it may take several days for documents to appear. For example, Executive Order 13491 (Ensuring Lawful Interrogation) was signed by President Obama on January 22, 2009, but wasn't published until five days later, on January 27.

Executive orders are a special challenge to researchers. The first executive order was issued in 1789, but executive orders were not numbered or issued uniformly until 1907. At that time, the State Department began a numbering system and designated an 1862 order establishing a provisional court to function during the military occupation of Louisiana as executive order #1. Orders issued between 1789 and 1862 are referred to as unnumbered executive orders. There was no governmental compilation of executive orders prior to the 1930s (when they were included in the *CFR*). See the listing of meta sites, above, for options for locating executive orders.

Compilation of Messages and Papers of Presidents, 1789–1897 is also known as the Richardson Set. In April 1895, James Richardson, a representative from Tennessee, was charged with compiling all of the official papers of the presidents. This compilation contains most of the presidential papers through Grover Cleveland's second administration ending March 4, 1897. The index volume (volume 10) also contains many of the papers of the earlier presidents which had been omitted from the previous volumes as well as the papers of President McKinley relating to the Spanish-American War. Sadly for those hoping for comprehensive coverage, there are interesting omissions, such as Lincoln's

Gettysburg Address so researchers of presidential materials from this first century will need to seek out materials in addition to this compilation. This compilation was updated in an edition published by the Bureau of National Literature to include Presidents Benjamin Harrison through Woodrow Wilson. Because there is both a public version and a repaginated privately published version, citations are confusing. A more comprehensive review of this title is available in Schmeckebier (1939: 311).

The *Public Papers of the Presidents of the United States* (1929–1933, 1945–present) is published by the Office of the Federal Register (OFR) and is the official publication of United States presidents' public writings, addresses, and remarks. (The gap in coverage corresponds to the FDR presidency, whose papers were published privately before this series began.) Each volume contains that year's papers and speeches of the president of the United States issued by the Office of the Press Secretary. This title does, in fact, overlap in coverage with the *(Weekly) Compilation of Presidential Documents.* Prior to the 1977 volume, the *Public Papers of the Presidents* was an edited version of the *(Weekly) Compilation of Presidential Documents.* Beginning with the Carter administration, the *Public Papers* were expanded to include virtually all materials published in the *Weekly Compilation,* plus a color photographic section.

The *(Weekly) Compilation of Presidential Documents* (1965–present) was originally issued every Monday and contains statements, messages, and other presidential material released by the White House during the preceding week (see figure 8.1). It includes such material as proclamations, executive orders, speeches, press conferences, communications to Congress and federal agencies, statements regarding bill signings and vetoes, appointments, nominations, reorganization plans, resignations, retirements, acts approved by the president, nominations submitted to the Senate, White House announcements, and press releases. Prior to the Carter administration, materials in the *Weekly Compilation* were not necessarily included in the *Public Papers of the Presidents,* so libraries needed to keep both titles to ensure a complete record, and the *Weekly Compilation* came out much more quickly that the *Public Papers* so it had current awareness value. Starting with the Obama administration, on January 29, 2009, the *Weekly Compilation* has been replaced by the *Compilation of Presidential Documents.*

Don't forget the *Congressional Record* (and predecessors) and the *Serial Set* (both covered in chapter 3). While we typically think of the *Record* as a place to find congressional debates, votes, sometimes the texts of bills, and more, the *Record* includes many important speeches, documents, and correspondence from the president and executive departments. The Gettysburg Address, for example, is found there on January 16, 1895 (although its inclusion was 32 years after the actual address!). State of the Union addresses are also included in the *Record* (because they are delivered to Congress) and the *Serial Set,* as are many more speeches, veto messages, and pieces of correspondence. These congressional sources are widely held by libraries in print or digital editions, and are important sources when researching the presidency or presidential actions.

The State of the Union, Inaugural Addresses, Vetoes, and More

Article II, section 3 of the Constitution says the president "shall from time to time give to the Congress information of the state of the union, and recommend to their consideration such measures as he shall judge necessary and expedient. . . ." This *state of the union* message is one of the few constitutional requirements of the president; as a result, copies of these speeches are thick on the ground by comparison with other materials from the president. It is interesting to note that until the 20th century, many of these speeches were not delivered in front of Congress (though some were), but were sent to Congress in written form. Because this is information delivered to Congress, these also appear in the *Congressional Record* (and its predecessors, the *Congressional Globe,* the *Register of Debates in Congress,* and the *Annals of Congress*); in the *Congressional Serial Set* and predecessor *American State Papers;* and, of course, in the *Public Papers of the Presidents* and the Richardson compilation. Online, they are available from 1790 forward at the American Presidency Project.

Inaugural addresses are also easy to locate. There are occasional volumes produced by congressional inaugural committees that compile all of the addresses, such as *Inaugural Addresses of the Presidents of the United States from George Washington 1789 to George Bush 1989* (the latest was printed as Senate document 101–10). They are also found in the Richardson compilation, in the *Public Papers of the Presidents,* at the American Presidency Project, and some are reproduced in the *Serial Set* individually.

There are many individual veto messages printed as part of the *Serial Set* and the *Compilation of Presidential Documents.* Two committee prints, *Presidential Vetoes, 1789–1988* (SuDoc:Y1.3:S.Pub.102–12) and *Presidential Vetoes, 1989–2000* (SuDoc:Y1.3:S.Pub.107–10) provide a comprehensive list of all vetoes to 2000, indicate if there was a message along with the veto (and provide a document number), and note whether the veto was sustained or overridden. Vetoes are covered more in chapter 3 as part of the process of a bill becoming a law (or not).

Treaties

In addition to legislation, regulation, and the courts (covered in chapters 4–7), a final major piece of law is treaties. Treaties are international agreements negotiated between sovereign powers. Article II, § 2 of the Constitution gives the president the "Power, by and with the Advice and Consent of the Senate, to make Treaties, provided two thirds of the Senators present concur" (US House of Representatives, 2007: 7). Article VI of the Constitution provides that treaties made under the authority of the United States have the same legal authority and force as statutes.

Unlike the legislative process discussed in chapter 3, treaties do not follow the usual bicameral legislative process. The Constitution assigns the task of negotiating treaties to the president (or those he designates), who then submits the treaty to the Senate. If the Senate ratifies the treaty, the treaty has the force of law.

There are generally two types of treaties: bilateral treaties, between two nations, which are often on specific topics such as trade or extradition; and multilateral treaties, which are between multiple nations, and usually cover global issues such as human rights, oceans, or the Antarctic. In a famous example of the treaty process, the United States signed the Kyoto Protocol on climate change in 1998, but the Senate never ratified it (actually, no president ever even presented it to the Senate to consider for ratification), so the

United States' signature on the treaty is largely symbolic, and the treaty is not law in the United States.

Cohen notes that "the determination of the effective date of a treaty is sometimes confusing because of the several significant dates involved in treaty making." The six referenced dates may include the date of signing, the date on which the ratifications are exchanged with the other signatory, the effective date specified in the treaty, the date of Senate approval, the date of ratification by the president, and the date of proclamation (Cohen et al, 1989: 457–8).

Until 1950, all treaties to which the United States was a party were published in the *U.S. Statutes at Large.* Two early volumes, volumes seven and eight, include all treaties from 1776 to 1845. Beginning in 1950, *United States Treaties and Other International Agreements (UST)* became the official compilation of ratified treaties. *UST* lags far behind in currency; recent treaties are published in slip form (individually) in the set *Treaties and Other International Acts Series (TIAS).* For content prior to 1950, you can also refer to *Treaties and Other International Acts of the United States 1776–1949.* This set is often known by the name of its editor, Bevans, and is available via HeinOnline. The *United Nations Treaty Series (UNTS)* is a standard compilation of treaties, bilateral and multilateral, worldwide.

Treaties in Force lists and indexes treaties to which the United States is a current party, and is available online or in print, updated annually. It contains sections for bilateral treaties and multilateral treaties. The bilateral section is arranged first by country, and then by subject; the multilateral section is arranged by subject. Each treaty contains its title, date, and citation in *TIAS, UST,* or the *U.S. Statutes at Large,* and the *UNTS,* as appropriate. The free *UNTS* database is searchable by name, participant, or full text.

In-depth treaty research is often best done with the more robust treaty resources available commercially via the databases in Lexis, HeinOnline, or Westlaw. A useful free resource is EISIL: Electronic Information System for International Law (www.eisil.org), from the American Society for International Law, which includes many multilateral treaties and agreements. The US Department of State (www.state.gov/s/1 /treaty/text/) and the United Nations (https://treaties.un.org/) both have extensive treaty sites that review sources and provide other material on treaties.

Finally, the International Court of Justice (also known as ICJ or the World Court) arbitrates certain disputes between nations and about treaties. ICJ rulings, unlike treaties ratified by the Senate, are not necessarily law in the United States.

Conclusion

What does the president do in a day? More than just sign laws or give speeches—though that is part of the job. Foreign affairs, executive orders, proclamations, policies—all of these are the result of public and private meetings, political decision making, and "strategery." Presidential documents are an interesting mix of public and executively controlled documents—and with every word and action being documented for posterity, they are a rich source of American political history that keeps researchers busy.

Exercises

1. When listening to or reading the news, listen for mentions of the president and think about which of the four categories of presidential documentation may apply to that particular news story.
2. If a researcher wants a letter from Teddy Roosevelt to his wife, where would they look? What about his correspondence with John Muir?
3. The day after an inaugural address, where would you look for the speech text? What are your options six years later?
4. If the president sends a BlackBerry message to a cabinet secretary, into which of Hirshon's categories of documents does this fall?
5. Are there any current examples of classified documents emanating from the current president that you can think of? What about older examples not included in this chapter?
6. What is the update on the immigration controversy? What has happened since the new policy was announced?

Sources Mentioned in This Chapter

Sources mentioned in this section do not duplicate the references that follow.

Executive Orders, Legislation, and Cases (Chronological Order)

National Security Act of 1947, P.L. 80-253, 61 Stat. 495, Chap. 343 (1947).

Presidential Libraries Act of 1955, P.L. 84-373, 69 Stat. 695 (1955).

Presidential Records and Materials Preservation Act, P.L. 93-526, 88 Stat. 1695 (1974).

Nixon v. Administrator of General Services, 433 U.S. 425 (1977).

Presidential Records Act of 1978, P.L. 95-591, 92 Stat. 2523 (1978).

National Archives and Records Administration Act of 1984, P.L. 98-497, 98 Stat. 2280, 44 U.S.C. §§ 2201–2207 (1984).

Presidential Libraries Act of 1986, P.L. 99-323, 100 Stat. 495 (1986).

Exec. Order No. 12667, 54 Fed. Reg. 3403 (January 18, 1989).

Exec. Order No. 13233, 66 Fed. Reg. 56025 (November 1, 2001).

Exec. Order No. 13489, 74 Fed. Reg. 4669 (January 21, 2009).

Presidential Speeches

Lincoln, Abraham. "National Military Park, Gettysburg, PA." 27 Cong. Rec. 1039 (1895).

Monroe, James. *Message of the President of the United States, at the commencement of the First Session of the Eighteenth Congress.* American State Papers (ASP05 For.re1.360), December 2, 1823.

Roosevelt, Franklin. "First Inaugural Address, Saturday, March 4, 1933." In *Inaugural Addresses of the Presidents*. Washington, DC: Government Printing Office, 1989.

Special Message to the Congress on Urgent National Needs, 107 Cong. Rec. 8887 (1961).

Other Sources

American Presidency Project, www.presidency.ucsb.edu.

CFR, Title 3, The President. http://purl.access.gpo.gov/GPO/LPS494; SuDoc: AE 2.106/3:3 (online) or GS 4.108/2. The *CFR* is widely available in print and online through public and commercial sites. Most depository libraries have good collections of Title 3 of the *CFR*.

Codification of Presidential Proclamation and Executive Orders (1945–1989), www.archives.gov/federal-register/codification/index.html.

Compilation of Messages and Papers of Presidents, 1789–1897, (Richardson set) available as *Serial Set* volumes 3265–1 through 3265–10 (H. misdoc 210); printed separately as SuDoc:Y4.P93/1:3/; online as http://catalog.hathitrust.org/Record/001137867 and available through several of the meta sites listed above.

[Weekly] Compilation of Presidential Documents (1965–present), from 1993–present available at http://purl.access.gpo.gov/GPO/LPS1769; SuDoc: AE 2.109: (online) or GS 4.114, and available through several of the meta sites listed above.

Congressional Record, http://purl.access.gpo.gov/GPO/LPS1671; SuDoc: X 1.1/A:.

Declassified Documents Reference System (DDRS), www.gale.cengage.com.

EISIL: Electronic Information System for International Law, www.eisil.org.

Executive Orders and Presidential Proclamations (ProQuest). www.proquest.com/products-services/databases/Executive-Orders-and-Presidential-Proclamations.html. *CIS Index to Presidential Executive Orders & Proclamations 1789–1983*. Washington, DC: Congressional Information Service, c1986–c1987.

FDsys, www.fdsys.gov.

CFR, Title 3, The President. http://purl.access.gpo.gov/GPO/LPS494; SuDoc: AE 2.106/3:3 (online) or GS 4.108/2. The *CFR* is widely available in print and online through public and commercial sites. Most depository libraries have good collections of Title 3 of the *CFR*.

Federal Register, http://purl.access.gpo.gov/GPO/LPS1756; SuDoc: AE 2.106 (online), AE 2.7, or GS4.107. The *Federal Register* is online at GPO 1994–present, commercial sites may have longer runs.

Goldsmith, William M. 1974. *The Growth of Presidential Power: A Documented History.* New York: Chelsea House.

HeinOnline, www.heinonline.org.

Inaugural Addresses of the Presidents of the United States from George Washington 1789 to George Bush 1989 (S.doc. 101–10), SuDoc:Y 1.1/3:101–10.

International Court of Justice (also known as ICJ or the World Court), www.icj-cij.org/homepage.

Library of Congress Archival Finding Aids by Name, www.loc.gov/rr/mss/f-aids/mssfa.html.

Miller Center of Public Affairs at the University of Virginia, http://millercenter.org/president/papers.

Presidential Libraries (National Archives), www.archives.gov/presidential-libraries.

Presidential Vetoes, 1789–1988, SuDoc:Y1.3:S.Pub.102–12.

Presidential Vetoes, 1989–2000, SuDoc:Y1.3:S.Pub.107–10.

Public Papers of the Presidents of the United States (1929–1933, 1945–present), available at http://purl.access.gpo.gov/GPO/LPS4752 (1991–), complete series at University of Michigan Digital Library, http://quod.lib.umich.edu/p/ppotpus; SuDoc: AE 2.114: (online) or GS 4.113, and also available through several of the meta sites listed above.

Savage, Charlie. 2007. *Takeover: The Return of the Imperial Presidency and the Subversion of American Democracy.* New York: Little, Brown.

Secrecy News, Federation of American Scientists, www.fas.org/blog/secrecy.

Treaties and Other International Acts Series. Washington, DC: Department of State. www.state.gov/s/1/treaty/tias/index.htm.

Treaties in Force: A List of Treaties and Other International Acts of the United States In Force On. . . . Washington: Government Printing Office. 1941—www.state.gov/s/1 /treaty/tif/index.htm.

United Nations Treaty Series (UNTS). New York: United Nations. 1946–. https://treaties.un.org/pages/UNTSOnline.aspx?id=1.

United States Presidential Library (HeinOnline). http://heinonline.org/HeinDocs/US%20Presidential.pdf.

United States Statutes at Large. Washington, DC: Government Printing Office (1789–1874 published by Little, Brown). Recent volumes available at www.gpo.gov/fdsys/; unofficial historical volumes at www.constitution.org/uslaw/sal/sal.htm.

United States Treaties and Other International Agreements (UST). Washington, DC: Department of State.

University Press of America. 1980–2004. *Documents of the National Security Council,* multiple supplements.

US *Congressional Serial Set,* http://purl.access.gpo.gov/GPO/LPS839, Final bound version SuDoc:Y 1.1/2:.

Warren G. Harding–Carrie Fulton Phillips Correspondence, www.loc.gov/collections/warren-harding-carrie-fulton-phillips-correspondence/.

Westlaw, www.westlaw.com.

WhiteHouse.gov.

References

Baker, Peter, and Shailagh Murray. 2005. "Bush Defends Supreme Court Pick; President Reassures Conservatives on a Range of Issues." *Washington Post,* October 5: A01.

Bush, George W. Exec. Order No. 13233, 66 Fed. Reg. 214 (November 5, 2001).

Clinton, William J. 1994. "Interview on MTV's 'Enough is Enough' Forum" *Weekly Compilation of Presidential Documents.* April 19: 836–49. www.gpo.gov/fdsys/pkg/WCPD-1994–04–25/pdf/WCPD -1994–04–25-Pg836.pdf.

Cohen, Morris L., Robert C. Berring and Kent C. Olson. *How to Find the Law.* 1989, 9th edition. St. Paul: West Group.

CQ Press. 2008. *The Powers of the Presidency,* 3rd ed. Washington, DC: CQ Press.

Doder, Dusko. 1984. "President Said to Voice 'His Secret Dream'; Moscow Calls Reagan's Quip 'Self-Revealing.'" *Washington Post*, August 15: A26.

General Accounting Office, 1992. *National Security: The Use of Presidential Directives to Make and Implement U.S. Policy* (GAO/NSIAD-92-72). Washington, DC: US General Accounting Office, 1992.

Hirshon, Arnold. 1974. "The Scope, Accessibility, and History of Presidential Papers." *Government Publications Review* 1: 363–390.

Johnson, Jeh. 2014. *Exercising Prosecutorial Discretion with Respect to Individuals Who Came to the United States as Children and with Respect to Certain Individuals Who Are the Parents of U.S. Citizens or Permanent Residents.* Memorandum, November 20, 2014. www.dhs.gov/sites/default/files/publications/14_1120 _memo_deferred_action.pdf.

Kandel, William A. et al. 2015 *The President's Immigration Accountability Executive Action of November 20, 2014: Overview and Issues* Washington, DC: Congressional Research Service. February 24, 2015. ProQuest Congressional Research Digital Collection.

Los Angeles Times. "Torture Memos: How Did We Get Here? Justice Department Writings Reveal the Origins of 'Enhanced' Interrogation." April 4, 2008. http://articles.latimes.com/2008/apr/04/opinion/ed-y004.

Nakamura, David, Robert Costa, David A. Fahrenthold. 2014. "Obama announces immigration overhaul shielding 4 million from deportation." *Washington Post.* November 20, 2014.

National Archives and Records Administration. 2010. "George W. Bush Presidential Library." www.georgewbushlibrary.gov.

National Archives and Records Administration. 2015a. "Presidential Records Act (PRA) of 1978." www.archives.gov/presidential-libraries/laws/1978-act.html.

National Archives and Records Administration. 2015b. "Presidential Libraries, A Brief History." www.archives.gov/presidential-libraries/about/history.html.

Obama, Barack. 2014. "Address to the Nation on Immigration Reform." *Compilation of Presidential Documents.* November 20, 2014. www.gpo.gov/fdsys/pkg/DCPD-201400877/pdf/DCPD-201400877.pdf.

Pincus, Walter. 2002. "Under Bush, the Briefing Gets Briefer: Key Intelligence Report by CIA and FBI Is Shorter, 'More Targeted,' Limited to Smaller Circle of Top Officials and Advisers." *Washington Post,* May 24: A33.

ProQuest History Vault, 1961–63. *Appointment Book of President Kennedy, 1961–1963, Oct. 01, 1962—Oct . 1, 1962.* American Politics and Society from Kennedy to Watergate. http://congressional.proquest.com/histvault?q=002240–002–0630.

ProQuest History Vault, 1960–1975. *Documents of the National Security Council, 3rd Supplement.* Vietnam and American Foreign Policy, 1960–1975. http://congressional.proquest.com/histvault?q=002955–001–0007.

Ragsdale, Lyn. 2014. *Vital Statistics on the Presidency: Washington to Clinton.* Washington, DC: Congressional Quarterly. http://dx.doi.org/10.4135/9781452299914.n5.

Relyea, Harold C. 2008. *Presidential Directives: Background and Overview.* Washington, DC: Congressional Research Service, Government and Finance Division. November 26, 2008. ProQuest Congressional Research Digital Collection.

Roosevelt, Franklin. Exec. Order No. 9066, 42 Fed. Reg. 1563 (February 19, 1942). www.presidency.ucsb.edu/ws/?pid=61698.

Ruger, Todd. 2015. "Democrats File Court Brief Backing Obama Immigration Orders" *Roll Call.* April 06, 2015.

Savage, Charlie. 2007. *Takeover: The Return of the Imperial Presidency and the Subversion of American Democracy.* New York: Little, Brown.

Schick, Frank L., Renee Schick, and Mark Carroll. 1989. *Records of the Presidency: Presidential Papers and Libraries from Washington to Reagan.* Phoenix: Oryx Press.

Schmeckebier, Laurence F. 1939. *Government Publications and Their Use.* Washington DC: Brookings Institution.

Smith, Donald C. 1989. "The Rhetoric of the *(Weekly) Compilation of Presidential Documents:* 'We Make that Decision on a Daily Basis.'" Government Publications Review 16: 213–217.

US House of Representatives. 2007. *Constitution of the United States as Amended.* (H.doc 110–50), July 25.

Yoo, John. 2003. "Memorandum for William J. Haynes II, General Counsel of the Department of Defense, Re: Military Interrogation of Alien Unlawful Combatants Held Outside the United States." United States Department of Justice, Office of the Deputy Assistant Attorney General, Washington, DC. March 14. www.aclu.org/sites/default/files/field_document/yoo_army_torture_memo.pdf.

PART II

Government Information in Focus

CHAPTER 9

The Executive Branch

CASSANDRA HARTNETT

Introduction

When Americans make a mental diagram of the three branches of government, often the executive branch is represented by an image of the White House. Although the Executive Office of the President resides in the executive branch, so do hundreds of other agencies. The executive branch is a coordinated group of agencies authorized by Congress to carry out the laws of the land (see chapter 6 for a discussion of the executive branch's regulatory function). Notably, with the exception of the president and vice president, it contains no elected officials. We refer to this executive sector of government as administrative or bureaucratic. Bureaucracy "is a government apparatus that elected officials employ to implement policies that they enact, and one that elected officials empower to make and enforce policies of its own" (Lavertu, 2010). The organization of US federal agencies has changed dramatically over time. Some relatively recent changes include the establishment of the cabinet-level Department of Veterans Affairs (upgraded from the Veterans Administration); the Department of Homeland Security (established in January 2003 by the Homeland Security Act of 2002, P.L. 107–296, 116 Stat. 2135); the Bureau of Ocean Energy Management, Regulation, and Enforcement (formerly Minerals Management Service); and the coordination of intelligence agencies into an Intelligence Community, with the Office of the Director of National Intelligence (DNI) beginning its operations in April 2005.

Executive branch literature offers readers an unparalleled view of government functioning over the years, and a glimpse of American society of the time. Think of the stories government agency publications might tell during just the 20th century:

- The development of federal guidelines for modern aviation by a Hoover administration bureau, the Aeronautics Branch
- World War II–era War Relocation Authority manuals providing instruction on the relocation and internment of those of Japanese ancestry

- Atomic Energy Commission and later Nuclear Regulatory Commission reports revealing the brave new world of nuclear energy and warfare
- The surgeon general's report in January 1964 demonstrating with clinical evidence the negative health effects of smoking
- The declassified Department of Energy reports showing government radiation experiments conducted on human subjects without proper consent
- The public remarks of former Federal Reserve Chair Ben Bernanke following the Great Recession, to which Americans listened with heightened interest
- USDA pamphlets promoting household cleaning methods now seen as unsafe (see figure 9.1)

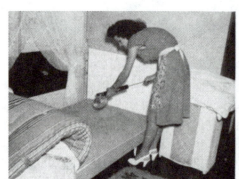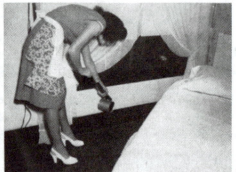

Treating Mattress for Bedbugs   Spraying Baseboard for Bedbug Control

FIGURE 9.1
Excerpt from a 1949 USDA Consumer Pamphlet That Encouraged Americans to Spray the Insecticide DDT, Banned since 1972 as a Harmful Substance, Directly onto Mattresses and Baseboards in the Home

Learning about executive branch structure can strengthen the overall information skills of any information specialist.

To better understand the executive branch, start by becoming more familiar with the names and functions of government agencies. Begin with the agencies most relevant to everyday life, and be willing to learn about agencies that are complete mysteries. Perhaps you have already heard of the Office of Head Start or the National Eye Institute, but what about the National Portrait Gallery, the Federal Grain Inspection Service, or the Migratory Bird Conservation Commission? This is not to neglect the US Military Academy at West Point, the Prints and Photographs Division of the LC, the Office for Victims of Crime, the Secret Service, the Selective Service, the St. Lawrence Seaway Development Corporation, or the Institute of Peace. All of the aforementioned federal entities have a publishing history, are represented in the SuDocs numbering scheme, have had their publications distributed to depository libraries, and, in addition, are actively publishing online.

The work of many specific executive agencies is scattered throughout this book, especially in chapters 10–18 with the topics of statistics, education, health information, and more.

Two items should be in every librarian's arsenal for understanding executive branch structure; both are already mentioned in this book. First is the A–Z list of agencies at www.usa.gov/directory/federal/index.shtml, and second is the *U.S. Government Manual,* discussed in chapter 2. For decades, the opening chapters of the *Manual* have included the Declaration of Independence, the Constitution, and an organizational chart of the federal government (see figure 9.2). The manual now has its own domain, www.usgovernmentmanual.gov. A third title, a print-only publication, *Guide to U.S. Government Publications,* is for those needing a comprehensive look at federal publishing patterns as reflected in the depository library program. The book, long referred to as Andriot after its original editors, is organized by agency and SuDoc class stem (the part of the classification number before the colon). It provides a list of series titles and types of materials published under each SuDoc stem, inclusive dates, and importantly, agency genealogy—which agencies have ceased, which have changed names, and which new ones have been established, with the exact chronology.

> **It's in the Details**
>
> The simple details of American daily life reveal the pervasive presence of the bureaucratic state—the dollars in our wallets, printed by the Treasury Department; the peanut butter we eat, subsidized and regulated by the US Department of Agriculture (USDA); the pain medications we take, approved and governed by the Food and Drug Administration (FDA); the cars we drive, produced in factories regulated by the Occupational Safety and Health Administration (OSHA) and themselves regulated by the Environmental Protection Agency (EPA) and the National Highway Traffic Safety Administration; the national parks and forests, in which we ski, fish, hike, hunt, climb, and camp, governed by the Forest Service and the Department of Interior; and the $425.3 billion in checks that our elderly and disabled receive annually from the Social Security Administration.
>
> *—Professor Daniel Carpenter of Harvard University (Carpenter, 2005: 41)*

With a quick glance at Andriot, one can discover that the Office of Federal Employees' Compensation existed only from 1972 to 1974; produced three different types of publications (annual reports, general publications, and pamphlets); and was replaced by the Office of Workers' Compensation Programs (Batten, 2016: 613).

Cabinet-Level Departments

Under the large central box in figure 9.2, the executive office of the president, small boxes show the 15 departments frequently referred to as cabinet-level agencies. Although the cabinet is a top-level advisory body, Bledsoe and Rigby point out that "membership in the president's cabinet is not limited to the secretaries of the executive departments . . . presidents are free to promote any [other] government official they please to cabinet-rank status" (1997a: 77). Since the earliest days of our government, four of the departments have been those pertaining to foreign affairs (Department of State), military affairs (Department of Defense, originally the Department of War), the legal system (Department of Justice, but originally a single Attorney General), and fiscal affairs (Department of the Treasury). Today, a secretary heads each department (except

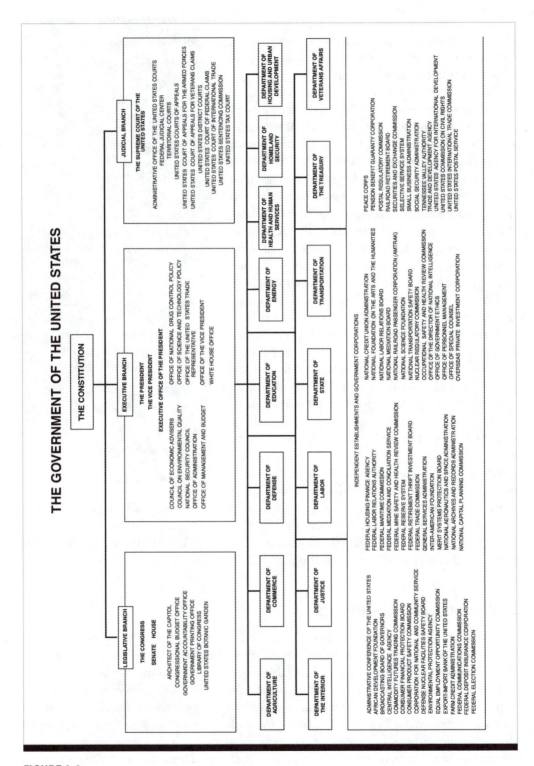

FIGURE 9.2
US Federal Government, an Organization Chart

for Justice, headed by the attorney general). Secretary positions are filled via nomination by the president, with confirmation following in the Senate. According to Article II, Section 2 of the US Constitution, the president "shall nominate, and with the advice and consent of the Senate, shall appoint . . . Officers of the United States" but may allow agency heads to appoint their own "inferior officers" as needed (Bledsoe and Rigby, 1997b: 145). The publication *U.S. Government Policy and Supporting Positions,* also known as the Plum Book, available via www.fdsys.gov, lists more than 7,000 presidentially appointed federal employees, excluding the judges of the judicial branch. It is released after every change in presidential administration.

Each department contains a number of agencies and subordinate offices; these are described in the *Government Manual,* in numerous other general guides to government, and on the agencies' own websites. Although it is conceivable that a government agency might exist that would be wholly uninteresting to the public or to librarians, the authors have not found one yet. There is simply too close a tie between government functioning and our everyday lives.

Independent Agencies and Government Corporations

Beneath the cabinet-level departments is a box listing the independent agencies and government corporations (see figure 9.2), those that do not fall under a larger department. The chief administrators and governing boards of these agencies are accountable to Congress and the president, and are required to post their notices and regulatory updates in the *Federal Register.* Some of the best-known such agencies include the EPA, the Nuclear Regulatory Commission, the Peace Corps, and the US Postal Service. Bledsoe and Rigby (1997b) group these bottom-listed agencies into three categories: regulatory agencies (example: the Federal Communications Commission or FCC, which regulates broadcast, wire, satellite and cable communications), independent executive agencies (example: National Aeronautics and Space Administration or NASA), and government corporations (example: the National Railway Passenger Corporation or AMTRAK). "A government corporation has a board and directors and managers, but it does not have any stockholders . . . [one] cannot buy shares of stock. If the government corporation makes a profit, it does not distribute the profit as dividends [nor does it pay taxes on the profits, the profits remain with the corporation]" (Schmidt et al., 2009: 503). An administrator of these freestanding executive branch units may or may not serve in the president's cabinet.

The US Postal Service

The creation of post offices was originally called for by Article I, Section 8 of the Constitution, and for decades the Post Office was part of the president's cabinet. With the passage of the Postal Reorganization Act of 1970 (P.L. 91–375, 84 Stat. 719), the US Postal Service became an independent federal agency, with an appointed board of governors, and the postmaster is no longer a member of the cabinet. The agency is self-sustaining, supporting itself by charging for postage and other products and services. It cannot close down rural post offices simply because they don't make money: it is a government agency mandated to connect the nation by relaying correspondence. It both competes and collaborates with the private sector.

The Quasi-Government

There's actually a misleading aspect to the organizational chart (figure 9.2): not all federally affiliated entities are included. One can find dozens more listed in the *Budget of the United States* and in the back of the *U.S. Government Manual* under Boards, Commissions, and Committees, Quasi-Official Agencies, Selected Multi-Lateral Organizations, and Selected Bilateral Organizations, with a further note that the *Manual* completely omits yet another category: federal advisory commissions. None of these are found on the organizational chart, perhaps for visual simplicity, but also because some are more nongovernmental than governmental. Their creation was mandated and/or partly funded by Congress, but their operations and infrastructure resemble a private, for-profit organization, except that their initial charters may include extra benefits or privileges not usually accorded the private sector, and their activities are prescribed by their government charters. Scholars have dubbed this sector the quasi-government.

One could categorize the array of quasi-governmental agencies on a numbered scale, with 1 being a purely governmental agency (both its funding and mission generated by government); 2 being a *quago* (mostly a government organization with some private sector attributes, for example the Legal Services Corporation); 3 being a *quango* (a private organization with some governmental sector attributes, such as the Red Cross); and 4 being a purely private organization (funding and mission established privately) (Moe and Kosar, 2005). Quasi-governmental agencies would fall in a range of fine gradations within 2 and 3, due to the many different types of organizations. The Boy Scouts of America, for example, cannot be considered purely private. The Boy Scouts were granted a federal charter in 1916 (P.L. 64-94, 39 Stat. 227, Chap. 148); they must forever remain nonprofit and file a report to Congress on April 1 each year detailing their activities (this can be found in the *Serial Set,* a compilation of congressional reports and documents). Thanks to the law, they retain sole and exclusive rights to their name and their emblems and badges. As the CRS notes, "There is nothing modest about the size, scope, and impact of the quasi government. Time will tell whether the emergence of the quasi government is to be viewed as a symptom of decline in our democratic government, or a harbinger of a new, creative management era where the purported artificial barriers between the governmental and private sectors are breached as a matter of principle" (Moe and Kosar, 2005: 2).

CRS analysts trace the era of the quasi-government era back to the establishment of the Communications Satellite Corporation (ComSat) in 1962 (Moe and Kosar, 2005: 5). Other examples of the quasi-government are government-sponsored enterprises (GSEs), hybrid financial structures such as the Federal Home Loan Bank System and the Farm Credit System. These exhibit legal characteristics of both public and private fiscal organizations. Quasi-government entities are not agencies as defined by Title 5 of the *United States Code,* and their publications may be more difficult to identify and access. For a detailed discussion of this topic, consult *The Quasi Government: Hybrid Organizations with Both Government and Private Sector Legal Characteristics* (Moe and Kosar, 2005).

Publications of Executive Branch Agencies

Agency Mission Is Paramount

Want to learn more about an agency's information output? First consider its purpose. As discussed in chapter 2 (Research Strategies—Strategy One) agencies are established by law and funded by Congress to carry out specific missions. For example, taxpayers expect the Internal Revenue Service to enforce tax laws and help us understand and meet our responsibilities, but not to establish new taxes or a higher rate of taxation (Congress does that) or to produce a fresh supply of pennies, nickels, and other coins (the job of the US Mint).

Leaders whose agencies drift too far off course may find Congress or the courts reviewing them for mission creep. One can easily discover agency mission statements in the *U.S. Government Manual* and on agency websites. Gormley and Balla (2008) note that an agency with a single, straightforward mission, such as the National Weather Service (NWS), is likely to perform its functions well and receive high ratings, especially when that mission enjoys wide support. But even the NWS can have its mission challenged, as in recent years' controversies about privately owned weather services competing with it (Murray and Bier, 2011). For tips on how best to navigate agency websites, refer to chapter 2.

Types of Agency Publications

The Superintendent of Documents (SuDocs) classification system (see chapter 1) provides a useful framework for understanding the different documents issued by federal agencies. In the SuDocs scheme, the numeral that comes directly after the first letter/number combination (i.e., after the department designation) indicates the subagency and *publication category:* annual reports; general publications; bulletins; circulars; laws; regulations, rules, and

---

The End of Term Harvests: The Universe of Born Digital Federal Documents

The End of Term Web Archive is a cooperative project of five major players in digital preservation: the California Digital Library, the Internet Archive, the LC, the University of North Texas, and the GPO. The 2008–2009 harvest documented what federal government websites looked like at the end of the George W. Bush presidency and the transition to the Barack Obama administration. (As discussed in chapter 8, the Presidency, government websites are most vulnerable to scrubbing during transitions in power.) The resultant digital archive of captured web pages is viewable and searchable at http://eotarchive.cdlib.org/index .html. James A. Jacobs, in a widely discussed white paper, quantifies the federal digital information boom (and the resulting problem of digital preservation) in the following way: Imagine comparing the 3 million items held in the FDLP to date, and all the coordinated effort of the library community to preserve these; then consider stewarding access to the 160 million URLs harvested in the 2008 End of Term Crawl (Jacobs, 2014). Scholarship in information science programs nationwide will inform practices as librarians, users, and the government officials themselves learn to understand the scope of federal information collections in our time and in the future.

instructions; handbooks, manuals, guides; bibliographies and lists of publications; directories; maps and charts; posters; forms; addresses and lectures; and so on.

What might be helpful about these categories, these types of publications? Some (laws, regulations, maps) are discussed elsewhere in this book. *Annual reports* can tell the story of agency accomplishments in a way not found elsewhere, but one must read them with the critical eye of a historian. *Bulletins and circulars* released at frequent intervals often provide the more everyday, on-the-ground picture of the topics in an agency's purview (be it aging, water pollution, or long-haul trucking), as do *handbooks, manuals, guides,* and *forms. General publications* make interesting browsing in SuDocs-ordered print-on-paper library stacks, giving the user a chance to see agency works that do not fit into easy categories. *Posters* have natural appeal as graphic objects and cultural artifacts. Bibliographies, especially those well annotated, provide a glimpse of the literature of the day, while *addresses* and *lectures* turn out to make fascinating reading as examples of the reflective thinking of the day.

When mining the riches of agency publications, expect most agencies to publish in at least these simple categories. In addition, many agencies may publish specialized titles or series directly related to the type of information the agency creates as it fulfills its mission. Spend some time perusing the *List of Classes* (see chapter 1) or the *Guide to U.S. Government Publications* to help create a broad mental map for executive agency output. This technique is helpful even now when the vast majority of government content is online, never published in a tangible form. Remember that your mental map of federal information has to incorporate vast blurry areas: instantly updated scientific data, interactive forms, transactional records, dashboards, user-generated tables, audio, video, social media channels, and every manner of customizable, continuously updated resources, the new normal in publishing everywhere.

How to Find Executive Branch Documents

Strategies

There are various strategies that can be used to find executive branch documents. Some have to do with the date the materials were published, and others with the kind of material.

Check the Catalog

In learning about executive branch publishing, look for transition in publishing patterns. A significant year for many documents librarians is 1976, when GPO instituted full online MARC cataloging. From 1976 forward, depository documents are simply easier to find in library catalogs, as full cataloging records were available for purchase commercially; in this sense, no special finding tips are needed for this period, as you can simply search WorldCat.org, your library's online catalog, or GPO's *Catalog of Government Publications.* For titles published prior to 1976, other strategies are needed.

Consider the Serial Set

As we discussed in chapters 1 and 2, the federal government funneled most of its reports through Congress in the 1800s, printed as part of the US *Congressional Serial Set*. We learned that the Public Printing and Binding Act (Mar. 1, 1907, P.L. 59-153, 34 Stat. 186, Chap. 2448) changed the distribution so that only a very few libraries (sometimes referred to as posterity libraries) continued to receive the more complete *Serial Set* which included large runs of executive branch materials. The two commercially digitized versions of the *Serial Set* (by ProQuest and Readex) have scanned from the fuller, posterity library editions. One can see vestiges of the earlier funneling-through-Congress well into the mid-20th century: in 1969, for example, one can still find the *Army Register,* a directory of US military personnel (SuDoc D 2.109) printed as part of the depository edition *Serial Set* (the *Army Register* is a good report to know about too). For more examples of ongoing executive branch serials included in the *Serial Set,* consult a guide produced by the College of Wooster library (*Agency Series Found in the Serial Set,* http://libguides.wooster.edu/congressionalserialsetfinding list) and see pages 11–13 of *The Serial Set: Its Make-up and Content* (Sevetson, 2013) for a general description. (The same book covers other historical executive agency topics such as agriculture, the Bureau of American Ethnology, the Survey of the Coast, the Civil War, and western exploration.) As a practice, for executive branch publications prior to about 1910, checking the *Serial Set* to see if the publication is included there is a critical step.

Format Distinctions and Vanishing Documents

From the late 1970s through the mid–1990s, microfiche was the dominant dissemination medium from GPO, with some recurrent reports fluctuating in format between paper, microfiche, sometimes to CD-ROM and then back to paper, and so on—making their use and bibliographic control quite a challenge. Also in this era, librarians were concerned with the privatization of government information and the trend of "Less Access to Less Information By and About the U.S. Government" (American Library Association, 2010) in the wake of the Paperwork Reduction Act (P.L. 96-511, 92 Stat. 1783 (1980)). When searching out a document in print-on-paper library collections or in online scanned repositories of the same (e.g., the HathiTrust), remember to double-check for microform or CD-ROM holdings, which are more likely to be undiscovered by digitization projects or cataloguing, and are more apt to be shelved in remote storage locations.

Could It Be on the Internet?

Starting in the 1990s and continuing today, the next challenge for information seekers was that of creating coherence (especially for time series data or a run of a government serial) in pre- and post-Internet publishing. Certain long-running publications disappeared in the Internet world, replaced by many separate web files. Familiar with working in the realm of multiple formats, librarians could once direct users to a section of their library's collection to find, for example, the latest economic census, including special reports arranged by industrial classification and state. Today's economic census is not released as tangible reports or even as PDFs; it is solely online as interactive data via American FactFinder (http://factfinder.census.gov/) or downloadable via FTP. The Census Bureau is not the only agency to radically change publication patterns in the Internet age, but it is a transformation that so typifies today's technology centric, downsized, yet necessarily forward-looking executive agencies. For information from the mid-2000s on (and sometimes much earlier), one should assume that agency publications are nearly completely born digital. But bringing coherence to this publishing stream and contextualizing it with previous output is the role of the government information specialist. Look for online guides that specifically address this range and transition.

CIS Index to U.S. Executive Branch Documents and Other Resources

Starting in 1990, a commercially produced index has made historical administrative documents more findable: the *CIS Index to U.S. Executive Branch Documents, 1789–1909 and 1910–1932.* Originally issued in print and silver halide microfiche, one can purchase both index and content today as a module of ProQuest *Congressional,* with the documents in PDF form (with coverage extending to 1939 and beyond). The beauty of this resource is that it provides users with subject/name, title, author, agency report number, and SuDocs number access to hundreds of thousands of agency publications, and metadata is available as bibliographic records, easily loaded into libraries' online catalogs or available through discovery services. This stands as a powerful way to access historical executive branch documents, along with the indexing provided for federal statistical publications by ProQuest *Statistical Insight* (the online successor to the printed *American Statistics Index,* from 1970 forward). The *Readex Non-Depository Government Publications* collection (on microform) is yet another source of federal executive material and more, covering the years 1953–2008.

Additional Tools and Everyday Searching

Today federal documents librarians have other aces up their sleeves. One useful meta-index is Public Documents Masterfile (PDM), a subscription database from Paratext. PDM combines index data from 26 different sources, including the *Monthly Catalog* from 1895–1976, GPO's shelflist, and a host of historical indexes. As of this writing, ProQuest is in the process of updating the content in their online *Monthly Catalog 1895–1976* offering and will be re-releasing it for sale in the near future. Using a mix of these resources, and benefiting from increased library cataloging of pre-1976 federal depository documents (records available via www.worldcat.org), and combined with seemingly limitless possibilities on the open Web, today's users are probably better positioned to find federal agency publications than they have been at any point in history. GPO even hosts a "government book talk" site (http://govbooktalk.gpo.gov/) for those who just want to find a good document to read. GovBookTalk highlights interesting or popular government releases and gives the public the chance to review and discuss works in an open forum. The HathiTrust is undertaking a US Federal Government Documents Initiative to expand and enhance access to GPO and non-GPO issued documents through the coordinated actions of its collective members (www .hathitrust.org/usgovdocs), a project worth watching.

Today most trained documents librarians start government searches with the open Web or WorldCat; there is no one database that captures all federal executive publications. Neither one of these resources would be as effective as it is today without the contributions of thousands of information specialists producing cataloging (WorldCat) and metadata (the open Web) or designing automated means of producing descriptive data. Experienced searchers learn when to search a mass digitization repository (Google Books, the HathiTrust, the Internet Archive), a specialized tool (FDsys), or the deep science web via www.ScienceAccelerator.gov.

Spotlight on Selected Federal Agencies and Departments

Many of the most important information-producing agencies are discussed elsewhere in this book; some are the subject of entire chapters. The following description of a small subset of agencies and their publications is meant as only a modest introduction, providing the reader with a launching point for learning more about the administrative branch of government. And in a broad sense, these very selected agencies provide a blueprint for the variety of publications and information available at all executive agencies. We have chosen to focus on the Departments of Commerce, Defense, and State. We also briefly address the Office of Management and Budget (OMB) because of its role in information policy, and the translations offered by the Foreign Broadcast Information Service (FBIS) and Joint Publications Research Service (JPRS). All of the cabinet-level departments and independent agencies have significant output and are worthy of ongoing study and attention.

Executive Office of the President, OMB, and the Budget

The Executive Office of the President (EOP), established in 1939, is a cluster of federal agencies directly serving the president. Some of the agencies, established by Congress or the president, have come and gone; others (like the White House Office and the Office of Management and Budget, originally called the Bureau of the Budget) have endured. In recent presidencies, the office has contained 9 to 15 distinct subagencies. There are also projects and initiatives administered here, such as First Lady Michelle Obama's LetsMove.gov program or the US Digital Service, the special user experience overhaul team for federal websites, launched in 2014. The EOP has been characterized variously as a "managerial or coordinative auxiliary, a national symbol, or a haven of political patronage" (Relyea, 2008: 1). The CRS provides a thorough 32-page history of the EOP in its *Executive Office of the President: An Historical Overview* (Relyea, 2008). So even the presidential office is a conglomeration of agencies, only one of which is the White House.

Established in 1939 as the Bureau of the Budget, and moved to within the EOP (and renamed) in 1970, OMB exists primarily to assist the president with the preparation of the federal budget and to establish government-wide management practices. Government documents librarians note OMB's roles with federal information. OMB promulgated Circular A-130 (Management of Federal Information Resources), a government rule defining *government information, government document, information life cycle,* and other terminology, bringing these concepts into the electronic age. In chapter 6 (Regulations), we discuss the fact that OMB review is a required step in the regulatory process, providing some uniformity across the complex universe of regulatory information. Observant readers have noticed that federal forms bear an OMB control number, denoting among other things that the form meets Paperwork Reduction Act requirements, minimizing respondents' time in replying. Over the decades, OMB's role has evolved to include the issuing of standards, regulatory guidance, and directives followed by all federal agencies. In collecting survey data, federal agencies must conform to OMB's five-race classification system, with two ethnicity possibilities (see sidebar). OMB developed these standards in coordination with 30 federal agencies to promote standardized record-keeping and reporting (Office of Management and Budget, 2000).

OMB's website, a branch of the WhiteHouse.gov tree, links to: About, OMBlog, The Budget, Management, Regulation & Information Policy, and Legislative Information. Critical content is hiding under About, then further under Agency Info: an archive of OMB's Bulletins, Circulars (back to 1952), Federal Register Notices, Memoranda, Policy Guidance, and Reports and Other Documents. Government transparency advocates, including some librarians, are concerned with OMB's extensive reach and the public's lack of knowledge about this blandly named federal agency. Such concerns are summarized on nonprofit foundation sites such as the Center for Effective Government http://foreffectivegov.org (a group monitoring OMB since 1983), in mainstream news articles, and in public policy literature. Reading the official OMBlog underscores OMB as implementer and enforcer of the president's vision. While not as partisan as Congress members' pages, OMBlog differs from the rest of OMB's site in that it contains less neutral content than might be expected from an executive agency; in Director Shaun Donovan's blog entry from April 30, 2015, for example, he critiques congressional Republicans, saying that their budget cut proposals take money away from working families and national security.

What Are the Requirements for Collecting Individual Data on Race and Ethnicity?

The OMB standards for data on race and ethnicity provide a minimum set of two categories for data on ethnicity:

- Hispanic or Latino and
- Not Hispanic or Latino,

and five categories for data on race collected from individuals:

- American Indian or Alaska Native,
- Asian,
- Black or African American,
- Native Hawaiian or Other Pacific Islander, and
- White.

Note: "other race" is not a response category. Respondents are to be offered the option of selecting one or more racial designations. Based on research findings, the recommended forms for the instruction are *Mark one or more, Select one or more,* or *Choose one or more* (not check all that apply).

Source: US Office of Management and Budget, 2006: 49–50.

OMB's function most evident to the public is the preparation of the federal budget, arguably one of the most essential documents of our time, both to the governed and the governing. Do not assume that newly appointed or elected officials understand the budget. University of Washington Associate Professor of Public Affairs Justin Marlowe authored a special July 2014 insert to *Governing* magazine precisely because so many public officials need to ramp up their finance skills rapidly (Kelly, 2014). When one imagines the physical publishing of the federal budget—its release is an annual media event—one needs to picture a multivolume set that does not have the same content or volume structure from year to year (it tends to vary by presidential administration). In recent decades, there was an effort to produce a citizen-friendly guide to the budget, so mere mortals could read a single-volume *Budget in Brief,* published annually from 1972 to 1990. (This content has been incorporated into the larger budget from 1991 forward.) A similar title, the *Citizen's Guide to the Federal Budget,* was published from 1996 to 2002. Most users will start by consulting the main volume, the *Budget of the United States.* To understand the budget by broad theme, the *Analytical Perspectives* volumes are useful; if seeking a time series back to 1940, try the *Historical*

CYBER SECURITY INITIATIVES

For necessary expenses for cyber security initiatives, including necessary upgrades to wide area network and information technology infrastructure, improvement of network perimeter controls and identity management, testing and assessment of information technology against business, security, and other requirements, implementation of Federal cyber security initiatives and information infrastructure enhancements, implementation of enhanced security controls on network devices, and enhancement of cyber security workforce training tools, [$5,000,000] *$8,000,000,* to remain available through September 30, [2016] *2017. (Department of Transportation Appropriations Act, 2015.)*

Program and Financing (in millions of dollars)

Identification code 069–0159–0–1–407	2014 actual	2015 est.	2016 est.
Obligations by program activity:			
0001 Cyber Security Initiatives (Direct)	9	8	8
0100 Direct program activities, subtotal	9	8	8
Budgetary resources:			
Unobligated balance:			
1000 Unobligated balance brought forward, Oct 1	8	3	....
Budget authority:			
Appropriations, discretionary:			
1100 Appropriation	4	5	8
1160 Appropriation, discretionary (total)	4	5	8

FIGURE 9.3
Funding in Billions of Dollars for the Department of Transportation's Cyber Security Initiatives

Tables. To get the most detail by agency, in a line-by-line format, consult the *Appendix.* The exact format of the budget has varied widely over the years. Remember that this is the president's proposed budget and not all sections will be passed by Congress. The president must submit the budget to Congress in February each year, and it is based on the coming federal fiscal year, or FY, running October 1 through September 30. Given the timing of the release of the budget (midway through the current fiscal year), plus the fact that amounts budgeted may not equal amounts ultimately appropriated or expended, the document presents different levels of precision based on the information available. For example, the FY 2016 budget includes *proposed* figures for FY 2016, *estimated* figures for FY 2015, and *actual* figures for FY 2014. Thus, for the current FY, the budget is primarily a *policy* document expressing the president's priorities (translated into budget dollars); the document's utility as a statistical source for real numbers applies only to earlier FYs that have "actual" dollars. Today, the budget is found at www.whitehouse.gov/omb/budget (try clicking through the historical tables with detail back to 1789) and via FDsys at www.gpo.gov/fdsys/browse/collectionGPO.action?collectionCode=BUDGET, where the "About the Budget" pages offer a useful overview of the process and its history. Or try GPO's mobile-optimized edition of the *Budget* at www.gpo.gov/mobile/. A more consumer-oriented (where is my money going?) approach can be found at Treasury's www.usaspending.gov.

Commerce Department

The US Department of Commerce (www.commerce.gov), which debuted as Commerce and Labor in 1903, and its subagencies and bureaus are key producers of government literature. First there are the sciences within Commerce: the National Institute of Standards and Technology (NIST); the National Oceanic and Atmospheric Administration (NOAA, addressed in chapter 14); the National Technical Information Service (NTIS, addressed in chapter 13); the National Telecommunications and Information Administration (NTIA); and the Patent and Trademark Office (USPTO) (chapter 17). Next are major economic, social science, and demographic publishers: the Bureau of the Census and the Bureau of Economic Analysis (BEA), both part of the Economics and Statistics Administration; see chapters 15 and 16. Here we will discuss some of the remaining agencies, the Bureau of Industry and Security (BIS), the International Trade Administration (ITA), and various online projects of the department.

The BIS monitors US exports, focusing on high technology and defense-related commodities that could increase a trading partner's military might. Its sister agency, the ITA, works to keep the United States strong in industry, trade and investment, promote fair trade, and ensure adherence to trade laws and agreements. Its Internet domain name reveals ITA's boiled-down purpose: www.trade.gov. The ITA is a more prolific publisher than the BIS, but examining both agencies' reports and documents shows the complexity of trade with other nations: the observance of treaties, the regulation of the flow of controlled commodities (including dangerous substances), and the enforcement of embargoes. USA Trade Online (https://usatrade.census.gov) focuses on import/export statistics, managed by the Census Bureau's Foreign Trade Division (covered in chapter 15). Additionally, the Department of Commerce is a core contributor to the free resources www.export.gov and www.tradestatsexpress.gov, addressed in chapter 15.

Defense Department

Maybe no other department website better captures our current government era than www.defense.gov. The military's vast social media sites (www.defense.gov/registeredsites/socialmediasites.aspx) demand attention as much as the links to the services (Joint Chiefs, Army, Marine Corps, Navy, Air Force, National Guard, and Coast Guard) or to the Unified Combatant Commands (Africa, Central, European, Northern, Pacific, Southern, Special Operations, Strategic, and Transportation). Thumbnail scroll panels surround a powerful central image, inviting users to explore photos, images, special reports, videos, and read Twitter updates from a recent briefing. A government institution usually characterized as the ultimate closed structure is transformed by the interactive Web. The promise of e-government is evident in many corners of the .mil domain.

The history of the United States military is the subject of innumerable books, studies, and documentary films. United States ground troops (Army) and naval and marine forces all date back to the country's founding (including the Continental Army of 1775); Congress established the Department of War in 1789 to coordinate all elements of wars. After World War II, the National Security Act of 1947 (P.L. 80-253, 61 Stat. 495) established the Department of Defense (DoD), originally (and briefly) called the National Military Establishment. The National Security Act Amendments of 1949 (P.L. 81-216, 63 Stat. 578) further delineated the new agency's structure, creating secretaries for the Army, Navy (including the Marine Corps), and newly established Air Force. The overall leadership structure today remains that of a civilian secretary of defense, three undersecretaries, and a nonvoting chair of the Joint Chiefs of Staff. The defense secretary also serves on the National Security Council, the highest-level forum on national security and foreign policy matters in the federal government. Today's Defense Department consists of more than 1.4 million active duty military personnel and 845,000 reserves. In today's gender-integrated military, the reports of the Defense Advisory Committee on Women in the Services, established in 1951, make excellent reading (Gender Studies librarians take note), see http://dacowits.defense.gov.

Since the DoD receives a notoriously large federal budget allocation ($581 billion in 2014), it is not surprising that its published output (found in libraries, at bookstores, and online) is substantial as well. Much DoD material concerns national security, may be highly technical or requires security clearance to access; such material falls outside the guidelines for wide distribution and cataloging via the depository library program or through sale to the general public. As with many other topic areas within government, it is still fascinating to see what *is* publicly released: material as far-ranging as poster-style prints of commemorative battle paintings; technical manuals (like the *Technical Manual for Batteries, Navy Lithium Safety Program Responsibilities and Procedures*); field manuals (like the classic *FM-76: Survival*); popular press items like *Soldiers* magazine; policy papers; innumerable pamphlets; recurrent reports on the nation's defense posture and world terrorism; and even music CDs from the United States Marine Band.

The Defense Department has its own publishing outlet for technical reports: the Defense Technical Information Center (DTIC), also addressed in chapter 13. DTIC offers an online index to its materials at www.dtic.mil/dtic/. DTIC's purpose is noted on the website,

> The Defense Technical Information Center (DTIC®) has served the infor-
> mation needs of the Defense community for more than 65 years. DTIC
> reports to the Assistant Secretary of Defense For Research and Engineering
> ASD(RE). Our mission is to provide essential, technical research, develop-
> ment, testing and evaluation (RDT&E) information rapidly, accurately and
> reliably to support our DoD customers' needs. More than 50 percent of the
> research records in the collection are available through the access controlled
> R&E Gateway, which is accessible to DoD personnel, defense contractors,
> federal government personnel and contractors, and selected academic insti-
> tutions . . . We also provide the general public and industry with access to
> unclassified, unlimited information, including many full-text downloadable
> documents, through this website. (DTIC, 2015)

Other agencies geared toward information gathering or dissemination are the Defense Information Systems Agency (www.disa.mil), the Defense Intelligence Agency, (www .dia.mil) and the National Geospatial-Intelligence Agency (NGA, www1.nga.mil). DISA is a combat support agency and safeguards the information systems serving US military operations, national leaders, and coalition partners; the DIA provides military intelligence for US military personnel, the Intelligence Community, and policy makers; and the National Geospatial-Intelligence Agency or NGA (formerly the Defense Map-ping Agency) develops imagery and cartographic intelligence resources for US naviga-tional and defense purposes. Chapter 13 (Scientific and Technical Information) touches on the world of military standards.

At least three military universities have played a major role in making military publi-cations more accessible to the general public, even if their primary objective is to assist the forces. First, in 1988, Air University began producing its online *Index to Military Periodicals* (www.dtic.mil/dtic/aulimp/). While it may not always link directly to the article's full text, it functions as a core index to 70 journals. The second is the *Staff College Automated Military Periodical Index* (www.dtic.mil/dtic/scampi/index.html), produced by the Joint Forces Staff College Ike Skelton Library. Third, the Naval Postgraduate School's Military Information research guide stands as one of the most useful library pages on this subject; see this and other subject guides at http://library.nps.edu/. The Naval Postgraduate School collaborates with the Department of Homeland Security in building and maintaining the *Homeland Security Digital Library* (HSDL), a virtual library of more than 160,000 documents culled from government sites and other content on the open Web. The materials are abstracted and brought together in a singularly use-ful collection built to aid first responders, academic researchers, and homeland security personnel. The HSDL is a respected core resource in government information today. Recently abstracted reports include the *National Security Implications of a Changing Cli-*

mate (www.hsdl.org/?view&did=765810) and the *2013 National Gang Report* (www
.hsdl.org/?abstract&did=762861).

Whether a user seeks academic content from a defense-related university, statistics on
military personnel, or annual reports of military subagencies, these materials are standard
depository library fare. Military history texts are some of the most appealing books distributed through the FDLP, with the publication quality of coffee-table books. Generally absent from the depository program are military newspapers, including the on-base
publication, *Stars and Stripes*. Libraries making special attempts to collect military newspapers have a particularly rich source of primary US historical material. World War I
military papers from the United States and other countries are included in a ProQuest
digital commercial product, *Trench Journals and Unit Magazines of the First World War*.
Military resources are expansive enough to warrant their own chapter or, indeed, book.
Professional organizations such as the Federal and Armed Forces Libraries Round Table
(FAFLRT) of the American Library Association and the Military Libraries Division of
the Special Libraries Association (founded in 1953) aim to foster continuing education
and believe that military libraries are essential to a strong defense.

State Department

The Department of State dates back to 1789. When one thinks of the State Department, what comes to mind? United States embassies all over the world, and foreign
embassies here in the United States? Diplomacy and the US Foreign Service? The issuing of passports and visas? The crafting of foreign policy? The admission of refugees?
All of these associations would be valid. Ask a government information specialist and
their first mental leap would be to State.gov as one of the government's most information rich and sophisticated online sites, customizable for users who wish to sign in
with their Yahoo, Google or other accounts via the MyStateDepartment service. For a
full list of *Major State Department Publications,* see www.state.gov/r/pa/ei/rls/dos/221
.htm. A small selection of these include the *Bilateral Relations Fact Sheets, Foreign Relations of the United States, Country Commercial Guides,* and *Country Reports on Human Rights
Practices.*

U.S. Bilateral Relations Fact Sheets, or simply *Fact Sheets,* previously known as *Background Notes* (www.state.gov/r/pa/ei/bgn/) are several-page overviews of individual
nations, compiled roughly annually; think of them as foreign relations cheat sheets.
Read the *Fact Sheet* on Ghana for a review of our formal relations with that country,
which began when Ghana gained independence in 1957. The profile for the US ambas-
sador is linked here as well as the address of Ghana's embassy in Washington, DC. The
Fact Sheet might even prompt the casual reader into an extended Internet diversion,
reading about Ghana's 10-year military partnership program with the North Dakota
National Guard!

The *Fact Sheet* links to State's landing page for Ghana: www.state.gov/p/af/ci/gh/.
From this page, with a Central Intelligence Agency (CIA) outline map and the Gha-
naian flag in the central pane, there are navigation links to the embassy, press releases,
Secretary of State's remarks on Ghana, African Development Foundation reports, and

the official State blog (DipNote) for Ghana http://blogs.state.gov/countries/ghana/. For factual information on the country, consult the links to the US Agency for International Development (USAID) projects in Ghana, the CIA *World Factbook* entry for Ghana, and the 382-page *Ghana: A Country Study* (sadly frozen in time in 1995 since the Library of Congress discontinued the much loved Area Handbooks series in 1998). The *CIA Factbook* is an indispensable reference book, an instant summary of the nation: its people, government, economy, political conditions, defense, transportation, and relations with the United States and other countries. One discovers that although English is the official language of Ghana, the next most widely spoken languages are Asante, Ewe, and Fanti, and the population of 25,758,108 is 71 percent Christian, in a nation slightly smaller than Oregon.

Suppose one wanted to dig into primary sources from US diplomatic history with Ghana, or any country. Look no further than another long-standing classic of government literature (back to 1861!), the *Foreign Relations of the United States (FRUS),* the world's first glimpse of diplomatic history as it unfolds. *FRUS* (http://history.state.gov/historicaldocuments/) is valuable enough that the release of new volumes is often covered by the news media, including the controversy surrounding the volumes released in 2001 regarding mid-1960s massacres in Indonesia. In *FRUS,* still issued in hardcover as well as online (and also included in the *Serial Set*), one finds now-declassified correspondence between top US and foreign officials. The whole world became more aware of the details transmitted via diplomatic wires in 2010 when over a quarter-million classified diplomatic cables were leaked in the Wikileaks "Cablegate" controversy (for ongoing coverage, see www.nytimes.com/interactive/world/statesecrets.html/). In recent years, *FRUS* content has included transcriptions from Oval Office audiotapes and material culled from a broader range of agencies, including the Intelligence Community (Department of State, Office of the Historian, 2010). The material included in *FRUS* has been declassified after a period of 30 years or more. In the case of Ghana, we can find a Confidential 1961 memo from Deputy Assistant Secretary of State for African Affairs (Mr. Penfield) to Assistant Secretary of State (Mr. Bowles). In it, Penfield explains that

> a withdrawal of the Western aluminum companies project would make it possible for the Soviets to create an extremely efficient aluminum production on the basis of what is considered the richest bauxite mine in the world and of the very cheap water power potential of the Konkoure River. (*Foreign Relations of the United States, 1961–1963, Volume XXI, Africa, Ghana:* 341)

FRUS has enjoyed an Internet life as a series picked up early for digitization. The University of Wisconsin Digital Collections offers a substantial portion of the series at http://uwdc.library.wisc.edu/collections/FRUS, a hundred-year span of nearly 400 volumes (1861–1960) to which one can add State's own offerings at https://history.state.gov/historicaldocuments (Truman to Carter administrations only) and the series was included in the *Serial Set* through the 1948 content, as well. Because the series is noncumulative, it is important for research libraries to retain every volume.

Country Commercial Guides. Preparing to open a new business venture in India, Peru, or Portugal? It would be wise to first consider if your product, service, or manufacturing plant is a good match for the local economy, and to consult the basic information vital to operating a business in those locales. To help foster well-informed American business ventures abroad, the State Department (in partnership with the ITA's US Commercial Service and other agencies) maintains up-to-date guides on the business climate of every nation. The Botswana *Guide,* for instance, reveals that the agriculture subsector commodities that are currently most in demand are "grains, dairy farming, pet foods, health foods, food service, ostrich farming and processing, leather, and fish farming" (Commercial Service, 2014: 30).

Country Reports on Human Rights Practices. Accurate reporting from the field is a critical component in the growing international attention to human rights. Since 1975, the State Department has compiled and submitted to Congress an annual report on the progress made in human liberty and dignity in various countries (not every country is included). The department collaborates with nongovernmental groups such as Amnesty International in bringing together verifiable accounts of each country's general treatment of women, children, and those arrested or imprisoned, as well as inhumane incidents known to have occurred since the previous edition. Although this is some of the most sobering reading within the government documents canon, it is important to know where to find even the grim truth. In Djibouti, the disturbing reality of female genital mutilation, as well as the efforts to end it, is noted. For Australia, the 2013 report noted, "657 anti-Semitic incidents, compared with 543 during the previous 12 months. These incidents included physical and verbal assaults, such as Jewish persons walking to and from synagogues being pelted with eggs; vandalism; and harassment" (Department of State, 2014: 17).

From State's home page, a user can go just about anywhere, browsing by country, foreign policy issue, and broad topic. Along with a substantial Media Center, Secretary of State's page, mobile-optimized documents, and offerings for youth or those interested in a diplomatic career, the site is critical for anyone traveling abroad, as it contains travel advisories and explicit directions on visas and passports. It even hosts a page about the United States, aimed at travelers here http://go.usa.gov/3gtfV.

Foreign Broadcast Information Service (FBIS) and the Joint Publications Research Service (JPRS)

The CIA administers another important cache of foreign relations material. For decades, its Foreign Broadcast Information Service (FBIS) has translated into English the radio, television, and newswire service broadcasts of non-English speaking countries. Such broadcasts often reveal pointed criticisms of US policies and useful intelligence about the conditions of everyday life in a specific country.

The FBIS translations are known as *Daily Reports.* In the early period (1941–1976), they were published five days a week in aggregated volumes, but from 1974–1996, the releases (divided into parts) corresponded to eight geographic areas covering the world. The reports have a unique numbering system. The format of the *Daily Reports* and its index changed multiple times over the years, making for a confusing mix: print (somewhat poor quality), microfiche, CD-ROM, then online through a database, *World News Connection (WNC),* which ceased December 31, 2013. The years 1941–1996 are now offered as a full text digital resource from Readex/NewsBank, broken into the year breakdown indicated above, with extra publications known as Annexes available as well. East View Information Services offers a full text digital subscription access to the *WNC* era archive, 1996–2013. One can also find some of the *Daily Reports* digitized at HathiTrust.

A similar operation within the CIA, the Joint Publications Research Service (JPRS) translated foreign government and industrial writings. Its reports were issued in print, then microfiche, from 1957–1995. It is now available as a full text digital subscription from Readex/NewsBank.

Conclusion

This chapter explored executive branch structure, noting cabinet-level departments, independent agencies, and a vast array of administratively linked entities and aids to find out about their mission and publications. We reviewed typical categories of publications (annual reports, handbooks, circulars, and more) and how to find historical documents (asking first "Was it published before 1976?" and "Could it have been published as part of the *Serial Set?*" and "Was it published outside the depository library program?"). We discussed the complexity of the current online environment, looking to end-of-term web-harvesting projects as a conceptual framing device to think about the high numbers of public interest documents residing on federal government servers. Many federal publications are no longer documents per se, but are constantly updated, customizable, or interactive online resources, databases, or repositories.

We looked to three federal departments (Commerce, Defense, and State) for a more focused introduction to government literature and the importance of an agency's mission to its publishing output. We discussed the role of the Office of Management and Budget and learned about the several different volumes of the *Budget of the United States*.

Output from the executive branch of government will be forever linked to the lives of the American citizens, as agencies—established, authorized, and funded by the people's legislature—aim to meet the challenges of our current age.

> **Did You Know? Academic Librarians and the State Department, 1990's Style**
>
> Early in its Internet history, the Department of State entered into an official GPO-recognized partnership with the University of Illinois at Chicago (UIC) to electronically archive its Web content, known as the Foreign Affairs Network (FAN). The DOSFAN project http://dosfan.lib.uic.edu/ERC/ was an early prototype of a public university helping with preservation of online government content. In addition to archiving many of State's electronic publications and web pages from 1990 to 1997, librarians at UIC helped answer informational questions about the Department of State in the days before websites included extensive FAQ and Ask Us pages.

Exercises

1. Search a library's online catalog for official government information concerning the response to Hurricane Sandy. List the names of the various agencies whose publications you found. How does this list differ from a search you might perform on the open Web, if you were to limit your search to the .gov and .mil domains?

2. Download organizational charts of the federal government and your state government on your phone or tablet. Quiz your friends and family; the same people who can name cities and their sports teams should be able to name the cabinet-level agencies in the federal and state government. If they are proficient, ask if they can name any of their local county or city government agencies.

3. Using DTIC and other government resources, what information can you find about the use of animals in military service, historically and currently?

4. Using the agency list at www.USA.gov, pick an agency with which you are unfamiliar. How easy is the website to use from a mobile device? For the agency chosen, can you locate the following on its official website? (Check all that apply.)

    ☐ Agency statutory authority
    ☐ Agency budget information, current and historical
    ☐ Apps
    ☐ Publications
    ☐ Streaming media

5. Using a list of either federal or state cabinet-level departments, select a department and imagine the possible consequences of eliminating that agency from government structure entirely (example: Department of Energy). Keeping your response nonpolitical, brainstorm probable changes to everyday life based on the absence of this particular agency. Consider impacts on the following dimensions: human health and safety, everyday conveniences, financial security, science and technology, information-seeking in this subject area, general provision of service in this area (i.e., where people might turn for needed services, if not the federal/state government).

Laws Mentioned in This Chapter (Chronological Order)

Public Printing and Binding Act. P.L. 59-153, 34 Stat. 186, Chap. 2448 (1907).
An Act To Incorporate the Boy Scouts of America. P.L. 64-94, 39 Stat. 227, Chap. 148 (1916).
National Security Act of 1947, P.L. 80-253, 61 Stat. 495 (1947).
The National Security Act Amendments of 1949, P.L. 81-216, 63 Stat. 578, (1949).
Postal Reorganization Act of 1970, P.L. 91-375, 84 Stat. 719 (1970).
Paperwork Reduction Act, P.L. 96-511, 92 Stat. 1783 (1980).
Homeland Security Act, P.L. 107-296, 116 Stat. 2135 (2002).

Sources Mentioned in This Chapter

Sources mentioned in this section do not duplicate the references that follow.

Agency Series Found in the Serial Set, College of Wooster Libraries, http://libguides.wooster.edu/congressionalserialsetfindinglist.
Analytical Perspectives, www.gpo.gov/fdsys/browse/collectionGPO.action? collectionCode=BUDGET/.
Andriot, see *Guide to U.S. Government Publications.*

Budget in Brief, 1972–1990, http://fraser.stlouisfed.org/publications/usbib/.

Budget of the United States, www.gpo.gov/fdsys/browse/collectionGPO action?collectionCode=BUDGET/.

Bureau of Industry and Security, www.bis.doc.gov.

Catalog of Government Publications, http://catalog.gpo.gov.

Center for Effective Government. http://foreffective gov.org.

Central Intelligence Agency, 1971—. *World Factbook,* www.cia.gov/library/publications/
the-world-factbook/.

*CIS Index to U.S. Executive Branch Documents, 1789–1909: Guide to Documents Listed in Checklist of U.S.
Public Documents, 1789–1909, Not Included in the U.S. Serial Set.* 1990. Bethesda, MD: Congressional
Information Service.

*CIS Index to U.S. Executive Branch Documents, 1910–1932: Guide to Documents Not Printed in the U.S.
Serial Set. 1996.* Bethesda, MD: Congressional Information Service.

Citizen's Guide to the Federal Budget, 1996–2002, www.gpoaccess.gov/usbudget/citizensguide.html.

Country Commercial Guides, www.buyusainfo.net.

Country Reports on Human Rights Practices, www.state.gov/j/drl/rls/hrrpt/.

Defense Advisory Committee on Women in the Services (DACOWITS), http://dacowits.defense.gov/.

Defense Information Systems Agency, www.disa.mil.

Defense Intelligence Agency, www.dia.mil.

Defense Technical Information Center, www.dtic.mil/dtic/.

Department of Commerce, www.commerce.gov.

Department of Defense, www.defense.gov.

Department of Health and Human Services. 1999. *Shoes and Socks, Take 'Em Off! If You Have Diabetes,
Have your Doctor Check Your Feet.* Bethesda, MD: US Department of Health and Human Services.

Department of State, www.state.gov.

Department of the Army. 1869–1976. *Army Register.* Washington, DC: Government Printing Office. Also
issued as a House document in the *Serial Set,* 1896–1969.

DipNote, http://blogs.state.gov.

DOSFAN (Electronic Research Collections), http://dosfan.lib.uic.edu/ERC/.

Executive Office of the President, www.whitehouse.gov/administration/eop/.

Federal and Armed Forces Libraries Round Table of the American Library Association, www.ala.org/faflrt/.

Federal Staff Directory. 2009. Mt. Vernon, VA: Staff Directories.

Federal Yellow Book. 2010. New York and Washington, DC: Leadership Directories.

Foreign Broadcast Information Service Daily Reports, 1941–1996 (description only), www.readex.com/
content/foreign-broadcast-information-service-fbis-daily-reports-1941–1996.

Foreign Relations of the United States, http://digital.library.wisc.edu/1711.dl/FRUS and http://history
.state.gov/historicaldocuments/.

Guide to U.S. Government Publications. 1973–. Detroit: Gale Cengage Learning.

Historical Tables (*Budget of the United States*), www.gpo.gov/fdsys/browse/collectionGPO.action?collection
Code=BUDGET.

Internal Revenue Service, www.irs.gov.

International Trade Administration, www.trade.gov.

Joint Publications Research Service Reports, 1957–1995 (description only), www.readex.com/content/
joint-publications-research-service-jprs-reports-1957–1995.

Less Access to Less Information by and about the U.S. Government, www.ala.org/ala/issuesadvocacy/
advocacy/federallegislation/govinfo/lessaccess/index.cfm.

List of Classes of United States Government Publications Available for Selection by Depository Libraries, www
.fdlp.gov/file-repository/collection-management/list-of-classes.

Military Libraries Division of the Special Libraries Association, http://units.sla.org/division/dmil/.

National Geospatial-Intelligence Agency, www1.nga.mil.

Non-Depository Government Publications, 1953–2008. Chester, VT: Readex.

Office of Management and Budget, www.whitehouse.gov/omb/.

Office of Management and Budget: Agency Information, www.whitehouse.gov/omb/agency/default/.

Pentagon Channel, www.pentagonchannel.mil.

ProQuest Statistical Insight, American Statistics Index, http://statistical.proquest.com.

ProQuest Trench Journals and Unit Magazines of the First World War (description only), www.proquest.com/products-services/trench.html.

Stars and Stripes, http://estripes.osd.mil.

U.S. Bilateral Relations Fact Sheets, www.state.gov/r/pa/ei/bgn/index.htm.

US *Congressional Serial Set,* www.gpo.gov/help/u.s._congressional_serial_set.htm.

US *Congressional Serial Set* Finding Guide, www3.wooster.edu/library/Gov/serialset/main.htm.

U.S. Government Annual Report, www.fms.treas.gov/annualreport/index.html.

U.S. Government Manual, www.gpo.gov/fdsys/browse/collection.action?collectionCode=GOVMAN/ or www.usgovernmentmanual.gov.

U.S. Government Policy and Supporting Positions, also known as the Plum Book, www.gpo.gov/fdsys/.

USA Trade Online, https://usatrade.census.gov.

USA.gov's A–Z list of agencies, www.usa.gov/directory/federal/index.shtml.

World News Connection (description only), www.eastview.com/online/globeonline.

WorldCat, www.worldcat.org.

References

Batten, Donna, ed. 2016. *Guide to U.S. Government Publications.* ed. Detroit: Gale Cengage Learning.

Bledsoe, W. Craig, and Leslie Rigby. 1997a. "The Cabinet and Executive Departments." In *Cabinets and Counselors: The President and the Executive Branch,* 2nd ed., 73–140. Washington, DC: CQ Press.

Bledsoe, W. Craig, and Leslie Rigby. 1997b. "Government Agencies and Corporations." In *Cabinets and Counselors: The President and the Executive Branch,* 2nd ed., 141–179. Washington, DC: CQ Press.

Bureau of Industry and Security. 2014. *Annual Report to the Congress for Fiscal Year 2014.* www.bis.doc.gov/index.php/about-bis/newsroom/publications.

Carpenter, Daniel. 2005. "The Evolution of National Bureaucracy in the United States." In *The Executive Branch,* edited by Joel D. Aberbach and Mark A Peterson, 41–71. Oxford; New York: Oxford University Press.

Commercial Service. 2014. *Doing Business in Botswana: A Country Commercial Guide for U.S. Companies,* www.buyusainfo.net/docs/x_633206.pdf.

Defense Technical Information Center. 2015. "About DTIC." www.dtic.mil/dtic/about/about.html.

Department of State, Office of the Historian. 2010. "About the Foreign Relations of the United States Series." http://history.state.gov/historicaldocuments/about-frus.

Department of State. 2014. "Country Reports on Human Rights Practices," Australia. www.state.gov/j/drl/rls/hrrpt/humanrightsreport/index.htm?year=2013&dlid=220179.

Foreign Relations of the United States, 1961–1963, Volume XXI, Africa, Ghana. 1995. http://history.state.gov/historicaldocuments/frus1961–63v21/pg_341.

Gormley, William, and Steven Balla. 2008. *Bureaucracy and Democracy: Accountability and Performance.* Washington, DC: CQ Press.

Huffman, J. Ford, and Tammy S. Schultz. 2012. *The end of Don't Ask Don't Tell: the impact in studies and personal essays by service members and veterans.* Quantico, VA: Marine Corps University Press. http://purl.fdlp.gov/GPO/gp023387.

Jacobs, James A. 2014. *Born-Digital U.S. Government Information: Preservation and Access.* Prepared for *Leviathan,* the Center for Research Libraries Global Resources Collections Forum. March 17. www.crl .edu/node/10225.

Kelly, Peter. 2014. "Budget or bust: Primer on public finance teaches government officials the basics." *UW Today.* July 25. www.washington.edu/news/2014/07/25/budget-or-bust-primer-on-public-finance -teaches-government-officials-the-basics/.

Lavertu, Stéphane. 2010. "Contemporary Bureaucracy: An Overview." *A History of the U.S. Political System: Ideas, Interests, and Institutions.* Ed. Richard A. Harris and Daniel J. Tichenor. Vol. 1, 391–405. Santa Barbara, CA: ABC-CLIO. *Gale Virtual Reference Library.*

Moe, Ronald C., and Kevin R. Kosar. 2005. *The Quasi-Government: Hybrid Organizations with Both Government and Private Sector Legal Characteristics.* Washington DC: Library of Congress, Congressional Research Service. May 18. http://digital.library.unt.edu/ark:/67531/metacrs6224.

Murray, Iain, and David Bier. 2011. "Do We Really Need a National Weather Service?" *FoxNews.Com.* www.foxnews.com/opinion/2011/08/27/do-really-need-national-weather-service/.

National Institute for Occupational Safety and Health. 2008. *Investigation of Employee Symptoms at an Indoor Waterpark* (HETA 2007–0163–3062). Washington, DC: National Institute for Occupational Safety and Health. June. www.cdc.gov/niosh/hhe/reports/pdfs/2007–0163–3062.pdf.

National Institute for Occupational Safety and Health. 2010. *Reducing Illnesses at Indoor Waterparks* (DHHS (NIOSH) Publication No. 2010–138). Washington, DC: National Institute for Occupational Safety and Health. March 2010. www.cdc.gov/ niosh/docs/wp-solutions/2010–138/pdfs/2010–138.pdf.

Office of Management and Budget. 2000. "OMB Bulletin No. 00–02: Guidance on Aggregation and Allocation of Data on Race for Use in Civil Rights Monitoring and Enforcement." March 9. www .whitehouse.gov/omb/bulletins_b00–02/.

Office of Management and Budget. 2006. "Memorandum for the President's Management Council: Guidance on Agency Survey and Statistical Information Collections." January 20. www.whitehouse .gov/sites/default/files/omb/assets/omb/inforeg/pmc_survey_guidance_2006.pdf.

Relyea, Harold C. 2008. *The Executive Office of the President: An Historical Overview* (Order Code 98–606 GOV). November 26. Washington, DC: US Congressional Research Service. www.fas.org/sgp/crs/ misc/98–606.pdf.

Schmidt, Steffen, Mack Shelley, and Barbara Bardes. 2009. *American Government and Politics Today, 2009–2010 edition.* Australia and Boston: Wadsworth Cengage Learning.

Sevetson, Andrea, ed. 2013. *The Serial Set: Its Make-up and Content.* Bethesda, MD: ProQuest.

CHAPTER 10

Statistical Information

AMY WEST AND ERIC FORTE

Introduction

How much statistical information does the US government produce each year? Well, at least 127 federal agencies engage in $500,000 or more of statistical activities, with 13 of them classified as primary statistical agencies (Office of Management and Budget, 2014). Data.gov has records for over 120,000 datasets from 83 agencies and it's not even comprehensive (Federal Agency Participation, n.d.)! While knowing how many agencies engage in statistical activities might be useful at bar trivia, perhaps we can say something more concrete and helpful about the scope of the government's statistical activities.

The US government, often in concert with state and local governments, collects at least a little bit of data on just about every possible thing. Datasets that leap to mind include the currently estimated number of galaxies, births, deaths, marriages, earthquakes, commute times, oil prices, expenditures on dining out, skateboard injuries, hours of sleep we get, air pollution, and national park visits.

The volume and variety of US statistical information make it a different kind of challenge to work with. For comparison, consider working with legislative information (chapter 3, Congressional Publications). There are specific types of documentation produced at specific points in the legislative process, and the primary challenge is remembering the sequence and the sources. That's not a trivial task and takes time and practice, but still, it's something you can ultimately have confidence that you've mastered.

Statistical information has different characteristics: very few datasets are as reliably published as legislative materials, there are many more of them, and they don't adhere to a single calendar or process. There is neither a central statistical agency overseeing statistics and data government-wide, nor a single database to search for all government data and statistics. *Don't panic!* There's good news, too: government statistics are increasingly easy to find with standard web tools, specialized tools are improving, and today's librarians have multiple networks of colleagues to call on for help.

This chapter will introduce the underlying mechanisms of data gathering, cover the overview publication *Statistical Programs of the United States Government,* briefly describe the 13 primary statistical agencies, and offer recommended strategies for finding US government statistical information in general. By the end of the chapter, you should feel comfortable handling (which does not necessarily meaning *answering*) requests for assistance such as

- Where do I look for statistics on welfare?
- I'm looking for US steel production from 1880–present.
- What percentage of US children are vaccinated?

Who Collects Data?

Data is being collected all around us—from the loyalty cards we have for our favorite stores, our online purchasing habits, work commutes, crime statistics, and emergency room visits. You name it, and data is being collected to better inform what should be stocked on the shelves, advertised to your computer, how often the buses or trains should run, and how the coffee shop and hospital should be staffed. While many data gathering efforts have their origins in the private sector and in trade, research, or interest groups, governments are the origin of many of our most core statistical data.

In the United States, the authority for every government counting effort should have its origin somewhere in the Constitution or in subsequent laws passed by Congress. Take the Census Bureau, for example. Its statistical duties go well beyond the decennial census. A law from 1954 is still on the books (amending earlier laws from the 1920s) requiring the Census Bureau to "collect and publish statistics concerning the amount of cotton ginned" (13 U.S.C. § 41). This type of specificity from Congress is not necessarily the rule. It's more common for Congress to establish some broader goals, such as those that lead to the plethora of surveys and reports that the Census Bureau produces about social and economic characteristics. It is often useful to understand the authorizing law for specific statistical efforts to better understand the reasons behind them.

How Statistics Are Gathered

It is also extremely useful to understand how the data is compiled. Such understanding not only informs efforts to find and use statistics, it helps determine if the data is even likely to exist. Governments use three general counting methods: collecting statistical samples via surveys; conducting a census (which may be a survey but is asked of every instance of a population, and is a complete enumeration); and aggregating administrative records.

A statistical sample is a subset of the potential population about which data is to be gathered, where participants are chosen by some random method, and which is large enough to yield survey results considered statistically accurate for the desired larger population. Although there are dozens of different, ongoing government statistical samples, many citizens may go a lifetime without ever being asked to participate in a government survey outside of the decennial census. Still, such surveys yield highly accurate statistical portraits. Consider the largest effort to measure health indicators of Americans, the annual National Health Interview Survey (NHIS, the source of many basic statistics about the health of Americans). The NHIS surveys approximately 35,000 households annually, covering some 87,000 people. Participants answer a series of questions regarding their health and their demographic characteristics. While this sample of 87,000 people equates to just three out of every 100,000 people, the sample size is nonetheless large enough to provide statistically sound health data for the whole nation and subset groupings by some basic demographic characteristics, such as race, sex, age group, and income range. Similarly, the government surveys prices of a sample of consumer products (rather than trying to measure the price of every single product!) in order to measure inflation.

Note that while the random sample is conducted to ensure that no geographic area or region is overly represented (we wouldn't, for instance want 80,000 of the 87,000 people surveyed to be from the West Coast, and then claim that represents the entire nation), the sample is *not* large enough to provide data for specific states, cities, or smaller geographic entities. If you want data on the health of the people of Topeka, Kansas (a city of a bit more than 100,000 people), those three interviews are not nearly enough to learn anything about the health of the city's entire population. This is a key point: the smaller the geographic area, the less likely it is that you can find statistics about it. Like the National Health Interview Survey, most statistics based on samples are big enough to provide data only for the United States as a whole, or sometimes for a United States region (such as Northeast, West, South, or Midwest). The same sample is likely too small to yield sound data for states, and it would definitely be too small to yield data for cities.

A census, on the other hand, is a complete enumeration, which means every single instance is counted. Among statistics about the entire US population, the decennial census is the only complete enumeration of the US population (it being no small feat to ask over 300 million people questions), although the Census Bureau also conducts censuses of every *business* in the country. These are therefore unique in that data about every single person or business, rather than just a sample, is counted. The difference is significant: in the large sample above three in every 100,000 people were asked; in the population census, all 100,000 are asked. Overall, the census (covered in even more detail in chapter 16) asks questions of over 100 million households, covering over 300 million people. That's a lot of tick marks.

While a census is much more laborious (and thus more costly) than a survey, the upside to all those tick marks is the ability to get detailed information about smaller geographic entities, something a survey sample cannot do. Not only can one get census statistics about the people in states, counties, cities, and small towns, but one can even go down to ZIP codes and smaller census units called census tracts (neighborhood sized), block groups (yes, like a group of some city blocks) and census blocks (more or less equivalent to a single city block). So to apply the geographic lesson that we just learned:

if you need data for these small geographic entities and you can see that the data was covered in the decennial census, you might be in luck.

The third category, administrative records, usually acts more as a complete enumeration, albeit one with some specific audience or subject. Much data is collected in the course of conducting government business, and a great deal of this data is often compiled and published. For instance, new US citizens are counted this way. Governments also coordinate collection of birth and death statistics in cooperation with hospitals and county health departments, leading to, among other data, statistics on the cause of death. Nearly everyone files taxes, so data on tax revenue from IRS statistics is based on everyone's taxes (not just a sample). Grant makers keep track of awards, so one can find data on recipients of research funding from the National Institutes of Health. The Social Security Administration keeps data on all the checks it sends out—whether for social security, welfare programs, or disability programs—data which is compiled into aggregate statistical data. Governments also collect much scientific data, such as hourly weather conditions; daily pollution samples; nearly real-time stream flow data; and endless sets of cartographic, seismological, meteorological, and other scientific data. Like the decennial census, a few government surveys are mandatory to answer. Some business statistics are collected this way, as are many educational statistics—schools are sent surveys every year and the data collected and published. All told, governments have numerous administrative functions that yield useful data.

An important point to note is that in almost every government statistical undertaking, confidentiality of respondents is required by law. For instance, one cannot find out the identity of a particular living respondent to a government survey. This goes for individuals and businesses; just as one cannot see the individual answers to a survey of a private citizen, nor can one see the individual answers from a private business. The same is true of administrative records. For instance, even when political candidates show the public their tax returns, they do it by choice; citizens cannot ask for or view such personal information. Not every government data collection is confidential, however. Most contributions to political candidates are required by law to be public. And the most notable, partial exception is the decennial census: those records become public 72 years after each census. For instance, if a patron's grandmother is 95 years old, it's possible to go back and access the 1940 census schedules (the actual forms used to gather data) and see what her family filled out, names and all. This and the ability to access a few other types of government records (such as old immigration forms, with which one could research the same grandmother's immigration paperwork) are essentially genealogical questions rather than statistical questions. For more about genealogical/historical research, see chapter 18.

How Statistical Data Is Compiled: Microdata

Finally, before we begin to understanding the key statistical agencies, the actual details of data collection are illuminating and increasingly important when finding government statistical information, and it can be informative to understand the route from the 'data'—by which we mean the immediate, complete results from a statistical gathering operation—to statistics, by which we mean data collated and formatted into something most anyone could reasonably read and interpret. In early years, before technological improvements, statistical compilation was actually done by making tick marks and adding them up. And while the concept of counting is unchanged, technology now allows those tick marks to be tabulated by computer. A basic understanding of the difference between these tick marks (the raw data, also called microdata) and the tables that are eventually published is of increasing importance, for "when quantitative analysis lies behind a reference question, anxiety and confusion can color even the most competent reference librarian's response" (Gerhan, 1999: 166).

At a glance, it's not too complicated. Generally, data from a survey is entered and coded into microdata files, essentially very large, and not clearly defined, spreadsheets. For instance, examine a tiny piece of the microdata for 2007's National Health Interview Survey (figure 10.1). Each row of numbers corresponds to one respondent; each column corresponds to one question; and a "codebook" or some other documentation explains what each column represents. In this case, the first two columns for all 10 respondents in the example below is "30," which the NHIS codebook identifies as meaning they are in the "Adult Sample." The next four digits identify the year of the survey, all "2007," and so on.

Our abbreviated, sample microdata file includes, among others, the following data:

- Column 39 specifies sex (labeled u; 1 for male, 2 for female).
- Columns 48–49 specify age (labeled vv, in years).
- Column 50 specifies marital status (labeled w, many values; for what is included below, "1" specifies married and living with spouse, "5" divorced, "6" never married, "7" separated).
- Columns 709–710 specify, for smokers, the number of cigarettes smoked per day (labeled xx).
- Columns 722–723 specify number of times of vigorous exercise per week (labeled yy; "95" means never).
- Columns 781–782 specify the number of hours of sleep per night (labeled zz).

Further columns specify geographic location, race, and hundreds of other health indicators about each person. Remember, this abbreviated raw data is just a tiny bit of the file, equivalent to a postage stamp on a basketball court. The example includes only some 50 columns; the actual file includes over 1,000 uninterrupted columns representing the answers to the many questions. Vertically, meanwhile, this abbreviated sample includes only 12 respondents, a far cry from the 87,000 in the actual sample.

A statistician or data expert using statistical software could take the raw file shown here and using the documentation, pull out data by a nearly infinite range of criteria and turn it into something we could read. Figure 10.2 shows a snapshot of selected data including those defined in figure 10.1.

Most users, however, are not experts with statistical software packages and are unable to easily go from the raw data to usable data as done in figure 10.2. Instead, we seek and

```
                                  u              vvw         xx       yy       zz
    30200700000211  \   6403177012120101 01721  \  00   /   95   \   11
    30200700000910  /   1573128021120202 02601  /  00   \   03   /   08
    30200700001110  \   3523209021120303 03421  \  30   /   95   \   06
    30200700001210  /   7924271022120101 01621  /  00   \   95   /   08
    30200700001310  \   7303180011120101 01625  \  00   /   95   \   07
    30200700001611  /   0033170021120101 01321  /  00   \   03   /   08
    30200700001810  \   9351047021120101 01416  \  09   /   95   \   06
    30200700002011  /   2182081021120101 01311  /  00   \   00   /   07
    30200700003311  \   7383131012120101 01491  \  00   /   95   \   06
    30200700003411  /   3651041021120101 01587  /  40   \   95   /   06
    30200700003810  /   7351941021120101 01297  \  20   /   95   \   08
    30200700004011  /   9653441022120101 01197  /  10   \   07   /   03
```

FIGURE 10.1
A Small Extract of Microdata from *National Health Interview Survey Sample Adult File*
Source: www.cdc.gov/NCHS/nhis/nhis_2007_data_release.htm.

Sample?	Year?	Sex	Age	Marital Status	If smoker, cigarettes/day	Vigorous exercise: times/wk.	Sleep: hours/night
30	2007	2	72	1	—	95	11
30	2007	1	60	1	—	3	8
30	2007	1	42	1	30	95	6
30	2007	2	62	1		95	8
30	2007	1	62	5		95	7
30	2007	1	32	1		3	8
30	2007	1	41	6	9	95	6
30	2007	1	39	1		0	7
30	2007	2	49	1		95	6
30	2007	1	59	7	40	95	6
30	2007	1	29	7	20	95	8
30	2007	2	19	7	10	7	3

FIGURE 10.2
Small Microdata Extract Transformed into a Readable Chart

rely on published output from the agency. The data culled from the National Health Interview Survey is the basis for many published reports and statistical tables. So figure 10.3 is just one table from the report *Health, United States,* which is the National Center for Health Statistics' flagship annual statistical publication. *Health, United States* features key results from the NHIS and numerous other surveys and data collection efforts.

Table 73 (page 1 of 2). Leisure-time physical activity among adults 18 years of age and over, by selected characteristics: United States, 1998, 2005, and 2006

[Data are based on household interviews of a sample of the civilian noninstitutionalized population]

This table has been updated since the printed book

Click here for spreadsheet version

Characteristic	Inactive[1]			Some leisure-time activity[1]			Regular leisure-time activity[1]		
	1998	2005	2006	1998	2005	2006	1998	2005	2006
	Percent of adults								
18 years and over, age-adjusted[2,3]	40.5	40.5	39.5	30.0	29.3	29.5	29.5	30.2	31.0
18 years and over, crude[3]	40.2	40.5	39.5	30.0	29.3	29.6	29.8	30.1	30.9
Age									
18–44 years	35.2	35.9	34.9	31.4	30.5	30.4	33.5	33.7	34.6
18–24 years	32.8	33.5	34.8	30.1	29.1	27.1	37.1	37.4	38.1
25–44 years	35.9	36.7	35.0	31.8	31.0	31.6	32.4	32.4	33.4
45–64 years	41.2	41.2	39.7	30.6	29.7	30.8	28.2	29.1	29.5
45–54 years	38.9	39.5	38.2	31.4	30.1	30.7	29.8	30.4	31.1
55–64 years	44.9	43.6	41.9	29.3	29.2	30.9	25.8	27.2	27.2
65 years and over	55.4	53.9	53.4	24.7	24.9	24.5	19.9	21.3	22.0
65–74 years	49.1	47.8	48.0	26.5	27.0	25.8	24.4	25.3	26.2
75 years and over	63.3	60.6	59.6	22.4	22.6	23.1	14.3	16.8	17.3
Sex[2]									
Male.	37.8	39.1	38.5	28.7	29.2	28.4	33.5	31.8	33.1
Female.	42.9	41.7	40.3	31.1	29.5	30.7	26.0	28.8	29.0
Sex and age									
Male:									
18–44 years.	32.0	34.4	34.2	30.7	30.5	28.8	37.2	35.1	36.9
45–54 years.	37.7	40.2	39.0	29.6	29.4	28.4	32.6	30.4	32.7
55–64 years.	44.5	43.4	41.1	26.9	28.0	30.6	28.6	28.7	28.2

FIGURE 10.3
Table 73 from *Health, United States,* 2007

Statistical Programs of the United States Government

The publication *Statistical Programs of the United States Government* (or simply *Statistical Programs*) provides an overview of US statistical information gathering. It identifies what it calls the 13 primary statistical agencies and provides overviews of the statistical programs and any budget increases or decreases that would cause changes to statistical programs for all executive branch cabinet-level agencies, as well as very short overviews of a few additional agencies such as the Environmental Protection Agency (EPA) and Institute for Museum and Library Services. To be a primary statistical agency is to be "an agency or organizational unit of the executive branch whose activities are predominantly the collection, compilation, processing, or analysis of information for statistical purposes" (Office of Management and Budget, 2014). These agencies, organized by parent agency, are:

Department of Agriculture
- Economic Research Service
- National Agricultural Statistics Service

Department of Commerce
- Bureau of Economic Analysis
- Census Bureau

Department of Education
- National Center for Education Statistics

Department of Energy
- Energy Information Administration

Department of Health and Human Services
- National Center for Health Statistics

Department of Justice
- Bureau of Justice Statistics

Department of Labor
- Bureau of Labor Statistics

Department of Transportation
- Bureau of Transportation Statistics

Department of the Treasury
- Internal Revenue Service

Social Security Administration
- Office of Research, Evaluation and Statistics

National Science Foundation
- National Center for Science and Engineering Statistics

Missing from this list are the departments of Defense, Homeland Security, Housing and Urban Development, Interior, State and Veterans Affairs. Does this mean these agencies don't produce and publish considerable amounts of data? Of course not, but none of them includes a subagency that meets the very specific criteria for a "primary statistical agency program." Instead, they have program missions that support statistical information-tion gathering as a secondary activity.

An indirect, but important use of *Statistical Programs* is to demonstrate that statistics don't just happen. Agencies collect data and publish statistics because a funded program exists for that purpose. Funded programs come out of the federal budget process, for example, as a result of legislative action. The work an agency carries out is either a reflection of what legislators think is important or what legislators don't consider important enough to defund. To put it another way, US government statistical information is inherently political from start to finish, an idea we will return to in the last section of this chapter.

If statistical information gathering originates from congressional funding/action, then so should its discontinuation. Since *Statistical Programs,* from the perspective of its authoring agency, is a budget document, it includes information on statistical information gathering activities that have ceased due to flat or reduced budgets for those agencies it covers. You can see all three elements in action in this excerpt from the section on the Bureau of Labor Statistics (BLS):

> BLS, of the Department of Labor (DOL), is a principal source of Federal labor and safety statistics. BLS is responsible for measuring labor market activity, working conditions, and price changes in the economy. BLS collects, processes, analyzes, and disseminates data on: employment and unemployment; projections of the labor force and employment by industry and occupation; prices and inflation at various. levels of the economy; consumer expenditures; wages and employee benefits; occupational injuries and illnesses; and productivity and technological change in U.S. industries . . .
> The FY 2014 appropriation of $592.2 million for BLS was $21.6 million below the FY 2014 President's request and $15 million above the FY 2013 appropriation. At this funding level, BLS curtailed the Quarterly Census of Employment and Wages program. (Office of Management and Budget, 2014)

Counting conservatively, this one paragraph describes 18 different datasets BLS creates, and indicates that one BLS program will be decreasing its efforts in the coming fiscal year. True, it doesn't tell *how* that program will change, but users will undoubtedly want to know why they can't locate the same data for the most recent year. This kind of information from *Statistical Programs* can help a librarian figure out why not, (and learn about other BLS statistical series along the way). Should you find you need similar kinds of information about statistical information not covered in this publication, you can still find it in the *Budget of the United States* (discussed in chapter 9), but this may be a more complicated process given the complexity and size of each year's budget documents. Attentive government information specialists can expect to use *Statistical Programs* occasionally, but once familiar with the information in the following section of this chapter, they will consult it mostly to learn if a program has been added or subtracted from an agency's activities.

The 13 Primary Statistical Agencies

In most cases the likely content of a statistical agency's work will be obvious from the name. For example, the Bureau of Justice Statistics (BJS) is pretty straightforward. Telling you that the BJS is where you would look for statistics on crime, incarceration, and the justice system would presumably tell you nothing you didn't already know just by reading the name. Because it is a primary statistical agency and produces so much information, attempting to summarize all of its activities is of limited value. Conversely, attempting to comprehensively describe each agency and its statistical activities is simply not feasible. So this section will be very selective and focus on notable characteristics of each agency. When it comes to finding actual numbers, you should expect to either dig into the agency's website or make the best use search tools (discussed later) on a case-by-case basis.

Bureau of Justice Statistics   *www.bjs.gov*

Many of the statistics on the BJS website come from either the Uniform Crime Reports (UCR), the National Crime Victimization Survey (NCVS), or a combination of the two. Between them, BJS provides data on the people experiencing crime, the people presumed to have committed the crimes, and the crimes themselves. The UCR is an interesting data source because the FBI administers it; however the content comes from individual reports submitted by local law enforcement. The UCR is not unusual in coming from a mix of federal and local efforts. Indeed lots of putatively federal data sources wouldn't be possible without active collaboration with state and local agencies. BLS has a moderately easy-to-use website with a mix of interactive tables and static publications containing charts and graphs. Like all agencies, BLS has plenty of jargon, but it also usually provides clear explanations.

Bureau of Labor Statistics   *www.bls.gov*

In addition to labor statistics—employment, unemployment, wages, hours, strikes, union memberships and productivity—BLS also conducts surveys that might not be so obvious. These include the Consumer Expenditure Survey and the American Time Use Survey and they provide exactly the data you would expect, namely on how we spend our money and time. BLS also calculates the Consumer Price Index (CPI). The CPI is one of the most heavily used and referenced statistics produced by the government because it measures inflation and everyone at every income level has a stake in the inflation rate. The CPI has two main components. The first is to check the prices on a standard set of goods on a regular basis across the United States; believe it or not, BLS sends people to stores to look on the shelves and scan the prices. The second component is to take the gathered data and make it comparable across time. The BLS provides layperson-appropriate explanations in each month's CPI summary press release, and more detailed explanations are readily available to users who would like to know more. The BLS website is generally easy to use although it is densely packed. BLS clearly presumes users come to its site because they know what they want and understand what those things mean. Novices can still use it, but they will need to spend time reading the copious documentation provided. BLS still uses a Java applet for one of its interactive tools and its performance on Macs is unpredictable. The text file versions of many of its files can be rather baroque; users would be advised to avoid the text files unless they are already familiar with the data.

Bureau of Transportation Statistics *www.bts.gov*

Like many statistical agencies, the Bureau of Transportation Statistics (BTS) publishes a yearbook of representative data. *National Transportation Statistics* contains expected tables such as miles of highway in the United States and length of air travel delays, but also tables such as worldwide passenger car production from 1961–present. One might not think that a transportation agency that mostly deals with the transportation system would include information on manufacturing production, but apparently the topical tie-in is close enough, a publishing style adopted by other agencies besides BTS. Expect surprises from agencies and try not to get into too much of a rut when searching for data or you might hide a perfectly good table from yourself.

Census Bureau

There's an entire chapter on the Census Bureau in this book (chapter 16). Read it.

Economic Research Service *www.ers.usda.gov*

The Economic Research Service (ERS) of the Department of Agriculture has one of the less helpful agency names. It's accurate yet not informative, for in addition to providing data on the economic side of agriculture, it provides some data that might not be obvious. For example, as noted above, BLS tracks general consumer spending. One might expect *all* data on consumer spending to come from BLS. However, much like car production and the BTS, the topic area of the ERS—agricultural economics—rules. Thus ERS is a key source of data on food expenditures, since knowing what people want to buy is important for farmers when they are deciding what to grow. Not only does ERS research what people buy, but they also research where people go to get the food. Thus, ERS has data on food deserts in urban areas even though most people equate agriculture with rural areas only. A food desert is an area, almost always urban, where there is little or no access to fresh, farm-produced food. ERS also produces an atlas of rural America. What's interesting about the atlas is that it consists of data from other agencies such as BLS and the Census. The repackaging by one agency of data from other agencies such as the *Atlas of Rural and Small Town America* is, if not common, not particularly rare either. The advantage of this practice is that sometimes the repackaging agency does a better job presenting the data than the original source agency!

National Agricultural Statistics Service *www.nass.usda.gov*

The National Agricultural Statistics Service (NASS) now manages the Census of Agriculture (previously this work was conducted by the Census Bureau) along with a number of other statistical programs that together provide agricultural statistics back to the mid-1800s. The census itself is only available online at NASS from 1997 forward. For prior years, the finding methods described for the decennial census in the Census chapter (chapter 16) would apply. NASS works with BLS to produce the Farm Labor Survey and also has an arrangement with Cornell University in which Cornell's Mann Library hosts historical publications containing NASS statistics. The venture with Cornell is unique in its exact form, but there are a few other agencies that partner with non–government data archives to host their data. This is another example of how agencies interact with organizations external to themselves.

Bureau of Economic Analysis *www.bea.gov*

Bureau of Economic Analysis (BEA) is charged with calculating US national accounts, for example, measures of economic activity for the nation as a whole. The signature dataset the BEA produces is gross domestic product and BEA has calculated it from 1929–present. BEA's website is aimed at knowledgeable users, although they do provide lots of documentation. However, the explanations may also take some time and study to understand. BEA and BLS both have responsibility for measuring major components of US economic activities; even though they cover different areas, they often create parallel, but different, datasets. While this creates the potential for confusion, it also provides more options for users. For example, both agencies have data on consumer expenditures, however, not only are these datasets drawing from different source material, they use different categories. While BLS provides statistics on expenditures on health insurance in the Consumer Expenditure Survey, BEA provides statistics on expenditures on nursing homes. BEA is also a source of data related to international trade (as is USDA, the Census, and a host of other agencies) in the form of statistics on foreign direct investment (investments in the United States by people and companies from other countries and multinational enterprises).

Energy Information Administration *www.eia.gov*

The Energy Information Administration (EIA) collects data on exactly what its name suggests (see chapter 14 for additional information). In addition to creating its own data and drawing on other agencies' data, EIA also makes use of privately produced data such as New York Stock Exchange futures data (since petroleum is a traded commodity) and trade association data for figures not otherwise obtainable. EIA's website is fairly easy to use with a predictable structure and good documentation. Many agencies provide multiple ways to view their data with an emphasis on mapping and EIA is no different. However, few agencies provide the kinds of sophisticated tools for retrieving and analyzing their data that EIA does. Usually, you would encounter this on sites producing scientific data that needs a specialized tool. For example, the EIA has recently introduced an Excel plug-in that researchers and business people may use to easily download and refresh EIA energy data and economic data from the Federal Reserve Bank's FRED datasets (the latter data is discussed in chapter 15, Business, Economic, and Consumer Information).

National Center for Education Statistics *nces.ed.gov*

The National Center for Education Statistics (NCES) provides lots of data for use by novice users and it is a heavily used resource for more detailed research as well. For example, NCES is the source for No Child Left Behind assessment data, so researchers, school districts, parents, and state and local government agencies all have a common resource to meet their different needs for this data.

In many cases, to get the most out of NCES data, users will need to use restricted use versions. Access to these versions is entirely at the discretion of NCES staff and the requirements for use are not trivial (NCES has a manual for restricted dataset users which is 56 pages long). The data are restricted because there will be versions containing personally identifiable information. Among other things, in order to use a restricted dataset, applicants must explain why public use versions (those without identifying information) do not support the applicant's research needs and how the data will be secured. Unless your user has a long-term, profession-critical need for restricted data, it's probably in their best interest for you to point them towards other versions of those datasets. NCES seems to be particularly well served by their new Data Inventory search tool (http://datainventory.ed.gov). The Data Inventory allows users to search by data item to see which survey or surveys ask about the item. For example, there are questions about study abroad participation in one wave of the Baccalaureate & Beyond Survey (B&B), but you would never know this from the summary B&B description. With the inventory, users can skip the time-consuming process of reading all the documentation of all the surveys until they get to the right one. This is even more useful for the many longitudinal surveys NCES oversees. Often, the questions asked will change from cohort to cohort, so just looking at the documentation for one iteration of the survey may be misleading. The Data Inventory solves the problem by letting users search across surveys and telling them exactly where to go to find what they need. Not every agency has a documentation navigation tool like this, although most could benefit from one.

NCES is also one of the agencies partnering with an external entity, in this case the Inter-university Consortium for Political and Social Research (ICPSR). ICPSR, headquartered at the University of Michigan, provides archival support for some NCES data although users can work entirely within the NCES website most of the time. The NCES is discussed in more detail in chapter 12 on Education.

National Center for Health Statistics *www.cdc.gov/nchs*

The National Center for Health Statistics (NCHS) is part of the Centers for Disease Control. NCHS is responsible for many national surveys on health conditions and practices as well as the national Vital Statistics report. Originally, vital statistics—births, deaths, marriages, divorces—were produced by the Census Bureau, but after numerous agency shifts over the years, ended up with the NCHS. Even though there is a whole series devoted just to these statistics, you will probably find it most effective to navigate health statistics by using the NCHS Fastats tool (www.cdc.gov/nchs/fastats/default .htm). Essentially an A-Z index of NCHS statistics, it has a predictable structure that includes some statistics in each entry as well as links to more detailed datasets. This is helpful for vital statistics because it turns out they're fairly complex with provisional and final versions as well as linked birth and death datasets (for examples, a linked birth and death dataset can provide insights by linking data around a birth with data around the same child's infant death). If a user needs that kind of data, Fastats will get to it—but if not, Fastats will also retrieve simpler information. Fastats is also the best place to find straightforward numbers on newsworthy health topics such as immunization rates for children. NCHS is covered in more detail in chapter 11 on Health Information.

Internal Revenue Service *www.irs.gov*

The Internal Revenue Service (IRS) statistical branch Statistics of Income (SOI) (www .irs.gov/uac/SOI-Tax-Stats-Statistics-of-Income) produces the statistics you would expect: statistics on individual, business, and nonprofit income and assets as reported on tax returns. It also has data on US investments abroad and foreign investments into the United States. If you think this sounds like the Foreign Direct Investment data from BEA, you're not alone. However, they are different datasets. What you find in the Tax Stats web pages (www.irs .gov/uac/Tax-Stats-2) are instead studies such as taxes paid by foreign-owned companies operating in the United States and vice versa, as well as "foreign trusts" in which a US citizen is the recipient of the trust. The Foreign Trusts dataset (www.irs.gov/uac/SOI-Tax –Stats-Foreign-Trusts) includes what may be the best title of a table: "Forms 3520 With Gratuitous Transfers." Gratuitous transfers, by the way, are transactions in which property is transferred to foreign trusts for less than fair market value, or for no consideration at all. Not the most common usage of gratuitous, but then the IRS also continues to use the word alien to describe taxpaying noncitizens, an archaic and thankfully rare usage.

Office of Research, Evaluation and Statistics

www.ssa.gov/policy/about/ORES.html

The Office of Research, Evaluation and Statistics (ORES) is the statistical branch of the Social Security Administration (SSA) and reports on all Social Security related data. The SSA supports both older Americans and disabled Americans. Thus ORES is one home for statistics on disability. The Census Bureau's American Community Survey is another. Neither provides a complete picture, so it's typical to look at both sources. In general, ORES provides data on Americans receiving benefits, and the amount of benefits dispersed. The SSA also produces one of the more fun datasets out there, albeit not through ORES. It's the Baby Names Dataset. Because SSA needs a person's name in order to issue a Social Security Card and because it uses death records to determine when to deactivate a decedent's Social Security Number and/or benefits, it has developed an extensive dataset of names. Researchers use this dataset to analyze, among other things, influences on behavior and language changes, and prospective parents can use it to avoid picking the same name everyone else is picking. If this chapter's author's parents had had access to the Baby Names tool, she probably would not have been one of the 26,239 children named Amy in her birth year.

National Center for Science and Engineering Statistics

www.nsf.gov/statistics

The National Center for Science and Engineering Statistics (NCSES) of the National Science Foundation provides data on the workforce and overall state of competiveness of the US science and engineering sector. For instance, NCSES workforce data is particularly interesting as it provides demographic detail on how heavily white men dominate this sector's workforce. Its data has spurred numerous recent efforts at many different educational levels to increase the retention of nonwhite men, women in all demographic groups, and all people with disabilities in the science and engineering sector.

Whew! That's the 13 principal statistical agencies down! What should be remembered from such a fast run through?

1. The principal statistical agencies cover an entire human's life and most activities in it: birth, death, education, employment, health, aging, and disability.
2. The principal statistical agencies cover the basics of the nation's activities: taxation, education, transportation, social services, crime and punishment, and health care.
3. Agencies work with each other and share data.
4. Agencies work with state and local agencies and share data.
5. Agencies work with nonprofit and for-profit entities when they need to, and sometimes include nongovernment-produced data in their reports.
6. It's rare for an agency to be the sole source of data on a topic.
7. It's not unusual for agencies to repackage each other's data to better serve their own constituents.

We didn't take an exhaustive tour of the US government data landscape to prove it, but you should be aware that while you can expect, with practice, to commit to memory some agency datasets, you will almost certainly never commit them all to memory. *That's ok!* Why? Because, as we'll discuss in the next section, strategic use of a small number of tools will take care of most questions you'll receive and for the ones they don't, there are professional networks that come to the rescue.

Recommended Strategies for Finding US Government Statistical Information

You may be thinking to yourself, fine, great, this is all very interesting, but what am I going to do when someone comes to me with an actual question and I don't know the answer? Well, after a moment of calm, invoke these options in this order:

1. Use the Statistical Abstract of the United States
2. Use search engines more effectively
3. Use Data.gov and other starting points for government statistics
4. Use professional networks

Statistical Abstract of the United States

The *Statistical Abstract of the United States* (hereafter *Statistical Abstract*) is your new best friend. This book is worth spending time with even when you're not being asked a reference question, except for when you're flying. Apparently TSA considers the posses-sion of almanacs in regular life inherently suspicious ("Exclusive: TSA's Secret Behavior Checklist to Spot Terrorists," 2015).

The *Statistical Abstract of the United States* has three uses: as a source of an answer to a question, as a pathfinder for more detailed data, and as a time-series dataset.

As the source of an answer, your odds are good: the 2012 edition has 1,406 tables. Most of the tables are from government sources, but a further feature of the *Statis-tical Abstract of the United States* is the inclusion of some privately produced data not otherwise available at a reasonable cost, such as tables derived from private market research. Examples include tables on leisure activities in the United States produced by GfK Mediamark Research & Intelligence, LLC, and data on religious identification in the United States from the Institute for the Study of Secularism in Society and Culture.

As a pathfinder, the *Statistical Abstract of the United States* gives you those 1,406 start-ing points on virtually every topic of personal and public interest and a very predictable structure, making it very fast to scan during a reference interaction. Each table includes the title, the units/scale of the information presented, relevant footnotes, and links to the original sources where available.

When you look at the publication across its entire run (which began in 1878), some tables are present for significant numbers of years, which makes the *Statistical Abstract of the United States* a dataset of its own. Additionally, many of those regularly recurring tables were ones created just for the *Statistical Abstract of the United States,* making it a source of unique content. These tables will refer in the source section to "unpublished data." Even though you might be disappointed that there are no hints for further sources, this is still helpful because at least then you know you don't need to keep searching for data like it.

The Census Bureau published the *Statistical Abstract* from 1878 to 2012 until budget cuts resulted in the elimination of the branch that produced it, a decision (to eliminate what was arguably among the most useful federal government publications) enacted over the protest of its users. Subsequently, the private sector publisher ProQuest picked up production of the print title in nearly the exact same form as the Census Bureau. In addition, ProQuest developed an online version with robust search features, added file formats, and included suggested citations for academic users. Regional libraries in the Federal Depository Library Program typically have the entire run of the *Statistical Abstract of the United States,* often in multiple forms with subscriptions to the print and online ProQuest products to boot.

With the change from government-produced to private sector production, some librar-ies may opt to not purchase the current online ProQuest version (or the print version from Bernan). For the historical material, there is an alternative, but it is labor intensive. The Census Bureau digitized all of the issues of the *Statistical Abstract* and posted them to their website. However, these are merely image files without any text search. Library staff can add text search capabilities by downloading each issue and using Adobe Acro-bat Professional or other software to OCR the text. This is not a speedy process, nor is it free given the labor required and the additional software. The essential point is that the *Statistical Abstract of the United States* is worth some effort and/or financial expen-diture because it is as close as it gets to a single source for all US government statistical information. For simple pathfinding, it's probably safe to say that any edition of the

Statistical Abstract would be useful for roughly five years past its publication date. However, most libraries should anticipate adding at least the print edition to their budgets for 2018 and after.

In short, the *Statistical Abstract of the United States* remains indispensable for understanding and discovering US government statistics regardless of how experienced a researcher you may be with respect to statistical information. Keep a copy in your preferred form close at hand!

Use Search Engines More Effectively

The following strategies are based on use of Google, but in testing they held for DuckDuckGo and Bing unless noted otherwise.

First, use the site limiter. The syntax is site:XXXX where XXXX can be just gov or census.gov or edu, and so on. Second, use the filetype limiter: filetype:XXXX where XXXX can be any file extension. Since this chapter is about statistics, you will get the best bang for your buck if you specify text files such as *.csv and *.txt or Excel extensions such as *.xls and *.xlsx. Google will claim that it only searches for specific filetypes, but experience indicates otherwise. For the most precise search, combine both limiters with your keywords. A search for *site:gov housing filetype:xls* will return data files. A search for *housing data* returns web pages and maybe data files. Cut out the uncertainty and go for precision. Obviously, you should use the limiters with care. If your starting assumptions about where to find the data or what format it's in are incorrect, then you will miss out on relevant results. Therefore, unless you know for certain that a particular agency has the data you want, use site:gov rather than trying to guess which agency is the right one. The same goes for the filetype. By using limiters strategically, you will have the best balance of precision and search scope.

> ### Google and Privacy
>
> Google has a feature that can help librarians, but which has some serious privacy implications. Google's Web History keeps track of all of the web pages you have clicked on. If you opt-in to use Web History, then Google will know more about your online activity and will share some, or all, of that information with other commercial entities and governments. However, government websites often have many pages with similar titles so quick access to a previously used page or source can be very helpful in a reference interaction. Still, like everything, the Web History service comes with a price. In this case, the price isn't in dollars, but information sharing.

Use Data.gov and Other Starting Points for Government Statistics

In addition to making better use of search engines, you can draw on many of the generalizations in this chapter so far to help you make better educated guesses in the first place. For example, remember how the *Statistical Programs of the United States Government* demonstrates the inherently political nature of government statistical information gathering? Well, when a user is asking for help with data with which you have no prior experience, ask yourself whether there's a likely political use for that data. If so, then ask yourself, in consultation with the *Statistical Abstract of the United States,* which agency might be a likely gatherer. Even if you don't feel confident in your guess about a possible agency, that's fine, just limit your search to site:gov.

While you will likely use general purpose search engines more often than not, the federal government also has a catalog of some of its datasets in www.data.gov. Data .gov also includes state and local datasets which may be a benefit—it depends on the circumstance. What Data.gov does that is definitely beneficial is provide a tidy, organized list of the data contained therein. Sometimes agencies put the data directly into Data.gov, but that's probably less common than pointing back to their own websites. Regardless it gives you or your user the ability to browse for data by topic and by agency. Its interface includes facets, so users with experience using library resources will be able to reuse those skills when using Data.gov. Data.gov results don't seem to be included in general web searches, but it is unclear whether this is a result of inadequate search engine optimization by Data.gov or search engine customization based on users' prior search habits. Because Data.gov results may not routinely appear at the top of search results, librarians should make a habit of going to Data.gov directly.

Nearly all of the sources and tools covered in this chapter are freely available online, part of the depository library program, or both. A commercial product, ProQuest Statistical Insight, is a powerful database aiming to index statistical data broadly from government and many private and organizational sources. By striving to comprehensively index statistical publications—and especially the content *inside* specific statistical tables—it provides potentially broader access and discovery to statistical publications and tables. Discovery of relevant datasets is also enhanced by allowing many special search limiters, such as searching for data by geographic, demographic, and other criteria. ProQuest Statistical Insight is based on three classic products from the Congressional Information Service (see chapter 3): the *American Statistics Index (ASI),* which indexes and abstracts federal government statistical sources since 1973; the *Statistical Reference Index (SRI),* which indexes and abstracts state, industry, and about 1,000 other nonfederal statistical publications since 1980; and the *Index to International Statistics (IIS),* which indexes and abstracts about 2,000 international organizations' statistical sources since 1983. Each has a full-text portion available as well, with the ASI segment starting with publications in 2004, and SRI and IIS both starting with publications in 2007. In addition to these three segments, there is a Statistical Tables module where hundreds of thousands of statistical tables, starting in 1999, selected from the three publication modules are individually indexed to ensure precise search and retrieval. The SRI module makes Statistical Insight especially useful for the indexing of nongovernmental sources, as well.

Use Professional Networks

Everything we've covered in this section so far should cover almost all of the questions you receive about finding US government statistical information. But what do you do when these tools don't work?

You turn to your colleagues! One way to do this is to search for site:edu guide XXXX. The results will be from institutions with *.edu addresses and will capture the resource guides that academic librarians enthusiastically create for their local clientele. Sometimes there will be lots of guides on a topic, such as the decennial Census, but in other cases, there may only be a few or even one. Occasionally, even when there are lots of guides on a topic, they still may not cover every angle. When guides don't help, then you move on to actively seeking help from colleagues.

Chapter 2, How to Think Like a Government Documents Librarian, discusses Other Help including your network and other points of assistance. In addition to those strategies, if you are in a depository library, but not the government information specialist, go talk to the depository librarian. If he doesn't know the answer, he will likely direct you to the Regional Depository Library for your area and the staff there. If the Regional can't help, then she'll point you to someone she thinks can. Next, consider joining the International Association for Social Science Information Service and Technology (IASSIST) for its e-mail list. IASSIST is the primary source of expertise on social sciences data in the United States (much of which comes from governments). The membership costs are very reasonable and worth every penny. Not only are IASSIST members experts, but they are true data nerds. They *want* people to use data and are always glad to help colleagues. Why only wonder if a given resource might help when someone else will be happy to confirm that the resource will help (or that it won't, but that there are lots of others that will and here is an annotated bibliography)?

Where does this leave us?

- The United States has no central statistical agency.
- Taken as a whole, the United States has a massive statistical information gathering effort.
- That effort covers every aspect of life for the nation, for humans and for a large number of flora and fauna.
- Just as there is no single statistical agency, there is no single search tool.
- But the *Statistical Abstract of the United States* gets pretty close.
- Moreover, general web searching is getting pretty good, especially with two small tweaks. (Remember to use limiters!)
- And the government is trying to help in an unfunded voluntary mandate sort of way with Data.gov.
- Your colleagues are even better than search engines and you can find them via
  - GOVDOC-L, an independent listserv of librarians interested in government information
  - Federal Depository Program and its network of librarians
  - IASSIST

You may now consider yourself introduced to US government statistical information!

Exercises

1. How many US military casualties in the Global War on Terror have had an unknown cause?

2. Which state has the lowest current unemployment rate?

3. Is it true that Minnesota winters are getting warmer? Find statistics on the average mean temperature during winter since 1895.

4. A user is concerned about bridge safety in the United States. Find statistics on the condition of US bridges.

5. Extra Credit: Find the definitions of *structurally deficient* and *functionally obsolete* provided by the Federal Highway Administration. Would these definitions resolve the user's concern about safety?

6. Extra Extra Credit: Is there really a Rat Information Portal? Who would produce such a thing?

Sources Mentioned in This Chapter

AirData Website Home Page, Environmental Protection Agency, www.epa.gov/airdata.

American Community Survey, www.census.gov/acs/www.

American Time Use Survey: Charts by Topic: Sleep, Bureau of Labor Statistics, www.bls.gov/tus/charts/sleep.htm.

Atlas of Rural and Small-Town America, Economic Research Service, US Department of Agriculture, www.ers.usda.gov/data-products/atlas-of-rural-and-small-town-america.aspx.

Baby Names (dataset), www.ssa.gov/oact/babynames.

Beyond Our Solar System: Overview, National Aeronautics and Space Administration, http://solarsystem.nasa.gov/planets/profile.cfm?Object=Beyond.

Births, Marriages, Divorces, and Deaths: Provisional Data for 2009, Centers for Disease Control, www.cdc.gov/nchs/data/nvsr/nvsr58/nvsr58_25.htm.

Budget of the United States Government, Executive Office of the President, www.gpo.gov/fdsys/browse/collectionGPO.action?collectionCode=BUDGET.

Bureau of Economic Analysis, www.bea.gov.

Bureau of Justice Statistics, www.bjs.gov.

Bureau of Labor Statistics, www.bls.gov.

Bureau of Transportation Statistics, www.bts.gov.

Commuting/Place of Work/Travel Time, US Census Bureau, www.census.gov/hhes/commuting/data/commuting.html.

Consumer Expenditure Survey, Bureau of Labor Statistics, www.bls.gov/cex/.

Cushing, OK Crude Oil Future Contract 1 (Dollars per Barrel), Energy Information Administration, www.eia.gov/dnav/pet/hist/LeafHandler.ashx?n=PET&s=RCLC1&f=D.

Data.gov.

Data Inventory search tool, Department of Education, http://datainventory.ed.gov.

Earthquakes, United States Geological Survey, http://earthquake.usgs.gov/earthquakes.

Economic Research Service, www.ers.usda.gov.

Energy Information Administration, www.eia.gov.

Fastats, National Center for Health Statistics, www.cdc.gov/nchs/fastats/default.htm.

Foreign Trusts, Internal Revenue Service, www.irs.gov/uac/SOI-Tax-Stats-Foreign-Trusts.

Immunization, Fastats, www.cdc.gov/nchs/fastats/immunize.htm.

Internal Revenue Service, www.irs.gov.

International Association for Social Science Information Services & Technology (IASSIST), www.iassistdata.org.

Inter-university Consortium for Political and Social Research (ICPSR), www.icpsr.umich.edu.

National Agricultural Statistics Service, www.nass.usda.gov.

National Center for Education Statistics, nces.ed.gov.

National Center for Health Statistics, www.cdc.gov/nchs.

National Center for Science and Engineering Statistics, www.nsf.gov/statistics.

National Crime Victimization Survey (NCVS), www.bjs.gov/index.cfm?ty=dcdetail&iid=245.

National Electronic Injury Surveillance System (NEISS), Consumer Product Safety Commission, www.cpsc.gov/en/Research—Statistics/NEISS-Injury-Data.

National Park Service Visitor Use Statistics National Reports, National Park Service, https://irma.nps .gov/Stats/Reports/National.

National Transportation Statistics, www.rita.dot.gov/bts/sites/rita.dot.gov.bts/files/publications/national _transportation_statistics/index.html.

Office of Research, Evaluation and Statistics, www.ssa.gov/policy/about/ORES.html.

ProQuest, www.proquest.com/products-services/statabstract.html.

ProQuest Statistical Insight, http://cisupa.proquest.com/ws_display.asp?filter=Statistical%200verview.

Statistical Abstract of the United States, Census Bureau, www.census.gov/compendia/statab.

Statistics of Income (SOI), www.irs.gov/uac/SOI-Tax-Stats-Statistics-of-Income.

Tax Stats, Internal Revenue Service, www.irs.gov/uac/Tax-Stats-2.

Uniform Crime Reports (UCR), www.fbi.gov/about-us/cjis/ucr/ucr.

US Census Bureau, www.census.gov.

Vital Statistics of the U.S., 1850–Present, University of Minnesota Libraries Guide, www.lib.umn.edu/ govpubs/vitalstats_guide.

References

"Exclusive: TSA's Secret Behavior Checklist to Spot Terrorists." 2015. *The Intercept.* https://firstlook.org/ theintercept/2015/03/27/revealed-tsas-closely-held-behavior-checklist-spot-terrorists.

"Federal Agency Participation." n.d. *Data.gov.* www.data.gov/metrics.

Gerhan, David. 1999. "When Quantitative Analysis Lies behind a Reference Question." *Reference & User Services Quarterly* 39, no. 2: 166–175.

Office of Management and Budget. 2014. *Statistical Programs of the United States Government Fiscal Year 2015.* www.whitehouse.gov/sites/default/files/omb/assets/information_and_regulatory_affairs/ statistical-programs-2015.pdf.

CHAPTER 11

Health Information

ANN GLUSKER

Introduction

Few concerns are as central to our lives as health. With the complexity of health information and the variety of sources available, searching for health information can be a bewildering process for researchers, consumers, and others. Compounding these difficulties is the specialized vocabulary of the medical profession, which can be impenetrable to an untrained information seeker. An additional challenge is the recent proliferation of health information, especially on the Internet, which is often unreliable and can, at its worst, be dangerously inaccurate. Government-created or -sponsored sources can often cut through some of the chaos and offer clear and trustworthy resources.

This chapter will focus mainly on materials that come from the executive branch, since it contains most of the variety of independent government agencies that actively engage in health-related activities (see chapter 9, The Executive Branch, for more information).

The National Institutes of Health and the National Library of Medicine: Centuries of Progress

The National Institutes of Health (NIH), a subagency of the United States Department of Health and Human Services, produces much of the federal government's output related to health information. The National Library of Medicine (NLM) is the central organization responsible for its collection, organization, and dissemination. To understand where these agencies stand today, and to be able to do research that spans back over decades, it is helpful to get a sense of their history.

The National Institutes of Health

The United States Department of Health and Human Services (HHS) is the agency under which most federal activity related to health and health care takes place. Specifically, its subagency, the NIH, is "the nation's medical research agency . . . [and] the largest source of funding for medical research in the world." As such, it is a prolific creator of health-related government documents, and medical advances made by NIH-funded researchers have been central to the history of medicine. The NIH is made up of 27 separate institutes and centers, each with its own research focus (National Institutes of Health, 2015a).

In the late 1800s, American physicians were becoming increasingly aware of the work being done by European researchers related to infectious organisms. Newly trained in bacteriological methods, Dr. Joseph Kinyoun established the nation's Hygienic Laboratory under the Marine Health Service, to expand upon the work being done overseas. Over the next decades, the laboratory moved to Washington, DC, and extended its purview to include noncontagious diseases and other health conditions, as well as the production of vaccines and antitoxins. Hygienic Laboratory personnel were central in exploring and suggesting ways to improve health conditions among the military during both world wars. In 1930, the laboratory was formally named The National Institute of Health, and study fellowships were established.

The years following World War II saw tremendous growth for NIH. Many new institutes were founded. The first was the National Cancer Institute (which was designated a component of the NIH only several years after its creation). Subsequently, the development of new condition-specific institutions created the current NIH structure of categorical disease-based constituent agencies and centers. Funding was also expanding rapidly in this period; the total NIH budget went from $8 million to $1 billion between 1947 and 1966. However, by the early 1980s, the state of the economy and competition for federal funding slowed this growth. NIH turned its attention to maintaining its preeminence as a broadly based research organization, and to developing collaborations and connections with similar institutions in other countries. The National Library of Medicine has been a central resource in this effort.

The National Library of Medicine

The National Library of Medicine (NLM) "is the world's largest medical library. The Library collects materials and provides information and research services in all areas of biomedicine and health care" (National Library of Medicine, 2015a). Today, NLM is a subagency of the NIH, which is itself a subagency of HHS.

The NLM, like the HHS, has military origins, and its existence is heavily indebted to two men in particular. The first is Dr. Joseph Lovell, who was appointed the first surgeon general of the United States Army in 1818. It is his reference collection that is the foundation of what is now NLM. His collection was so extensive in its day that in 1836 it was officially named The Library of the Office of the Surgeon General, United States Army (National Library of Medicine, 2015g).

The second central figure in the history of NLM is Dr. John Shaw Billings. He assumed direction of the Army Surgeon General's library after the Civil War, at a time when there was a substantial influx to the library of discarded books from army and other military hospitals. Billings was a dynamo, and during his tenure, from about 1867 to 1895, he turned his library into the largest medical library in the Americas, and one of the largest in the world. He was a tireless collector and visionary. Not only did he expand the collection many times over (from 2,300 to 124,000 volumes), but he created an index-catalog of its holdings, and launched the *Index Medicus,* which will be discussed in more detail below. He even came up with the idea of the punch card, which he suggested to Census Bureau head Herman Hollerith for use in tabulating data from the 1890 census, and which eventually revolutionized information processing (for more on Hollerith, see chapter 10, Statistical Information, and chapter 16, The Census) (National Library of Medicine, 2015d).

After Billings's tenure, the Library was renamed the Army Medical Library (1920) and later the Armed Forces Medical Library (1952), before becoming part of the Public Health Service (PHS) and being named the National Library of Medicine in 1956. In the next decades NLM created a system of Regional Medical Libraries (today's National Network of Libraries of Medicine) and developed information systems which were the basis of its current central resource, PubMed, which will be discussed further in the next section. It also produced the consumer health resource MedlinePlus, released in 1998, which provides reliable, librarian-vetted consumer health information.

The National Library of Medicine and the Organization of Health Information

Figure 11.1 shows the manner in which the library that Billings inherited from his predecessor was first cataloged; its contents were listed (not indexed) primarily by author and secondarily by subject (for example, Hamilton on Female Complaints). The innovative Billings cataloged his library with not only author, but also—unusually for the time—subject indexes. Given the extent of the library's holdings, this catalog was considered an exhaustive resource of the medical literature of the time.

However, this was an era in which periodicals were becoming a major source of medical information, meaning that the volume of publications increased dramatically. Billings's main cataloging project couldn't keep pace with these new publications, and so he created a separate indexing system for medical periodicals. This became known as *Index Medicus,* which was published monthly by the library starting in 1879. Today's MEDLINE is the modern outgrowth of the printed *Index Medicus* (maintained by NLM until 2004), a chronology of which appears in figure 11.2.

By the mid-1960s, NLM was able to take the enormous step of computerizing *Index Medicus,* which was still being published in paper form. After some experimentation, the Medical Literature Analysis and Retrieval System (MEDLARS) was launched, using *Index Medicus* as its input. By 1971, MEDLARS was able to be accessed online, and was called MEDLINE (MEDlars onLINE), which still exists today and is the major component of PubMed. Central to the efficient indexing and retrieval of articles within

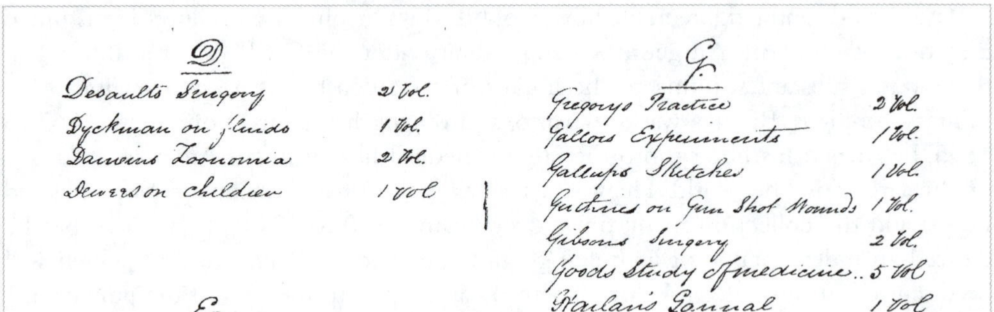

FIGURE 11.1
Facsimile of Page from "The First Catalogue of the Library of the Surgeon General's Office, 1840"
Source: National Library of Medicine, 1961.

these tools was the introduction, in 1960, of a new list of Medical Subject Headings, known as MeSH (Katcher, 1999). Its structure, which has had an enormous impact on access to health information, has been recognized as a model for controlled vocabulary creation in other arenas and forms the basis of subject searching in both MEDLINE and PubMed (Lipscomb, 2000).

PubMed is "the freely accessible online database of biomedical journal citations and abstracts created by the US National Library of Medicine" (National Library of Medicine, 2015e), and is the recommended starting point for any health literature search, whether for government documents or other sources such as citations of articles published in peer-reviewed journals. It is one of the most comprehensive and valuable tools in existence for finding such literature (including the broader Internet). Its building blocks are MEDLINE, with its indexing for 5,400 journals from around the world (although note that PubMed does include indexing and abstracts in addition to that

QUESTION: How do I find older medical journal articles?

ANSWER:

To identify articles published from:

- 1946–present, search PubMed®. Your retrieval will include both MEDLINE® and OLDMEDLINE records, as well as some other citations not indexed with Medical Subject Headings (MeSH®).
- Before 1946, there are a small number of citations included in PMC: PubMed Central, searchable via PubMed. Otherwise, there are no online sources from NLM except for IndexCat™. You need to use Index Medicus® and the other print sources that are described below. These sources can be found at many medical and large university libraries. Note: Index Medicus® ceased hard copy publication with the Dec. 2004 edition (Volume 45).

Index title	Years	NLM call number	Number of volumes	Publisher	Description
Index Medicus (IM)	1879–1926	ZW1 I383	45 volumes in 3 series; 1879–1899, 1903–1920 including war supplement 1914–1917, 1921–1926	Edited by John Shaw Billings, Robert Fletcher, et al.; Published by F. Leypoldt, Carnegie Institution, etc.	Journals, books, pamphlets indexed; Subject arrangement with author indexes; intended to supplement the Index-Catalog, contains some material not in the Index-Catalog.
Bibliographia medica	1900–1902	ZW1 B5836	3 volumes	Edited by Marcel Baudouin; Published by Institut de Bibliographie, Paris	Publication of *Index Medicus* was suspended from 1899–1902. In the interval, a similar index was issued in Paris by the Institut de Bibliographie. In French.
Index-Catalog of the Library of the Surgeon-General's Office (ICLSGO) IndexCat	1880–1961	Z 675 .M4 I38	61 volumes in 5 series; 1880–1895, 1896–1916, 1913–1932, 1936–1955, 1959–1961	Library of Surgeon-General's Office, Army Medical Library, Armed Forces Medical Library, and GPO (Government Printing Office)	Journals, books, pamphlets, theses indexed; Journal articles listed only under subject; Subject-author arrangement each series A-Z, except Series 4 which is A-Mn only. Series 5 excludes journal articles and was published in 3 volumes: Volume 2 is in A-Z subject arrangement.
Quarterly Cumulative Index to Current Literature (QCICL)	1916–1926	ZW1 Q4	12 volumes	American Medical Association	Journal articles indexed; lists of new books, publishers, new gov't pubs; aimed at English-speaking, clinical, American doctors; alphabetical dictionary arrangement.

FIGURE 11.2

Finding Older Medical Journal Articles. *Source: National Library of Medicine, 2015b.*

Index title	Years	NLM call number	Number of volumes	Publisher	Description
Quarterly Cumulative Index Medicus (QCIM)	1927–1956	ZW1 Q3	60 volumes	American Medical Association; Carnegie Institute helped finance 1927–1931	Journal articles indexed; list of books and publishers; dictionary arrangement.
Current List of Medical Literature (CLML)	1941–1959	ZW1 C969	36 volumes	Army Medical Library; Armed Forces Medical Library	Journal articles indexed; table of contents arrangement with author, subject indexes; *use jointly with QCIM since indexed Journals not the same;* 1957–1959 the ONLY index.
Index Medicus/ Cumulated Index Medicus (IM/CIM)	1960–2004	ZW1 I384	1960–2004, 45 volumes	Index Medicus: NLM ; Cumulated Index Medicus: American Medical Association (1960–1964), NLM (1965-2004) [GPO]	Searchable on PubMed. Monthly issues with annual cumulations; subject, author indexes with complete entry under each. Publication ceased with December 2004 edition (Volume 45).

FIGURE 11.2   (continued from previous page)

from MEDLINE), and MeSH (NLM's controlled indexing vocabulary). Understanding these building blocks makes using PubMed searching far more effective.

MEDLINE citations are useful not only because of the consistency of the record structures retrieved by PubMed, but also because each citation is indexed using these medical subject headings, or MeSH terms. The MeSH terms constitute a controlled vocabulary applied to each MEDLINE entry by NLM indexers. Using these terms is an invaluable tool for creating searches with consistent search strategies, and addressing possible differences in terminology between lay and professional language. For example, articles about the substance vitamin C will be indexed with the MeSH term *ascorbic acid* (this is an example of vocabulary control). However, not every article about that substance will contain the exact wording *vitamin C*. Using the MeSH term *ascorbic acid* for the search ensures that the search will find all related articles, whether or not they use the wording *vitamin C*. In this case, there is an added benefit in that MeSH contains many "entry terms" which cross-reference related terminology. Vitamin C is an entry term for ascorbic acid; PubMed knows that if the user types in vitamin C, the MeSH term *ascorbic acid* should be applied by default. Not every common term is an entry term in this way, however.

Using MeSH terms also connects a search in the most efficient way possible to the underlying structure of MEDLINE indexing. MeSH terms themselves are structured in a hierarchy, and searching can be more productive if the search terms are refined according to a particular term's place in that hierarchy. PubMed users can see the MeSH terms related to their initial search terms as part of the search results and can revise them interactively. A searchable graphic of the MeSH hierarchy is also available through PubMed. Not every phrase a user types in has a corresponding MeSH term, so one should always explore the hierarchy and possible related terms that might yield a tighter search. For example, the term *health care costs* appears in two different tree structures, with varying related terms and concepts, which in turn may suggest previously unconsidered search strategies (see figure 11.3).

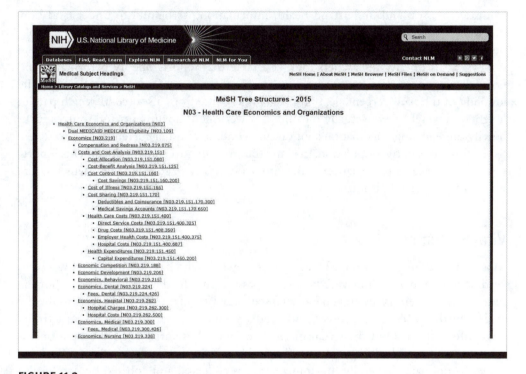

FIGURE 11.3
MeSH Tree Structures for the Term "Health Care Costs"
Source: Screenshot of MeSH Browser, 4/27/2015.

Another innovation from NLM regarding the organization of health information was the development of its own classification system, in use in many health sciences and other libraries (although not all libraries use the NLM classification, preferring to place corresponding materials in the LC's "R" class).

> NLM *Classification* covers the field of medicine and related sciences.
> The scheme is a system of classification intended to be used for the shelf
> arrangement of all library materials, regardless of format . . . [It] is a system
> of mixed notation patterned after the Library of Congress (LC) Classification

where alphabetical letters which denote broad subject categories are further subdivided by numbers. NLM *Classification* utilizes schedules QS–QZ and W–WZ, permanently excluded from the LC Classification Schedules and is intended to be used with the LC schedules which supplement NLM *Classification* for subjects bordering on medicine and for general reference materials. (National Library of Medicine, 2015f)

Where Does Health Information Come From?

In order to assess and understand health information, it's helpful to understand how that information was created, and the cautions that may apply to using it. For example, obesity researchers know that people underreport their weight when asked about it in surveys. So, if obesity researchers look at a table that reports obesity percentages and notes a survey as its data source, they can assume that the percentage reported is on the low side of the true percentage, unlike data that come from a source in which patient height and weight were actually measured. Government documents and sources focus heavily on reporting information about health conditions, using current figures to reflect the health status of the population. In many (but not all) government documents reporting statistics, health information comes from one of three sources: vital statistics, surveys, and research/clinical trials.

Vital Statistics

Most of us are familiar with vital statistics data; anyone who has ever had to show a birth certificate to apply for a driver's license or passport has held a vital statistics reporting instrument in their hands. In general, vital statistics data refer to central events in the life cycle—births, marriages, divorces, and deaths—which are vital milestones in citizens' lives. Information about these transitions is considered essential to government operations. Communicable disease information and hospitalizations are also often considered vital statistics data. Generally this information is collected and collated by state health departments from individual reports of events by health care providers, agencies, hospitals, and so on. Designated forms are used, with reporting requirements governed by state codes. The relevant government website or government publication, rather than a secondary source, should be the starting place for checking any of these figures.

Vital statistics data are uniquely valuable, because they cover the entire population which experiences an event. Not only is there complete population coverage, but the data are collected using forms that contain many items of detail about the people involved. If, for example, researchers are interested in levels of mothers' education, they might be better off researching this question in a state that includes this item on the birth certificate because by using birth certificate data, they are getting information about every birth that occurred in the state, as opposed to using survey data, which would give them information about only the sample of the population that was asked that question. Vital statistics also offer fairly consistent collection of information through the use of standard certificates. As long as one is fairly sure that the information is filled out completely and accurately for this item on the certificates, there is a high degree of certainty that the levels reported are close to the truth (there are often systemic and other issues with completeness and accuracy of filling out certificates, but that is another discussion). In addition, these data sources can sometimes be linked and considered in conjunction with one another. One such source is infant deaths, which reflect deaths among infants in the first year of life, per 1,000 live births; this information is obtained from linked birth and death records (information from the death certificates of all babies who die under the age of one year are linked, using specific data fields, to the corresponding infant's birth certificate).

Vital statistics data can only go so far, however. They are collected at a particular point in time and with relation to a specific event, and they don't ask questions related to health behaviors and various health conditions. They can't give information such as whether new mothers continue to breastfeed six months after giving birth, whether younger people are more likely to use seat belts than older people, or whether medical expenditures are higher for men or women. For information about health behaviors such as these, and a host of other questions, one must turn to survey data.

Survey Data

Survey data most often come from information gathered from a sample of the population, usually collected following scientific methods that ensure that the sample is representative of the population at large. In general, the kind of survey data reported in government documents come from surveys sponsored and/or administered by government entities. The following are some of the health surveys conducted nationally and/or at the state level that are commonly used in health research and government reporting: the Behavioral Risk Factor Surveillance System; the National Health Interview Survey; the National Health and Nutrition Examination Survey; the National Health Care Surveys; the Medical Expenditure Panel Survey; the Youth Risk Behavior Surveillance System; and some questions on the American Community Survey and the Current Population Survey, both from the Census Bureau.

Survey data can be exciting because they can report on health questions directly. For example, if researchers want to know what percentage of the population gets an annual flu shot, they can ask survey respondents rather than trying to gather that information from health care providers. Survey data are therefore more flexible and responsive to current conditions than vital statistics data. However, this flexibility comes at a price; surveys are very expensive to administer, and therefore often don't completely cover an entire population of interest (for example, people who speak only limited English are commonly underrepresented in surveys). Also, since only a sample of the population is being questioned, the data being reported is an approximation, with associated error. A sample percentage, even if statistically manipulated, may not represent the true rate in the population.

Another issue with survey data is that they can't go into a great deal of depth. For example, phone surveys are kept to a maximum of about 45 minutes of questioning, in order to ensure participation. Surveys also may not focus on a particular issue of interest;

for example, a researcher who wants to study attitudes toward binge drinking may find that available surveys ask only two or three questions about alcohol consumption, and nothing about attitudes.

Furthermore, a recent challenge in conducting phone surveys is the rise of cell-phone-only households, and the problems of tying them to a geographic location (since the phone's location reflects only the place of initiation of the contract, not the residence of its owner). Figuring out selection of respondents, which used to be done by selecting from a random list of land lines, is now a challenge because some people have both land lines and cell phones, which could cause them to be double counted in a methodology using both types of contact. The current practice is to sample cell phone-only and land line-only phone respondents separately, but also to allow for respondents who have both but mostly use their cell phones. This is much more cost-effective than a strict separation of types. (Centers for Disease Control and Prevention, 2015b).

Research/Clinical Trials

For a more in-depth look at a question, a research study may be called for. This is particularly the case if the information being sought is clinical in nature. The range of medical research is vast and beyond the scope of this discussion, including studies funded by private foundations, issue-oriented organizations, pharmaceutical companies, and other entities with health-related interests. For government-sponsored medical research, funding is generally supplied by the NIH in a competitive process. Loosely defined, the funded research may be basic medical research, focusing on laboratory findings, or a clinical trial, which measures the effects of an intervention on human subjects. It may take place in federal, state, or local government agencies, in universities, in health care settings, in freestanding laboratories and research institutions, or a variety of other settings. In addition, researchers who get NIH funding must share the data generated by their research with other researchers.

A final note: remember that in almost all cases, it takes some time for health data to become available to the public. Typically, vital statistics data for a calendar year will become available 12 to 18 months after the end of the year of interest (sometimes longer). Survey data are usually available within about a year of the completion of the survey data collection, depending on the sample size. These delays are due to the time required to gather the information from all sources, and additional time to process it; clean it (for example, remove values where there have been data entry errors, such as a person's age entered as 199 years); test it; analyze it; and prepare data sets, tables, and figures for release to the public.

Federal Resources and Organizations

The array of types and creators of health information is vast, and it can improve search processes to have some familiarity with the main resources and organizations involved with the production and dissemination of publications, websites, and other material.

This section covers print resources and websites created and maintained by federal-level agencies and organizations.

Health information is contained in the publications of each federal governmental branch (Boorkman et al., 2004). However, while government publications correspond to all three branches of government, for health information the most important of them come from the executive branch. Publications distributed via the Government Publishing Office can be found in the *Catalog of U.S. Government Publications* (http://catalog.gpo .gov) and its predecessor, the *Monthly Catalog of United States Government Publications*, both discussed in detail in chapter 2.

The specific question being researched will to some extent determine which agencies' publications to consult. As discussed, HHS is a central organization for health-related information and oversees many federal agencies with associated agendas, such as the National Institutes of Health (which contains the NLM), the Centers for Disease Control and Prevention, the Agency for Healthcare Research and Quality, the Health Resources and Services Administration, the Food and Drug Administration (FDA), and the Centers for Medicare and Medicaid Services.

Each agency's website has a research/data section with lists of publications. One agency that does not fall under HHS but is a central resource for health-related information is the independent Environmental Protection Agency (EPA), which has a mission of protecting not only the environment but also human health. The EPA is discussed in more detail in chapter 14.

Print Resources

Whatever the research topic, consider starting with classic publications that are still issued in print format. Seeing a report in print can give a better sense of its big picture than exploring it piecemeal online. Tables can be easier to find and use in a printed hard copy than in its online counterpart. Looking at printed reports can be especially valuable for researching health-related trends and other historical questions; regular periodic reports may only have older print versions from the pre-Internet days, and thus the print copies may be the only way to look at a series over time. Also consider looking at publications from agencies which are not normally considered health-related.

The *magnum opus* of print publications related to health is *Health, United States,* published each year by HHS. *Health, United States, 2013* was the 37th such report issued. It has nearly 500 pages, including 135 detailed figures and tables and a chartbook with 29 figures, as well as a special section on prescription drugs (each year's report has a focused section on a current health topic). Each year "*Health, United States* presents trends and current information on measures and determinants of the Nation's health. It also identifies variation in health status, modifiable risk behaviors, and health care utilization among people by race and ethnicity, gender, education and income level, and geographic location" (Centers for Disease Control and Prevention, 2015d). In addition to outlining health disparities, the report discusses access to health care and available resources, and health care insurance costs and expenditures, drawing from vital statistics and survey data. *Health, United States* is available both online and in hard copy. However, the information presented in a given year's report will be from the previous year or before, and the report is not likely to have information on a topic at any geographical area smaller than the state level.

Another important print publication is the *Morbidity and Mortality Weekly Report,* or *MMWR,* from the Centers for Disease Control and Prevention. "Often called 'the voice of CDC,' the MMWR series is the agency's primary vehicle for scientific publication of timely, reliable, authoritative, accurate, objective, and useful public health information and recommendations" (Centers for Disease Control and Prevention, 2015a). The exciting aspect of this publication is that it is willing to present preliminary data in the interests of timeliness, which allows swifter tracking of current trends and information than can be found in some of its larger counterparts (such as *JAMA* or the *New England Journal of Medicine,* whose articles often are considered breaking news in the media). While centrally managed, it also reflects information submitted by health departments from all over the United States, many of them local jurisdictions, and it covers a wide range of topics, often crucially important to health care practitioners. The CDC also has more of a stake in surveillance (tracking health and disease patterns in populations) than do some more research-oriented agencies. This makes the *MMWR* (which is searchable via PubMed) the go-to source for questions related to trends in certain health conditions or practices. Another publication focusing on population-level health is *Public Health Reports,* the journal of the United States Public Health Service (first published in 1878).

Increasingly, venerable publications which have long been central to health information are no longer issued in print (if at all). While these reports are no longer being issued in print format, the older volumes are invaluable resources for historical health-related research, and are still held in many depository libraries. Most are also available online, along with newer and current releases of ongoing series.

An example of this is the *Vital and Health Statistics Series* from the National Center for Health Statistics (a division of the CDC), in which it reports on various areas of its work. This is also known as the Rainbow Series (because the original print volumes were printed on different colors of paper). Another prominent publication no longer in print (but a version of which is still available online) is the *Healthy People* series, currently at *Healthy People 2020,* which sets out desired health status standards and targets for communities. In addition, the Census Bureau's *Statistical Abstract,* which had a Health/Nutrition section that was useful in gathering information from a variety of sources into one unified set of tables, is no longer being published by the Census Bureau; ProQuest is now producing a close approximation, discussed in chapter 10 on Statistical Information.

Websites

Websites with health-related government information abound. These may be gateways to download the publications issued by an agency; they may be databases or interactive query systems to allow access to information; or they may be cross-agency information compendia. The NLM website (www.nlm.nih.gov) is a good place to explore, with its thoughtful, organized presentation of trusted sources. Not only can it be used in order to discover a range of websites, agency and otherwise, but it also includes an extensive listing of databases and other electronic resources. While it's not usually a problem to find a report if you know its name or the name of the issuing agency, the NLM site will facilitate finding reports and resources otherwise.

Another fruitful source of website resources can be found in the intersection of medical and government librarianship. Broadly conceived, these two types of librarians approach health-related questions in different ways; the medical librarian tends to start a search process with a focus on the subject matter, and the government documents librarian starts with a focus on relevant agencies, jurisdictions, and statistical sources. However, they will eventually meet in the middle, and their websites are each full of rich guides to best tools. Consider looking at the sites of health sciences libraries for pages listing government documents sites, and at the sites of government documents libraries for pages on medical and health-related sites. Examples are the Columbia, Purdue, University of Delaware, and University of Washington pages listed in the "Sources Mentioned" section below. Also be sure to look at the corresponding professional organizations' sites. An example is the "Public Policy" page of the Medical Library Association.

The following are some of the best federal-level government sites, which all health information seekers should have in their toolkits:

Articles and Databases

- **PubMed (www.pubmed.gov)**
  PubMed "comprises more than 24 million citations for biomedical literature from MEDLINE, life science journals and online books." Its content tends towards the academic, and therefore sophisticated search techniques (for example, incorporating MeSH headings into the search strategy, and/or using the advanced search option) can yield better results.
- **National Library of Medicine Catalog (www.ncbi.nlm.nih.gov/nlmcatalog)**
  The catalog "provides access to NLM bibliographic data for journals, books, audiovisuals, computer software electronic resources and other materials."
- **National Technical Information Service (www.ntis.gov)**
  Discussed in more detail in chapter 13, this broad repository of scientific, technical, engineering, and business reports offers on the order of three million publications, many of them health-related.

Consumer Health Information

- **MedlinePlus (www.medlineplus.gov)**
  One of the best and most reliable consumer health websites currently available. Its content is user-friendly, and while it links to outside sites that are not government-produced, all of its links are vetted by librarians from NLM, and are trustworthy.
- **Healthfinder (www.healthfinder.gov)**
  This HHS site overlaps MedlinePlus in some aspects (for example, both offer health encyclopedias), but is broader in scope and focuses more on connecting with services, and taking action toward healthy living.

Research Findings

- **ClinicalTrials (www.clinicaltrials.gov)**
  This site is a registry of clinical research projects and results involving human subjects. It is useful for both patients and researchers, and includes non-United States entries.

- **PubMed Health (www.ncbi.nlm.nih.gov/pubmedhealth/)**
  PubMed Health is also useful for patients and researchers, as it gathers a range of research findings in one site to address clinical effectiveness (what works). It has both summaries and full text of relevant research reports.

Statistics

- **FastStats (www.cdc.gov/nchs/fastats/)**
  This service of the National Center for Health Statistics (a sub-agency of the CDC) is good for quick statistics, such as the current death rate from heart disease. From allergies to whooping cough, a full spectrum of topics is covered. Each has a page that lists the most current national statistics, links to the source reports (this can be useful itself), and gives additional resources of interest.

- **CDC Wonder (http://wonder.cdc.gov)**
  This site from the CDC has a wide scope of data available with which users can run their own analyses.

- **Health Services Research Information Central: Data, Tools and Statistics (www.nlm.nih.gov/hsrinfo/datasites.html)**
  This comprehensive listing of health statistics sites includes many government-created resources.

Public Health/Environmental Health

- **Public Health Partners (www.phpartners.org)**
  The result of a "collaboration of U.S. government agencies, public health organizations, and health sciences libraries," this site is aimed at the public health workforce, which comprises a number of professional roles and needs, and is one of the more comprehensive health-related sites. Features include Public Health Topics and links to Current Public Health News.

- **Environmental Protection Agency (www.epa.gov)**
  The EPA site contains a wide range of information on environmental concerns, including health-related publications and data.

- **TOXNET (Toxicology Data Network) (http://toxnet.nlm.nih.gov)**
  This NLM site allows searching on a range of databases on toxicology, hazardous chemicals, environmental health, and toxic releases.

Miscellaneous

- **Agency for Healthcare Research and Quality (www.ahrq.gov)**
  The AHRQ works to improve the nation's health care system, including resources such as the National Guidelines Clearinghouse for evidence-based health care.

- **Health Resources and Services Administration (www.hrsa.gov)**
  HRSA works to improve access to the nation's health care system, including issues such as access to affordable care and access to providers in shortage areas.

- **Food and Drug Administration (www.fda.gov)**
  The FDA ensures the safety and efficacy of many of the substances and machines that come into contact with our bodies, and as such has many resources and reports related to health concerns.

- **Centers for Medicare and Medicaid Services (www.cms.gov)**
  This agency works to improve life conditions for older adults and people with financial or medical need; some of its many health-related resources include directories of health care providers and locations.

State, Local, Tribal, and International Resources

Exploring resources produced by local, state, tribal, and international government agencies and organizations can yield valuable information in addition to that published by the federal government. For example, if you are interested in health questions at the county level, often federal publications do not contain data at that level of detail, while state health departments may publish that information in print and on the Internet. Likewise, many larger local health jurisdictions will publish health information for areas smaller than counties. It is harder to find subcounty information for rural areas than it is for urban areas, as the small population sizes in rural areas usually don't allow for data analysis and presentation. In fact, much of the health information available at any level is driven by population or survey sample size.

State and local health departments often develop resources that are updated regularly, so it is worth checking back with agencies of interest on a consistent basis. An example of this kind of resource at the state level is the *Vital Statistics Annual Reports* from the Texas Department of State Health Services. Similar examples of locally produced resources are the *Annual Morbidity/Communicable Disease Reports* series, from the County of Los Angeles Department of Public Health, and the *Annual Drinking Water Quality Report* from the City of Madison, Wisconsin.

When looking for state and local health information resources on the relevant agency's website, consider searching within the site using the following terms: statistics, vital statistics, data, publications, reports, and annual reports. Often an agency will have a link to its materials using one of these headings.

For resources related to the health of American Indians, Alaska Natives, and Native Hawaiians, be sure to look for information published by the tribe or organization (regardless of whether the group is recognized by the federal government), as well as that released by federal, state, and local governments. Nationally, the Urban Indian Health Institute (www.uihi.org) and the HHS Indian Health Service sites (www.ihs.gov) can be excellent sources of information on the health of these groups.

In addition, even if a question is not specifically international in focus, looking at information from international government sources, as well as intergovernmental organizations such as the World Health Organization, can suggest avenues of inquiry and questions that might not occur to someone in the United States context. For example, tables that include statistics on maternal mortality are common in the context of the developing world, and can cast light on the question of maternal mortality causes and prevention here in the United States.

Indicator Websites and Additional Sources

With the variety of sites with available data increasing, a useful genre of website in the health information world is the health indicator website. Health indicators are generally data points which suggest the relative health of populations and groups; for example, life expectancy at birth and infant mortality are considered two basic indicators of a community's health. The creators of indicator sites gather such information and synthesize it, saving information consumers from the laborious process of doing it themselves. In particular, these compilations of wide varieties of information from many sources can be very helpful when researching across topics. They may be produced by governmental or nongovernmental organizations, but they almost always use a substantial amount of government-created content.

Some well-known sites of this type are the Health Indicators Warehouse (www .healthindicators.gov) from the HHS; the Annie E. Casey Foundation's KIDS COUNT Data Center (datacenter.kidscount.org); and the United Health Foundation's America's Health Rankings (www.americashealthrankings.org). There are also a variety of state- and local-level indicator websites, such as the New York State Community Health Indicators Reports (New York State Department of Health, 2015). Entering the words *health indicator site* in a search engine will yield a number of hits. You can also do a search on the health indicator title itself (for example, life expectancy) if you know it. Three cautionary notes: always double-check that the data included are recent, critically assess their trustworthiness (perhaps using the site:gov limiter in a Google search), and be careful when using data from a website that reports a health index (a combined measure created from various separate pieces of health information) unless there is a clear understanding of the components of the index and the method used to combine them.

Last but not least, be persistent in searching for sources, especially grey literature: material that has not been formally published and is often difficult to find through regular channels. The New York Academy of Medicine Library publishes a Grey Literature Report (www.greylit.org) that outlines the latest such health-related publications, some of them government-produced (Association of College and Research Libraries, 2004). Consider exploring materials from legislative and judicial sources. And most importantly, just as one might use Google Scholar as a complement to a PubMed search, remember that any given search engine does not yield a reliable search of the entire Internet—always get a second opinion by repeating searches using a different search engine.

A Word on Consumer Health and Health Literacy

Many of us may never need to research any health topic beyond those related to our own personal situations. These kinds of searches fall under the term *consumer health*. Many resources will differentiate these kinds of questions from those focused on research or academic topics, in order to better serve information seekers' needs. A 2013 report by the Pew Internet and American Life Project and the California Health Care Foundation stated that 59 percent of American adults have looked online for health information in the past year, and 35 percent of American adults were online diagnosers who used their Internet searching to figure out the diagnosis for a condition they or a friend or relative were experiencing (Pew Internet and American Life Project, 2013).

Clearly, this trend toward using the Internet as a source of personal health information, which has spawned the term *e-patient,* is a phenomenon to be reckoned with, especially with the growing population of digital natives, many of whom are power users of technical applications. It raises questions such as: where are information seekers finding their information? Are the websites they consult accurate and reliable? Current? Free from bias? Do searchers know how to assess the quality of a website—a crucial concern if they are acting on the medical information found online? Are they health-literate, defined as, according to The Patient Protection and Affordable Care Act of 2010, Title V, "the degree to which individuals have the capacity to obtain, process, and understand basic health information and services needed to make appropriate health decisions" (Department of Health and Human Services, 2015c)? Among other things, health information seekers urgently need user-friendly tools and techniques for assessing websites' quality. A useful checklist is presented in the NLM's "MedlinePlus Guide to Healthy Web Surfing."

The role of government-produced publications in this scenario is central, since their function is to deliver the most trustworthy information available. Government agencies by their very nature have a vested interest in making reliable information available in user-friendly formats and well-publicized sites. An important effort along these lines is the increasing use of social media to reach citizens. Most government figures and many agencies, at federal, state, and local levels, have Facebook and Twitter accounts, and increasingly there are platforms for crowdsourcing (such as during disaster response) and other more dynamic and community-based forms of social media. There is even a coordinating body, the Social Media Community of Practice, which "unite(s) more than 500 Federal social media managers in a community dedicated to identifying and solving shared challenges" (Kapadia, 2014; DigitalGov.gov, 2015). Another effort has been to simplify the Web addresses of resource pages, so that users don't need to search for or remember complex strings. Hence, users can access sites such as aids.gov, cancer.gov, and so on.

More remains to be accomplished, both in educating users about available resources, and in teaching users how to use those resources most effectively. Consumer health librarians are working hard to partner with organizations that can get the message out, and to lobby for ever-improved materials.

In addition to education about availability and use of consumer health resources, health information seekers need a heightened awareness of quality issues related to current health news stories on the Internet and in other news outlets. Media portrayal of health news items should be taken with a grain of salt, no matter what the perceived quality of the information source. Every statistic or finding mentioned is worthy of healthy skepticism.

An example is an article from the *New York Times* published March 23, 2010. In it, Denise Grady (2010) wrote, "Caesarean section has become the most common operation in American hospitals." This is a strong and seemingly clear statement. Grady's source was a recently released report on cesarean deliveries by Menacker and Hamilton of the National Center for Health Statistics. They wrote, "In 2006, cesarean delivery was the most frequently performed surgical procedure in U.S. hospitals" (Menacker and Hamilton, 2010). This statement is very different than the one reported in the *Times.* First, the underlying data was four years old at the time of the *Times'* reporting, but the *Times'* wording implied the information was current; secondly, the terms *operation* and *surgical procedure,* while they may mean the same thing to a layperson, do not have the same meaning in the health care arena (the latter is a more specific term). Digging deeper, it seems that Menacker and Hamilton's statement was referencing yet another source. That source, by C. Allison Russo, Lauren Wier, and Claudia Steiner of the Agency for Healthcare Research and Quality (2009), stated "C-sections were, overall, the most commonly performed operating room procedures in U.S. hospitals in 2006." Considering that not all surgical procedures in hospitals are done in operating rooms, it seems that Menacker and Hamilton and Grady would each have done better to stick with this original study's language. Their slight changes in wording made for differences in meaning that could have a substantial effect on the usefulness of the information for certain seekers. The moral is, if you see a statistic, question it, dig for the original source, and assess its usefulness for the information need at hand.

Health Information Case Study:
The Patient Protection and Affordable Care Act

In 2010, after many months of planning and intense negotiations, President Obama signed into law the Patient Protection and Affordable Care Act (known as the Affordable Care Act, or Obamacare). The full act contained many provisions related to health care costs, insurance and insurers, but the most important for the purposes of consumer health (and this case study) were those related to the individual mandate requiring the purchase of health insurance coverage. In practice, these came into effect in October of 2013, with the aim of citizens obtaining insurance coverage beginning on January 1, 2014. The story of the launch and first months of the federal marketplace, HealthCare .gov, is a torturous, complex, and contentious one, which illustrates the vast challenges inherent in trying to disseminate information about a new program, and create an online mechanism for engaging with it.

Under the ACA, many Americans without health insurance (who were not a member of a variety of exempted groups) either had to purchase an approved insurance plan, or pay a penalty when they filed their income tax returns. Actually, as the American Public Health Association pointed out, the fact that people could choose the penalty rather than the insurance meant that it was not technically a mandate, although many in the public saw it as such (American Public Health Association, 2015). Options for the purchase of an eligible plan were to be made available through marketplaces including ACA-compliant plans from a range of insurers. These marketplaces would be coordinated either at the state or federal level, depending on states' preferences. In order to efficiently sign up the hundreds of thousands of eligible people and families for insurance plans, online interfaces were created, sometimes called insurance "exchanges."

Several months before the October 1 launch of the federal marketplace site, HealthCare.gov, there were both public relations issues and website readiness concerns. The provisions of the law were so complex, and therefore difficult to communicate, that millions of people did not realize that they might be eligible for subsidies (CNN Money, 2013). And, as early as March of 2013, the Obama administration was informed by a private consulting company that the October launch was "fraught with risks," in part due to the fact that the requirements for the system were constantly changing as it was being developed, and inadequate allowance was made for testing the many adjustments that had been made (Eilperin & Somashekhar, 2013).

The launch itself was disastrous. On October 12, 2013, the *New York Times* reported that millions were unable to even log in, and estimates of the fixes required ranged from two weeks to two months. A government shutdown occurring at the same time, everyday politics, regulatory requirements for government contracts, and lack of resources were each blamed for the "glitches" (Pear et al., 2013). The interface itself created bottlenecks: users were not able to browse for plans (they had to create accounts with personal information to even check out plan options), and account information had to be verified with data from nine or more federal agencies, before a consumer could make a choice of plan. In addition, after the consumer selected a plan, there were communication errors between the federal marketplace and chosen insurers, so that consumers could not be sure they were covered even if their application appeared to be successful on the federal site. (Buchanan et al., 2013) However, eventually the problems were mainly fixed, and by December 11, although sign-ups were still behind hoped-for levels, the HHS expressed confidence that they would sign up the expected seven million consumers by the deadline of March 2014 (Horsley, 2013). Eventually, eight million Americans signed up for health insurance using the federal marketplace, and sign-ups in the second year of ACA open enrollment (autumn of 2014) were virtually glitch-free, with 2.5 million signed up in the first month of site availability. (Alonso-Zaldivar, 2014; Mangan, 2014).

The costs, both financial and political, were high for this enormous information project. An August 2014 HHS report stated that the government had issued 60 contracts related to the Federal Marketplace, totaling $1.7 billion (Office of the Inspector General, 2014), and a July 2014 Government Accountability Office report noted that the "CMS [The Centers for Medicare and Medicaid Services (cms.gov), which had responsibility for the federal marketplace interface] incurred significant cost increases, schedule slips, and delayed system functionality for the FFM and data hub systems due primarily to changing requirements that were exacerbated by oversight gaps" and suggested that the "CMS take immediate actions to assess increasing contract costs and ensure that acquisition strategies are completed and oversight tools are used as required, among other actions" (US Government Accountability Office, 2014). While such an enormous information need may not arise again for many years, the lessons learned on this one highlight the issues facing government information campaigns of all sizes.

Besides the challenges related to providing information enabling the public to sign up for insurance (the brunt of which was borne by CMS), the ACA presented challenges to a perhaps unprecedented number of government agencies, which were impacted by its provisions and in turn needed to educate both consumers and professionals about those impacts. A list of additional agencies affected, by no means exhaustive, includes

- the White House (WhiteHouse.gov), which provided much of the response to the press
- the Internal Revenue Service (IRS.gov), of particular interest due to the tax penalty
- the Social Security Administration (SSA.gov) and other government agencies that were involved in verifying eligibility in the online marketplaces
- the Congressional Budget Office (cbo.gov), Department of Commerce (commerce.gov), and Department of Labor (dol.gov), which analyzed effects of the act on the economy, small businesses, employment rates, and so on
- policy-related agencies such as the Health Resources and Services Administration (HRSA.gov) and the Agency for Healthcare Research and Quality (AHRQ.gov)
- the National Library of Medicine (nlm.nih.gov), the consumer health arm of the Federal Trade Commission (consumer.ftc.gov), and other agencies responsible for providing consumer health information
- agencies such as the State Department (state.gov) and the Immigration and Customs Enforcement Department (ice.gov), which handled eligibility questions from Americans living abroad and foreign-born immigrants and residents in the United States
- state and local governments (especially in states that did not participate in the federal marketplaces) to which citizens turned for local assistance in enrollment

An addition to the above list is HealthIT.gov, which is related to the personal electronic health record. Along with insurance reform, the ACA contained extensive provisions for health system reform, among which was the mandated adoption of electronic health records by 2014 for all patients and providers (an instance of the government reaching far into the everyday provision of health care). The result is that electronic health records (EHRs) are a central aspect of the health information scene in the United States (Bradbury, 2009). The newly created Office of the National Coordinator of Health Information Technology oversees related concerns. Its public interface is the HealthIT website (HealthIT.gov), which states: "Health information technology (health IT) makes it possible for health care providers to better manage patient care through secure use and sharing of health information. Health IT includes the use of electronic health records (EHRs) instead of paper medical records to maintain people's health information."

While EHRs do not themselves constitute government information, as individuals' personal and health information is increasingly held in electronic format, and in varied databases which can all be related to each other, health research will be revolutionized. Interconnected electronic databases will allow analyses of previously unanswerable and complex health-related research questions, which in turn may have impacts on government. Both from the researchers' position and from the standpoint of protections needed by research subjects in this scenario, regulatory interventions beyond those already in place are sure to be required. It will be fascinating to see how it all plays out.

Exercises

1. A patron tells you that her mother has an appointment for an EKG. Her mother is anxious, since she doesn't understand English (she is a speaker of Korean) and doesn't understand what the test is for. What do you ask her to be sure you find the right source, and where do you look first?

2. Search PubMed for articles related to cancer screening. Develop a list of five topic areas which you might want to research further (for example, genetic testing might be one of the topics).

3. As you do the searches above, jot down the MeSH headings that correspond to the terms you are entering (you can find them in the "search details" box after conducting the search). How much did they vary from the terms you entered?

4. Read your favorite newspaper in either print or online form. Looking at the health-related stories, do you see any that cite statistics that were originally released in government documents? Can you find the document that the statistic came from, and is it accurately reported in the newspaper article?

5. Track the legislative history of The Patient Protection and Affordable Care Act (P.L. 111-148, passed on March 23, 2010). For a detailed account, see the *Law Library Journal* article "A Legislative History of the Affordable Care Act: How Legislative Procedure Shapes Legislative History" by John Cannan (Cannan, 2013).

6. Check out the Twitter account of the US Surgeon General (https://twitter .com/Surgeon_General). Of the tweets you see, which is most compelling for you personally? Which might be most helpful for library patrons at public libraries, vs. academic libraries?

Sources Mentioned in This Chapter

Agency for Healthcare Research and Quality, AHRQ.gov.

America's Health Rankings, www.americashealthrankings.org.

Centers for Disease Control and Prevention, CDC Wonder, wonder.cdc.gov.

Centers for Medicare and Medicaid Services, cms.gov.

City of Madison, Wisconsin, Annual Drinking Water Quality Report, www.cityofmadison.com/water/water-quality/annual-drinking-water-quality-report.

Clinical Trials, clinicaltrials.gov.

Columbia University Libraries, US Government Documents, Ready Reference Collection: Health and Social Services, http://library.columbia.edu/subject-guides/usgd/federal/rref/health.html.

County of Los Angeles, Department of Public Health, Acute Communicable Disease Control, http://publichealth.lacounty.gov/acd/Report.htm.

Environmental Protection Agency, epa.gov.

FastStats, www.cdc.gov/nchs/fastats.

Food and Drug Administration, www.fda.gov.

Health Indicators Warehouse, www.healthindicators.gov.

Health Resources and Services Administration, HRSA.gov.

Health Services Research Information Central: Data, Tools and Statistics, www.nlm.nih.gov/hsrinfo/datasites.html.

Health, United States, www.cdc.gov/nchs/hus.htm.

HealthCare.gov, www.healthcare.gov.

Healthfinder, healthfinder.gov.

HealthIT.gov, healthit.gov.

Healthy People, www.healthypeople.gov.

Index Medicus, www.nlm.nih.gov/bsd/num_titles.html.

Indian Health Service, www.ihs.gov.

KIDS COUNT Data Center, datacenter.kidscount.org.

Medical Library Association, Public Policy, https://www.mlanet.org/about/public-policy.

MedlinePlus, www.nlm.nih.gov/medlineplus.

MedlinePlus Guide to Healthy Web Surfing, www.nlm.nih.gov/medlineplus/healthywebsurfing.html.

MeSH Browser, www.nlm.nih.gov/mesh/MBrowser.html.

Morbidity and Mortality Weekly Report, www.cdc.gov/mmwr.

National Library of Medicine, www.nlm.nih.gov.

National Library of Medicine Catalog, www.ncbi.nlm.nih.gov/nlmcatalog.

National Library of Medicine Catalog of US Government Publications, catalog.gpo.gov/F.

National Technical Information Service, www.ntis.gov.

The New York Academy of Medicine, Grey Literature Report, www.greylit.org.

Partners in Information Access for the Public Health Workforce, http://phpartners.org.

Public Health Reports, www.publichealthreports.org/Issues.cfm.

PubMed, www.ncbi.nlm.nih.gov/pubmed.

PubMed Central, www.ncbi.nlm.nih.gov/pmc.

PubMed Health, www.ncbi.nlm.nih.gov/pubmedhealth.

Purdue University Libraries, Government Documents on Health. http://guides.lib.purdue.edu/govhealth.

Texas Department of State Health Services, Vital Statistics Annual Reports, www.dshs.state.tx.us/chs/vstat/annrpts.shtm.

ToxNet, toxnet.nlm.nih.gov.

University of Delaware Library, US Government Information: Health, http://guides.lib.udel.edu/c.php?g=85404&p=548920.

University of Washington Health Sciences Libraries, Public Health Toolkit, http://hsl.uw.edu/toolkits/
  public-health.
Urban Indian Health Institute, www.uihi.org.
Vital Statistics of the United States, www.cdc.gov/nchs/products/vsus.htm.

References

Alonso-Zaldivar Ricardo, 2014. "Probe exposes flaws behind HealthCare.gov rollout." http://apnews
  .excite.com/article/20140731/us-health-overhaul-de4c72c273.html.
American Public Health Association, 2015. "ACA Frequently Asked Questions." www.apha.org/
  topics-and-issues/health-reform/aca-frequently-asked-questions.
Association of College and Research Libraries. 2004. "Gray Literature: Resources for Locating Unpub-
  lished Research." www.ala.org/ala/mgrps/divs/acrl/publications/crlnews/2004/mar/graylit.cfm.
Boorkman, Jo Anne, Jeffrey T. Huber, and Fred W. Roper, eds. 2004. *Introduction to Reference Sources in the
  Health Sciences.* 4th ed. New York: Neal-Schuman.
Bradbury, Danny. 2009. "Obama and e-Health Records—Can He Really?" *The Guardian* (London),
  March 18. www.theguardian.com/society/2009/mar/18/electronic-medical-records.
Buchanan, Larry, Guilbert Gates, Haeyoun Park and Alicia Parlapiano, 2013. *The New York Times.* www
  .nytimes.com/interactive/2013/10/13/us/how-the-federal-exchange-is-supposed-to-work-and-how
  -it-didnt.html?ref=politics&_r=2&.
Cannan, John. 2013. "A Legislative History of the Affordable Care Act: How Legislative Procedure
  Shapes Legislative History." *Law Library Journal,* Volume 105, Number 2. www.aallnet.org/mm/
  Publications/llj/LLJ-Archives/Vol-105/no-2/2013–7.pdf.
Centers for Disease Control and Prevention. 2015a. "About the Morbidity and Mortality Weekly
  Review (MMWR) Series." www.cdc.gov/mmwr/about.html.
Centers for Disease Control and Prevention. 2015b. "BRFSS Overview: 2012." www.cdc.gov/brfss/
  annual_data/2012/pdf/Overview_2012.pdf.
Centers for Disease Control and Prevention. 2015c. "CDC Adding Households with Cell Phone Service
  to the National Immunization Survey (NIS), 2011." www.cdc.gov/vaccines/imz-managers/coverage/
  nis/child/dual-frame-sampling.html.
Centers for Disease Control and Prevention. 2015d. "Health United States: 2013." www.cdc.gov/nchs/
  data/hus/hus13.pdf.
Centers for Disease Control and Prevention. 2015e. "MMWR Publications." www.cdc.gov/mmwr/
  publications/index.html.
CNN Money, 2013. "Millions eligible for Obamacare subsidies, but most don't know it." http://money
  .cnn.com/2013/04/23/news/economy/obamacare-subsidies/index.html.
Department of Health and Human Services. 2015a. "Historical Highlights." www.hhs.gov/about/
  hhshist.html.
Department of Health and Human Services. 2015b. "Operating Divisions." www.hhs.gov/about/foa/
  opdivs/index.html.
Department of Health and Human Services. 2015c. "Full Text: Patient Protection and Affordable Care
  Act." www.hhs.gov/healthcare/rights/law/patient-protection.pdf.
DigitalGov.gov. 2015. "Social Media." www.digitalgov.gov/communities/social-media/.
Eilperin, Juliet and Sandhya Somashekhar, 2013. "Private consultants warned of risks before HealthCare.
  gov's Oct. 1 launch." *The Washington Post.* www.washingtonpost.com/politics/private-consultants
  -warned-of-risks-before-healthcaregovs-oct-1-launch/2013/11/18/9d2db5f4–5096–11e3–9fe0
  -fd2ca728e67c_story.html.

Grady, Denise. 2010. "Caesarean Births Are at a High in U.S." *The New York Times*. www.nytimes.com/2010/03/24/health/24birth.html.

Horsley, Scott, 2013. "Enrollment Jumps at HealthCare.gov, Though Totals Still Lag." www.npr.org/blogs/health/2013/12/11/250023704/enrollment-jumps-at-healthcare-gov-though-totals-still-lag.

Kapadia, Shefali. 2014. "Agencies 'Open the Door' to Innovative Uses of Social Media." www.federalnewsradio.com/445/3547907/Agencies-open-the-door-to-innovative-uses-of-social-media.

Katcher, Brian S. 1999. *MEDLINE: A Guide to Effective Searching*. San Francisco, CA: The Ashbury Press.

Lipscomb, Carolyn. 2000. "Medical Subject Headings (MeSH)." *Bulletin of the Medical Library Association* 88, no. 3 (July): 265–266.

Mangan, Dan, 2014. "HealthCare.gov enrollment hits nearly 2.5 million." www.cnbc.com/id/102273913.

MedlinePlus.gov. 2015. "MedlinePlus Guide to Healthy Web Surfing." www.nlm.nih.gov/medlineplus/healthywebsurfing.html.

Menacker, Fay, and Brady E. Hamilton. 2010. "Recent Trends in Cesarean Delivery in the United States." NCHS Data Brief no, 35, National Center for Health Statistics, Hyattsville, MD. March 2010. www.cdc.gov/nchs/data/databriefs/db35.pdf.

National Institutes of Health. 2015a. "About the National Institutes of Health." www.nih.gov/about.

National Institutes of Health. 2015b. "Institutes, Centers, and Offices." www.nih.gov/icd.

National Library of Medicine. 1961. "The First Catalogue of the Library of the Surgeon General's Office, Washington, 1840." www.nlm.nih.gov/hmd/pdf/library.pdf.

National Library of Medicine. 2015a. "About the National Library of Medicine." www.nlm.nih.gov/about/index.html.

National Library of Medicine. 2015b. "FAQ: Index Medicus Chronology." www.nlm.nih.gov/services/indexmedicus.html.

National Library of Medicine. 2015c. "MEDLINE, PubMed, and PMC (PubMed Central): How are they different?" www.nlm.nih.gov/pubs/factsheets/dif_med_pub.html.

National Library of Medicine. 2015d. "National Library of Medicine: John Shaw Billings Centennial." www.nlm.nih.gov/hmd/pdf/john.pdf.

National Library of Medicine. 2015e. "NCHS Published Report Series." www.nlm.nih.gov/nichsr/usestats/Example16_NCHS_published_report.html.

National Library of Medicine. 2015f. "NLM Classification." www.nlm.nih.gov/pubs/factsheets/nlmclassif.html.

National Library of Medicine. 2015g. "The Story of NLM Historical Collections." www.nlm.nih.gov/hmd/about/collectionhistory.html.

New York State Department of Health. 2015. "New York State Community Health Indicator Reports (CHIRS)." www.health.ny.gov/statistics/chac/indicators/.

Office of the Inspector General, United States Department of Health and Human Services, 2014. "An Overview of 60 Contracts That Contributed to the Development and Operation of the Federal Marketplace: Complete Report." http://oig.hhs.gov/oei/reports/oei-03–14–00231.asp.

Pear, Robert, Sharon LaFraniere and Ian Austen. 2013. "From the Start, Signs of Trouble at Health Portal." *The New York Times*. www.nytimes.com/2013/10/13/us/politics/from-the-start-signs-of-trouble-at-health-portal.html?hpw&pagewanted=all.

Pew Internet and American Life Project. 2013. "Health Online, 2013." www.pewinternet.org/2013/01/15/health-online-2013/.

Russo, C. Allison, Lauren Wier, and Claudia Steiner. 2009. "Hospitalizations Related to Childbirth, 2006." Statistical Brief #71. Rockville, MD: Agency for Healthcare Research and Quality, Healthcare Cost and Utilization Project (HCUP). www.hcup-us.ahrq.gov/reports/statbriefs/sb71.jsp.

United States Government Accountability Office. 2014. "Healthcare.gov: Ineffective Planning and Oversight Practices Underscore the Need for Improved Contract Management." www.gao.gov/products/GAO-14-694.

CHAPTER 12

Education Information

SUSAN EDWARDS

Today, education is perhaps the most important function of state and local governments. Compulsory school attendance laws and the great expenditures for education both demonstrate our recognition of the importance of education to our democratic society. It is required in the performance of our most basic public responsibilities, even service in the armed forces. It is the very foundation of good citizenship.

—*Brown v. Board of Education, 347 U.S. 483 (1954)*

Introduction

We are all deeply affected by education—as children, as parents, as citizens. Education has a profound impact on the quality of life and economic well-being of individuals and communities, and is one of the largest expenditures of towns, cities, and states. Conducting education research can be challenging and complex, partly because education is at once both highly decentralized and subject to extensive and complex government oversight, policy, and standardization at all levels of government. Funding for education provides one example of the decentralization. The Census Bureau's May 2014 report on public education finances shows that in 2012, the federal government provided about 10 percent of the total funding for public elementary and secondary schools, while the states contributed about 46.5 percent and local governments provided 44.5 percent (Bureau of the Census, 2014).

Unlike many other countries, the United States has no national core curriculum—though 43 states and the District of Columbia have adopted the Common Core State Standards Initiative (www.corestandards.org). There is no national agreement on what is required to graduate from high school, or the age at which a student begins, or is allowed to leave, school. Decisions about what and how to teach have historically been controlled at or below the state level and can be highly contentious within and even between states, as demonstrated by ongoing battles over whether or how to teach evolution.

Yet within this historical backdrop of decentralization, there is an important and growing federal role in educational assessment, policy, funding, and research. This is in addition to the historic role of promoting equal access to educational opportunities, and preventing discrimination based on sex, race, ethnicity, national origin, or disability. For librarians and researchers, it's particularly important to know that the US Department of Education plays a crucial role, both currently and historically, in collecting and disseminating information and data from the states about education—including at the local level.

Education reference questions can be challenging for librarians, and frequently have real-life implications for the patrons who ask them. They often combine the personal and the political, the local and the federal, as in this question: "My child is eight years old and has cerebral palsy. What does the research show is the best practice for children like her? What does the law say she's entitled to, and how can I work with my daughter's teacher and school to make sure she is getting the best education possible?" In this chapter we will explore using government information from a variety of local, state, and federal sources to answer these and many other questions.

Government Involvement in Education

The 10th Amendment of the US Constitution (the final item in the Bill of Rights), enacted in 1789, provides that "the powers not delegated to the United States by the Constitution, nor prohibited by it to the States, are reserved to the States respectively, or to the people." Since education was not explicitly mentioned in the Constitution, it was deemed a state, not federal, function. However, since education touches on other fundamental rights established by the Constitution, and because it is so integrally related with the nation's economic and political well-being, the federal government's involvement in education has expanded greatly since World War II through civil rights legislation, federal court decisions, and executive action. (Cross, 2010: ix–x)

State Sources

We think of the United States as having a core commitment to free public education, but this has evolved over time and historically was determined by the state, or even the city or town. The first statewide law requiring free public schools was enacted in 1826 by Massachusetts, which was also the first to make attendance compulsory, in 1852. (We'll see later, however, that in at least one town in Massachusetts, education was compulsory only for three months of the year!) School attendance

Anti-Education Laws?

At the same time that education was becoming more available for some, it was becoming illegal for others. In 1830, Louisiana passed the first law that prohibited teaching slaves to read; Georgia, Virginia, Alabama, and North and South Carolina passed similar laws between 1831 and 1835 (Goldin, 2006: 2–390).

didn't become mandatory in all states until 1918—though reflecting the decentralized nature of education, many cities passed free school legislation prior to their states' enactment of public school laws (Goldin, 2006: 2–390).

Some states and local governments published (and continue to publish) annual reports that complement, and may precede, the federal education sources. The titles vary, and it can take a bit of sleuthing in the library catalog or in a secondary source to determine the exact title. In New York, for example, the *Report of the Superintendent of Common Schools* from 1823 provides information on school funding and on the number of students attending school.

As was discussed in chapters 5–7, states each have their own statutes, case law precedent, and administrative law which will include education law. Education librarians should be familiar with the main sources for their state. The state department of education also may have a website that provides a helpful entry point for state and federal legislation related to education in your state.

Federal Collection and Dissemination of Information

In 1867, the US Bureau of Education was established to collect and disseminate information on schools and teaching, a role it continues to fill today through its successor, the US Department of Education. The Bureau published an annual *Report of the Commissioner of Education* from 1869 through 1917 and provides rich descriptive information on a wide variety of topics related to education. It contains reports from all the states, including many from towns and cities. These reports, like other primary sources, give a vivid sense of the attitudes, prejudices, and concerns of the time. For example, the *Report* of 1873 offers the following quote from a bishop in Dakota:

> Our missions are placed among a wild people, who, from the oldest down
> to the youngest, have never known any control, but have lived independent,
> idle lives, with no higher law than the whim of the moment. It is not easy
> to induce the children of such people to come to a day-school, and their
> parents would not think for a moment of compelling them. But they will
> come to a boarding-school, for there they find what they do not know in
> their own homes, regular meals, good clothing, and comfortable beds. These
> wild children become quite docile in the schools and their improvement is
> decided. (Bureau of Education, 1874: 479)

The *Report* includes articles on special topics, such as *On the Instruction of Deaf Mutes* by E. M. Gallaudet (first superintendent of what was to become Gallaudet University). In addition to his report on the pedagogy of the Clarke Institution for Deaf Mutes in Northampton, Massachusetts, he takes the time to report on an off-topic, but intriguing, overlap between the signs used by American Indians and the sign language of the deaf, including "identical or strikingly similar" signs for love, hate, fear, death, anger, river, and other words (Bureau of Education, 1874: 503).

But the bulk of the *Report* consists of detailed informational essays and statistics about the schools, libraries, museums, orphanages, and institutions for the deaf and blind. It's hard to imagine where else we could learn that in Pittsfield, Massachusetts, in 1873, school attendance was compulsory for three months of each year for children between the ages of 8 and 14, of which only six weeks need be consecutive; or that in Mississippi eight years after the end of the Civil War, black parents were "forcing the question of mixed schools in cases where there are but two or three colored children in a subdistrict" (Bureau of Education, 1874: 222).

Congress and Higher Education

In 1862 Congress passed the Morrill Land Grant Act, which gave federal land to states which they could use (or sell, and use the proceeds) to found colleges of mechanical arts, military science, and agriculture. This was of great value to the states, but not everyone benefited equally. African Americans were not allowed to attend some of the original land-grant institutions, and in 1890 Congress passed the Second Morrill Land Grant Act. This act gave the Office of Education responsibility for administering support for the original land-grant colleges and universities and also mandated that the facilities be open to all students, or the state must establish separate institutions. In response, the Southern states then established 16 African American land-grant colleges, part of the historically black colleges and universities (HBCUs).

In 1944 Congress passed the G.I. Bill (you can find the official name in chapter 5!) which included funding for vocational training and higher education for veterans returning from World War II. The G.I. Bill had a profound economic and social impact, making a college education attainable for many students who were the first in their families to attend. In 1947, the peak year, veterans made up 49 percent of college admissions. By 1956, when the original bill expired, almost half of all veterans (7.8 million out of 16 million) had participated in an education or vocational training program.

The Higher Education Act of 1965 included provisions for federally funded financial aid for needy college students. It was extended in 1973 with the federal Pell Grant program, and further extended when Congress passed the Taxpayer Relief Act of 1997, establishing the Hope Tax Credits, tax credits for lifelong learning, education IRAs, and the ability to deduct interest on student loans. Today, the federal government is the major source of financial aid for students in higher education. The FAFSA (Free Application for Federal Student Aid) is the gateway to federal aid, administered by the Department of Education.

The Supreme Court and Education

The Supreme Court has decided several key cases involving constitutional rights and education. For example, *Plessy v. Ferguson,* 163 U.S. 537 (1896), upheld racial segregation (including the resistance to integration that resulted in the land-grant funded historically black colleges and universities) with the "separate but equal" doctrine. This validation of racial segregation remained in effect until 1954, when it was overturned by the Supreme Court in *Brown v. Board of Education.* Other education-related Supreme Court decisions include *West Virginia Board of Education v. Barnette,* 319 U.S. 624 (1943), in which the Court held that students could not be compelled to salute the flag; *Engel v. Vitale,* 370 U.S. 421 (1962), which established that states could not require public prayer in schools, even if students were permitted to remain silent or leave the room while the prayer was recited; *University of California Regents v. Bakke,* 438 U.S. 265 (1978), where the Court ruled that while race could be a factor in admissions, racial quotas even in support of affirmative action violated the equal protection clause and could not be used to determine admission to a state-supported school; and *Plyler v. Doe,* 457 U.S. 202 (1982), which held that Texas could not deny access to a free public education to undocumented school-age children.

Federal Education Legislation

The first comprehensive federal education legislation was passed in 1958 in response to the Soviet launch of Sputnik during the Cold War. The goal of the National Defense Education Act (NDEA) was to help Americans remain academically competitive with the Soviets. The NDEA included loans for college students, as well as provisions to improve science, mathematics, and foreign language instruction in elementary and secondary schools (Department of Education, 2010).

In 1965 Congress passed the Elementary and Secondary Education Act (ESEA), the main federal law affecting education from kindergarten through high school. In order to promote equal access to education, ESEA included (and still includes) Title 1 funding. Title 1 directs funding to local school districts to improve teaching and learning for students in high-poverty schools. Sex discrimination in education was prohibited by Title IX of the Education Amendments of 1972, and Section 504 of the Rehabilitation Act of 1973 prohibited discrimination based on disability. In 1975, Congress passed the Individuals with Disabilities Education Act (IDEA) to ensure services to children with disabilities, and to govern how states and public agencies provide early intervention and special education (http://idea.ed.gov/).

In 2001, Congress reauthorized ESEA as the No Child Left Behind Act (NCLB). NCLB expanded the role of the federal government in education by mandating increased accountability from the states, school districts, and schools with the goal of ensuring that no child (or group of children) would be "left behind" in underperforming, high-poverty schools. NCLB required states to implement statewide accountability systems covering all public schools and students based on rigorous state standards. It also required states to measure statewide progress toward meeting the objectives set by the state with assessment results broken out by poverty, race, ethnicity, disability, and limited English proficiency (www2.ed.gov/nclb/overview/intro/execsumm.html).

> The No Child Left Behind Act of 2001 transformed the federal government's role in education, moving it, in a musical sense, from second-chair status in the orchestra to the conductor's podium. The government now is almost literally in the position of setting the stage for all the other players. The conductor can call in the string section (highly qualified teachers), cue the wind section (supplementary-service providers), maintain the drama through the

percussionists (adequate yearly progress), and conclude with a stunning finish that brings everyone to their feet (accountability). (Cross, 2010:158)

Education Resources: Getting Started

The US government provides numerous resources for education research, including information about education at the state and local level. The first two, the *Condition of Education* and ED.gov, are easy to use and can provide quick answers to some education reference questions. *Teachers* from the LC is a unique source for teachers wanting to integrate primary sources into their lesson plans. Education Resources Information Clearinghouse (ERIC), is a much larger, more complex and powerful resource, so it is covered here in more depth.

The Condition of Education

The *Condition of Education* (http://nces.ed.gov/programs/coe/) is a congressionally mandated report of education in the United States. Published annually since 1975, it provides a national (not state or local) portrait of trends in early childhood through postsecondary education. It includes statistics and a narrative summary of student achievement, educational outcomes, and school environments and resources. Each year also provides in-depth coverage of a specific topic which varies from year to year. For example, the 2014 *Condition of Education* focuses on financing higher education in the United States, showing a fourfold increase (in constant dollars) of grant aid from 2000 to 2010 and a 2.5 percent increase in loans—for a total in 2011 of $146 billion in student financial aid in grants and loans.

ED.gov (US Department of Education)

ED.gov (ED) from the United States Department of Education is *the* portal for information about education from preschool through graduate school. Educational policy is a particular strength of the site, and ED provides access to an extensive network of legislation, regulation, and policy guidelines on elementary and secondary education, higher education, adult education, special education and rehabilitative services, and vocational education. ED provides ED links to research publications and reports, and has a frequently updated news section and blog. ED also delivers content with Web 2.0 technology, including Facebook, Twitter, and YouTube.

According to the department's website, ED's mission is to promote student achievement and preparation for global competitiveness by fostering educational excellence and ensuring equal access. ED supports these goals through:

- Establishing policies on federal financial aid for education, and distributing as well as monitoring those funds.
- Collecting data on America's schools and disseminating research.

- Focusing national attention on key educational issues.
- Prohibiting discrimination and ensuring equal access to education.

The Library of Congress: Teachers

The LC provides a deep and rich body of materials to help classroom teachers effectively use primary sources, including lesson plans that meet Common Core standards, state content standards, and the standards of national organizations. The teaching resources are on a wide range of topics including the Japanese American Internment, the Harlem Renaissance, the Dust Bowl, Jim Crow and Segregation, and many more. Sources include photographs, cartoons, documents, and multimedia.

ERIC

ERIC, the Education Resources Information Clearinghouse (www.eric.ed.gov), from the US Department of Education, is the world's largest digital library of education resources. ERIC indexes published and unpublished scholarly and professional literature in education. One of ERIC's historic and current strengths is to provide access to material that has not been formally published (also called grey literature or fugitive literature). This includes conference papers, dissertations, and material from research centers, policy and professional organizations, and federal, state, and local agencies. In addition, ERIC indexes hundreds of education and education-related journals.

ERIC began in 1966, and in the early years provided subscribing libraries with the unpublished material on microfiche. In 1993 ERIC began migrating to the Web (Weiner, 2009), and has actively worked to convert the microfiche to digital form. Much, but not all, of this material (1966–1992) is now available online. Digital conversion is an ongoing effort, as ERIC seeks permission from copyright holders of this unpublished material to make the remaining documents available online. Some libraries are removing the content available online, while others are choosing to keep the complete microfiche collection "just in case."

ERIC is not the only tool used to find education research, though it is the only one that is freely available as a government resource. In 2007 Jean-Jacques Strayer analyzed the indexing coverage of ERIC and compared it with some of the commercial databases. He determined that the commercial databases Academic Search Premier, Web of Science, and PsycINFO also uncovered useful education research depending on the topic and the depth of the researcher's information need, but stated that "[a] strong case can be made for starting with the ERIC database" (Strayer, 2008: 91). Not included in his comparison was the relatively new Education Source (developed from a merger of databases from EBSCO Publishing and H. W. Wilson, including Education abstracts, Education index retrospective, Education full text, Education research complete, and more than 200 additional full-text journals) and it would be interesting to see how the indexing coverage compares with ERIC. But even without this analysis, the fact remains that ERIC is a government-published database that is essential to all education researchers.

One of ERIC's strengths is its powerful search interface based on the *Thesaurus of ERIC Descriptors* (Thesaurus). Like the MeSH subject headings covered in chapter 11, the Thesaurus provides controlled vocabulary to increase search precision. A word in the Thesaurus (called a descriptor) is not the same as a keyword. A descriptor is applied to the article by an editor to describe what the article is about, as opposed to a keyword, which is any word that appears in the bibliographic record—but which may or may not be the focus of the content. Controlled vocabulary also ensures that related words with the same meaning are brought together into one term. And as terminology changes over time, the descriptors provide links from earlier terms to current terms.

Like all disciplines, education has its own terminology (or jargon, depending on one's perspective) and using the Thesaurus is particularly helpful for the searcher new to the discipline. For example, the Thesaurus category of Reading further subdivides into areas such as Reading Aloud to Others, Reading Difficulties, Reading Fluency, Speed Reading, and provides links to additional terms on related topics. Once you find a helpful term it can be added easily to the advanced search query and combined with other descriptors or limits.

Let's look at how to use ERIC's thesaurus to help our parent trying to find research on the best educational practice for children with cerebral palsy. Searching the Thesaurus for cerebral palsy, she sees that it is listed, but is also part of the larger category of Disabilities. By browsing Disabilities, she can see the array of subtopics available including related and relevant terms, such as Speech Impairment and Multiple Disabilities, which could be added to broaden the search, if cerebral palsy doesn't find enough material. After adding cerebral palsy to the Advanced Search, ERIC displays the results and a panel on the left side of the screen lets her restrict the results in a variety of ways—by date, audience (whether the article is oriented towards teachers, researchers, parents, or another group), source (name of journal), education level, or publication type. Our parent cares most about the grade level, so she chooses to limit by Elementary Education and finds quite a few articles that are worth exploring.

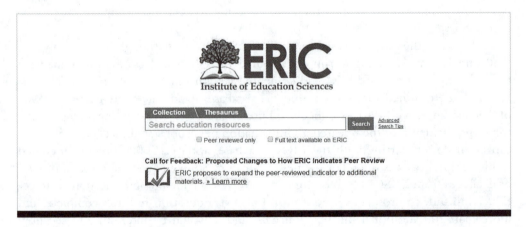

FIGURE 12.1
ERIC

ERIC Research Tip

Today's searchers are used to typing in a few words and relying on the search engine to retrieve the most relevant results. Sometimes this approach fails—which is when they come to a reference librarian. Power searching a structured database with editor-added content like the Thesaurus and field restrictions can help them locate the precise information they need.

Statistics

Statistics questions are common in education reference, and most frequently involve the demographics of students and staff, school funding and expenditures, and educational attainment or achievement. Our patrons want us to help them find the one number that provides the hard data to support their argument. But statistics are squishy, as this recent newspaper article shows:

> State officials are claiming the state dropout rate declined by almost 11 percent over the last year, but critics say the data being used is flawed and doesn't accurately reflect what's going on in Texas schools. (Associated Press, 2010)

The article elaborates that a state report claims the dropout rate in Texas is 9.4 percent, while other studies estimate a much higher number of dropouts—up to 31 percent according to an independent education advocacy group. How can there be such a difference of opinion on what seems like such a basic question?

The graduation rate, which seems so simple, is actually quite complex—partly because there are different definitions of a dropout and different ways to count them. Different states use different methodologies, as do the Census Bureau and the National Center for Education Statistics. Some of the differences include whether the dropout rate includes students who left school but received a GED, whether students are counted who leave that school and move to another state or country, if students (including students with disabilities or with limited English proficiency) must graduate within four years in order to be counted with their cohort, and whether to count students who are expelled or who are removed to child protective services (Wolfe, 2009).

Different measures have different goals—determining the dropout rate of a given high school for school accountability purposes is a very different goal from measuring the total number of 16- to 24-year-olds who aren't in school and don't have a high school diploma or GED. And different data sources use different methodologies. All of the census data, unlike administrative data, relies on a sample of the population and is self-reported. State data come from administrative records and is more comprehensive— but it is not consistently handled from state to state, and has the built-in problem of not tracking students who leave school. For difficult to find (or understand!) statistics, one approach is to search ERIC with a limit by the publication type Numerical/Quantitative. The resulting articles can help explain the numbers, as well as the strengths and weaknesses of the different methodologies. And the sources cited may lead to the exact statistic needed.

An important part of the statistics reference interview is to determine the geographic level of the question. Is the patron interested in national level data? Or does s/he need the information broken out for a state, school district, or one particular school? Another important question is whether the information needs to be cross-tabulated by a particular variable. For example, does the patron want just the dropout rate by high school, or does she also want it broken down by (cross-tabulated with) race or gender?

The number of statistics reported from more than 14,000 local school districts up to the state and the national level is growing, partly in response to No Child Left Behind and other standards-based reforms that require measurable progress towards educational goals. However to answer some questions, you still need to consult district or individual school sources. One example of a question that requires using the local data is per pupil spending for each school within a district, an important aspect of analyzing comparability.

Comparability

Since 1965, Title 1 of the Elementary and Secondary Education Act has included additional funding for local school districts based on the number of children who are economically disadvantaged in order to provide comparability and "ensure that all children have a fair, equal, and significant opportunity to obtain a high-quality education" (US Department of Education, 2005). Measuring whether equity in funding has been achieved, both at the school and the district level, has been challenging—in part due to a lack of data. For instance, *No Child Left Behind* does not require that districts report the actual salary data for school personnel. As long as all the schools in the district use the same salary scale, and the schools with the greatest poverty have the same proportion of teachers as the wealthy schools, they are seen as comparable. Recognizing this limitation, the United States Department of Education gathered data on state and local spending on school-level personnel and non-personnel resources (Klein, 2015). The first data (from school year 2008–2009) was released in December 2011, and showed that about 40 percent of the variance in per pupil funding occurred within school districts (Spatig-Amerikaner, 2015) and that 4.5 million low-income students attending higher-poverty schools received on average $1,200 less per pupil than students in other schools in the same district (Hanna et al., 2015). A study of comparability in California schools undertaken by the Center For American Progress (which implemented its own school-by-school finance data collection prior to the federal requirement) showed that "the aggregated salary gap between two otherwise identical schools with the average number of teachers, one with a student poverty rate of 50 percentage points higher than the other, amounts to approximately $76,000" (Miller, 2010). This discrepancy is attributed to teachers with more experience, and therefore higher pay, moving from high-poverty schools to low-poverty schools.

Statistical Sources

This selective list of sources provides a wide range of education-related statistics. A particular source may focus on finance, achievement, demographic, or higher education statistics, but most contain a combination of these elements. All of the federal sources contain statistics for the states; some also have statistics for smaller geographic areas including school districts. Congressional hearings (discussed in chapter 3) can also be a good source of statistics.

National Center for Education Statistics (NCES) *nces.ed.gov*

NCES is the primary federal entity for collecting and analyzing data related to education, located within the US Department of Education and the Institute of Education Sciences. NCES publishes numerous reports and datasets each year. Some NCES databases are individually covered in more depth within this list.

Digest of Education Statistics *nces.ed.gov/programs/digest/*

A good starting place, the *Digest,* from the NCES, covers a wide variety of subjects including the number of schools and colleges, teachers, enrollments, graduates, educational attainment, finances, federal funds for education, libraries, and international education. All material is nationwide in scope, and spans from prekindergarten through graduate school. The *Digest,* like the *Statistical Abstract of the United States* covered in chapter 10, also provides helpful information on the source of each of the statistics in the tables.

American FactFinder *factfinder.census.gov*

American FactFinder (from the US Census Bureau and covered in chapter 16), provides access to education-related statistics for the country as a whole, as well as for specific geographic areas, based on answers to questions from recent decennial censuses and the American Community Survey. For a quick start, select a geographic area in the Community Facts search box, and then expand Education on the left of the screen to see which statistics are available on a subtopic such as educational attainment or school enrollment (see figure 12.2).

The American Community Survey (ACS), also covered in chapter 16, offers a vast array of education-related data for states, cities, and even school districts. The ACS tables on the subject of Education: School Enrollment and Educational Attainment are listed below. In the Advanced Search screen of American Factfinder, you can enter the desired table number (the alphanumeric code on the left of the title of the table) and geographic area and then pick the desired dataset (ACS 1, 3, or 5 year estimates):

B06009	Place of Birth by Educational Attainment in the United States
B07009	Geographical Mobility in the Past Year by Educational Attainment for Current Residence in the U.S.

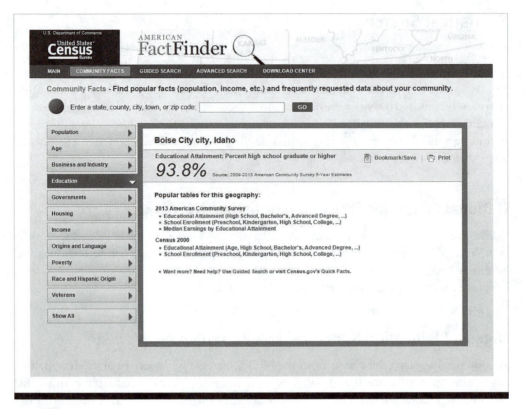

FIGURE 12.2
American FactFinder Community Facts

B07409	Geographical Mobility in the Past Year by Educational Attainment for Residence 1 Year Ago in the U.S.
B13014	Women 15 to 50 Years Who Had a Birth in the Past 12 Months by Marital Status and Educational Attainment
B14001	School Enrollment by Level of School for the Population 3 Years and Over (Note: Tables B14002 and B14003 further break this down by Type of School and Level of School.)
B14004	Sex by College or Graduate School Enrollment by Type of School by Age for the Population 15+
B14005	Sex by School Enrollment by Educational Attainment by Employment Status for the Population 15+
B14006	Poverty Status in the Past 12 Months by School Enrollment by Level of School for the Population 3 Years and Over
B15001	Sex by Age by Educational Attainment for the Population 18 Years and Over
B15002	Sex by Educational Attainment for the Population 25 Years and Over (Note: this table is further broken down by Race/Ethnicity in tables C15002A–C150021.)

B15004	Poverty Status in the Past 12 Months by Sex by Educational Attainment for the Population 25 Years and Over
B16010	Educational Attainment and Employment Status by Language Spoken at Home for the Population 25 Years and Over
B17003	Poverty Status in the Past 12 Months of Individuals by Sex and Educational Attainment

---

Hispanic Classification

When using current census-based data, remember that "White Alone" includes Hispanics! By Office of Management and Budget definitions (OMB), Hispanic is not a race—Hispanics can be any race, including white, black, or some other race. Most researchers working with race/ ethnicity will want to use White, Not Hispanic or Latino instead of simply White Alone.

Education Demographic and Geographic Estimates (EDGE)

nces.ed.gov/programs/edge/

EDGE (formerly School District Demographics System, SDDS) provides user-friendly access to some of the education related ACS data, plus some additional surveys, tailored to the school district level. EDGE doesn't include all the education data in ACS, but does provide easier to use tools for mapping school related data.

Public School System Finances *www.census.gov/govs/school*

Since 1977, this Census Bureau survey includes financial data for all public school systems that provide elementary or secondary education. The data include revenue by source (local property tax, monies from other school systems, private tuition and transportation payments, school lunch charges, direct state aid, and federal aid passed through the state government), and expenditure by function and object. Since 1992, it also includes direct state aid for several different programs, including; federal aid for Title I of the Elementary and Secondary Education Act; Children with Disabilities, and Impact Aid programs; salaries and employee benefits by function; maintenance, transportation, and business activities; and spending for instructional equipment.

National Assessment of Educational Progress (NAEP, also known as The Nation's Report Card) *nces.ed.gov/nationsreportcard/*

NAEP is the only national assessment of America's students in mathematics, reading, science, writing, the arts, civics, economics, geography, US history, and beginning in

2014, Technology and Engineering Literacy (TEL). NAEP provides results for populations of students (e.g., all fourth-graders) and groups within those populations (e.g., female students or Hispanic students). NAEP does not provide scores for individual students or schools, although state NAEP can report results for selected large urban districts.

State Education Data Profiles *nces.ed.gov/programs/stateprofiles/*

The Profiles provide easy access to elementary and secondary education characteristics and statistics on finance, postsecondary education, public libraries, assessments, and selected demographics for all states. Via dropdown box or a map of the United States, users can select up to four states for comparison, or view US averages as a whole.

Common Core of Data (CCD) *nces.ed.gov/ccd/*

CCD annually collects fiscal and non-fiscal data about all public schools, public school districts, and state education agencies in the United States. The data are supplied by state education agency officials and include information for schools and school districts, including name, address, and phone number; descriptive information and demographics about students and staff; and fiscal data, including revenues and current expenditures. (This database is challenging; most users will need some help!)

State Contacts and Information
www2.ed.gov/about/contacts/state/index.html

This site provides a quick place to look for contact information (phone numbers, e-mail, address, and website) for state education agencies and education-related organizations.

IPEDS: Integrated Postsecondary Education Data System
nces.ed.gov/ipeds/

This is the place to go for answers to in-depth questions requiring higher education statistics. IPEDS gathers information from every college, university, and technical and vocational institution that participates in the federal student financial aid programs. It includes data on student characteristics (race/ethnicity, gender, and age); institutional characteristics; institutional prices; enrollment; student financial aid; degrees and certificates conferred; graduation rates; and the institution's human and fiscal resources.

Historical Statistics

The first education statistics for the United States as a whole come from the 1840 decennial census (see chapter 16 for more on Census). Slavery in the United States was legally sanctioned at that point, and free white men and women were asked whether they were literate (in any language). In 1850 and 1860 all free inhabitants, regard-

less of race or gender, were asked about literacy. In 1850 the census added a question about
school attendance, but surprisingly school attainment (the highest grade completed) wasn't
asked until 1940 (Goldin, 2006: 2–468). The
Historical Census Browser (http://mapserver
.lib.virginia.edu/index.html) from the University
of Virginia provides an easy to use interface for
locating education statistics to the state or county
level from the Decennial Census through 1960.

> **CONTACTING AGENCIES DIRECTLY**
>
> Sometimes the state education agency (or even the school or school district) has additional data that are not included in the published national or state sources. Personal contact may turn up that extremely elusive statistic that a patron needs. When calling or e-mailing, let the agency representatives know they are speaking with a librarian, and list the resources already searched. It establishes the librarian's appreciation for their expert knowledge and respect for their time.

In 1867 the Bureau of Education (precursor to
the cabinet-level Department of Education) was
established, and the *Report of the Commissioner of
Education* (title varies, also called *Annual Reports
of the Commissioner of Education*) was published
from 1869–1870 through 1916–1917. The original
Reports may be difficult to find, but fortunately for
librarians and researchers, these *Reports* were included in the US *Congressional Serial Set,*
which is also commercially available online (the *Serial Set* is discussed in chapters 2 and 3),
and many are now freely available online via HathiTrust Digital Library (http://catalog
.hathitrust.org/Record/009164574). The *Reports* were continued by the *Biennial Survey
of Education in the United States* through 1957–1958, followed by the *Digest of Education
Statistics* from 1962 to the present. Selected statistics from these series are also included
in the *Historical Statistics of the United States* as discussed in chapter 10.

For those who want a bit less detail with their statistics, the National Center for
Education Statistics published *120 Years of American Education: A Statistical Portrait.* Covering 1870–1990, this is also available on the Web (http://nces.ed.gov/pubs93/93442
.pdf) and lists historical sources, a brief history of education statistics, and statistical
tables.

Some states (and even some school districts) have collected and published a variety
of education-related reports including statistics on school finance, student demographics, and student achievement. In many cases these reports provide much more detailed
information than the national compilations, and may even predate them. Many of these
statistics are not found online; they exist only on paper and can be difficult to locate
through a library catalog. As discussed in chapter 10, it's important to think about who
might have collected the data, and then to be creative with searching for agencies as
authors in a library catalog. For example, a patron is interested in education in Oakland,
California, in the late 19th and early 20th centuries. Searching U.C. Berkeley's library
catalog with simple keywords of education, California, and Oakland retrieves *Rules and
Regulations of the Board of Education of the City of Oakland, California,* from 1897. The
full record leads us to the corporate author entry of "Oakland (Calif.). Board of Education." Finding this access point allows us to retrieve many relevant titles, including
the *Annual Report* of Oakland's Board of Education from 1872 to 1918. Note that the
corporate author is a very useful access point for historical government documents; it
frequently retrieves more titles than searching by subject heading.

Since many education questions have a local focus, it's helpful to familiarize yourself with the sources available for your state and local area, as well as with how your library has cataloged them.

Emerging Trends in Education Research

Evidence-based practice is "a new educational and practice paradigm for closing the gaps between research and practice to maximize opportunities to help clients and avoid harm" (Gambrill 2006, 339). Evidence-based policy initiatives in education such as the 2001 No Child Left Behind legislation emphasize research as a necessary prerequisite for program support. In 2002, Congress created the Institute of Education Sciences (http://ies.ed.gov) to conduct and disseminate scientifically valid education research using methods from science and medicine such as randomized controlled trials and meta-analysis of the literature. As the IES website states:

Our mission is to provide rigorous and relevant evidence on which to ground education practice and policy and share this information broadly. By identifying what works, what doesn't, and why, we aim to improve educational outcomes for all students, particularly those at risk of failure. (Institute of Education Sciences, 2015).

The implementation of these initiatives in education has not been without controversy. Some of the definitions of "what works" used by the What Works Clearinghouse have been criticized, and some have questioned whether test scores might rise as a result of "teaching to the test" rather than increasing the literacy and/or math skills of the students. There are concerns that standardized tests and accountability measures don't adequately take into account the impact of our long history of racial and socioeconomic disenfranchisement in education, and the difficulty of hiring and retaining skilled teachers in poorer school districts (Willinsky, 2014, also noting research of Banks and Darling-Hammond). More fundamentally, there is a sense that some of the emerging research is itself methodologically flawed, and that teachers are expected to improve student performance even though rigorous studies have exposed major deficits in the curricula that they are required to use (Begley, 2010). These criticisms are not a condemnation of using research to inform educational policy, but a plea to generate and disseminate more high-quality educational research.

Resources for evidence-based practice in education include the following:

- ERIC (www.eric.ed.gov) indexes research based on evidence- based practice as well as information produced and disseminated by the What Works Clearinghouse (http://ies.ed.gov/ncee/wwc/), the 10 Regional Educational Laboratories (http://ies.ed.gov/ncee/edlabs/), and the Research and Development Centers (http://ies.ed.gov/ncer/randd/).
- Best Evidence Encyclopedia: Empowering Educators with Evidence on Proven Programs (www.bestevidence.org), from Johns Hopkins University School of

Education's Center for Data-Driven Reform in Education, provides reviews of evidence-based programs.

- Doing What Works: NCLB Proven Methods (www2.ed.gov/nclb/methods/whatworks/list.jhtml) offers research-based education practices online from the US Department of Education.
- The Wing Institute (www.winginstitute.org) is an independent, nonprofit organization promoting evidence-based education policies and practices.
- The Campbell Collaboration: What helps? What harms? Based on What Evidence? (www.campbellcollaboration.org) provides a library of systematic reviews on the effects of interventions in education.

Open Access

As discussed in chapter 1 and again in chapter 13, open access is the free, immediate, online availability of research articles, coupled with the rights to use these articles fully in the digital environment. Open access is a growing movement to ensure access to research—especially research funded at least in part by public monies. The American Educational Research Association has recently joined the OA movement by launching AERA Open. "*AERA Open* aims to advance knowledge related to education and learning, cumulatively and incrementally. It also seeks to serve as a venue for innovation, novel inquiry and ideas, interdisciplinary bridge building, and research that fosters the connection of research to practice." This is an encouraging development, but most academic education research is still not freely available on the Web. Remember our parent looking for information about how to help her child with cerebral palsy get the best education possible? Although the citations indexed in ERIC are freely available to anyone with access to the Web, many of the articles she located are not freely available online. Without open access, the work of educational researchers remains isolated within the academy.

Conclusion

As librarians, we have an important role in helping to ensure that educators, researchers, parents, and policy makers have meaningful access to the information they need. Education research is particularly challenging, because it frequently requires federal, state, and local government sources, as well as scholarly publications and the extensive grey literature produced by think tanks, nonprofits, and government agencies. As government documents librarians, we are fortunate to have some very powerful research tools available to us—and once we learn to use them, we can help parents, students, and researchers find the information they need.

Exercises

1. Using your library catalog (or WorldCat, if that's appropriate), what is the earliest government education source for your state?
2. Using American FactFinder (http://factfinder.census.gov), type the name of your city or town into the box under Community Facts. Select the Education facet on the left.

   - What is the educational attainment of the population 18–24 years—the percent with a high school degree or higher?
   - What is the percentage for males? For females?
   - What is the poverty rate for those with less than a high school degree?

3. Using NAEP State Profiles (http://nces.ed.gov/nationsreportcard/states/), take a look at the report for your state. Did your state test higher or lower than the national average for eighth-grade math? Now navigate to http://nces.ed.gov/nationsreportcard/statecomparisons/ and select eighth-grade math and the latest year available, which lets you also select different student groups. Was there a gap in achievement based on gender? On race?
4. A student is interested in current, quantitatively based articles on the black-white achievement gap in high school. In ERIC, should you use Blacks or African Americans as a descriptor? (Hint: look at the Thesaurus for the terms and read the scope notes.) How would you restrict the search to articles with a quantitative focus?

Sources Mentioned in This Chapter

Sources mentioned in this section do not duplicate the references that follow.

Legislation and Court Cases (Chronological Order)

Agricultural and Mechanical Colleges Acts (Morrill Acts), (July 2, 1862, 12 Stat. 503).

Second Morrill Act (August 30, 1890, 26 Stat. 417).

Plessy v. Ferguson, 163 U.S. 537 (1896).

West Virginia Board of Education v. Barnette, 319 U.S. 624 (1943).

Servicemen's Readjustment Act of 1944 (G.I. Bill), P.L. 78-346, 58 Stat. 284 (1944).

Brown v. Board of Education, 347 U.S. 483 (1954).

National Defense Education Act, P.L. 85-864, 72 Stat. 1580 (1958).

Engel v. Vitale, 370 U.S. 421 (1962).

Elementary and Secondary Education Act, P.L. 89-10, 79 Stat. 27 (1965).

Higher Education Act of 1965, P.L. 89-329, 79 Stat. 1219 (1965).

Education Amendments of 1972 (includes Title IX), P.L. 92-318, 86 Stat. 235 (1972).

To amend the Education Amendments of 1972 . . . (Pell Grants, also known as Basic Educational Opportunity Grants), P.L. 93-35, 87 Stat. 72 (1973).

Rehabilitation Act of 1973, P.L. 93-112; 87 Stat. 355 (1973).

Education for all Handicapped Children Act, P.L. 94-142, 89 Stat. 773 (1975); the name was changed by P.L. 101-476 to the Individuals with Disabilities Education Act (104 Stat. 1103, 1990).

University of California Regents v. Bakke, 438 U.S. 265 (1978).

Plyler v. Doe, 457 U.S. 202 (1982).

Taxpayer Relief Act of 1997, P.L. 105-34, 111 Stat. 788 (1997).

No Child Left Behind Act, P.L. 107-110, 115 Stat. 1425 (2002); overview at http://www2.ed.gov/nclb/overview/intro/execsumm.html.

American Recovery and Reinvestment Act of 2009 (ARRA), P.L. 111-5, 123 Stat 115 (2009).

Department of Education

120 Years of American Education: A Statistical Portrait, http://nces.ed.gov/pubs93/93442.pdf.

Common Core of Data (CCD), http://nces.ed.gov/ccd/.

Condition of Education, http://nces.ed.gov/programs/coe/.

Department of Education (ED.gov), www.ed.gov.

Digest of Education Statistics, http://nces.ed.gov/programs/digest/.

Doing What Works: NCLB Proven Methods, www2.ed.gov/nclb/methods/whatworks/list.jhtml.

Education Demographic and Geographic Estimates (EDGE) http://nces.ed.gov/programs/edge/.

Education Resources Information Clearinghouse (ERIC), www.eric.ed.gov.

FAFSA: Free Application for Student Aid, https://fafsa.ed.gov.

IPEDS: Integrated Postsecondary Education Data System, http://nces.ed.gov/ipeds/.

National Assessment of Educational Progress (The Nation's Report Card), http://nces.ed.gov/nationsreportcard.

National Center for Education Statistics (NCES), http://nces.ed.gov.

Public School System Finances, www.census.gov/govs/school/.

Regional Educational Laboratories, http://ies.ed.gov/ncee/edlabs/.

Research and Development Centers, http://ies.ed.gov/ncer/randd/.

State Education Data Profiles, http://nces.ed.gov/programs/stateprofiles/.

What Works Clearinghouse, http://ies.ed.gov/ncee/wwc/.

Other Sources

American Community Survey, www.census.gov/acs/.

American FactFinder, http://factfinder.census.gov.

Best Evidence Encyclopedia: Empowering Educators with Evidence on Proven Programs, www.bestevidence.org.

Campbell Collaboration, www.campbellcollaboration.org.

Common Core State Standards Initiative, www.corestandards.org.

Historical Census Browser, http://mapserver.lib.virginia.edu/index.html.

Library of Congress: Teachers, www.loc.gov/teachers/.

Public School System Finances, www.census.gov/govs/school/.

Statistical Abstract of the United States, www.census.gov/compendia/statab/ and www.proquest.com/products-services/statabstract.html.

Wing Institute: Evidence-Based Education, www.winginstitute.org.

References

Associated Press. 2010. "State Report Pegs Dropout Rate at 9.4%." *Education Week,* July 16. www
.edweek.org/ew/articles/2010/07/16/366028txdropoutratetexas_ap.html.

Begley, Sharon. 2010. "Second Class Science: Education Research Gets an F." *Newsweek,* May 10. www
.newsweek.com/2010/04/30/second-class-science.html.

Bureau of the Census. 2014. *Public Education Finances 2012.* May. www2.census.gov/govs/school/
08f33pub.pdf.

Bureau of Education. 1874. *Report of the Commissioner of Education for the Year 1873.* Washington, DC:
Government Printing Office.

Cross, Christopher. 2010. *Political Education: National Policy Comes of Age.* Updated Edition. New York:
Teachers College Press.

Department of Education. 2010. "The Federal Role in Education." Accessed August 20. www2.ed.gov/
about/overview/fed/role.html.

Gambrill, Eileen. 2006. "Evidence-Based Practice and Policy: Choices Ahead." *Research on Social Work
Practice* 16, no. 3: 338–357.

Goldin, Claudia. 2006. "Education." In *Historical Statistics of the United States (online),* Susan B. Carter,
Scott Sigmund Gartner, Michael R. Haines, Alan L. Olmstead, Richard Sutch, and Gavin Wright, eds.
Millennial ed. Cambridge, England; New York: Cambridge University Press.

Hanna, Robert, Max Marchitello, Catherine Brown. 2015. "Comparable but Unequal." *Center for American Progress.* Accessed April 6. www.americanprogress.org/issues/education/report/2015/03/11/
107985/comparable-but-unequal/.

Institute of Education Sciences. 2015. "About Us." http://ies.ed.gov/aboutus/.

Klein, Alyson. 2015. "As Congress Rewrites NCLB, Arne Duncan Highlights 'Title I Comparability
Loophole.'" *Education Week—Politics K-12.* Accessed April 6. http://blogs.edweek.org/edweek/
campaign-k-12/2015/03/can_an_nclb_rewrite_close_the_.html.

Miller, Raegen T. 2010. "Comparable, Schmomparable: Evidence of Inequity in the Allocation of Funds
for Teacher Salary within California's Public School Districts." May. Washington, DC: Center for
American Progress. www.americanprogress.org/issues/2010/05/pdf/comparable_schmomparable.pdf.

Spatig-Amerikaner, Ary. 2015. "Unequal Education." Center for American Progress. Accessed April 6.
www.americanprogress.org/issues/education/report/2012/08/22/29002/unequal-education/.

Strayer, Jean-Jacques. 2008. "ERIC Database Alternatives and Strategies for Education Researchers."
Reference Services Review 36, no. 1: 86–96.

US Department of Education. 2005. "Title I—Improving The Academic Achievement Of The Disadvantaged." Laws. December 19. www2.ed.gov/policy/elsec/leg/esea02/pg1.html.

Weiner, Sharon A. 2009. "Tale of Two Databases: The History of Federally Funded Information Systems
for Education and Medicine." *Government Information Quarterly* 26, no. 3: 450–458.

Willinsky, John. 2014. The New Openness in Educational Research. In A. D. Reid, E. P. Hart, and M. A.
Peters (Eds.), *A Companion to Research in Education* (pp. 575–582). Springer Netherlands. Retrieved
from http://link.springer.com/chapter/10.1007/978–94–007–6809–3_75.

Wolfe, Christine O. 2009. *The Great Graduation-Rate Debate.* Washington, DC: Thomas B. Fordham Institute. July. www.eric.ed.gov/PDFS/ED508051.pdf.

CHAPTER 13

Scientific and Technical Information

KATHRYN W. TALLMAN

Introduction

The United States government is one of the most prolific producers and publishers of scientific and technical information in the world—so prolific that it can be difficult to know where to start. The material produced, published, or distributed by the government ties directly to the legislatively mandated responsibilities of individual executive branch agencies such as the Department of the Interior and independent agencies such as the Environmental Protection Agency and NASA. The content ranges from fact sheets geared to a general audience to technical publications aimed at specialists in science disciplines. Scientific and technical information can be found on agency websites, department databases and catalogs, federated search engines, subscription databases, and more. A single publication may be discoverable and accessible through multiple channels, while a closely related work may only be found in one location. Therefore, locating and accessing government scientific and technical information can be confusing at times. However, the Internet, federal policies, and a general trend towards open and unrestricted access to research have all increased our knowledge of and access to scientific information from all levels of government. This chapter will untangle this web of government scientific and technical information while reviewing its origin, evolution, and accessibility.

Open Government Initiatives and Scientific and Technical Information

In 2013, two major announcements from the White House impacted the government scientific and technical information landscape. The first came on February 22, 2013, when the White House Office of Science and Technology Policy (OSTP) released a memorandum titled "Increasing Access to the Results of Federally Funded Scientific Research." This memo directed federal agencies with more than $100 million in annual research and development disbursements to make the results of scientific research publically available within 12 months of their publication (Office of Science and Technology Policy, 2013). Compliance with this mandate requires agencies to publish the data and research results of federally funded research. Both of these elements, the data and the resulting research, must be made accessible to the public for free. Compliance is decentralized, meaning that there is no one place for agencies to deposit this information. To make matters more confusing, both the data and the resulting research may be published in different locations. To get a better idea of how each agency is complying with this mandate, a simple search for the agency name and the Public Access Plan can be performed in any Internet search engine. For example, a search for "Department of Defense Public Access Plan" results in a memorandum from the Under Secretary of Defense directing the agency's authors to "submit final, peer-reviewed journal manuscripts to the Defense Technical Information Center (www.dtic.mil/dtic/) system upon acceptance for publication" (Department of Defense, 2014). While some agencies, like the Department of Defense, are using existing infrastructure to comply with this mandate, others are creating new repositories for department-affiliated scientific research. One example can be found in the Department of Energy, which has created a new public access database for federally funded research called DOE Pages (www.osti.gov/pages/).

The second announcement came on May 9, 2013, when President Barack Obama issued Executive Order 13642 to make "open and machine readable the new default for Government Information" (Executive Order 13642, 2014). One example of how federal agencies are responding to this open data mandate can be found on NASA's new open government website, Open NASA (http://open.nasa.gov). This site offers two different databases, one with petabytes of freely accessible data (http://data.nasa/gov) and the other with open source software code (http://code.nasa.gov), enabling citizen developers to create apps and manipulate data in new and innovative ways. Other agencies have submitted data sets to Data.gov, the US government's public access data repository. The National Transportation Library (http://ntlsearch.bts.gov/repository/index.do), for example, advises users to search Data.gov for all public access datasets produced by the Department of Transportation. Regardless of how federal agencies comply with these directives, there is no doubt that these unprecedented actions by the White House will increase public access to high quality government-funded scientific and technical research in the years to come. For more information on White House science policies, see the OSTP National Science and Technology Council (NSTC) website for a list of documents and reports (www.whitehouse.gov/administration/eop/ostp/nstc/docsreports/).

Access to Scientific and Technical Information

Although the federal government has multiple channels for information distribution, there are three main methods relevant to this discussion: sale and distribution to depository libraries by the Government Publishing Office (GPO), sale and distribution by the National Technical Information Service (NTIS), and distribution through the Internet on agency websites and publication warehouses. Publications available through NTIS are often called technical reports, although that term can be applied equally to much of the information distributed by the GPO and federal agencies. When searching for a known item, particularly a technical report, it is wise to extend the search beyond the NTIS to other resources such as federal agency websites, Science.gov, USA.gov, digital archives like the Wayback Machine (http://archive.org/web/), and Internet search engines with results limited to specific domains like .gov and .mil. In the pre-Internet days, unraveling the various access points presented significant challenges. Now that the Web is a mature delivery platform, it is fairly easy to locate information about known items.

Government Publishing Office

As discussed in more detail in chapter 1, materials published by the GPO are distributed to a network of depository libraries around the country. While not every library receives every publication, the library serving as a regional depository should have copies of all publications distributed by GPO through the program. Especially since the advent of GPO cataloging in 1976, many depository libraries have added records for government information to their catalogs. With a nationwide network of libraries and catalog records in local catalogs and bibliographic networks, most materials that are not available locally should be available through interlibrary loan.

Access points for materials distributed to depository libraries by GPO include the Catalog of Government Publications, or CGP (http://catalog.gpo.gov; discussed in chapter 2) and the Federal Depository Library Directory (www.fdlp.gov/about-the-fdlp/federal-depository-libraries), which provides contact information, links to depository websites, and library catalogs. The Catalog of Government Publications is a good place to begin a search for citations to scientific and technical information published by the legislative, executive, and judicial branches of the US government. An increasing number of electronic documents are accessible by persistent URLs (PURLs) and can be downloaded as PDF files. The CGP is not a union catalog and will not point to records in individual library catalogs.

Another good source of government-produced scientific and technical information is the United States Congress. Hearings, reports, and debates on issues such as climate change or wildlife conservation are full of good information and can point to further research and specialists in a particular field of study. The Federal Digital System (FDsys, www.gpo.gov/fdsys/) and Congress.gov (www.congress.gov) are two free access points for this type of information. For example, a search for "climate change and ocean" in FDsys results in over 2,000 hearings, including one titled "Effects of Climate Change and Ocean Acidification on Living Marine Organisms," with written statements from a retired navy admiral, an oceanographer, and other experts. Congressional hearings and other congressional publications like CRS reports are written for members of Congress. Therefore, the information contained in these publications should be accessible to most readers and is an excellent source of background information on many scientific and technical topics.

National Technical Information Service

The National Technical Information Service (NTIS) provides a separate distribution mechanism for scientific and technical information. There is some overlap in coverage with the materials distributed by the GPO and some federal agencies. NTIS serves as a permanent repository of more than 2.5 million bibliographic records and provides full-text access to over 800,000 publications via the National Technical Reports Library (NTRL). Many of these documents are categorized as technical reports, and while most people have a general notion about what we mean when we use the word *science,* technical reports are more difficult to define. In essence, technical reports summarize the results of federally funded research. They may include the research methodology, data, conclusions, and most importantly, the successes and failures of a given project. It is important to note, however, that technical reports are not necessarily peer reviewed or otherwise part of the more traditional scientific publishing process. Ellen Calhoun defines a technical report as "an account of work done on a research project that a scientist compiles to convey information to his employer or sponsor or to other scientists." She further observes that, while there is great variability in the quality of the writing or presentation, technical reports "usually represent the first appearance in print of current scientific investigations" (Calhoun, 1991: 163). Too often overlooked, these reports provide a wealth of scientific and technical information that may not be discovered elsewhere.

Before the Internet matured, NTIS was the first place to look for technical reports. While it is still a rich tool for government-funded scientific and technical research, its status as the premier tool has been somewhat diminished by the availability of individual agency-developed publications databases, whose contents are often searchable via a regular, web search engine. On the other hand, the scope of the NTIS database has also changed: NTIS has greatly expanded the subject coverage of the database so that it is no longer limited strictly to technical reports. Researchers may now uncover conference proceedings, journal articles, patent applications, and even CRS reports (covered in chapter 3), among many other types of documents.

The organization now known as NTIS has gone through several name and mission statements since its founding shortly after World War II. The original purpose was to translate and disseminate captured German scientific and technical documents to speed the development of military technology. Over time that role expanded to include indexing and distribution of federally funded scientific and technical information. In 1992, the American Technology Preeminence Act (P.L. 102-245) was amended to require "all costs associated with bibliographic control to be recovered by fees." Therefore, until 2014 NTIS charged for full-text access to documents as it relied on the sales of reports, indexing tools, and specialized databases for its continued existence. Users had to order individual technical reports from NTIS or visit an institution with subscription access to the National Technical Reports Library (NTRL). This is no longer the case, as the NTRL has expanded free access to all electronically available documents in the NTIS collection.

In 2014, NTIS unveiled this new public access model for the National Technical Reports Library. Public access to this database now requires a simple registration, log-in, and password. The user is limited to a basic search and can download any existing full-text

PDF, and must purchase documents that are not already available in digital format. Alternatively, public patrons can contact their regional federal depository library to inquire about access to the NTRL digital-on-demand service. Once a document is digitized, it becomes accessible to all users of the NTRL database. NTRL offers two additional subscription products: Premium Access NTRL and Institutional Premium Access NTRL. Institutional and Premium Access NTRL offers expanded search functionality and personalization options, while the Institutional level allows users to select documents for Digital-on-Demand delivery. Digital-on-Demand requests are restricted to five documents per week, per institution, and must be approved by administrators, making this a rather cumbersome process. Additionally, larger documents can take weeks to be digitized. International users must subscribe to Premium Access NTRL in order to access any documents in the NTRL. There are many issues with the new NTRL interface. Default search results are ordered by date rather than relevance, and some public users have reported problems with logging in and having to reset their accounts. NTRL is most convenient to use via subscription. However, subscription pricing may be prohibitive to small or medium-sized libraries (see table 13.1).

The move to provide the American public with free access to documents in the NTRL database came partly in response to legislation that threatened to terminate NTIS

Let Me **GOOGLE** That for You Act
Senate Bill 2206 113th Congress (2013-2014)

An act to streamline the collection and distribution of government information

Sponsor: Sen. Coburn, Tom [R-OK] (Introduced 04/03/2014)

Committees: Senate - Commerce, Science, and Transportation

Latest Action: Read twice and referred to the Committee on Commerce, Science, and Transportation.

Selected Excerpts:

- No Federal agency should use taxpayer dollars to purchase a report from the National Technical Information Service that is available through the Internet for free.
- Future technological advances will ensure that the services offered by NTIS are even more superfluous for essential government functions than they are today.

2012 GAO Report:

- Of the reports added to NTIS's repository during fiscal years 1990 through 2011, GAO estimates that approximately 74 percent were readily available from other public sources.
- These reports were often available either from the issuing organization's website, the Federal Internet portal (http://www.USA.gov) or from another source located through a web search.
- The source that most often had the report [GAO] was searching for was another website located through http://www.google.com.
- 95 percent of the reports available from sources other than NTIS were available free of charge.

Source: Congress.gov

FIGURE 13.1
Let Me Google That For You Act

operations. The Let Me Google That for You Act (figure 13.1) was introduced to the Senate in April 2014 and addressed the redundancy of specialty government tools such as NTIS' database, and freely available web indexing tools such as Google Scholar. While it died in Congress, it may well be reintroduced in future Congresses in some form. The report that triggered this legislation was a 2012 Government Accountability Office investigation which found that the majority of publications located in the NTIS repository were available elsewhere on the Web using a simple Google search. Of those publications found using Google, 95 percent were available to the public, free of charge (Government Accountability Office, 2012).

TABLE 13.1
NTRL Access Levels

Feature	Public Access	Premium Access	Institutional Access
Cost	$0	$200 (US)/$300 (Int'l)	Varies
Search Functionality	Basic	Basic/Advanced	Basic/Advanced
E-mail Documents	No	Yes	Yes
Save Notes	No	Yes	Yes
Save Favorites	No	Yes	Yes
Export to Endnote	No	Yes	Yes
Digital on Demand	No	No	Yes
Usage Statistics	No	No	Yes
Institutional Branding	No	No	Yes

Source: www.ntis.gov/products/ntrl.

Agency Websites

Most federal agencies have large and well-developed websites. Once found, they can be a virtual treasure trove of scientific and technical information. Content on these websites can range from datasets, maps, and research to consumer-oriented publications and discovery tools. Agency websites are good for drilling-down to specific resources, as well as searching for known items. Science.gov, for example, provides a basic and advanced search box in addition to a section to browse for websites by topic. Many of these sites have developed mobile phone applications, such as NASA's Spinoff App which highlights technologies that have transferred from NASA research to our everyday lives. Federal agencies also promote research, projects, and programs on social media networks such as Facebook and Twitter. For example, the Environmental Protection Agency (EPA) has over 130,000 followers on Facebook, as well as a popular Twitter account called EPA Research, with new and timely research publications, media, and infographics posted every day. Hopefully, these open access and social engagement initiatives will continue to lead to more interesting, accessible, and discoverable scientific information.

Tips for Locating Agency Websites for Scientific and Technical Information

For scientific and technical information, a subject-based approach is often most useful. While the website USA.gov (described in chapter 2) provides a comprehensive list of government agencies, Science.gov (www.science.gov) has science-specific tools to help guide users to scientific government resources by topic. Although it lacks a complete directory of agencies by name or organizational structure, Science.gov provides one-stop shopping for scientific and technical information by searching over 60 federal databases and 2,200 websites. In addition to simple and advanced search features, the site includes menus of scientific information arranged by topic and subtopic. For example, the Environment and Environmental Quality subject is further subdivided into 16 narrower topics such as Climate Change and Radiation. Each subdivision then provides a list of agencies or projects with descriptions. The subtopic Radiation, for example, contains links to two programs in the Department of Energy: the National Atmospheric Release Advisory Center (NARAC) and the Low Dose Radiation Research Program. The Science.gov Index (www.science.gov/browse/topiclist.htm) provides an alphabetical list of scientific topics with associated websites. Browsing for federal agencies and programs using this index is especially useful for researchers who are not familiar with a particular area of study.

Agency Publication Warehouses and Bibliographic Databases

The US government produces a number of bibliographic databases and full-text collections that are described in this section. Databases that began as bibliographic databases, such as Agricola, are intended as true, comprehensive discipline databases, and so index a mix of governmental (public domain) and commercially published (copyrighted) materials. This mixture of resources means that while some of the material indexed is freely available online, some of the information remains inaccessible except to subscribers. Other government bibliographic databases, such as SciTech Connect, are organized solely with the purpose of exposing government-sponsored and authored research to the general public, and do not attempt to index nongovernmental publications. Treesearch, a database of research from the Forest Service, follows another pattern. Because the material it indexes is authored only by government employees, all of the material is in the public domain and available at no charge, regardless of whether it was published in a commercially-produced journal. The availability of research located in these databases will undoubtedly increase in wake of the White House open data and open access directives described above. Users can hope that these initiatives will continue to exert pressure on other federal agencies to follow the Treesearch model. However, the true impact of these policies is still unknown and an area for further study. The following section, organized by federal agency, will describe the content, scope, and full-text availability of the database(s) found within each agency. Table 13.2 summarizes the following key agencies' databases.

Department of Agriculture: Agricola, National Agricultural Library Digital Collections (NALDC), PubAG

- Agricola (http://agricola.nal.usda.gov), or the National Agricultural Library Catalog, serves as the official catalog for the National Agricultural Library (NAL). Agricola has been the go-to citation database for both USDA resources and general agricultural research for many years. The National Agricultural Library Digital Collection (http://naldc.nal.usda.gov) is the NAL's digital repository and a good database for primary resources and some USDA-authored publications. The Department's newest offering, PubAg (http://pubag.nal.usda .gov), provides full-text access to USDA publications and citations to peer-reviewed journal articles.

- Agricola is especially useful as a bibliographic index, with citations to books and journal articles located within the National Agricultural Library. Full-text access is provided for some publications through the NALDC; however, most records point to the publisher's website and access is determined by subscription. The NALDC and PubAg, on the other hand, are particularly useful for accessing freely available USDA-authored publications. As mentioned above, the NALDC also provides some primary resources, such as photographs and historic documents. One such collection, the USDA Pomological Watercolor Collection, contains beautiful, detailed paintings of plant specimens from 1886–1942. PubAg, on the other hand, provides free full-text access to over 40,000 articles written by USDA employees. However, PubAg also contains citations to peer-reviewed journal articles, many of which are limited by subscription barriers. It is important to remember that some of the content provided for free, by the USDA, may not be accessible through Google Scholar—although Google Scholar may find a full-text version of research located using PubAg if the researcher has submitted the report to an open-access repository of scholarly work.

Department of Defense: Defense Technical Information Center (DTIC)

As noted earlier, the Defense Technical Information Center, or DTIC (www.dtic.mil/ dtic/), has been designated as the public access database for federally funded research in the Department of Defense. DTIC provides access to defense-related scientific information for the defense community, which includes the various agencies of the Department of Defense (DoD), contractors, and those seeking potential contracts with the DoD. Since the DoD needs information on everything from the readability of gauges on flight controls to the durability of uniforms to weapon systems, it maintains an interest in many scientific and technical disciplines. While some of the information is restricted to registered users who meet certain eligibility requirements, the site provides access to a wide array of nonclassified materials. If the full text is not available from DTIC, declassified materials can be ordered from NTIS using the accession number in the National Technical Reports Library. A simple search for aerial drones in the technical reports collection yielded more than 2400 citations for a variety of documents, including technical reports, CRS reports, graduate theses, and more.

Department of Energy: SciTechConnect, DOE Pages

In 2013, the Department of Energy consolidated the contents of its two most popular public resources, OSTI's Information Bridge and the Energy Citations Database, into one database: SciTech Connect. SciTech Connect (www.osti.gov/scitech/) provides access to free, publically available Department of Energy research and development results. It boasts over 2.5 million citations to technical reports, books, journal articles, multimedia, and data on subjects ranging from engineering and nuclear technologies to renewable energy and national security. SciTech Connect uses an innovative semantic search technique that mimics search engines like Google, rather than the more traditional term-based algorithms used by most library catalogs and bibliographic databases. This keyword-to-concept mapping expands search results to include related concepts for all of the keywords used in the search. For example, a search for terms *wind energy* will prompt the database to search for related concepts such as *wind turbines* and *renewable energy*. See the SciTech Connect FAQ page (www.osti.gov/scitech/faq) for more information on this semantic search.

SciTech Connect allows for basic and advanced searching, as well as subject-based browsing. For example, a browse on the subject of fossil fuels presented a new screen offering many options to narrow the topic by document type, publication date, and keyword. A subject browse for full-text books on liquefied natural gas resulted in eight results, including *Alternative Fuel Transit Buses: DART's (Dallas Area Rapid Transit) LNG Bus Fleet Final Results*. This step-by-step process of browsing and narrowing scientific concepts is useful for users who are unfamiliar with a particular subject. This site allows registered users to create alerts, export data and bibliographies, and save searches. SciTech Connect is an excellent place to search for information on alternative fuels and other energy-related topics. Are you curious about how biomass can be used as a renewable source of energy? Check out *Turning Algae into Energy in New Mexico*, a video by Los Alamos and New Mexico State University scientists available on SciTech Connect.

The newest product from the Department of Energy is DOE Pages—Public Access Gateway for Energy and Science (www.osti.gov/pages/). This database was created to comply with the OTSP memorandum on federally funded scientific and technical research. As of December 2014 it is still in the beta period, but users will soon be able to access 20,000–30,000 manuscripts and articles published by department-affiliated researchers.

DOE resources are covered in more detail in chapter 14 on Energy and Environment Information.

Department of Interior: USGS Publications Warehouse

The US Geological Survey (USGS) has been a prolific publisher of scientific information since the 1880s, with an emphasis on geology, mapping, flora, fauna, water supply, coal, oil and gas fields, minerals with economic potential, and other topics. The USGS Publications Warehouse (1880–present; http:// pubs.er.usgs.gov) provides bibliographic citations for all series publications, with full text available for more than half of the publications. The site provides a list and brief description of past and ongoing USGS series with titles such as *Professional Papers, Bulletins, General Interest Publication,* and *Scientific Investigations Reports.* Format and access to these publications vary. Recently the USGS began adding citations to book and journal literature published by commercial publishers to the Publications Warehouse. The number of non–USGS publications is growing quickly, and while the database provides Digital Object Identifiers (DOIs) to publisher index pages, the full-text may be found elsewhere, such as a local library or on the Internet. When full text of USGS publications is unavailable, the site provides instruction on how to obtain copies directly from the agency or from depository libraries. Advanced search allows the user to limit by series, contributing agency, publication type, and more. Budding gold miners, for example, can read publications such as *Introduction to Geology and Resources of Gold* and *Mineral Facilities of Latin America and Canada.*

Department of Transportation—Transportation Research International Documentation (TRID)

The Transportation Research International Documentation database, or TRID, (http:// trid.trb.org), combines bibliographic records from the Transportation Research Information Services (TRIS, 1900–present) and the International Transportation Research Documentation Database (ITRD). This database is managed by the Transportation Research Board of the National Academy of Sciences under the sponsorship of the US Department of Transportation. TRID contains over 1 million bibliographic citations to books, technical reports, conference proceedings, and journal articles in the field of transportation research. Subject matter includes transportation-related environmental impact statements, highways, transit, railroads, maritime issues, aviation, pipelines, pedestrians, and bicycles. A limited amount of full text is available from this site, but some states have transportation libraries where the full text can be accessed. Because TRID indexes both commercially produced and noncommercial information sources, some materials are hidden behind subscription barriers.

Environmental Protection Agency: National Service Center for Environmental Publications (NSCEP)

The Environmental Protection Agency, with a mission to "create a livable environment," has jurisdiction over many aspects of the air, water, and land of the United States. Its interests range from air and water pollution to solid waste and emergency response to toxic substances, especially with regard to the human health effects of exposure to pollution. EPA's National Service Center for Environmental Publications (NSCEP), 1970–present; (www.epa.gov/nscep/), provides access to over 1,500 print and 65,000 digital documents. Materials in stock can be ordered at no charge. Digital copies of publications are available for download in PDF, TIFF, and plain text formats. The NSCEP also has a large selection of foreign language documents. A search for "radon" retrieved consumer-oriented publications such as *Basic Radon Facts 2013,* as well as more technical material such as *Radon Mitigation Research Improved Technology for Environmental Protection.* The EPA is covered in more detail in chapter 14 on Energy and Environment Information.

Forest Service: Treesearch

Treesearch (www.treesearch.fs.fed.us) provides access to publications written by scientists in the US Forest Service. Their goal is to make available all books, chapters, and articles written since 2004 and to add older publications as rapidly as possible. Treesearch now offers 40,000 full-text, publicly available documents, with thousands being added each year. The site offers the largest freely available collection of forestry research in the world. Since all publications in Treesearch were written by employees of the Forest Service, they are in the public domain. Whereas many government databases built on the open access concept post manuscript versions of articles, this public domain status allows the developers of Treesearch to include final published versions of journal articles from subscription-based journals. Treesearch employs a very simple and intuitive search function. In addition to searching by title, author, and keyword, Treesearch also allows the user to search by research station. An added feature is GeoTreesearch (www.fs.fed.us/research/products/geotreesearch/), a map-based research tool that combines keyword searching with geographic filters.

NASA: NASA Technical Reports Server and Open.Nasa.Gov

NASA and its predecessor agency, the National Advisory Committee for Aeronautics (NACA), have been publishing information relating to aeronautics, astronautics, space exploration, remote sensing, and other topics since 1915. The NASA Technical Reports Server (http://ntrs.nasa.gov) simultaneously searches multiple collections including the NACA collection (1915–1958), NASA collection (1958–present), and NIX (NASA Image Exchange). Search results can include bibliographic citations with order information, full text, images, and video. If the full text is not available online, the site provides information on how to order copies.

NASA's Technology and Innovation team recently released a new collection of publically accessible databases through Open.nasa.gov (http://open.nasa.gov) with the intent of continuing NASA's efforts to meet the White House's open data policy. This website offers a data repository and a collaborative code repository. The data portal (http://data.nasa.gov) provides a simple search box and a menu of data collections. A search for lunar data retrieved over 10 data sets, including the *Lunar Sample Atlas* and the *Lunar Map Catalog.*

Gateways to Scientific and Technical Information

In addition to the various agency bibliographies, databases, and warehouses, several projects aim for one-stop shopping to government scientific information. Science.gov is emerging as the premier website for scientific and technical information from the federal government due to its cross-agency coverage of scientific information. It provides a single search interface for 60 databases and more than 2,200 federal websites from 15 federal agencies. According to the website, Science.gov is the gateway to 200 million pages of authoritative government information. In addition to simple and advanced searching, the site includes a site map and index that lead users to information by topic.

TABLE 13.2
Agency Pubication Warehouses and Citation Databases

Title	Web address	Dates of Coverage	Content	Full Text Coverage
Agricola	http://agricola.nal.usda.gov/	Unknown	Books, Articles, Department-Affiliated Publications, Datasets, Multimedia	Some
National Agricultural Library Digital Collections	http://naldc.nal.usda.gov/	Unknown	Books, Articles, Department-Affiliated Publications, Multimedia	All
PubAg	http://pubag.nal.usda.gov/	Unknown	Articles, Department-Affiliated Publications	Some
Defense Technical Information Center	http://www.dtic.mil/dtic/	Unknown	Articles, Department-Affiliated Publications, Technical Reports, Annual Reports, Military Standards, Datasets, Conference Recordings, Budget Information	Some
DOE Pages	http://www.osti.gov/pages/	2009- present	Articles, Department-Affiliated Publications	Some
SciTech Connect	http://www.osti.gov/scitech/	1943- present	Articles, Technical Reports, Datasets, Multimedia, Patents and Patent Applications, Dissertations and Theses	Some
USGS Publications Warehouse	http://pubs.er.usgs.gov/	1880–present	Books, Articles, Department-Affiliated Publications, Chapters, Patents, Technical Reports, Annual Reports, Speeches, Conference Papers, Datasets, Multimedia	Some

Transport Research International Documentation Database (TRID)	http://trid.trb.org/	1900–present	Books, Articles, Department-Affiliated Publications, Projects	Some
National Service Center for Environmental Publications	http://www.epa.gov/nscep/	1970–present	Articles, Department-Affiliated Publications, Reports, Fact Sheets	All
Treesearch	http://www.treesearch.fs.fed.us/	1902–present	Books, Articles, Department-Affiliated Publications, Reports, Conference Proceedings	All
NASA Technical Reports Server	http://ntrs.nasa.gov/search.jsp	1915–present	Articles, Department-Affiliated Publications, Technical Reports, Patents, Datasets, Conference Proceedings, Multimedia	Some
Open.NASA.gov	http://open.nasa.gov	Unknown	Datasets, Software Code, Project Plans	N/A

Developed by the same Office of Scientific and Technical Information (OSTI) within the US Department of Energy that created Science.gov, WorldWide Science (www.worldwidescience.org) uses federated search technology to locate geographically dispersed information from over 100 science databases and portals from more than 70 countries. WorldWide Science is overseen by an alliance represented by government agencies from around the world, including the Canada Institute for Scientific and Technical Information, the Institute of Scientific and Technical Information of China, the LC, and others. Ten languages are currently supported on this site and much of the material retrieved is otherwise invisible to conventional search engines. The site features both simple and advanced search features. Results screens include facets that can be used to narrow an existing search. It also provides the ability to narrow the results with additional keywords or terms. Search results can include a mix of full text and bibliographic citations.

Data.gov, previously discussed in chapter 10 on Statistical Information, is the federal government's portal to government data (www.data.gov/about). It indexes over 138,000 datasets from 235 organizations, including international, federal, state and local agencies, universities, and commercial or nonprofit organizations. For example, Data.gov contains datasets from the California Institute of Technology Jet Propulsion Laboratory, the Millennium Challenge Corporation, and the National Oceanic Atmospheric Administration. Data from this repository has been used to create hundreds of mobile applications, maps, graphics, and other information resources. For a fascinating look at how this data is used, check out Data.gov's applications page (www.data.gov/applications). A simple search box allows the user to search for datasets using basic keywords, and the search results may be filtered by geographic location, dataset type, publisher, date, and more. Researchers may also browse by topic. The climate topic page offers information on four subthemes: coastal flooding, ecosystem vulnerability, food reliance, and water.

It also provides a list of datasets and additional resources. Most interestingly, the climate topic page also contains a list of data innovation challenges. These challenges, sponsored by federal agencies and private corporations, encourage citizen scientists to manipulate data, spur innovation, and create solutions. Some of these challenges offer a cash reward. For example, a NASA and USGS Challenge for Imagining Data Applications for Resilience offers up to $35,000 in cash rewards for innovative, data-driven applications to help improve climate resilience and prepare for climate change.

Scientific and Technical Collections Hosted by Nongovernmental Agencies

The National Academies Press (NAP; www.nap.edu) publishes manuscripts and reports issued by the National Academy of Sciences, the National Academy of Engineering, the Institute of Medicine, and the National Research Council, each of which serves in an advisory capacity to Congress. Much like CRS reports (covered in chapter 3), which provide context and easy-to-digest summaries of important issues to members of Congress, NAP publications are useful for acquiring detailed background information on topics of interest to legislators. Reports and publications can be read online, ordered, or, for more than 5,000 titles, downloaded in their entirety at no charge. The record for each title contains a table of contents, summary, and research tools in addition to a list of options for accessing the title. Some publications have multimedia associated with the title. For example, *Hidden Costs of Energy: Unpriced Consequences of Energy Production and Use* includes a nine-minute podcast titled *Hidden Costs of Energy*. In addition to pure science, the site also provides analysis of current policy for some topics. In 2013 the NAP released *Effects of U.S. Tax Policy on Greenhouse Gas Emissions*, written by researchers for the National Research Council.

The Technical Report Archive and Image Library (TRAIL) (pre-1974, www .technicalreports.org), a project of the Greater Western Library Alliance and the Center for Research Libraries under the leadership of the University of Arizona, represents a large-scale effort to digitize federal technical reports published before 1975. The site provides access to eight series, including the Atomic Energy Commission, National Advisory Committee for Aeronautics, National Bureau of Standards, National Earthquake Information Center, Office of Saline Water, Office of Technical Services, and the US Fish and Wildlife Service. Additional series are in production mode. A basic search for the phrase gold mine produces over 100 results, with one publication, *Summarized Data of Gold Production,* dating to 1929 and providing statistics on global gold production in the 1920s.

Standards

Standards are an important component of scientific and technical research. They define the requirements for an object, method, technology, or practice to "work properly, safely, and efficiently to the benefit of society" (Bobick and Berard 2011, 125). They are used by businesses, industries, scientists, researchers, and developers in both the private sector and the government. Standards are developed and sold by hundreds of regional, national, and international organizations, making it quite difficult to unravel and locate the precise standards that are needed. Although there is no single clearinghouse of standards, the US government does provide guidelines for acquiring standards on the website Standards .gov (www.nist.gov/standardsgov/). Some agencies, such as the General Services Administration and the Department of Homeland Security, have their own websites with agency-specific standards. The LC Science, Business, and Technology division, for example, maintains a large collection of current and historical standards from various organizations such as the American Welding Society and the International Electrical Commission. Standards.gov has information about these resources, among many more, in their finding standards section (www.nist.gov/standardsgov/findingstandards.cfm).

Military Standards

Military standards developed by the Department of Defense are among the most plentiful and sought-after standards produced by the US government. The Acquisition Streamlining and Standardization Information System, or ASSIST, provides direct access to specifications, standards, and related documents cataloged under the Department of Defense Standardization Program. The database, Assistdocs.com (www.assistdocs.com) provides access to unclassified information distributed by Defense Standardization Program Office. Although the site has a dot-com address, it is an official site of the Department of Defense. Businesses hoping to develop and sell products for the Department of Defense must comply with standards established by the various agencies under the department. The Assistdocs site collects and provides one-stop access to these standards. Abbreviations and document numbers associated with military standards can be confusing. However, Assistdocs makes it easy to search by document ID, number, and keywords in the title. While military standards and handbooks frequently reference standards from nongovernmental standards organizations such as the American Society for Testing and Materials and the Society of Automotive Engineers, Assistdocs includes only official government standards. This can be a source of confusion for some users, who should be referred to engineering collections for nongovernmental standards.

Patents

The founders who drafted the Constitution recognized the need to "promote the progress of science and the useful arts" by granting inventors exclusive rights to their discoveries for a limited period of time (Article I, Sec. VIII of the United States Constitution). This protection is granted in the form of patents. From detailed drawings and specifications to equations and references, patents contain an abundance of scientific and technical information that might not be found elsewhere. Since 1952, the US Patent and Trademark Office, an agency of the Department of Commerce, has been charged with

examining and issuing patents. While the emphasis of this section is on scientific information, it is also worth noting that the Patent and Trademark Office is also responsible
for protecting trademarks: the word, name, symbol, or device that distinguishes the
goods made by one company from those made by another. The Patent and Trademark
website (www.uspto.gov) provides search features for existing patents and patent applications as well as trademarks.

Patents are a key scientific government resource, and are covered in-depth in chapter
17 on Patents, Trademarks, and Intellectual Property.

Conclusion

Equipped with a few simple concepts and a basic understanding of the best ways to
track down government information, any librarian can provide scientific and technical
information to patrons. While some of the terminology may be daunting, the fundamentals of information gathering remain the same. When a user asks for scientific or
technical information, take a deep breath and ask yourself a few questions: (1) which
agencies of the government might be interested in this topic? (2) How do I find their
websites? and (3) What keywords should I use for the search? Having read the information in this chapter, you should have a good idea of where to start. It is also important
to keep in mind that government scientific and technical resources are always in flux.
Much has changed in the past five years, with the OSTP memorandum on federally
funded research and the executive order on open data access opening up access to scientific research. Federal agencies and producers of federally funded research are looking for new, innovative ways to comply with these mandates. New databases, websites,
blogs, and activities on social media channels will inevitably lead to an increase in the
availability and demand of scientific and technical information. By understanding the
basic resources for accessing this information, any librarian can help answer even the
most difficult questions.

Exercises

1. I am building a new home and would like to use radon-resistant construction
   materials. Where would I go to find more information about this?
2. A patron is interested in selling pistol holsters to the military. Where would you
   find the necessary standard?
3. What safety improvements did NASA make after the Columbia disaster? What
   were some of the lessons learned from this tragedy?
4. Bark beetles have destroyed millions of trees in the Rocky Mountains over the past
   few years. What is the Forest Service doing to prevent the spread of bark beetle?
5. A patron is concerned about the chemical 'carbaryl' which is used in some
   insecticides. Where is this insecticide used and have there been any studies on
   the potential health impacts in humans?

Sources Mentioned in This Chapter

Agricola, http://agricola.nal.usda.gov.

Assistdocs.com, www.assistdocs.com.

Catalog of Government Publications (CGP), http://catalog.gpo.gov.

Congress.gov, https://www.congress.gov.

Data.gov, http://data.gov.

Defense Technical Information Center (DTIC), www.dtic.mil/dtic/.

DOE Pages, www.osti.gov/pages/.

EPA's NSCEP, www.epa.gov/nscep/.

Federal Depository Library Directory, www.fdlp.gov/about-the-fdlp/federal-depository-libraries.

Federal Digital System (FDsys), www.gpo.gov/fdsys/.

GeoTreesearch, www.fs.fed.us/research/products/geotreesearch/.

GPO Bookstore, http://bookstore.gpo.gov.

NASA Technical Reports Server (NTRS), http://ntrs.nasa.gov/search.jsp.

National Academies Press (NAP), www.nap.edu.

National Agricultural Library Digital Collections (NALDC), http://naldc.nal.usda.gov/naldc/home.xhtml.

National Science and Technology Council, https://www.whitehouse.gov/administration/eop/ostp/nstc/docsreports.

National Technical Reports Library (NTRL), http://ntrl.ntis.gov.

National Transportation Library, http://ntlsearch.bts.gov/repository/index.do.

NASA Code, http://code.nasa.gov.

NASA Data, http://data.nasa.gov.

NASA Open, http://open.nasa.gov.

NTIS home page, www.ntis.gov.

Patent and Trademark, www.uspto.gov.

PubAG, http://pubag.nal.usda.gov/pubag/home.xhtml.

Science.gov, www.science.gov.

SciTech Connect, www.osti.gov/scitech/.

Standards.gov, www.nist.gov/standardsgov/.

Technical Report Archive and Image Library (TRAIL), www.technicalreports.org.

Transportation Research International Documentation database (TRID), http://trid.trb.org.

Treesearch, www.treesearch.fs.fed.us/.

USA.gov, www.usa.gov.

USGS Publications Warehouse, http://pubs.er.usgs.gov.

Wayback Machine, Internet Archive, www.archive.org.

WorldWideScience.org: The Global Science Gateway, www.worldwidescience.org.

References

Bobick, James E., and Lynn Berard. 2011. *Science and Technology Resources: A Guide for Information Professionals and Researchers.* Library and Information Science Text Series. Santa Barbara, Calif: Libraries Unlimited.

Calhoun, Ellen. 1991. "Technical Reports De-Mystified." *Reference Librarian,* no. 32: 163–175.

Department of Defense, Under Secretary of Defense. Memorandum. 2014. "Public Access to the Results of Department of Defense-Funded Research," July 9. http://dtic.mil/dtic/pdf/PublicAccessMem02014.pdf.

Executive Order 13642 of May 9, 2013, Making Open and Machine Readable the New Default for Government Information. *Code of Federal Regulations,* title 3 (2014): 244–246, www.gpo.gov/fdsys/pkg/CFR-2014-title3-v011/pdf/CFR-2014-title3-v011-e013642.pdf.

Government Accountability Office. 2012. *National Technical Information Service's Dissemination of Technical Reports Needs Congressional Attention.* GAO-13-99. Information Management. www.gao.gov/assets/660/650210.pdf.

Office of Science and Technology Policy, Executive Office of the President. Memorandum. 2013. "Increasing Access to the Results of Federally Funded Scientific Research," February 22. www.whitehouse.gov/sites/default/files/microsites/ostp/ostp_public_access_memo_2013.pdf.

US Senate, 113th Congress, 2nd Sess. "S.2206 Let Me Google That for You Act," April 3, 2014. Available on: Congress.gov. https://www.congress.gov/bill/113th-congress/senate-bill/2206/all-info.

CHAPTER 14

Environment and Energy Information

JESSE SILVA AND LUCIA ORLANDO

Introduction

Energy powers our homes, businesses, and cars, as well as producing the many goods and services that we rely on to function and thrive. Our energy needs are most frequently met using coal, oil, and gas—finite sources that have a well-established negative environmental impact. And, the public is also increasingly interested in information on renewable sources of energy, including solar, wind, and geothermal. The Department of Energy (DOE) and Environmental Protection Agency (EPA) are the two major federal agencies concerned with energy and the natural environment and provide an abundance of knowledge and data about energy research and policy. The DOE focuses on research, development, and management of all types of energy, while the EPA focuses on regulations, research, and strategies to address pollution risks in air, water, and ground. Types of pollution regulated include noise, toxic substances, and radiation. These agencies sometimes overlap, as well as complement, each other's programs, research, and regulations, making it important to have a basic understanding of each agency. Because Congress (covered in chapter 3) and the White House (covered in chapter 8) influence the policy and direction of agency actions, it's also necessary to consult the White House policy pages on the subject (www.whitehouse.gov/energy, www.whitehouse.gov/energy/our-environment) and relevant congressional committees in order to track the direction of current and future legislation, plans, and policies. While DOE and EPA are the two major sources of federal information and data on energy and the environment, be aware that other agencies cover specific areas and may provide extensive, specific data resources which relate to energy and the environment, such as the Occupational Safety and Health Administration, the Commerce Department, the Bureau of Reclamation, and many others (chapter 2 provides some great strategies on searching across multiple agencies).

Energy Information Sources

Brief History of the Department of Energy (DOE)

Like many contemporary federal agencies, the agency known today as the Department of Energy is composed of multiple programs and offices that were once spread across various agencies throughout the executive branch. The department's early development can be traced back to the development of atomic weapons and energy—the Manhattan Project in 1942 followed by the Atomic Energy Commission in 1946. Subsequent development and growth of the commercial nuclear power industry coupled with the 1970s energy crisis compelled Congress and the executive branch to consolidate existing functions and programs into a single DOE (P.L. 95-91; 91 Stat. 565 (1977)). Combining programs, offices, and functions into the DOE as a cabinet-level office allowed comprehensive, balanced coordination of federal energy policy, plans, and programs.

Over the next several years and coming decades, our aging power grid and sources of energy are sure to become very hot topics, revealing the politicization of energy. While this politicization is not new (oil embargos in the 1970s, regulation/deregulation of electricity producers, energy policy authored by energy companies, etc.), it is something to be aware of when looking for sources and the information contained in them.

DOE's Mission

DOE's mission "to ensure America's security and prosperity by addressing its energy, environmental, and nuclear challenges through transformative science and technology solutions" (Department of Energy, 2014) means they oversee almost all large-scale energy issues in the United States. This includes research and development related to energy technology, energy conservation, overseeing energy regulatory programs, responsibility for the nuclear weapons program, and energy data collection and analysis. While their mission seems straightforward, determining whether or not DOE is responsible for a specific aspect of an energy issue is complicated in practice due to overlap with related programs managed by other agencies such as EPA, the Departments of the Interior, Agriculture, Defense, or Homeland Security, and state and local government entities. For example, although DOE regulates the operation of power plants, EPA is responsible for regulating pollutants emitted during the plant operations. Furthermore, DOE engages in joint projects where missions overlap with other agencies. Examples include the Energy Star program and Fueleconomy.gov, the website developed to guide consumers in choosing fuel-efficient vehicles, which is coproduced with EPA. DOE approaches energy issues from the standpoint of conserving resources and maximizing efficiency, while EPA focuses its efforts on limiting pollution caused by corresponding emissions.

Energy.gov

DOE's website Energy.gov is a good place to start when researching energy resources, whether seeking statistics about energy usage, information about energy alternatives, or research related to energy production. Content on Energy.gov is directed to a variety of audiences, including consumers, schoolchildren, students, researchers, policymakers, and businesses. The main page is geared toward consumers and general audiences with links to the official blog that showcases recent developments and historical events, along with current news releases from DOE, as well as engaging thematic maps and tools that visually represent topics like consumer spending or consumption of energy at the national and state level. The search tool allows keyword searching as well as filtering of search results by type of resource (article, map, web page) or topics related to the search query.

DOE's information is organized into five categories:

- Public Services: Targeted to residential consumers and businesses, includes energy saving tips for homes and commercial buildings, programs and calculators by energy type, vehicle emissions and fuel savings manufacturing, clean energy, national security, funding and financing programs.
- Science and Innovation: Developments and projects at the national labs, scientific research, electric power, energy sources, energy efficiency, science education, and climate change.
- Energy Saver: Tips for saving energy and money in residential and commercial buildings, advanced manufacturing, energy management, renewable energy development and programs.
- About Energy.gov: Mission, leadership, organization, data, including open data initiatives, contact directories, and agency history.
- Offices: Listing of program offices like the Office of Science, research labs, and staff offices such as Congressional and Intergovernmental Affairs.

Statistics

Good policy comes from good analysis, and good analysis comes from good data. Compiling and analyzing reliable energy data are the responsibility of the Energy Information Administration (EIA), the major federal statistical agency within DOE. The agency's reports and data products serve a diverse audience including policymakers, consumers, academic researchers, and energy and financial analysts. EIA collects and publishes non-partisan data and analysis for both domestic and international energy products such as oil. Their robust website includes current and future trends related to domestic energy production, demand, consumption, technology, and energy reserves. Domestic data is compiled nationally, regionally, and at the state level. The user can browse the website by source or type of energy, including renewables, as well as for consumption and efficiency data. The topic section includes projections, analytical reports, environment (greenhouse gases, power plant emissions), and market and financial data. The geography section includes national data, data by US states, or data by country. The geography section also includes both static and dynamic maps showing where oil, coal, and gas are produced, and greenhouse gases are emitted, as well as static maps showing where types of energy are produced and even where real-time power disruptions due to storms are occurring.

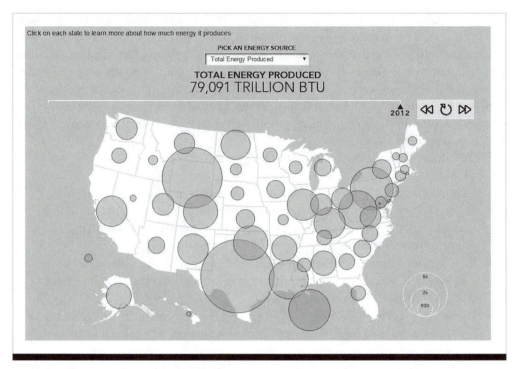

FIGURE 14.1
US Energy Production through the Years
Source: http://energy.gov/articles/us-energy-production-through-years.

Many datasets include data in chart and table form, with the option to download all corresponding data into a spreadsheet. Some of the more popular and comprehensive data products include interactive visualization and multimedia tools to enhance understanding of the data product, as seen in figure 14.1.

Two of the most popular EIA datasets are

- Monthly Energy Review: Current and historical data going back 65 years for fossil and renewable fuels, emissions, consumption, sectors, and energy markets.
- Annual Energy Outlook: Focuses on the US energy system, including energy production, consumption, technology, market trends, legislation, and regulation.

DOE makes much of its data available on Data.gov (discussed further in chapter 10), under its own topic area at energy.data.gov. EIA participates in open data initiatives to make its data sharable and to increase usability and interactivity. Some of this is accomplished through releases of API (Application Programming Interface) data, that is, data specifically structured to allow programmers outside of DOE to openly use the public data in other computer-based applications.

Development, production, and consumption of energy resources are global in scope. For this reason EIA also collects limited data on the energy situation of 219 other countries. Basic data for these countries focuses on the production and consumption of crude oil, coal, and electricity as well as total energy and carbon dioxide emissions. EIA provides detailed analysis briefs for 36 countries, which include domestic consumption, exploration and production, and imports and exports of energy resources. The Organisation for Economic Co-operation and Development (OECD) also tracks energy data through the International Energy Administration (IEA). Basic data and reports are available for free, but more detailed data for OECD member countries require a subscription to the IEA data module in the OECD iLibrary. Another free source is UNdata, from the United National Statistics Division. It provides country-specific energy data on production, consumption, exports, and stockpiles.

Finally, another major source of data and statistics is the Federal Energy Regulatory Commission (FERC). FERC (www.ferc.gov) is an independent regulatory commission with authority for setting rates for coal, electric, natural gas, oil, and renewable energy markets. FERC data is provided in report form as pdfs, making it necessary to manually enter data to build a dataset. Reports and analyses are available under the Market Oversight tab (www.ferc.gov/market-oversight/market-oversight.asp). Types of reports include analysis of domestic energy markets, reliability assessments by season, and annual State of the Market presentations. While FERC provides a detailed list of the data sources used to develop their assessments, much of it is from fee-based commercial sources.

Renewable Energy/Energy Efficiency/Consumer Information

Over the last couple decades, the need for sustainable energy resources, more efficient building material, and clean energy transportation has been gaining momentum. The Office of Energy Efficiency and Renewable Energy (EERE, www.eere.energy.gov) monitors development of clean-energy generation projects using geothermal solar, wind, and water resources. This includes research into renewable energy technologies, efficient building design and materials, and efficient vehicles and fuels. This extends to bringing new technology to market through programs, technical assistance, and guidance for consumers, businesses, and state and local governments. The National Renewable Energy Laboratory (NREL, www.nrel.gov), a federal lab, also performs vital work to research and brings new clean energy technologies to market. Finally, the Office of Scientific and Technical Information (OSTI) disseminates federal R&D and grant-funded research, primarily in the form of technical reports through Science.gov. More information on OSTI is available in chapter 13. Another source to be aware of is http://worldwideenergy.org. This site, maintained by OSTI, allows users to search across several energy databases, not only from the United States but also from countries participating in the Energy Technology Data Exchange (www.etde.org). DOE also provides tools and calculators that provide informative and useful ways to interact with the data on a personal level, making us better informed about costs associated with our energy lifestyle. For example, it's possible to calculate the cost savings associated with Energy Star–rated products, estimate the costs for owning a vehicle, and perform home energy audits. While there is no single list of calculators, they are featured prominently on applicable pages when available.

Consumer Information from DOE

The DOE also aims to make information available to general audiences. DOE partnered with the EPA to develop two popular programs to help inform consumers and businesses about savings and energy efficiency:

Energy Star (www.energystar.gov): Created in 1992, the Energy Star logo signifies a product or building has been independently certified to save energy and therefore lower operating costs and reduce greenhouse gases. The Energy Star website helps consumers find qualified products, in addition to providing home assessment tips and tools, and discover tax credits or rebates specific to the user's local area.

FuelEconomy.gov (www.fueleconomy.gov): Provides information on fuel demand by vehicle type, estimates of carbon footprint, and comparative fuel efficiency across car models and years. It also provides tips for driving efficiently to maximize savings and emissions, and supplies calculators to track personal fuel expenses. The site also discusses how hybrid and electric cars work, provides information about available tax credits, and alternative fuels.

Environmental Information Sources

Brief Histories of EPA and NOAA

Although environmental activism began over one hundred years ago, historians and environmentalists trace contemporary interest in environmental issues back to the 1962 publication of Rachel Carson's *Silent Spring*. While the book focused on pesticides, it brought environmental concerns to the public conscience. Over the next several years after its publication, other environmental issues garnered national interest, such as the Ohio's Cuyahoga River catching on fire, a massive oil spill off the coast of California, and intense smog in major American cities. While Congress had taken some steps to protect the environment prior to the publication of *Silent Spring* by passing the Federal Water Pollution Control Act (P.L. 80-845, 62 Stat. 1155 (1948)) as early as the 1940s and the Clean Air Act (P.L. 88-206, 77 Stat. 392 (1963)) in the 1960s, it was clear that competing agency missions reduced the overall power of the federal government to protect the environment. However, it wasn't until 1970 when President Richard Nixon announced a government reorganization in a message to Congress that the EPA was established as an independent executive branch agency (Nixon, 1970). In this same message, Nixon also announced the creation of the National Oceanic and Atmospheric Administration (NOAA). Since then, the EPA has been an agency with a very broad mission that often overlaps with many other agencies.

EPA's Mission

EPA's mission is to protect human health and the environment, and it is interested in how waste and pollution in the water, air, and land affect human health, ecosystems, and the environment (Environmental Protection Agency, 2015a). Its mission focuses on implementing federal environmental regulations, developing pollution reduction technologies and strategies, and gathering and publishing data. Much like DOE, EPA's broad mission often interacts with different agencies, and in some instances it is unclear to the layperson (and even to experienced professionals) where the boundaries lie. In answering environmental reference questions, you may need to consult publications from the Department of Interior, DOE, Department of Agriculture, OSHA, and the other state and local government agencies. In some cases the EPA website will link you to the appropriate supplemental site (or original data source); in other cases it will not. Due to both its size and interest in issues also monitored by multiple agencies, the EPA can be an intimidating agency to explore, but knowing a few strategies and tools can help you navigate its website (www.epa.gov) rather quickly.

Resources from the EPA

In addition to Tips for Navigating Agency Websites (chapter 2, sidebar), items specific to the EPA include

- My Environment (www.epa.gov/myenvironment) provides environmental information at the local level for such topics as current air quality, nearby hazardous waste sites, and more. Enter an address or a zip code and My Environment produces an interactive map (see figure 14.2 of Beaumont, Texas). My Environment also links to different EPA and non-EPA databases for more in-depth analysis.
- Regulatory Development and Retrospective Review Tracker, also known as Reg DaRRT, (http://yosemite.epa.gov/opei/RuleGate.nsf), provides quick access to proposed rules from the EPA. While Regulations.gov (see chapter 6 on Regulations) allows searching across new regulations, EPA's Reg DaRRT allows for more complex searching limited to environmental regulations and discovering regulations on topics such as Children's Health, Local Governments, or Unfunded Mandates. Reg DaRRT also links directly to Regulations.gov so one can provide comment and/or view other public comments on active or recently passed rules and regulations.
- National Service Center for Environmental Publications, or NSCEP (www.epa.gov/nscep), is probably the best source for discovering EPA's research and published output from the formation of the agency to present. Many of the historic publications have been digitized and made available; others are only available for order in paper.
- After the published record has been exhausted, a final strategy for finding specific information is to contact the agency directly. The EPA divides the US into 10 different regions (see map: www.epa.gov/osp/regions/images/RegionsMAP.jpg). Knowing these regions can help you locate the office or lab to contact about an environmental issue in a specific part of the country. Local offices can also be a source of publications that were never distributed through the FDLP.

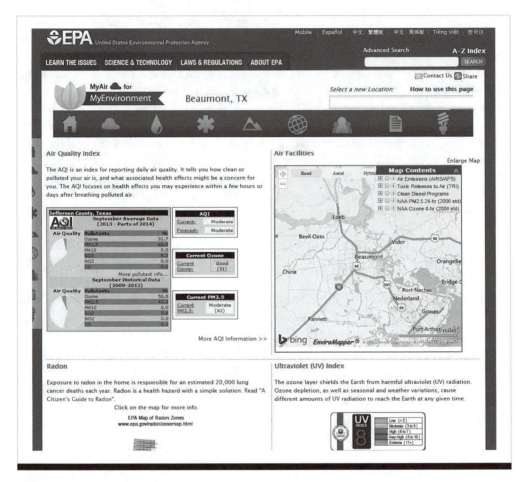

FIGURE 14.2
Air Quality Index for Beaumont, Texas, from the EPA's My Environment
Source: www.epa.gov/myenvironment.

Data and Statistics

EPA collects and publishes a great deal of statistics and numeric data (many, but not all, of which can be discovered via www.data.gov). EPA also maintains a portal to find numeric data by topic or keywords (www.epa.gov/datafinder/). In addition to these and the sources mentioned below, keep in mind that other agencies' data may be used in conjunction with EPA data, such as population data from the Census Bureau combined with TRI data (described below) to see how a particular chemical release may affect the area's human population.

One environmental term to know is the *emission factor,* which is a numeric value that attempts to relate the amount of a particular pollutant released to the atmosphere with an activity associated with its release. Emission factors are used for developing emissions inventories for air quality management decisions and in developing emissions control strategies. A tool for discovering this information is *AP-42, Compilation of Emission*

Factors (www.epa.gov/ttnchie1/ap42, known simply as AP-42). It contains emission factors and process information (a high level description of how a product is manufactured) for more than 200 industries. The current edition was published in 1995, but more recent draft updates are available on its website. WebFIRE (http://cfpub.epa.gov/webfire/) is another tool one can search for current emission factors and hazardous air pollutant statistics, but lacks the manufacturing process information contained within AP-42. WebFIRE also allows bulk data download.

Another prominent program is the *Toxic Release Inventory* (www2.epa.gov/toxics-release-inventory-tri-program), which monitors the release of more than 650 chemicals known to cause cancer or other chronic human health effects, have significant adverse acute human health effects, or have significant adverse environmental effects (Environmental Protection Agency, 2015b). Every business must report the release of these chemicals, which are then gathered and published by the EPA. Users can access the data via bulk data download or by using several of the tools available on the site (such as TRI Explorer or TRI.net) that allows for data visualization. TRI data can also be found in other government databases, such as the National Library of Medicine's Toxnet (http://toxnet.nlm.nih.gov), which is covered in more detail in chapter 11. All TRI tools have detailed instructions that can assist a novice user.

Weather, Climate, and Climate Change

One cannot discuss the environment without also talking about the weather and climate. NOAA, within the Commerce Department, produces information on climate and weather, among other resources. While NOAA is the agency that tracks climate and weather, growing attention to climate change and global warming has increased collaboration between NOAA, EPA, and other agencies (more on this below). In this context, the biggest difference between NOAA and EPA specifically is the regulatory work. NOAA is primarily a research agency that gathers and shares information, while its regulatory work focuses on oceanic topics such as fisheries. NOAA garners more attention for its research work, while the EPA attracts just as much attention for its regulations as its research.

Weather forecasts viewed across the United States are based on data provided by NOAA's National Weather Service (NWS). Weather.gov (www.weather.gov) provides current local forecasts from the NWS by city and zip code, while the National Centers for Environmental Information (NCEI, a new agency that subsumed the former National Climatic Data Center) provides historical weather information and data. The Weather and climate section of NCEI's website (www.ncei.noaa.gov) allows searching for precipitation, temperature, and wind speeds for many locations across the United States and limited locations outside the country. Each dataset title gives a hint of its contents; for example, "Surface Data, Daily U.S." contains data on the minimum and maximum temperature, wind gusts, and other pertinent information at the surface each day. The NCEI is also a great source for time-series data (data collected over a set period of time) on the weather. This can help users track climate change. Depending on the location, some datasets go back one hundred years or more. Annual summary data can also be generated looking at the temperature and precipitation using the "Annual Climatological Summary" data set (see figure

U.S. Department of Commerce
National Oceanic & Atmospheric Administration
National Environmental Satellite, Data, and Information Service

Elev: 50 ft. Lat: 38.913° N Lon: 76.970° W
Station: **NATIONAL ARBORETUM DC, DC US COOP-186350**

Annual Climatological Summary
(2015)
Generated on 01/11/2016

National Centers for Environmental Information
151 Patton Avenue
Asheville, North Carolina 28801

Date	Temperature (F)														Precipitation (inches)									
Elem->	MMXT	MMNT	MNTM	DPNT	HTDD	CLDD	EMXT		EMNT		DT90	DX32	DT32	DT00	TPCP	DPNP	EMXP		TSNW	MXSD		DP01	DP05	DP10
	Mean Max.	Mean Min.	Mean	Depart. from Normal	Heating Degree Days	Cooling Degree Days	Highest	High Date	Lowest	Low Date	Number Of Days				Total	Depart. from Normal	Greatest Observed		Snow, Sleet			Number Of Days		
											Max >=90	Max <=32	Min <=32	Min <=0			Day	Date	Total Fall	Max Depth	Max Date	>=.10	>=.50	>=1.0
Month																								
1	41.3	24.9	33.1	-2.4	985	0	66	05	10	08	0	5	25	0	3.07	-0.02	0.53	13	4.4X	3	07	10	2	0
2	38.8X	19.8X	29.3	-9.1		0	67	09	4	20	0	5	24	0	1.73X	-1.17	0.85	22	8.0X	4X	18	5	1	0
3	51.7X	30.8X	41.2	-5.0		0	76	27	12	06	0	1	16	0	4.18X	0.46	0.61	05	6.0X	5	06	10	5	0
4	68.0	45.9	57.0	0.6	246	12	82	19	34	01	0	0	0	0	3.21	-0.30	0.98	20	0.0X	0	0	8	2	0
5	81.4X	61.0X	71.2	5.3			92	29	48	02	3	0	0	0	2.12X	-2.16	1.07	19	0.0X	0	0	4	1	1
6	85.0X	68.3X	76.6	1.5			95	24	58	04	12	0	0	0	12.90X	8.82	2.85	02	0.0X	0	0	12	7	5
7																								
8																								
9																								
10																								
11																								
12																								
Annual	61.0*	41.8*	51.4*		1231*	12*	95*	Jun*	4*	Feb*	15*	11*	65*	0*	27.21*		2.85*	Jun*	18.4*	5*	Mar*	49*	18*	6*

Notes

(blank) Data element not reported or missing.

+ Occurred on one or more previous dates during the month. The date in the Date field is the last day of occurrence. Used through December 1983 only.

A Accumulated amount. This value is a total that may include data from a previous month or months or year (for annual value).

B Adjusted total. Monthly value totals based on proportional available data across the entire month.

E An estimated monthly or annual total.

X Monthly means or totals based on incomplete time series. 1 to 9 days are missing. Annual means or totals include one or more months which had 1 to 9 days that were missing.

T Trace of precipitation, snowfall, or snowdepth. The precipitation data value will equal zero.

Elem Element types are included to provide cross-reference for users of the NCDC CDO system.

Station Station is identified by: COOP ID, Station Name, State

S Precipitation amount is continuing to be accumulated. Total will be included in a subsequent monthly or yearly value. Example: Days 1-20 had 1.35 inches of precipitation, then a period of accumulation began. The element TPCP would then be 0013SS and the total accumulated amount value appears in a subsequent monthly value.

* Annual value missing; summary value computed from available month values.

FIGURE 14.3
Annual Climatological Summary for the National Arboretum in Washington, D.C.
Source: www.ncei.noaa.gov.

14.3 as an example). Again, the data is available only for places where the information was collected, so if the patron is looking for weather information for a small town during the first half of the 20th century, the data may not be available.

Another NOAA site, Climate.gov (www.climate .gov), makes browsing for recent climate data much easier than NCEI's site, but lacks the historic data. Climate.gov also includes information on future climate simulations where a user can, for example, simulate rainfall patterns in a changing global climate. The site also provides instructional materials and lesson plans for teaching climate.

As stated before, the EPA's work often overlaps with other agencies. One area where this has garnered attention and has led to several partnerships in recent years is in climate change. Climate change is a broad and sometimes controversial issue that does not fit neatly into one particular agency's mission, so the US Global Change Research Program (USGCRP) integrates the work of 13 interested departments and agencies into a single program. The continually updated USGCRP website (www.globalchange.gov) enables the discovery of the major government reports on this topic. The list of agencies participating in USGCRP (Department of Defense, DOE, Commerce, etc.) provides a roadmap one might explore further, not only for resources about global climate change, but about environment and energy in general.

In the international arena, the Intergovernmental Panel on Climate Change (IPCC) is the international scientific body that studies climate change and attempts to coordinate a global response. IPCC's website (www.ipcc.ch) is brimming with reports and data. Another international agency working on climate change is the United Nations Framework Convention on Climate Change (UNFCCC). The main difference between these two bodies is that the UNFCCC focuses on the policy and IPCC focuses on the science. The Bonn climate talks of June 2010 was held under the aegis of the UNFCCC, as were the meetings that resulted in the Kyoto Protocol of 1997. The IPCC allows governments to nominate experts to write its scientific reports so a diverse group of scientists that covers different views, expertise, and geographies can present nonpartisan findings. UNFCCC's Newsroom (http://newsroom.unfccc.int) has useful data and reports on global warming, as well as data on each nation's progress in meeting climate targets and signing and ratifying environmental treaties.

NOAA is also involved with and monitors marine debris (garbage floating in the ocean) through its Marine Debris Program (http://marinedebris.noaa .gov). This program was started by the Marine Debris Research, Prevention, and Reduction Act of 2006 (P.L. 109-449, 120 Stat 3333, (2006)). While the program may sound benign, it has been monitoring a couple of major issues that have garnered national interest the last few years:

Great Pacific Garbage Patch, a large, floating mass of garbage in the Pacific Ocean (http://marinedebris.noaa.gov/info/patch.html).

Japanese Tsunami of 2011 and its effect on the ocean and beaches of the US West Coast and Hawaii (http://marinedebris .noaa.gov/tsunamidebris/faqs).

Public Lands

Land controlled by the federal government makes up one-quarter to three-quarters of most western states and is known as public land. Four agencies provide most of the management of these lands: National Park Service (NPS), Bureau of Land Management (BLM), US Fish and Wildlife Service (FWS), and the US Forest Service (FS). While each of these agencies has its own unique mission, the main difference is preservation (NPS and FWS) versus multiple uses (BLM and FS). For example, the FWS, which carries out research on endangered species, manages the Endangered Species Act Documents Library (www.fws.gov/endangered/esa-library/index.html).

Public Land Resources

A large portion of information related to government work on public lands can be discovered in Environmental Impact Statements (EIS). Each public land agency goes through a periodic planning process through which EISs or other management plans are created. Each of these documents takes into account current and proposed activities on the land, alternatives, and their environmental impact. EISs must be written for any activity having an impact on federal lands. Since the federal government owns nearly 650 million acres of land—almost 30 percent of the land area of the United States—the EIS process is both a common and an important activity (Vincent, 2014). These EISs are announced each week in the *Federal Register,* but can also be found in EPA's *Environmental Impact Statement Database* (www.epa.gov/compliance/nepa/eisdata.html). EISs have their origins in the National Environmental Policy Act (NEPA) (P.L. 91-190, 83 Stat. 852 (1970)) which requires that federal agencies "integrate environmental values into their decision making processes by considering the environmental impacts of their proposed actions and reasonable alternatives to those actions" (Environmental Protection Agency, 2015c). In addition to EISs, other planning reports are also created, and these can provide additional information. For instance, when the counterculture festival Burning Man wanted to expand the number of participants in its festival, the BLM issued a detailed Environmental Assessment Report in order to renew their permit (US Bureau of Land Management, 2012).

A concern with EPA's Environmental Impact Statement Database, as well as with EIS searching (and with other information produced by the government as well) is that some of these materials are not distributed through the FDLP. With the advent of e-government, many are often not published in print at all. And while there is a requirement that these statements be published, there is no requirement that they be preserved. Most national forests and other public land divisions post their recent EIS and other documents on their websites; in many cases these reports are current only. If a needed report is not on the site, a phone call, e-mail, or even a visit to a specific office might be necessary. When looking for older, historic reports, keep these strategies in mind:

- Check WorldCat to see if a library has managed to collect the item.
- The Northwestern University Transportation Library's Environmental Impact Statements (www.library.northwestern.edu/libraries-collections/evanston-campus/transportation-library/services/reference-services/search-eis) is the largest privately held collection of EISs. They claim to hold every EIS issued by federal agencies from 1969 to the present, whereas EPA's library covers only 1970 to 1990.

- Cambridge Scientific Abstracts provides full-text EISs from 2003 to the present in their commercial database *Environmental Impact Statements.*

Recreation

As mentioned previously, responsibility for public land spans several federal agencies. Visits to areas managed by the NPS are the chief way the public interacts with federal land in the United States. When planning a visit to a national park, wildlife, or heritage site, it's most helpful to consult the website directly to learn about unique attractions, recreational opportunities, wildlife, and hazards. While NPS is perhaps the most well-known single agency, other agencies such as the FS, FWS, and even the National Archives, also encourage the public to enjoy the land and cultural resources they manage. Twelve of these agencies partnered to create Recreation.gov which serves as a gateway to discovering places to visit, and more importantly make reservations at thousands of destinations across the United States. However, when looking for information about federal recreational land regulations, business opportunities, scientific research or other publications, it's important to consult the agency or subagency's website. Depending on the query, it might be necessary to use both the federal search engine USA.gov and the search tool or site index located on the agency's web page to find specific information.

Conclusion

Managing our energy needs and human impact on the environment falls primarily to the Department of Energy and the EPA. These agencies provide vital links to research, data, regulations, and new technologies that help sustain our energy infrastructure and environmental standards. The work of these federal agencies is also vital to good policy decisions. Congress and the president rely on the information and data produced by the DOE and EPA to enact sound legislation, support regulations, and craft policy that will benefit the United States and world. While these agencies produce much of the information, numerous other federal, international, regional, and state agencies are also producers and repositories of publicly available data on these topics.

Exercises

1. Describe the weather in Washington, DC, on the date of President Franklin Roosevelt's first inauguration in 1933.
2. Find a new environment-related regulation proposed by the EPA (or other agency) on a topic that interests you. What is the regulation about? Submit a comment stating your personal opinion either for or against the regulation.

3. Look up any environmental hazards around your home, school, or work. Did you know much about the hazard before looking it up?

4. Find two ways you can reduce water usage in your home. Now see if you can also find two ways to reduce energy consumption in your home.

5. Compare the gas mileage per gallon (MPG) for two cars that you like.

6. Find some information on hydraulic fracturing. Are there any hazards associated with it, and if so, what?

7. What does the EPA say about recycled water? Is it safe?

Sources Mentioned in This Chapter

Legislation (Chronological Order)

Federal Water Pollution Control Act, P.L. 80-845, 62 Stat. 1155 (1948).

Clean Air Act, P.L. 88-206, 77 Stat. 392 (1963).

National Environmental Policy Act (NEPA), P.L. 91-190, 83 Stat. 852 (1970).

Department of Energy Organization Act, P.L. 95-91; 91 Stat. 565 (1977).

Marine Debris Research, Prevention, and Reduction Act of 2006, P.L. 109-449, 120 Stat. 3333 (2006).

Other Sources

Climate.gov, www.climate.gov.

Department of Energy, Energy.gov.

Department of Energy Office of Energy Efficiency and Renewable Energy, http://energy.gov/eere/office-energy-efficiency-renewable-energy.

Energy Information Administration, www.eia.gov.

Energy Information Administration, Analysis and Projections, www.eia.gov/analysis.

Energy Star, www.energystar.gov.

Environmental Protection Agency, www.epa.gov.

Environmental Protection Agency, *Compilation of Emission Factors, AP-42*. www.epa.gov/ttnchie1/ap42.

Environmental Protection Agency, Environmental Impact Statement Database, www.epa.gov/compliance/nepa/eisdata.html.

Environmental Protection Agency, My Environment, www.epa.gov/myenvironment.

Environmental Protection Agency, National Service Center for Environmental Publications, www.epa.gov/nscep.

Environmental Protection Agency, Regulatory Development and Retrospective Review Tracker, http://yosemite.epa.gov/opei/RuleGate.nsf/.

Environmental Protection Agency, Toxic Release Inventory. www2.epa.gov/toxics-release-inventory-tri-program.

Environmental Protection Agency, WebFIRE, http://cfpub.epa.gov/webfire/.

Federal Energy Regulatory Commission, www.ferc.gov.

FuelEconomy.gov, www.fueleconomy.gov.

Great Pacific Garbage Patch, http://marinedebris.noaa.gov/info/patch.html.

Intergovernmental Panel on Climate Change, www.ipcc.ch.

Japan Tsunami Marine Debris, http://marinedebris.noaa.gov/tsunamidebris/faqs.

Marine Debris Program, http://marinedebris.noaa.gov.

National Centers for Environmental Information, www.ncei.noaa.gov.

National Oceanic and Atmospheric Administration, www.noaa.gov.

National Weather Service, www.weather.gov.

Northwestern University Transportation Library Environmental Impact Statements, www.library
.northwestern.edu/libraries-collections/evanston-campus/transportation-library/services/
reference-services/search-eis.

Online Computer Library Corporation, Worldcat, www.oclc.org/worldcat.en.html.

US Global Change Research Program, www.globalchange.gov.

United Nations Framework Convention on Climate Change, http://newsroom.unfccc.int/.

United States Bureau of Land Management, www.blm.gov.

United States Fish and Wildlife Service, www.fws.gov.

United States Fish and Wildlife Service, Endangered Species Act Documents Library, www.fws.gov/
endangered/esa-library/index.html.

United States Forest Service, www.fs.fed.us.

United States National Park Service, www.nps.gov.

References

Department of Energy. 2014. "Mission—Department of Energy." http://energy.gov/mission.

Environmental Protection Agency. 2015a. "EPA. Our Mission and What We Do." www2.epa.gov/
aboutepa/our-mission-and-what-we-do.

Environment Protection Agency. 2015b. "Learn about the Toxics Release Inventory." www2.epa
.gov/toxics-release-inventory-tri-program/learn-about-toxics-release-inventory#What%20are%20
TRI%20toxic%20chemicals?.

Environment Protection Agency. 2015c. "National Environmental Policy Act (NEPA)." www.epa.gov/
compliance/nepa/.

Richard Nixon 1970. "Annual Message to the Congress on the State of the Union," January 22. The
American Presidency Project. www.presidency.ucsb.edu/ws/?pid=2921.

US Bureau of Land Management. 2012. *Burning Man Final Environmental Assessment, 2012–2016*.
www.blm.gov/epl-front-office/projects/nepa/28954/37412/39212/Burning_Man_DOI-BLM-
NV-W030–2012–0007-Final_EA.pdf.

Vincent, C. H., et al. 2014. *Federal Land Ownership: Overview and Data*. Washington, DC: Library of Congress Congressional Research Service. http://fas.org/sgp/crs/misc/R42346.pdf.

CHAPTER 15

Business, Economic, and Consumer Information

JESSICA JERRIT AND ERIC FORTE

Introduction

The business of America is business.
President Calvin Coolidge's famous misquote—he actually said, "After all, the chief business of the American people is business" (Coolidge, 1925)—rings true when considering the amount of government effort and government information that exists to support business enterprise. It's impossible to imagine the study and analysis of US economics, business, and industry without the use of data collected, processed, and disseminated by governments, especially the US federal government.

> The federal government is a friend of business when it comes to producing information. Most economic indicators, forecasts, and other macroeconomic data are the result of long-standing cooperation among the companies that fill out forms, the government that collects and tabulates the data, and private and government economists who interpret the results. (Boettcher, 2005: 19)

Look at the broad contents of the 2012 edition of the *Statistical Abstract of the United States* (that most popular of government documents—2012 is the last government-produced version, though the title continues via the publisher ProQuest—see chapter 10 for details). In terms of business and economics coverage, of the 30 browsable sections in the *Statistical Abstract,* nearly half are directly focused on economics, business, and industry:

- Accommodations, Food, and Other Services
- Arts, Recreation, and Travel
- Banking, Finance, and Insurance
- Business Enterprise

- Construction and Housing
- Energy and Utilities
- Foreign Commerce and Aid
- Forestry, Fishing, and Mining
- Income, Expenditures, Poverty, and Wealth
- Information and Communications
- Labor Force, Employment, and Earnings
- Manufactures
- Prices
- Wholesale and Retail Trade

Another eight categories (at least) also contain key information about US business and economics:

- Agriculture (think of the business of agriculture—even the US Department of Agriculture produces scores of market research reports)
- Federal Government Finances and Employment (think of the US budget and federal income tax data)
- Geography and Environment (think of the interplay between industry and the environment)
- Health and Nutrition (health care use and expenditures, health insurance, and even disease incidence all figure prominently in the ever more interdisciplinary world of the business reference librarian)
- Population (think of marketing and demographic data)
- Science and Technology (think of R&D expenditures and other measures of the entrepreneurial environment)
- Social Insurance and Human Services (think of philanthropy and the activities of nonprofit organizations)
- State and Local Government Finances and Employment

Governments serve numerous functions related to business and commerce:

- measure business and economic activity
- define and classify business ventures via systems widely adopted by major private business information products (e.g., the Standard Industrial Classification [SIC] Code and North American Industry Classification System [NAICS])
- Measure and support the nation's labor force (US Bureau of Labor)
- regulate everything from certain operations of small businesses, to accounting practices of public corporations, to Wall Street, to food and drugs, to foreign trade
- support US business productivity and success (US Department of Commerce and the Small Business Administration)

While the government produces all of this business, economic, and consumer data, it is not always easy to find, and packaging the data for easy public consumption is not necessarily government's first priority. Note that many fee-based business information products analyze or expand upon government information, making it more usable. "Proprietary business-resource databases distinguish their services by providing value-added analysis, organization, and one-stop convenience. As a general rule, one should expect to consult a variety of government sources to obtain equivalent information supplied in commercial databases" (Scott, 2009).

This chapter will address the source of much of this data: the major business, economic, and consumer information available from governments, primarily the US federal government.

Types of Business and Economic Information

Much government-produced business information relates to categories spelled out by the most famous of economic inspirations for the United States, economist and father of capitalism Adam Smith. In Book V, chapter 1 of *The Wealth of Nations* (Smith, 1819), Smith discusses public goods and government duties in some detail. These state duties include, for Smith, things such as national defense, police, and the justice system; protecting intellectual property such as patents and trademarks; enforcing contracts; building infrastructure; and regulating banking. Generally, these government functions are those which Smith did not think that free markets could adequately perform.

In addition, as particularly seen in the next chapter about the decennial census, governments in the United States quickly saw the benefit in measuring economic and business enterprise data alongside gathering population counts. Much government information about business, then, is data and statistics measuring the characteristics and output of the economy. This includes well known economic statistics—those widely reported in the media—such as inflation, unemployment, and retail spending, to less known but much more detailed measures, such as business activity by industry, types of business, and geography.

Several government surveys collect data about people, such as about their occupations and wages, and publish compilations of this data. Remember that in no instance is any individual's personal data revealed; law ensures privacy. In some instances the government publishes information about specific companies, such as public company financials (to inform investors), or specifics about company operations related to oversight in the more regulated industries, such as utilities, airlines, and communications. It also publishes and manages patents and other intellectual property, and handles business bankruptcies and antitrust actions.

Governments support businesses and consumers, providing help for new and existing businesses, protecting and educating its citizens as consumers, and regulating industries for the safety and benefit of citizens when the free market might not provide such protections.

Finally, the US government is particularly supportive of US businesses operating abroad, and publishes quite a bit of information in support of exporting and selling abroad. Other international data, such as foreign trade and exchange rates, are also popular, and published by various international government bodies.

Economic Indicators

Among the most prominent types of government business information are economic indicators, which are pieces of data commonly used by politicians, bureaucrats, scholars, and business people to measure the strength of our economy. These indicators, often produced monthly, frequently end up as lead stories in not just business news sources, but general news sources as well. Read the *New York Times* for a month and count how often economic data releases are covered on the first screen or front page. Depending on the news cycle and the content of the information, stories about economic data produced by the government may appear in a dozen top headlines in a month. The implications of these indicators can drive government policy in many ways. Unemployment data can influence government policy and funding of unemployment benefits; price and inflation data are key to actions of the Federal Reserve and its management of money supply (and the Fed's actions can, of course, have dramatic impacts on financial markets); exchange rates and trade balances influence government policies related to international trade; and occupational measures influence vocational and higher education priorities. In any case, understanding this data and identifying its sources—reports and statistical data sets—are frequent tasks in using government information.

Depending on how one defines an economic indicator, there could be hundreds of them. A wide variety of agencies contribute to our knowledge of our economy, and there is not currently a single compilation of all such releases from the government. However, a significant subset of the nation's most important economic indicators is compiled into the monthly *Economic Indicators,* transmitted to Congress from the president's Council of Economic Advisers. Among the 48 currently compiled statistics included are popularly reported data such as gross domestic product, unemployment, inflation and prices, interest rates, and foreign trade (see figre 15.1). All tables in each monthly issue generally include annual data for the last 10 years and quarterly data for the last 2 years.

Although *Economic Indicators'* paper and PDF format may not be extremely friendly to more robust statistical extraction, it does provide a consistent platform for this data as its publication dates back to 1948. The Federal Reserve Bank of St. Louis has extracted most of these indicators and makes them available through their FRED (Federal Reserve Economic Data) database, often back to the early 20th century. FRED is a constantly growing database and offers data downloads in many formats, custom charting, and links to data sources (http://research.stlouisfed.org/fred2/). FRED also contains the latest data revisions, which *Economic Indicators* and other paper and PDF sources will not reflect. FRED's companion database, ALFRED (ArchivaL Federal Reserve Economic Data, http://alfred.stlouisfed.org/) provides access to "vintage data," meaning that you can access economic data as it was at a specific moment in history. This is invaluable for scholars trying to analyze policy decisions in the past or replicate past research.

Another standard compilation of economic indicators and statistics across government is the annual *Economic Report of the President* (*ERP*), which is published annually by the Council of Economic Advisers (an agency within the president's office established by Congress in 1946). Nearly all of the categories mentioned above—prices, employment and unemployment, GDP and output by sector or industry, foreign trade, government spending, interest rates, and more than 100 additional items—are included

CONTENTS

General Notes

Detail in these tables may not add to totals because of rounding.
Unless otherwise noted, all dollar figures are in current dollars.
Symbols used:
p Preliminary.
r Revised.
c Corrected.
... Not available (also, not applicable).
NSA Not seasonally adjusted.

FIGURE 15.1
Economic Indicators Table of Contents

in the *ERP,* with most data available annually for 40, 50, and 60 years or more. In addition to its statistics section, it includes a prose description and analysis of the current economy, with chapters on various current issues. Both the *Economic Report of the President* and *Economic Indicators* are available in FDsys and are archived by the Federal Reserve in the Federal Reserve Archival System for Economic Research (FRASER, https://fraser.stlouisfed.org).

Most of the popular data releases from *Economic Indicators* come from three primary agencies: the Department of Commerce, the BLS (under the Department of Labor), and the Federal Reserve (the Fed). Each of these agencies provides a portal to their popular releases which many will consider easier to use than *Economic Indicators,* if not as complete. The Bureau of Economic Analysis (under the Department of Commerce) provides US Economy at a Glance (www.bea.gov/newsreleases/glance.htm); the BLS produces Economy at a Glance (www.bls.gov/eag/eag.us.htm); and the Board of Governors of the Federal Reserve System features a web page of its statistical data (www.federalreserve.gov/econresdata/statisticsdata.htm).

The Department of Commerce Economics and Statistics Administration website collects popular indicators produced by two of its bureaus: the US Census Bureau (www.census.gov) and the BEA (www.esa.doc.gov/about-economic-indicators). Prominent among these are retail sales, which are often reported on in media as consumer spending (think of news stories discussing how people are spending more, or less, and how that affects the economy), sales and construction of new and existing homes, Gross Domestic Product (GDP, the most used, complete indicator of the output of the nation's economy), and foreign trade (think of discussions of trade deficits).

BLS produces several prominent economic indicators as well, all available from its Economy at a Glance (www.bls.gov/eag/eag.us.htm). Unemployment is possibly its most cited indicator, but the agency's mission also includes measurement of a less intuitive statistic when one considers labor: prices. BLS's Consumer Price Index and Producer Price Index are the primary source for news articles about prices and inflation. Another popular indicator available from Economy at a Glance is productivity, a measure of how productive the nation's workers are. Also noteworthy is the fact that BLS unemployment indicators are also available for states and metropolitan areas at Economy at a Glance, and are the source of unemployment rates frequently reported for states and cities. Several other BLS data items are available for smaller geographies as well. The map interface at Economy at a Glance helps users to navigate to this data.

The third most prominent agency producing economic indicators is the Federal Reserve, whose mission is largely to manage the nation's money supply. As economic and monetary theory surrounding money supply has grown in prominence in recent decades, the Fed, and especially its chair, have become economic rock stars. The chair's every word is minutely scrutinized by the business media at a level more commonly attributed to celebrity watching. While key indicators from the Fed, such as those measuring consumer credit and money stocks, may not have quite the broad popularity of unemployment, prices, and home sales, markets and the financial industry pay very close attention to this data from the Fed. The most popular Fed action is its control of the interest rate (popularly known as the prime rate or the federal funds rate), which may change after a meeting of the Fed's Open Market Committee, and always makes front page news. Announcements of changes to the prime rate garner rapt attention from economists, politicians, bureaucrats, and the nation's world markets.

Economic data for states is largely derived from federal statistical efforts. For instance, the BEA measures economic output for states, while the BLS measures employment and prices for states and metropolitan areas. States usually have their own economic and/or commerce-related agencies, which may conduct some research on their own to supplement the federal data. City and local data follows the same pattern, except only a few of these economic indicators cover smaller geographies, and when they do, it's generally only for larger metropolitan areas. Many cities and counties are the subject of more in-depth local economic analysis, sponsored by local governments, or perhaps by a university, chamber of commerce, or research center nearby. Become familiar with the state and local resources most relevant to you. One interesting compilation of standard economic data (along with more detailed banking data) is the FDIC State Profiles, available at www.fdic.gov/bank/analytical/stateprofile/.

Business and Industry Data

The federal government produces quite a bit of information about the condition of particular industries and business enterprises. Some of this data has been referred to already: the BEA, for instance, tracks overall production by sectors of the economy (sectors are broad categories such as retail trade, manufacturing, mining, and services).

The Census Bureau has several survey programs that produce more robust business and industry data. Also, various government services produce intelligence about specific companies. This section addresses industry and specific company information available from the government.

Surveys of Business and Industry

Census Bureau surveys of business are the highlights of this category, and their major survey is the economic census. The economic census is similar to the decennial census (covered in chapter 16), but instead of surveying people, it surveys businesses. With some exceptions, nearly every business in the country that has employees receives an economic census questionnaire, and is required by law to complete it. Just as the regular decennial census gathers key data such as population, age, race, and sex, all by location, the economic census, currently taken every five years, asks every business questions so as to gather key economic data: type of business (for example, there are companies who manufacture car parts, companies that sell car parts, companies that sell cars, and companies that perform car repairs: all are in different industries); a measure of size, such as number of employees and payroll; a measure of output, such as value of shipments or services, or retail sales; and location, to allow all of this data to be available for states, counties, cities, and ZIP codes. The economic census yields a rich picture of the US economy, with data by industry and location.

History of the Economic Census

As Micarelli (1998) summarizes, the first economic census took place as part of the 1810 decennial census after Congress passed a law specifically calling for it. At that time, the economic census consisted of counting manufacturers by broad types of products (25 categories), with an estimate of their output. Results were compiled into a single volume as part of the 1810 census results: *A Series of Tables of Several Branches of American Manufacturers of Every County in the Union so far as they are returned in the reports of the Marshals, and of the secretaries and of their respective assistants, in the autumn of the year 1810: Together with returns of certain doubtful Goods, Productions of the Soil and agricultural stock, so far as they have been received.* These measures of economic activity continued as part of the regular census at the behest of Congress. Over the years, more and more data was compiled. In 1850, it was expanded beyond manufacturing to include mining and fishing. In 1880, transportation and communication industry information was gathered in response to the burgeoning railroad, steamer, and telephone industries.

The 20th century saw a continued expansion of the economic census, and it began to be staggered in time from the population census. For a time, the economic census was taken every two years. There was no economic census in 1945—the nation was busy at war—but the 1947 census of manufactures was notable for the introduction of standard classification codes for industries (up until this time, the Census Bureau created its own industry categories). This happened because in 1941, a predecessor to OMB created the *Standard Industrial Classification (SIC) Manual,* which became a standard classification of industries that, in revised form, is still sometimes used today. So the 1947 economic census classified each business according to categories defined in the *SIC Manual.* The North American Industry Classification System (NAICS) was developed to replace the SIC codes and was adopted in 1997.

The rest of the 20th century saw the modern economic census take shape: held every five years (in years ending in 2 and 7), covering all industries except for agriculture (which now has a separate census of agriculture), and with data available alongside population census data via the American FactFinder platform.

Finding and Using Economic Census Data

Data from the Economic Census is available through American FactFinder as well as the Census Bureau website (www.census.gov/econ/census). Currently, the most recent data available is 2012. The survey took place during 2013, and businesses provided data on the previous year, 2012. Data tabulation and publishing of results are occurring from 2014 through 2016. This lag between when the data is collected and when it is made available is one of the biggest weaknesses of the Economic Census as business researchers tend to want the most up-to-date information possible.

The data produced by the Economic Census covers thousands of industry groups from the very broad (such as manufacturing) to the specific (such as the manufacturing of frozen specialty food). Industries are classified using NAICS codes (see sidebar). One can further access this industry information for specific geographies like states, counties, metropolitan areas, and ZIP codes. Note that the confidentiality of individual businesses is treated similarly to that of individual people or households in the decen-

NAICS and SIC Codes

As noted above, the *SIC* (the letters are pronounced "S I C") *Manual* was first used by the Economic Census in 1947. In its most recent form it is divided into 10 broad categories:

Agriculture, Forestry, and Fishing

Mining

Construction

Manufacturing

Transportation, Communications, Electric, Gas, and Sanitary Services

Wholesale Trade

Retail Trade

Finance, Insurance, and Real Estate

Services

Public Administration

These 10 broad categories are then broken down into several dozen smaller categories designated by the first two digits of the SIC code, with further digits delineating the industries in more detail.

For example, the Services category includes two-digit industries, such as 75 Automotive Repair, 80 Health Services, and 83 Social Services. A tiny piece of the Services category looks like this:

73 Business Services

    734 Services to Dwellings and Other Buildings

        7342 Disinfecting and Pest Control Services

Within this breakdown, data is then available for pest control businesses.

NAICS (the North American Industry Classification System, pronounced "nakes") was developed in the 1980s and 1990s and both updated the SIC system and implemented a system more in line with standards. NAICS was first used in the economic census in 1997. It is similar to the SIC system in that it has broad and then more specific categories denoted by numbers. Unlike SIC, NAICS goes down to six digits. For example:

56 Administrative and Support and Waste Management and Remediation Services

    561 Administrative and Support Services

        5617 Services to Buildings and Dwellings

            56171 Exterminating and Pest Control Services

While the NAICS system has now been widely adopted to classify industries both by governments and private market research products, the SIC system is still sometimes used.

nial census: if a smaller level of geography only has one or a few establishments of any particular type, data will likely be suppressed so as to prevent publication of data that might be easy to attribute to a particular business.

Other Business and Economic Surveys

The Census Bureau conducts a number of other related surveys of business and industry. A popular data set is the *County Business Patterns* (CBP)/*ZIP Code Business Patterns* (ZBP)/*Metro Business Patterns* (MBP) series. These series are similar to the economic census in that they count the number of establishments by NAICS code and location. For each entry, there is also data on the size of the establishments (by number of employees and payroll). CBP/ZBP/MBP is published annually; that means it is usually more up-to-date than the Economic Census, but the key item that this series lacks is the all-important measure of output, whether that be sales, shipments, or receipts.

Current Industrial Reports (*CIR*) is another long-standing Census Bureau product. It produces quarterly reports on manufacturing activity by product. For instance, the report on socks details the number of socks manufactured in the United States by year and quarter, and by type of sock, such as by material (e.g., cotton, wool) and audience (e.g., women's socks, infant socks). CIRs cover only the entire nation; no smaller geography is available.

Several other Census Bureau surveys supplement the economic census. The Census Bureau's Business and Industry website (www.census.gov/econ/) leads to surveys and data by topic. And the BEA's Industry Economic Accounts data (www.bea.gov/industry/) features broad measures of output (such as GDP) by industry. The IRS makes broad business tax statistics available through the Statistics of Income program (www.irs.gov/uac/Tax-Stats-2). Occasionally, another agency has specific oversight of an industry and produces useful data about that industry. See the sidebar for some of the most useful.

Other Agencies with Useful Industry Data

Many diverse agencies produce data that is helpful when researching a specific industry. These are a few of the most helpful:

- **Agriculture:** USDA, National Agricultural Statistics Service (NASS) (www.nass.usda.gov)

- **Banking:** FDIC (https://www.fdic.gov/bank/)

- **Energy (including renewable and nonrenewable fuels):** The Energy Information Administration (www.eia.gov)

- **Fisheries:** NOAA (www.noaa.gov)

- **Forest products:** US Forest Service (www.fia.fs.fed.us)

- **Healthcare:** CDC, National Center for Health Statistics (www.cdc.gov/nchs/)

- **Mining:** USGS, National Minerals Information Center (http://minerals.usgs.gov/minerals/)

- **Transportation:** Bureau of Transportation Statistics (www.rita.dot.gov/bts/home)

Company Information

Just like information about citizens, information about companies gathered by federal and state governments is nearly always confidential. One can no sooner access the tax returns of the business down the street than could one see a neighbor's tax forms, census forms, or Medicaid application. There are exceptions, however, which are noteworthy. As Boettcher points out, the notion that there is no company-specific government information is a "long-standing myth" (2005, 19).

There are several laws and regulatory actions that result in select company information being made public. Perhaps the most noteworthy are the company financial reports from publicly traded companies. This information is gathered by the Securities and Exchange Commission (SEC) for the explicit purpose of making basic company financial information public for companies that are traded on a stock market. This effort began through laws passed after the 1929 market crash (see the Securities Act of 1933, P.L. 73-22, 48 Stat. 74, and the Securities Exchange Act of 1934, P.L. 73-291, 48 Stat. 881), and is intended to ensure that all investors have accurate financials about companies they may choose to invest in.

While these SEC company reports have been produced for years, until the Internet era they were not widely available outside of investment circles, and generally required a fee to acquire. Public information advocate Carl Malamud led efforts to put these reports online, for free, available to the public at large (Markoff, 1993). These reports are now published in the SEC's free EDGAR database (www.sec.gov/edgar .shtml). Different reports are published at various stages in the year and based on company actions affecting shareholders, but the most famous EDGAR report is the annual 10-K, which features much of the same data that companies share with shareholders via their own annual reports. Other important forms include the 10-Q (similar to the 10-K but quarterly rather than annual), the 8-K (major developments that don't make it into a 10-K or 10-Q), and the proxy statement (management salaries and any conflicts of interest). EDGAR reports are key government sources for investors and others researching companies.

Another relatively obvious source of government information about individual companies is patents. Covered in detail in chapter 17, both patent applications and actual granted patents are public. From a business standpoint, patents are frequently scoured by competitors and the media for clues to new products and services. For instance, in 2014 Amazon.com, Inc. filed an application for a patent (patent application number 14/495818) about a new fulfillment model that would allow customers to choose items in a physical store and then leave without interacting with a human cashier or an electronic pay station. Patent applications can give valuable intelligence about a company's future strategic direction and industries watch the patent space for new inventions, hoping to find clues as to future product development of competitors. This patent, new services like Amazon Locker (which allows busy people to pick up their order at a designated locker), and their experiments with drones paint a picture of a company that is focused on new ways of connecting customers with products. Note that this patent, like Nike's self-lacing, lighted sneakers (patent application number 2009/ 0272013) is an application only. There is no guarantee it will be approved, and even if it is, Amazon might choose not to make use of the technology.

Businesses that are contracting with, or doing business with, government generally have that relationship made public, and these records can serve as another source of company information. While the process for vendors to bid for, and win, government contracts and sales is complicated and beyond the goals of this chapter, it is notable that the primary portal for advertising opportunities for doing business with the government over $25,000, FedBizOpps.gov, allows one to search for award recipients by many criteria, including agency for which the work is to be done, industry (the nature of the work), and location. Another website, USAspending.gov, was specifically created to provide transparency on recipients of government contracts (it was created by the Federal Funding Accountability and Transparency Act of 2006, P.L. 109-282, 120 Stat. 1186, cosponsored by Senators Barack Obama and John McCain). It allows searching by various criteria. For instance, one can see government contracts awarded by agency, company, location, type of award, or product. Listed are awards to companies such as Halliburton, or Lockheed Martin and its $13.6 billion in federal contracts awarded in FY 2015.

Another public database containing company information is Federal Election Commission (FEC) campaign finance data. Law requires political donations to be public; the FEC provides a Campaign Finance Disclosure Portal to search such information at www.fec.gov/pindex.shtml. For instance, one can search Microsoft and find some $5 million in various political contributions in the last 15 years, including the candidates, parties, and political organizations contributed to. An alternative, privately produced interface to this data that is extremely useful is www.opensecrets.org.

Many other government agencies gather and publish some company information when the company operates in an industry that is subject to special regulation and reporting. A classic example is the MyEnvironment database from EPA, discussed in chapter 14. Companies that produce products and byproducts of various environmental effects— such as those that produce air pollutants, or that may have material run off into water sources—are monitored and required to report to EPA certain data, which is then made public via MyEnvironment. Enter a location here to see a list of companies or facilities in your location that produce emissions that are required to be reported to the government.

Various other government regulation efforts lead to company data. Airlines are regulated by the federal government, and airline data is published by the Bureau of Transportation Statistics (BTS) at www.rita.dot.gov/bts/. Want to see which airlines take in the most in baggage fees? Check the BTS releases. Fuel costs, profits/loss, and many other tables are available for US airlines. This company-specific data is only a fraction of the data available from the BTS. Also available are statistics like causes of flight delays, airline hub volume, tarmac times, chronically delayed flights, and rankings of airports by flight delays (hint: Salt Lake City, Portland, and Seattle are safer bets for non-delayed flights).

Another useful site with some company information is ClinicalTrials.gov (www .clinicaltrials.gov), which lists clinical trials for medical drugs and products. One can see which companies are conducting trials with which drugs, and where, and for what purpose. Several other sources from the government list company information (see Scott, 2009 for additional resources).

Market Research

Market research is generally any information about consumers and competitors that provides intelligence about a particular market, whether that market be widgets, food, or some service such as medicine. We've just seen government information that provides information about industries and sectors, and even sometimes about specific companies. But the most useful market research data gathered by governments is about its citizens, the nation's consumers. The federal government is the single biggest compiler of this market research in the country, and this is primarily for one reason: it conducts the decennial census and its companion the American Community Survey or ACS (both discussed in depth in the next chapter). These comprehensive surveys provide social, demographic, and economic information about the entire population, in such detail that data is available for even very small geographies, such as ZIP codes and smaller census-defined places such as census tracts and blocks.

While the details of the decennial census and the ACS are covered in the next chapter, what is important here is simply that the data gathered by these surveys provides the basic information about the population of the nation that forms the basis of most market research done by private market research firms. From these surveys, one can tell the population, age and sex characteristics, income, occupation, and much more information, about every place in the country. Private market research firms take this census data and repackage it, supplement it with other data, correlate it with privately compiled data, and make it more usable for business planners and marketers. Understanding how to use the census data covered in the next chapter allows anyone to understand the most core market research product in the country.

There are several other government surveys which provide information about the population that also acts as market research. The joint Census Bureau/BLS monthly Current Population Survey (CPS), while it primarily gathers data related to the labor market, also asks enough economic and social questions beyond the decennial census and ACS to make it useful as market research. Data on income and poverty, occupations, and health insurance are among its highlights. The CPS table creator (www.census .gov/cps/data/cpstablecreator.html) allows access to much of this data. Note that unlike decennial census and ACS data, CPS data is not available for smaller geographies such as cities and towns: the sample just isn't big enough.

Market research is primarily focused on learning about how people spend their money, and the decennial census doesn't really provide any clues to this. The BLS conducts a survey called the Consumer Expenditure Survey (CES, www.bls.gov/cex) covering more than 20 categories of spending: housing, such as mortgages, home repairs, and utilities; transportation expenses such as automobiles, gasoline, and mass transit; personal expenditures such as apparel, healthcare, and personal products; and entertainment and recreation expenditures. Like the census, the CES can form the basis of more in-depth, private market research products. Unlike the census, the CES only provides national data. While it is a useful portrait of the nation's spending, it is of lesser use to local business planners. It does break data down by some market segments, including age, race, region, broad occupation, income, and family type (e.g., single, dual earner, married with children).

Market research is a very broad topic, and much data is potentially useful. In addition to those just covered, statistical products such as those discussed earlier from the IRS are useful. Surveys such as the BLS's American Time Use Survey (www.bls.gov/tus), which asks people to measure how much time they spend on activities such as work, housework, entertainment, and education, can be useful to market researchers. Many other statistical programs and products covered elsewhere in this book (such as health data that can inform the market for health products and services, or education data that informs the market for educational products and services), can also be useful as market research, since they all provide intelligence about the nation and its citizens. Those seeking market research data from the government should creatively apply lessons from throughout this book in order to maximize the possibilities.

Labor

There is ample government information related to labor and employment. The government gathers data on occupations and wages, productivity, earnings, and more. This section will briefly summarize key information from the Department of Labor (and its subagency the BLS) beyond the key data on employment, unemployment, and prices covered in the earlier Economic Indicators section.

Some of the most popular government business information is related to occupations. BLS produces an annual survey of occupations called the *Occupational Outlook Handbook (OOH)*. The *OOH* looks at hundreds of occupations and provides several types of information for each one:

- the nature of the work
- the qualifications, schooling, training, and professional certificates necessary for the occupation
- the occupation's salaries and wages
- the outlook for the occupation: Is it in demand? Will more people be needed in these jobs in the future, or is there a glut of trained people already?

The *OOH* is a staple of any library that provides information about careers. A related product is BLS's compensation surveys. Wages by Occupation (www.bls.gov/bls/blswage .htm) provides median and average salaries and wages for over 800 occupations, and includes breakdowns for states and metropolitan areas. BLS compiles numerous other data related to occupations, employment, and prices. Its parent agency, the Department of Labor (DOL), serves labor broadly. DOL features much information helpful to workers, including data from the Occupational Safety and Health Administration (OSHA, discussed in the following section on law and regulations), information and support of employment for people with disabilities, information about job discrimination, rules about union activities, employer health insurance, workers compensation, and more.

Support for Business

Governments at all levels in the United States offer support for businesses. The federal government and each state government all have offices that give advice and information on starting and operating a business, including the legal basics such as how to register a business; practical tips on how to manage, grow, research, and document business activities; and how to access market research and other business intelligence sources available from the government.

The US Small Business Administration (SBA), and especially its website, www.sba .gov, is the starting point for business planning and is useful to any business or prospective business. The SBA is an independent agency that exists solely to help, nurture, and guide small businesses, and is meant to connect small businesses to intelligence, advice, and financial help. The "Starting and Managing a Business" section of the website features information and instructions on how to legally start and register a business, with information by state and even ZIP code; how to write a business plan; determining type of business (sole proprietorship, partnership, or some form of corporation); finding local zoning and real estate information; finding financing; and getting expert help. It is a must-use portal for anyone starting a business, as it pulls together information from across all appropriate parts of government—everything from the IRS to the EPA.

Other sections on the website include information about contracting opportunities, finding loans and grants, and tools to connect potential lenders and investors to start-ups in need of financial backing. Also notable from SBA are some of its expert help services. SCORE (Service Corps of Retired Executives) is an SBA program that has provided expert advisory services to small business owners for decades. There are hundreds of SCORE offices around the nation, covering most cities. SBA also administers Small Business Development Centers and Women's Business Centers, which also offer counseling to prospective small business owners and have physical offices throughout the nation.

The US Department of Commerce is another agency that provides key support for businesses, especially to US businesses looking to export or operate abroad. This will be covered below under Exporting and Doing Business Abroad.

Laws and Regulations

One intersection of business and government is in the regulation of business to ensure fair markets and to balance the needs of business with the needs of citizens and consumers. As noted earlier, none other than Adam Smith, the father of free market capitalism, discussed some of the instances where government needed to be involved in order to ensure a functioning free market (Smith, 1819). Debate about government's role in regulating business remains lively.

Government regulation of business is rooted in laws passed by Congress and the regulations promulgated by executive agencies in order to implement and enforce these laws. Chapters 3 and 6 discuss the process of making laws and making regulations, respectively, while chapter 5 discusses finding laws already on the books. Sources covered in those chapters can be used to find instances of regulation of business.

Many federal and local agencies provide support for new businesses as they research the laws and regulations that apply to them. Suppose you are interested in starting a small organic produce business. The Small Business Administration website (www.sba.gov) includes a section on business laws and regulations that summarizes the legal steps necessary to start and register a business, as well as the basics for complying with tax and finance, labor, and environmental laws. State business information portals will give information about local laws and regulations. While these steps are necessary and apply to starting any business, there are also laws and regulations pertaining to specific industries. In this example, for instance, using the skills and tools for finding laws and regulations discussed earlier in the book—and also the skills about finding executive branch information in chapters 2 and 9—one can find information about laws and regulations related to organic farming from the Department of Agriculture. For instance, see the National Organic Program (www.ams.usda.gov/AMSv1.0/nop, and related information at www.ers.usda.gov/topics/natural-resources-environment/organic-agriculture .aspx) as well as information from the EPA (www.epa.gov/agriculture/torg.html), specifically the Organic Foods Production Act of 1990 (P.L. 101-624, 104 Stat. 3359; current law after subsequent amendments at 7 U.S.C. § 6501) and the regulations at 7 CFR 205. There are countless other laws and regulations related to specific products, businesses, and business practices. While starting at the SBA.gov page noted above is helpful, it can still be daunting to figure out all applicable laws related to one's business without additional legal advice and support.

There are several other government sites that do help, however. EPA's Laws and Regulations section (www.epa.gov/lawsregs/) provides detailed information about environmental regulations, and makes finding environmental regulations a bit easier than using the *CFR*. The Department of Labor has a similar Compliance portal (www.dol .gov/compliance/) that leads users to laws and regulations regarding employees and the workplace, including those from the Occupational Safety and Health Administration.

Another agency involved in regulating commerce is the Federal Trade Commission (FTC). Much of the FTC's activity is related to antitrust, as it works to "ban unfair business practices and prevent mergers that harm consumers," which are prohibited by law. While one might associate FTC with only antitrust issues, and its work related to companies such as IBM, Microsoft, Google, airlines, and cable companies, FTC provides a variety of research and information materials aimed at business owners and consumers, everything from economic research reports on health care economics to "How to Avoid Bamboozling Your Customers," which addresses the use of bamboo in products. Both business owners and consumers can profit by concise, clear explanations in numerous publications, such as information about buying a home, getting a credit card, dealing with identity theft and business fraud, and complying with telemarketing rules such as the Do Not Call list.

Another aspect of business and the law is bankruptcy. Many people and businesses seek bankruptcy protection when they can no longer pay their debts and they seek some relief or a structured response. All bankruptcy cases are handled by special federal bankruptcy courts. There is information on the laws and processes for bankruptcy at www.uscourts.gov/FederalCourts/Bankruptcy.aspx.

Support for Consumers

Another key role of government involvement in business is to support citizens' and consumers' rights. Largely, this role is fulfilled via the law and rulemaking process already discussed. For instance, the Dodd–Frank Wall Street Reform and Consumer Protection Act (P.L. 111-203, 124 Stat. 1376, 2010) was a major overhaul of the financial industry in response to the 2007 financial crisis. In addition to many regulatory changes, it also created the Consumer Financial Protection Bureau, which is charged with protecting consumers by educating them, enforcing regulations, and analyzing the consumer financial services market. Laws and regulations are the key sources for information about consumer and citizen protections, whether they be financial, environmental, aimed at workers, and so on.

Executive agencies often have plain language summaries and compilations of laws and regulations; the EPA and OSHA are two good examples. Similarly for consumer information, there are several agencies that provide information relating to protection of consumers and summaries of applicable laws. The Federal Trade Commission, discussed earlier as a source to aid business owners, is also very useful to citizens. The FTC website provides many concise consumer education documents on topics such as credit, identity theft, health and the environment, buying a car or a house, getting an education or a job, and shopping online and avoiding online scams.

Another agency supporting consumers is the Consumer Product Safety Commission (CPSC). While FTC protects consumers broadly, CPSC is more narrowly focused on preventing injury caused by consumer products. The CPSC website lists recalls and safety warnings, but also provides publications to aid consumer safety, such as those on creating a safe baby nursery; keeping pools and playgrounds safe; preventing fire, electrical, and carbon monoxide hazards; and dangerous toys.

The Food and Drug Administration (FDA) also plays a vital role in protecting consumers through their regulation of industries such as food, drugs, medical devices, and cosmetics. Consumer information on the FDA website includes product recall announcements, medical procedure safety warnings, and advice on how to prevent food-borne illness.

Exports and International and Foreign Business Information

The global economy is a large and complicated entity. While the US federal government is unparalleled in its support for, and breadth of information about, its own business climate, there are nonetheless some key government and international organization resources that provide key global information. This section provides a brief, selective guide to major sources.

International Sources

UNdata, *World Development Indicators,* and the comparative international statistics section of the *Statistical Abstract of the United States*, all provide international economic and business data. UNdata (http://data.un.org) links to a number of useful databases compiled by various international organizations that work with countries to standardize and share data on economic topics.

Databases available via UNdata include:

- Energy Statistics Database—country by country data on production, imports, and exports of energy resources.
- FAO Data—from the Food and Agriculture Organization, country-by- country data on production and yield of crops, livestock, fertilizers, and land related to agriculture.
- INDSTAT—from the United Nations Industrial Development Organization, a rich database of data resembling that of the US Economic Census: country-by-country estimates of the number of establishments, employees, payroll, and output by industry.
- International Financial Statistics—from the International Monetary Fund, the premier compilation of country-by-country financials, not unlike the data for the United States available from the US Treasury Department.
- National Accounts databases—output and consumption for the world's nations, similar to data from the US BEA.
- LABORSTA—from the International Labor Organization, with prices and employment by economic activity, country-by-country, similar to the US BLS.

There are several other large, key databases of international economic activity, available from http://data.un.org/Explorer.aspx.

Trade

There are several sources for foreign trade statistics. For the United States, data on both exports and imports is gathered at ports of entry by Customs and Border Protection, a subagency of the Department of Homeland Security (until 2003, known as the US Customs Service, and an agency of the Department of Commerce). The Census Bureau compiles and publishes United States trade data. The most robust data is available via USA Trade Online (https://usatrade.census.gov/); this database is not free to the public at large and is available on a cost-recovery basis. USA Trade Online features data on the type of goods, the destination country (or origin for imports), the amount of goods, and the port. Federal Depository Libraries have limited free access to USA Trade Online, so users may be able to visit their local depository library to access the database at no charge.

Trade data is also available from the International Trade Administration (ITA), also in the Department of Commerce, although it's not as robust as USA Trade Online. ITA's primary trade statistics product is TradeStats Express (http://tse.export.gov/TSE/TSEHome.aspx), which provides total volume of US imports and exports by foreign nation. TradeStats Express also shows imports and exports by product, both for the nation as a whole, and for states. US foreign trade data is also available via databases at the Census Bureau (www.census.gov/foreign-trade/statistics/index.html) and the International Trade Commission (http://dataweb.usitc.gov). Note that trade data uses its own systems for product classification, different than the industry classifications in NAICS or the SIC Manual. For imports, it is the *Harmonized Tariff Schedule* of the United States. For exports, it is *Schedule B: Statistical Classification of Domestic and Foreign Commodities Exported from the United States.*

For trade between two countries where the United States is not one of the parties, such as between England and Argentina, there are several sources. The UN Comtrade database (http://comtrade.un.org) compiles trade data from several UN sources. It has monthly and annual data, and allows users to search by reporter, partner, and commodity. *Direction of Trade Statistics,* from the International Monetary Fund, is another time-honored source and is available in print and as an online subscription database. It covers data on the value of trade between any two countries, but not data about the product or commodities involved. The World Trade Organization, meanwhile, compiles and publishes data (www.wto.org/english/res_e/statis_e/statis_e.htm) about exports and imports of a country by commodity and product, but does not have this data specifically between any two countries.

Exporting and Doing Business Abroad

The ITA's Export.gov compiles information to help US businesses export and succeed in foreign markets. Export.gov is one of the more important government resources for business, and the highlight is the material in the Market Research Library (www .export.gov/mrktresearch/), from the US Commercial Service. The Market Research Library provides access to several key series:

- Country Commercial Guides (CCG). Prepared by US embassies, these annual guides for most of the world's countries are invaluable in their descriptions of the commercial climate of the country, as well as political and economic factors that affect American businesses' operations. CCGs describe characteristics of the labor force (will the American firm be able to find and hire qualified employees?), infrastructure (not just roads, but communications, such as the Internet), the law and justice system (is theft rampant, or piracy of intellectual property?), government regulation (is there corruption?), and banking and finance (is it safe to use a local bank?). There are usually extensive descriptions of good products and markets to enter, as well as details on exporting, whether about tariffs, shipping concerns, or legal considerations. CCGs also discuss strategies for entering the market, including franchising, finding a local distributor for your product, and how to make sales in the local climate. Finally, CCGs describe business customs and etiquette, such as prevalence of long lunches or appropriateness of electronic communication. CCGs also include extensive lists of local contacts (see figure 15.2).
- Market Research Reports. Market research reports, which are in-depth reports containing intelligence about a particular product or business type (and often in a specific location), are usually very expensive. But the US government, in order to support US business abroad, does produce or acquire a number of market research reports about foreign markets. While not comprehensive for any sector or country, one lucky enough to find an on-target market research report here has much of their research already done. Examples of titles are *Nicaragua Hotel and Restaurant Equipment, Mexico Agribusiness, Peru Electronic Commerce,* and *Russia: Biologically Active Supplements.*

Doing Business in Egypt: 2014 Country

Commercial Guide for U.S. Companies

INTERNATIONAL COPYRIGHT, U.S. & FOREIGN COMMERCIAL SERVICE AND U.S. DEPARTMENT OF STATE, 2010. ALL RIGHTS RESERVED OUTSIDE OF THE UNITED STATES.

- Chapter 1: Doing Business In Egypt
- Chapter 2: Political and Economic Environment
- Chapter 3: Selling U.S. Products and Services
- Chapter 4: Leading Sectors for U.S. Export and Investment
- Chapter 5: Trade Regulations, Customs and Standards
- Chapter 6: Investment Climate
- Chapter 7: Trade and Project Financing
- Chapter 8: Business Travel
- Chapter 9: Contacts, Market Research and Trade Events
- Chapter 10: Guide to Our Services

FIGURE 15.2
Egypt Country Commercial Guide Table of Contents

The US Commercial Service also provides extensive information on the mechanics of exporting abroad, online and in-person trainings, and a network of offices throughout the US and abroad. They can also provide personalized consulting and (for a fee) even connect businesses to potential partners abroad.

Another great source for researching the business environment in a country is Doing Business from the World Bank (www.doingbusiness.org). Doing Business ranks countries and selected cities or regions within those countries on factors like dealing with construction permits, getting electricity, and enforcing contracts. Their reports outline the steps a typical business would have to go through to accomplish each task.

State and Local Business and Economic Information

Most state and local business information is derived from the many federal government surveys and programs covered in this chapter. This local information includes decennial census data, economic census and the *County/ZIP Code/Metro Business Patterns,* unemployment and prices from the BLS, and more.

States generally have a state agency or office that produces some business and economic information. For instance, the Florida Legislature's Office of Demographic and Economic Research (http://edr.state.fl.us) prepares economic information for the state, and many other states have similar research offices associated with their legislative branches. You may also find data being produced by universities, local business associations, or local government. In Arkansas, the biggest producer of state data is the Institute of Economic Advancement out of the University of Arkansas Little Rock (www.aiea .ualr.edu). Downtownseattle.com, a collaboration of several local business groups, provides unique information for downtown Seattle, including demographics, pedestrian count data, and reports on leading sectors. Familiarize yourself with your appropriate state agencies or related institutions and their outputs.

Probably most important is the state and local information to help businesses. Much of this information is linked from the SBA website, and includes state data on registering a business, securing proper licenses, and complying with state and local regulations. Every state also has some information designed to support new and existing businesses. New York's business portal (www.ny.gov/services/business), for instance, features the New York Business Wizard (https://bw.licensecenter.ny.gov/BW/guestHomeAction .els) which allows one to enter a type of business and see regulatory and licensing requirements. Use the SBA website and an exploration of state websites to find these portals for your own state.

Local information is likewise sometimes available from federal and state sources. Beyond those, check your local city and county government sources; also check for research about your local economy wherever it might be published.

Conclusion

With a nation founded on a capitalist market economic system, business is very important to the American people and their government. Numerous government agencies produce information about the economy and business situation, aid business growth and success, and support the nation's consumers. An earlier chapter encouraged you to think like a government documents librarian. To find and use business information from governments, continue to use these civics skills—and also think like a businessperson.

Exercises

1. What is the current discount rate? What is the logic from the Fed regarding the latest discount rate, and where did you find it in government resources?
2. What is the SIC Code and the NAICS code for law offices? What is the total value of services from law offices in the United States for 2012? How many law office establishments were there in Chicago in 2013?
3. What federal or state agency handles child care center licensing in Missouri?
4. According to official SEC filings, what is Amazon's net income for the last two quarters of 2014?
5. What are the top five destinations for exports from the state of Tennessee in 2012?

Sources Mentioned in This Chapter

Sources mentioned in this section do not duplicate the references that follow.

Legislation (Chronological Order)

Securities Act of 1933, P.L. 73-22, 48 Stat. 74 (1933).

Securities Exchange Act of 1934, P.L. 73-291, 48 Stat. 881 (1934).

Organic Foods Production Act of 1990, P.L. 101-624, 104 Stat. 3359 (1990).

Federal Funding Accountability and Transparency Act of 2006, P.L. 109-282, 120 Stat. 1186 (2006).

Dodd-Frank Wall Street Reform and Consumer Protection Act, P.L. 111-203, 124 Stat. 1376, (2010).

Other Sources

ALFRED (ArchivaL Federal Reserve Economic Data), http://alfred.stlouisfed.org.

American Community Survey, www.census.gov/acs/www/.

American FactFinder, http://factfinder.census.gov.

American Time Use Survey, www.bls.gov/tus/.

Bankruptcy (United States Courts), www.uscourts.gov/FederalCourts/Bankruptcy.aspx.

Bankruptcy Statistics (United States Courts), www.uscourts.gov/statistics-reports/caseload-statistics
    -data-tables.

Bureau of Economic Analysis Industry Economic Accounts, www.bea.gov/industry/.

Bureau of Transportation Statistics, Data and Statistics, www.bts.gov/data_and_statistics/.

Census Bureau Business and Industry, www.census.gov/econ/.

Census Bureau Foreign Trade, www.census.gov/foreign-trade/.

ClinicalTrials.gov, www.clinicaltrials.gov.

Consumer Expenditure Survey, www.bls.gov/cex/.

Consumer Financial Protection Bureau, www.consumerfinance.gov.

Consumer Price Index, www.bls.gov/cpi/.

Consumer Product Safety Commission, www.cpsc.gov.

County Business Patterns, www.census.gov/econ/cbp/index.html.

Current Industrial Reports, www.census.gov/manufacturing/cir/index.html.

Current Population Survey Table Creator, www.census.gov/cps/data/cpstablecreator.html.

Decennial Census, www.census.gov/2010census/.

Department of Labor compliance portal, www.dol.gov/compliance.

Direction of Trade Statistics, www.imf.org/external/publications/index.htmEconomic Census, www
    .census.gov/econ/census/.

Economic Indicators, www.gpo.gov/fdsys/browse/collection.action?collectionCode=ECONI.

Economic Report of the President, www.gpo.gov/fdsys/browse/collection.action?collectionCode=ERP.

Economy at a Glance, www.bls.gov/eag/eag.us.htm.

EDGAR, www.sec.gov/edgar.shtml.

Energy Statistics Database, http://unstats.un.org/unsd/energy/edbase.htm; http://data.un.org/
    Explorer.aspx.

EPA's Laws and Regulations, www.epa.gov/lawsregs/.

Export.gov, www.export.gov.

FAO Data, http://faostat.fao.org/; http://data.un.org/Explorer.aspx.

FDIC banking data, www.fdic.gov/bank/statistical/index.html.

FDIC State Profiles, www.fdic.gov/bank/analytical/stateprofile/.

FEC Campaign Finance Disclosure Portal, www.fec.gov/pindex.shtml.

FedBizOpps.gov, www.fedbizopps.gov.

Federal Reserve System statistical data, www.federalreserve.gov/econresdata/releases/statisticsdata.htm.

FRASER (Federal Reserve Archival System for Economic Research) system, http://fraser.stlouisfed .org/publications/ei/.

FRED (Federal Reserve Economic Data), http://research.stlouisfed.org/fred2/.

Federal Trade Commission, www.ftc.gov.

Harmonized Tariff Schedule of the United States, http://hts.usitc.gov.

INDSTAT, http://data.un.org/Explorer.aspx.

International Financial Statistics, www.imfstatistics.org/imf/; http://data.un.org/Explorer.aspx.

International Trade Commission, http://dataweb.usitc.gov.

LABORSTA, http://laborsta.ilo.org/; http://data.un.org/Explorer.aspx.

Metro Business Patterns, www.census.gov/econ/cbp/index.html.

MyEnvironment, www.epa.gov/myenvironment/.

NAICS (the North American Industry Classification System), www.census.gov/eos/www/naics/.

Occupational Outlook Handbook, www.bls.gov/oco/.

OpenSecrets.org, www.opensecrets.org.

Producer Price Index, www.bls.gov/ppi/.

Schedule B: Statistical Classification of Domestic and Foreign Commodities Exported from the United States, www.census.gov/foreign-trade/schedules/b/.

SCORE (Service Corps of Retired Executives), www.score.org.

Small Business Administration, www.sba.gov.

Small Business Administration, Business Law & Regulations, www.sba.gov/category/ navigation-structure/starting-managing-business/starting-business/business-law-regulations.

Standard Industrial Classification (SIC) Manual, www.osha.gov/pls/imis/sicsearch.html.

Statistical Abstract of the United States, www.census.gov/compendia/statab/.

Statistics of Income; IRS statistics, www.irs.gov/taxstats/index.html.

TradeStats Express, http://tse.export.gov.

TreasuryDirect, www.treasurydirect.gov.

UN Comtrade, http://comtrade.un.org.

UNdata, http://data.un.org.

US Patent and Trademark Office, www.uspto.gov.

USAspending.gov, www.usaspending.gov.

USA Trade Online, https://usatrade.census.gov.

Wages by Occupation, www.bls.gov/bls/blswage.htm.

World Development Indicators, http://data.worldbank.org/data-catalog/world-development-indicators/.

World Trade Organization data, www.wto.org/english/res_e/statis_e/statis_e.htm.

ZIP Code Business Patterns, www.census.gov/econ/cbp/index.html.

References

Boettcher, Jennifer C. 2005. "Company Research Using U.S. Federal Government Sources." *Online* 29, no. 2: 19–24.

Coolidge, Calvin. 1925. "Address to the American Society of Newspaper Editors" (speech), January 17. www.presidency.ucsb.edu/ws/index.php?pid=24180.

Markoff, John. 1993. "Plan Opens More Data to Public." *New York Times,* October 22. www.nytimes
.com/1993/10/22/business/plan-opens-more-data-to-public.html.

Micarelli, William F. 1998. "Evolution of the United States Economic Censuses: The Nineteenth and
Twentieth Centuries." *Government Information Quarterly* 15, no. 3: 335–377.

Scott, Kerry, and Lucia Orlando. 2009. "Government Resources: Worth a Hard Look in Hard Times."
BRASS Business Reference in Academic Libraries Committee 4, no. 2. www.ala.org/ala/mgrps/divs/rusa/
sections/brass/brasspubs/academicbrass/acadarchives/v014n02/v014n02.cfm.

Smith, Adam. 1819. *An Inquiry into the Nature and Causes of the Wealth of Nations.* Edinburgh: Stirling and
Slade. http://catalog.hathitrust.org/api/volumes/oclc/2340521.html.

CHAPTER 16

Census

ERIC FORTE, KELLY SMITH, AND ANNELISE SKLAR

Introduction

The decennial census and the United States Census Bureau were introduced in chapter 10, but these resources are of such importance that they merit their own chapter. In many libraries, statistics are the most heavily requested genre of government information, and the decennial census, also known as the Census of Population and Housing, is far and away the largest single statistical undertaking in the nation.

To comprehend the massive scale of the decennial census, think for a moment about the *second* largest statistical effort in the United States, the related American Community Survey (ACS)—which will also be covered in this chapter. The ACS surveys a whopping 250,000 households each month, and so reaches some three million households annually. This is much larger than any other government statistical survey, or any other regular statistical survey, for that matter. Yet the decennial census—by counting each and every person in the entire United States every decade—is more than *100 times* bigger than the ACS, having counted some 310 million people in the year 2010.

The decennial census's core constitutional function is to determine the apportionment of representatives in the House of Representatives. But the census (especially now in combination with the American Community Survey) also provides the basic demographic and social statistics about our nation. It is the only nationwide statistical effort of sufficient scale to result in usable statistical data about even small cities and towns. In fact, this ability to access uniform, comparative data for these small geographies cannot be stressed enough. The size of the census, the data for small geographies, and the fact that it has been taken consistently for more than 200 years all make the census a singular and vital source of statistics.

Scientists, economists, and public policy makers use decennial census data heavily in research about the nation's populace. But perhaps the most important purpose beyond apportionment, and the one stressed in marketing campaigns designed to maximize voluntary census compliance, is census data's role in determining shares of billions of dollars in federal funds to states, cities, and communities. In fact, the Government Accountability Office (GAO) found that funding for all ten of the largest federal assistance programs—Medicaid, Highway Planning & Construction, State Fiscal Stabilization Fund-Education State Grants, Title I Grants to Local Education Agencies, Individuals with Disabilities Education Act Part B, Temporary Aid for Needy Families, Section 8 Housing Choice Vouchers, Community Development Block Grant, Federal Transit Formula Grants Programs, and the Children's Health Insurance Program—is determined largely based on census data (Orlando and Hyde, 2010). For instance, when Medicaid funds are distributed to states by the federal government, they are distributed based on population figures and characteristics taken from the census. Census figures also helped determine shares of redevelopment money after Hurricane Katrina, and the same goes for dozens of other government programs. Communities that most completely answer the census stand to win the most federal monies. In other words: when it comes to filling out the census, compliance literally pays.

The Census in the Constitution

While the Latin word *censere* more closely means estimate rather than count, the idea of a census has generally been associated with counting and especially counting people. Babylonians, Egyptians, Chinese, and indigenous Peruvians all appeared to conduct some type of census in ancient times (Halacy, 1980). In the Roman Empire, a census was often associated with either determining the numbers of men to potentially conscript for the purposes of war, or to count people for the purposes of taxing them. Neither reason is likely to have made a census a popular undertaking among citizens. Further, "the penalty for refusing to reveal how many people were in your household, how many slaves, how much livestock, was forfeiting it all and becoming a slave yourself" (Gibbs, 2010:56). A census also appears several times in the Bible; King David is "said to have been punished for ordering a census—though the punishment was inflicted on the very people being counted (2 Samuel 24:15)," because Satan had tempted him into the action (Browning, 2009); and one gospel says that Joseph and Mary went to Bethlehem to comply with the taxing purposes of a census (Luke 2:1–6). While citizen concerns about participating in a census remain and will be discussed later, such concerns are now more likely to be for reasons related to privacy and accuracy rather than fear of conscription, taxes, or a vengeful god.

The United States' decennial census has a completely different mission than these ancient efforts, and its fascinating history goes far in explaining how we arrived at our modern decennial census. As introduced in chapter 10, the decennial census is the original statistical program of the nation, drawing its statutory authority ultimately from Article I, Section 2 of the Constitution:

> Representatives and direct taxes shall be apportioned among the several
> states which may be included within this union, according to their respective

numbers, which shall be determined by adding to the whole number of free persons, including those bound to service for a term of years, and excluding Indians not taxed, three fifths of all other Persons. The actual Enumeration shall be made within three years after the first meeting of the Congress of the United States, and within every subsequent term of ten years, in such manner as they shall by law direct. (US Constitution, art. I, sec. 2)

Debate in drafting this particular clause included various suggestions related to whether race or wealth should be a factor in whether or not a citizen was even counted (Halacy, 1980). The framers eventually decided that slaves were to be counted as only three-fifths of a person, which was not only shameful policy but also cost certain states representation. This practice lasted through the 1860 census. In 1868, the 14th Amendment explicitly eliminated the notion of applying different weights when counting different groups of people, stating that "Representatives shall be apportioned among the several States according to their respective numbers, counting *the whole number* of persons in each State" (emphasis added).

The three-fifths clause was not the only portion of the founders' census article that was soon discarded. "Indians not taxed" referred to American Indians living free, a category that was largely gone by the end of the 19th century and officially retired in the 1940s. Indentured servants "bound to service for a term of years" similarly ceased to exist. The "direct taxes" line, meanwhile, was originally inserted to reduce temptation for a state to inflate its population in order to gain an unequal share of representation (for the greater the population, the greater the potential tax paid by the state). In practice, however, taxes were very rarely billed on the basis of census counts: only occasionally during early periods of wartime, although in the 1830s the federal government did distribute an *excess* of federal funds to states on the basis of census counts. The 16th Amendment, in 1909, removed the concept of direct taxes entirely from the census, thus meaning that four facets of the founders' original census clause eventually disappeared from the law.

Census Privacy

All census data is confidential for 72 years, although it was not until 1840 that census takers were specifically instructed to treat all information with confidentiality (Halacy, 1980). By 1880, confidential returns became law (13 U.S.C. § 9). Census data may only be used for statistical purposes; no taxation, conscription, or other punitive measures are to result from filling out a census form. An individual or household's census answers are even protected from subpoenas or search warrants, so they cannot be used as evidence in any legal proceeding. This privacy requirement applies to workers in the field, those working with data at the Census Bureau, and the published public data; what an individual provides on a census form will be nothing more than anonymous numbers for most, if not all, of his or her lifetime. On a related note, citizens who do not answer the census can be fined, although in practice this has almost never happened.

Conducting the Census

The first census, taken in August of 1790, was conducted under the nominal direction of the Secretary of State by US marshals, who traveled the nation on horseback and simply went looking for people. With citizens not always expecting or wanting to be found, the enterprise carried some danger. While these marshals received instructions in how to conduct the count, there were no official forms, and marshals were responsible for procuring paper and organizing it in such a way as to facilitate a count. It was a labor-intensive process (see figure 16.1).

Taking the census of an ever-expanding population remained a massive undertaking, especially as it continued to be taken by hand, in person. Although population growth made the census increasingly difficult to conduct with each passing decade, improved methods somewhat mitigated the increase in volume. In 1840, the government finally instituted an official form for the marshals to use. The census of 1870 saw the introduction of the first rudimentary counting machines. In 1871, the census contracted with

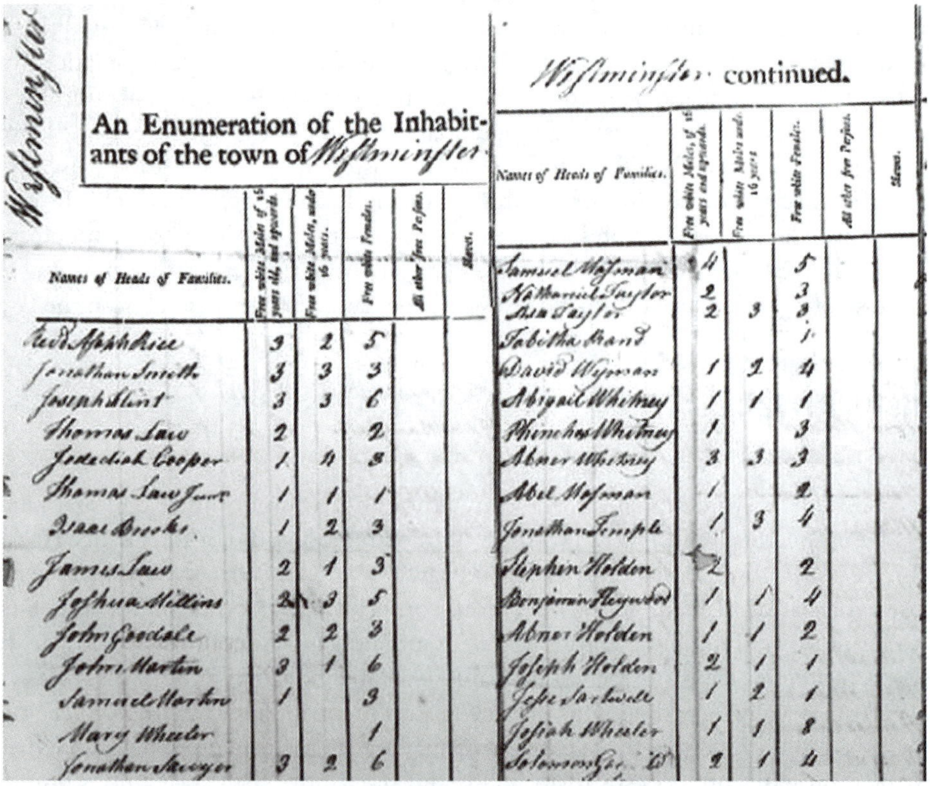

FIGURE 16.1
Excerpt from 1790 Census Schedules Showing Name of Head of Household and Tick Marks for Each Resident of the Home

a young scientist to devise a better tabulation machine in time for the 1880 census. The scientist, Herman Hollerith, famously succeeded in building a machine that could rapidly read encoded punch cards (figure 16.2), which later became the basis for the company IBM. The 1880 census also saw workers specifically dedicated and trained to conduct the census, creating the first large, once-a-decade class of temporary census workers. Counting was further eased in 1950 by the first use of an electronic computer to aid in tabulation. The 1960 census, meanwhile, saw the census recorded by the use of blackened dots which were microfilmed, and then read and tabulated by cameras and computers. Modern-day census data is tabulated in the manner discussed in chapter 10, with very large microdata files from which are made various specific reports and tables. Parts of contemporary decennial census microdata are available to the public, allowing researchers to create their own tables and reports out of the original data. See the section on Decennial Census Microdata later in this chapter for more information.

Amazingly, all of the censuses prior to 1970 were conducted in person—a huge undertaking with an increasingly large population. The 1910 census saw the first effort at a mail-in census; response was abysmal, and the effort was abandoned. The 1960 census again saw forms mailed to households. Households could not mail them back, but at least the forms would be filled out and ready to share when the census worker came knocking, saving time and expense. In 1970, the government finally stopped sending workers to every household and allowed citizens to mail back census forms; only nonrespondents now receive a personal visit from Census workers, who, like their US marshal forebearers, risk their personal safety—from being shot at (Osborn, 2013) to being killed by dogs ("Dogs Kill Census Worker," 2000)—to provide the most accurate population count.

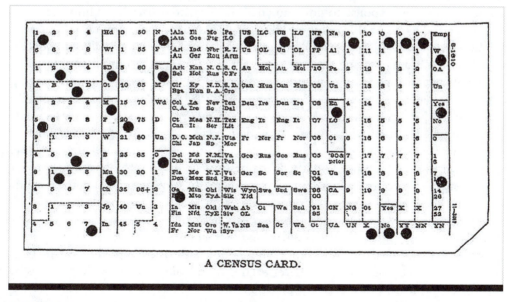

A CENSUS CARD.

FIGURE 16.2
Punchcard from 1910 Census Used to Encode Each Household's Answers, Which Were Then Tabulated by Machine

It's natural to wonder about the viability of taking an online census. Like online voting, fears about the integrity and security of such an effort kept an online census from occurring. In 2010, the most recent decennial census, forms were once again sent and returned via US mail, with nonrespondents receiving a personal visit or phone call. In 2013, however, recipients of the American Community Survey were finally given the option of responding online. Census 2020 is expected to be conducted primarily online, largely to secure cost savings and increase response rates (www.census.gov/2020census).

Census Content

The content of the questions is the single most important aspect of the census. If a question was asked as part of a decennial census, a wealth of data exists on that topic for the entire nation. The questions form the basis of available data and publications.

Almost from the beginning, the census evolved from the simple headcount called for by the Constitution to something with a more expansive purpose. As early as 1790, James Madison proposed using the opportunity of the census effort to gather additional information about the population. Despite some opposition—these early efforts were denounced by some as "a waste of trouble and supplying materials for idle people to make a book" (Cassedy, 1969: 216)—Congress soon acted on the potential to learn more about the nation via the census effort. Questions related to age, sex, ancestry, schooling, and wages presented a broader demographic portrait of the nation, while questions about the economic structure helped Congress understand the fast-evolving state of the nation's industry and agriculture. Over the ensuing years, these extra questions have come and gone in response to governmental or social concerns. In addition to many economic and demographic questions, the census has made some unique and interesting inquiries. For many years, people were asked about their place of religious worship, which aroused suspicion and some controversy in a nation built on religious freedom and individual privacy. (Law now forbids any government survey of religious worship, practice, or beliefs.) Citizens were asked how many and what type of bathroom facilities they had (i.e., indoor vs. outdoor), and how many insane or "idiotic" people, habitual drunkards, and tramps lived in the household (Halacy, 1980). Regardless of whether the questions make sense today, what had begun as a simple headcount had grown over two centuries into a census of hundreds of questions about health, education, housing, and ancestry, with even more separate questionnaires for American Indians, the recently deceased (filled out by surviving family members), and soldiers, among others.

The invaluable census publication *Measuring America: The Decennial Census from 1790 to 2000* includes a history of the census along with copies of every question asked and every form used in each census. Especially useful is a grid (excerpted in figure 16.3) that summarizes the subjects asked over each census, making it easy to see, census by census, if a particular piece of data was gathered.

While the specific questions asked shifted over the years, extra questions remained a staple of the census in one manner or another up through the 2000 census. The 2010 census, for reasons discussed shortly, saw these extra questions largely jettisoned with a return to what was the shortest and simplest census since the very first one in 1790.

Statistical Sampling

Asking the extra questions, as important as they were, eventually did begin taking a toll, as the more expansive census became both harder for citizens to answer and more expensive for the nation to conduct. Picture a census worker sitting in a household and asking over 100 questions. And then going next door. And so on, across the entire nation.

The mid-20th century saw two changes to address these issues. First, much of the extra data that the census had been gathering began to be covered by other surveys. For instance, a great deal of health and education data is now gathered by much smaller surveys such as the Current Population Survey (see chapter 10). Economic questions, which comprised many of the extra questions, were spun off into a separate economic census (covered in chapter 15). Finally, the extra questions that remained—and there were still dozens not related to the basic headcount used for apportionment—began to be asked of only a sample of the population, taken concurrently and as part of the census enumeration. In this scenario, 100 percent of households were still counted and asked basic questions such as age and sex; however, a smaller sample of the population would answer a census that included the extra questions. Since this extra data was not used for the constitutional apportionment, a statistical sample was and remains sufficient to gather this data, as modern statistical techniques ensure an accurate count of these questions.

Beginning in 1940 and continuing through Census 2000, approximately one in five to one in six of all households received the longer sample form, which included the basic questions and also the extra questions. This became known as the census long form. Everyone else received the census short form. The data from those who filled out the short form (plus the short form elements of those who filled out the long form) is referred to as 100 percent data, to make clear that this data is from all respondents to the census, unadjusted by sampling. The actual percentage of people receiving the long form varied by geography. Part of what makes the census so invaluable is its ability to provide data for even small geographies such as small towns. In a big city, one in six is still a massive sample and very statistically accurate. In a small city, though, asking only one in six does not yield enough data to get a true representation of the community. A larger portion of the population in smaller places and rural areas were given the long form in order to make the results statistically significant; as many as one in every two households in the smaller geographies were given the longer survey.

The content of these extra questions is always subject to debate and sometimes controversy. The Census Bureau receives thousands of suggestions for questions to include on the census, most of them related to a specific interest of a researcher or organization. For instance, if one is selling shoes, what better way to collect data about shoe usage or preferences than through the census? It's paid for by taxes and gathers data for even

Demographic characteristics	1790	1800	1810	1820	1830	1840	1850	1860	1870	1880	1890
Age	–	[1]X	[1]X	X	X	X	X	X	X	X	X
Sex	[1]X	[1]X	[1]X	X	X	X	X	X	X	X	X
Color or Race	X	X	X	X	X	X	X	X	X	X	X
Ancestry/Ethnic Origin	–	–	–	–	–	–	–	–	–	–	–
If American Indian, proportions of Indian or other blood	–	–	–	–	–	–	–	–	–	–	–
If American Indian, name of Tribe	–	–	–	–	–	–	–	–	–	–	–
Relationship to head of family or household	–	–	–	–	–	–	–	–	–	X	X
Married in the past year	–	–	–	–	–	–	[2]X	[2]X	X	X	X
Marital status	–	–	–	–	–	–	–	–	–	X	X
Number of years married	–	–	–	–	–	–	–	–	–	–	–
Age at or date of first marriage	–	–	–	–	–	–	–	–	–	–	–
Married more than once	–	–	–	–	–	–	–	–	–	–	–
If remarried, was first marriage terminated by death?	–	–	–	–	–	–	–	–	–	–	–
Number of years widowed, divorced, or separated	–	–	–	–	–	–	–	–	–	–	–

FIGURE 16.3
Excerpt of Grid Summarizing All Questions Asked in the Decennial Census from 1790 to 2000 (Excludes identification items, screening questions, and other information collected, but not intended for tabulation)

Demographic characteristics	1790	1800	1810	1820	1830	1840	1850	1860	1870	1880	1890
Social characteristics											
Free or slave	X	X	X	X	X	X	X	X	–	–	–
Per slave owner, number of fugitives	–	–	–	–	–	–	X	X	–	–	–
Per slave owner, number of manumitted	–	–	–	–	–	–	X	X	–	–	–
Physical and mental handicaps and infirmities											
Deaf or deaf mutes	–	–	–	–	X	X	X	X	X	X	X
Blind	–	–	–	–	X	X	X	X	X	X	X
Insane	–	–	–	–	–	X	X	X	X	X	X

FIGURE 16.3   (continued from previous page)

small geographies, so a shoe company could easily see which cities and towns bought which types of shoes. There is nearly no end to what people hope could be asked in the census, from the serious to the silly: "As long as we're spending all this money to reach so many people, imagine what we could find out. Which do you favor, . . . Smooth or chunky? Faith or works? Liberty or equality?" (Gibbs, 2010: 56). The Census Bureau, however, rejects nearly all such requests as outside the scope of the decennial census.

Census Controversies

The census has been central to numerous formative political and social controversies in American history. Simply figuring out how to use the population data to determine the size of the House of Representatives was contentious right from the first census effort. How big should the House be, and most importantly, what is the population threshold for a new representative? Disagreement over how to determine the allotment of representatives led to the very first presidential veto in the nation's history when George Washington vetoed the Apportionment Act on April 5, 1792.

The years leading up to the Civil War saw the census at the center of a number of very divisive arguments related to the balance of power between slaveholding and free states. In the published reports of 1860, the Census Bureau editorialized about what the numbers meant with regard to slaves and their potential freedom, suggesting that some combination of morality, barbarianism, and genetics would see the black population soon become either extinct altogether or totally absorbed into the white population—an example of official government racism (Kennedy, 1864). Less controversial but more famous, in 1890 the Census Bureau declared the closing of the American frontier as shown in the latest census figures.

Contemporary census controversies are both familiar and novel: familiar in that the census still scares some part of the population, who fear it as an intrusion into their privacy and a manifestation of a big brother government; novel in that the census's consistent inability to accurately count every person has raised the idea of using more sophisticated statistical means to make a more accurate census.

Privacy advocates have long resisted the extra questions on the census, arguing for keeping the census to only its strict constitutional role of counting inhabitants and apportioning representatives. Even the 2010 census—one of the shortest in history—had its detractors. Minnesota Representative Michele Bachmann, perhaps the most vocal of 2010 census critics, claimed at the time to be "leaving most of its form blank except for the question that asks directly how many people reside in her home. 'We won't be answering any information beyond that,' she said. She complained that the remaining nine questions are 'very intricate, very personal' and argued that 'the Constitution doesn't require any information beyond that'" (Colvin, 2010:41). Echoing concerns about government intrusion into private information, Representative Jeff Duncan (R–S.C.) and several cosponsors introduced the failed "Census Reform Act of 2013," which would have abolished virtually all census surveys except for a simple decennial count of the population. Despite such resistance, voluntary census response rates have remained steady over recent decades, with more than 70 percent of households returning the form via mail and the rest receiving personal visits.

While the law suggests that these privacy concerns are unfounded, census data has been abused in the past. The most notable instance was during World War II, when the Census Bureau provided the War Department names and addresses of those of Japanese ancestry living in the United States and thus aided efforts to identify them for internment (Holmes, 2000). Scholars Margo Anderson and William Seltzer, who discovered and reported this abuse of census data, have done extensive work related to government statistics and confidentiality (see https://pantherfile.uwm.edu/margo/www/govstat/integrity.htm). And although providing specially tabulated anonymous data on request is perfectly legal (and the Census Bureau now lists such requests on its website, www.census.gov/about/policies/foia/foia_library/custom_tabulations.html), the Census Bureau in 2004 caused alarm with civil liberties groups and Arab-American advocacy organizations by providing the Department of Homeland Security with population statistics on Arab-Americans, including how many people of Arab backgrounds live in certain ZIP codes (Clemetson, 2004).

The other great contemporary census controversy surrounds the problem of undercounting the population. Poor areas and racial minorities are especially prone to being undercounted, a phenomenon first truly noted when more African Americans registered for the World War II draft than were even thought to be in the country based on census data. As Holden summarizes, statisticians have long advocated for using statistical sampling to adjust the results to more accurate figures (2009). While sampling has been used for the extra questions, it had never been the basis for the apportionment data, which is taken from 100 percent results only. To address this in time for Census 2000, the Census Bureau proposed a plan to use limited statistical sampling to make population numbers more accurate, arguing that such methods were sound and fair and would represent a more accurate count. Before such a plan could be instituted, however, the Supreme Court, in the 5–4 decision *Department of Commerce v. U.S. House of Representatives* (525 U.S. 326), ruled sampling for apportionment purposes to be unconstitutional.

So to make the census as accurate as possible, the Census Bureau relies on vigilance, education, and outreach rather than statistical methods. It tries hard to make people understand that by not responding to the census, they only hurt themselves and their communities and they are essentially going unrepresented in the House of Representatives. To maximize an accurate count, the census even has a large-scale marketing campaign, which in 2010 saw the first ever census Super Bowl commercial. Successful outreach can be a difficult proposition, though. The homeless population, for a number of reasons well-articulated by Kearns (2012), is historically difficult to reach and enumerate. Undocumented immigrants, legally included in census enumerations, often have a distrust of the government that leads many to be fearful of providing personal information via census forms. Despite the efforts to ensure participation, the 2010 Census still missed millions of people, especially African Americans, Hispanics, and Native Americans.

Race, ethnicity, and sexual orientation are other often contentious issues in the decennial census, and changes in policy have made these demographics difficult to accurately compare over time. For example, the first time that respondents were able to identify themselves as more than one race was in the 2000 census. O'Hare (1998) provides background and a summary of federal statistical classification of race categories, including the change for Census 2000. This move has been both welcomed and criticized, and is indicative of ongoing sensitivity in the nation to issues of race. Ancestry questions (which ask respondents to identify their country of origin), meanwhile, are consistently dogged by claims of undercounts and concerns that respondents do not always willingly identify their ancestry. Complicating matters even more, studies have shown that many people are inconsistent in the way they identify their race and/or ethnicity (Cohn, 2014). It also wasn't until the 2010 census that the Census Bureau, at the direction of the Obama administration, counted and reported same-sex married couples. In 1990, when the "unmarried partner" option was first included to count unmarried heterosexual couples living together, the Census Bureau—because same-sex marriage was not yet legal in any states—edited the responses of same-sex couples who self-identified as "married" to make it appear that one member of the couple was of the opposite sex and "just made them a married [heterosexual] couple." In 2000, the Census Bureau retained the gender information as provided but recategorized couples who self-identified as "married" to "unmarried partners" and declined to release those numbers (Long, 2011).

Census Geography

Geography is key to the decennial census. Obviously, the census must count the people in each state in order to apportion representatives by state. But in order to distribute federal funds—not to mention for the benefit of research about the nation—the census also presents data that can describe smaller geographies, such as cities and towns. Data for smaller areas is needed by state governments to determine congressional district boundaries within their state, and is used by state and local governments to define electoral districts. To satisfy those needs, the census provides data for states, counties, cities and townships, and smaller geographies known as census tracts, block numbering areas, block groups, and blocks. This last geography is more or less akin to an actual city block. All of these smaller geographies, from census tracts on down, began in the 20th century, and it was not until the 2000 census that every place in the country was assigned a census tract. Previous decennial censuses, then, do not feature census tract (or equivalent) data for all places.

> **Census Geography, Major Divisions, Values for Address Shown in figure 16.4**
>
> 1. Census Region (of four regions: Northeast, Midwest, South, West): West
>
> 2. State: California
>
> 3. County or equivalent: Santa Barbara County
>
> 4. County subdivisions: n/a
>
> 5. Place (city or equivalent): Santa Barbara city
>
> 6. Census Tract (within a county, between 1,200–8,000 people; ideally 4,000): 5.02
>
> 7. Block group (within census tract, a cluster of blocks of 600–3,000 people): 4
>
> 8. Census Block (within block group, much like an actual city block): 4,000

Figure 16.4 shows an example of the census geography associated with a particular address.

While beyond the scope of this chapter, the Census Bureau also developed the TIGER (Topologically Integrated Geographic Encoding and Referencing) system, geographic reference files that, in addition to their use in census geography, helped spur the development of the world of GIS (geographic information system) data and software. These TIGER files were created by combining United States Geological Survey topographical maps with Census Bureau maps of addresses used by decennial census takers in the field. When used with GIS software, TIGER files combined with decennial census data enable creation of sophisticated maps, including features such as roads, rivers, elevation data, and legal and census boundaries, all mapped with demographic and socioeconomic data from the census.

Census Publications

Although neither the constitution nor later action by Congress called for publication of census results, publications did start with the first census, with a single 56-page report. In 1800, another single report was produced, of 74 pages. By 1840, there were well over 1,000 pages of decennial census reports; by 1880, 20,000; and by 1960, over 100,000

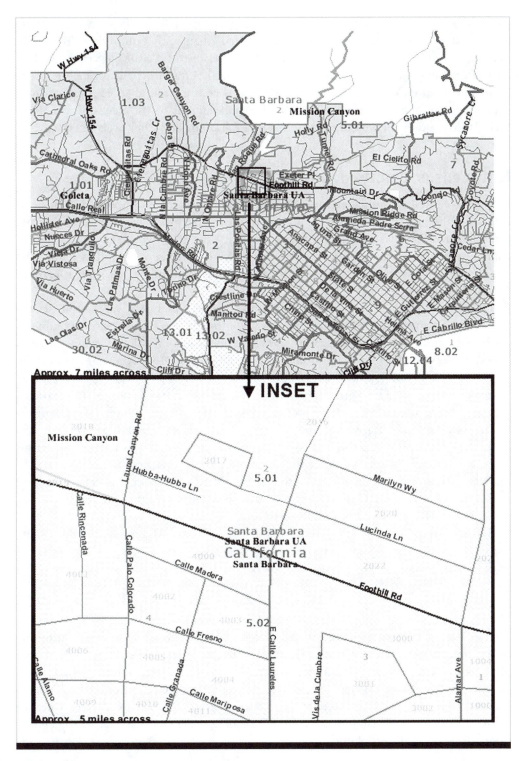

FIGURE 16.4
Census Map of Santa Barbara, California (top) and Inset (bottom) Showing Census Tract 5.02;
Block Group 4; and Block 4000

pages (Eckler, 1972). That's hundreds of times bigger than *War and Peace*. And the 1970, 1980, and 1990 censuses were much bigger than that, with hundreds of published volumes. As of 2000, most data and publications began to be available via the Web as part of the same rapid transition to web access that has transformed so much government information. Within one 10-year decennial census period, access evolved from these hundreds of printed reports (with limited and difficult-to-use electronic access via CD-ROMs and primitive online systems) to a full point-and-click web interface.

Early Census Reports: 1790–1840

Using the earliest decennial census reports is straightforward. As published in print or scanned online by the Census Bureau (www.census.gov/prod/www/decennial.html), these historical reports usually contain a summary table or two and several pages of data per state. The state data is further broken down by smaller geographies, namely, by county and city/town/place, and occasionally, a subdivision of a place, such as Harlem Division in figure 16.5.

The data published depends on the questions asked. For each relatively simple decennial census in this early period, there is only a volume or two of results: one volume of the basic population data by geography, and sometimes a second volume or two for extra data such as the economic or pensioner data. From 1790 to 1840, the census generally just took a count and gathered data by sex and a few basic age categories, and for free citizens versus slaves. The 1810 census saw a concurrent effort to count manufacturers, the result being some data on the number, volume, and type of manufacturing done in the nation, states, and for each county. Separate volumes were published to share this data. The 1820 census was the first to add an economic question as part of the census itself, with citizens noting whether they were employed in agriculture, commerce, or manufacturing. Again, a second volume was published to present this data. The 1830 and 1840 censuses more closely resembled the early censuses, although 1840 included some extra questions asked of military pensioners.

Accessing the data in these volumes is pretty straightforward. There is usually a summary page with general population data for each state, and then a chapter for each state with further breakdowns by county and town. This is important as it mirrors—in a simpler form—all census data throughout history, namely, with data grouped by geography.

Not all reports are online at the historical census reports website. The invaluable *Catalog of United States Census Publications 1790–1972* lists and describes every report in each census. Getting one's hands on these volumes is not always easy. While historical census reports have sometimes been republished by private publishers, it is mostly larger libraries that own significant runs of historical decennial census reports. The Census Bureau also has a print-on-demand program for reports that it has scanned. Finally, each state is home to a State Data Center (www.census.gov/sdc) that coordinates access to census data. Each of these sources can aid users in actually laying hands on the appropriate decennial census volume.

The Return for SOUTH CAROLINA having been made since the foregoing Schedule was originally printed, the whole Enumeration is here given complete, except for the N. Weftern Territory, of which no Return has yet been publifhed.

DISTICTS	Free white Males of 16 years and upwards, including heads of families.	Free white Males under fixteen years.	Free white Females, including heads of families.	All other free perfons.	Slaves.	Total.
Vermont	22435	22328	40505	255	16	85539
N. Hampfhire	36086	34851	70160	630	158	141885
Maine	24384	24748	46870	538	NONE	96540
Maffachufetts	95453	87289	190582	5463	NONE	378787
Rhode Ifland	16019	15799	32652	3407	948	68825
Connecticut	60523	54403	117448	2808	2764	237946
New York	83700	78122	152320	4654	21324	340120
New Jerfey	45251	41416	83287	2762	11423	184139
Pennfylvania	110788	106948	206363	6537	3737	434373
Delaware	11783	12143	22384	3899	8887	59094
Maryland	55915	51339	101395	8043	103036	319728
Virginia	110936	116135	215046	12866	292627	747610
Kentucky	15154	17057	28922	114	12430	73677
N. Carolina	69988	77506	140719	4975	100572	393751
S. Carolina	35576	37722	66880	1801	107094	249073
Georgia	13103	14044	25739	398	29264	82548
	807094	791850	1541263	59150	694280	3893635

Total number of Inhabitants of the United States exclufive of S. Weftern and N. Territory.	Free white Males of 21 years and upwards.	Free white Males under 21 years of age.	Free white Females.	All other Perfons.	Slaves.	Total
S. W. territory N. Ditto	6271	10277	15365	361	3417	35691

NEW-YORK.

NEW-YORK CITY and COUNTY.	Free white Males of 16 years and upwards, including heads of Families.	Free white Males under 16 years.	Free white Females, including heads of Families.	All other free Perfons.	Slaves.	Aggregate total.	More Females than Males.	More Males than Females.
City of New York	8328	5797	14963	1061	2180	31218	838	
Harlem Divifion	171	110	291	41	189	803	9	
Total,	8500	5907	15254	1101	2369	33131	847	
WEST CHESTER COUNTY.								
Morrifina	43	17	41	2	30	133	19	
Weft Chefter	217	112	411	49	142	1203	70	
Eaft Chefter	174	160	320	11	75	740	14	
Pelham	45	31	84	3	38	198	8	
Yonkers	265	120	458	12	170	1123		27
Greenburgh	330	323	616	0	122	1400		37
New Rochelle	170	130	277	26	89	692		23
Scarfdale	73	53	113	14	28	281		13
Mamaroneck	108	98	171	18	57	452		35
Rye	258	164	417	14	133	986	5	
Harrifon	242	120	453	35	54	1004		9
White Plains	130	106	218	8	49	505		12
Mt. Pleafant	501	412	909	8	84	1914		14
North Caftle	608	593	1205	43	29	1476	4	
Bedford	618	612	1181	10	33	1470		58
Poundridge	245	270	538	7		1062	21	
Salem	366	316	728	14	19	1453	30	
North Salem	266	239	509	16	28	1058	4	
Stephen	343	397	611	5	38	1497		18
York	386	381	771	28	40	1809	1	
Courtlandt	484	452	905	15	66	1932		31
Total,	5939	5330	10958	157	1419	24003	79	390
DUTCHESS COUNTY.								
Frederickftown	1437	1540	2811	41	63	5932	126	
Phillipftown	517	593	941	2	25	2079	168	
Southeaft Town	231	241	435	3	13	921	39	
Pawling	1031	1068	2098	91	41	4130	1	
Beckman	847	951	1682	11	106	3597	116	
Fifhkill	1366	1290	2643	41	601	5941	15	
Poughkeepfie	612	573	1092	48	190	2529	98	
Clinton	1171	1111	2115	31	170	4607	17	
Amenia	768	782	1449	154	52	3078	95	

FIGURE 16.5
1790 Census Summary Results for the Nation (left) and Part of New York (right)

Multivolume Reports: 1850–1930

Beginning in 1850 the amount of data gathered in the decennial census grew quickly and steadily. This was partly because more "extra" questions were asked and partly because of the nation's rapidly expanding population. The year 1850 was the first census to ask questions not only related to manufacturing and industry but also about education, literacy, and real estate, among other topics. The 1880 census was the first to ask questions related to health and health conditions, and 1910 saw the first use of census tracts and smaller geographic designations, for the first time allowing users to access data about particular parts of towns. Use of census tracts expanded over the following decades, mainly in metropolitan areas, but eventually the Census Bureau expanded the program to include the entire country by 2000.

By 1880, the decennial census had become undeniably long and the number of published reports numbered into the dozens. Extended social and demographic questions were asked, as well as many questions about agriculture, industry, and manufacturing. By this time finding the desired data becomes more complicated. Different volumes cover different geographies and different topics. Data for a particular place might appear in many different volumes, depending on the subject; similarly, data for a particular subject might appear in many different volumes, depending on geography.

To find specific data, consult the *Catalog of United States Census Publications, 1790–1972,* mentioned in the previous section. Like census reports from earlier eras, some of the reports from this period will be a part of the Census Bureau's historical census reports website; others will be owned by depository libraries, and perhaps State Data Centers.

Era of the Statistical Sample: 1940–2000

As mentioned earlier in the chapter, the 1940 census was notable for the introduction of statistical sampling. Census workers—still going door-to-door, remember—asked an extended set of questions to every 20th household. Sampling was refined over the following decades. With the growth of the nation and the census—data was also being tabulated for thousands of smaller geographic units, such as census tracts—published reports by this time number in the hundreds for each census, and finding the desired data can take some digging.

In 1970, published reports began to be split into separate series based on whether the data was from the 100 percent questions or the sample questions, which may be helpful in identifying the right volumes. For instance, there are single volumes of the basic 100 percent data for each state (covering places and smaller geographies within the state, too); there are also single volumes for each state with the sample data results, and volumes containing data by census tract for metropolitan areas. Many subject-based reports have been produced, too. In addition to the listing of all reports in the *Catalog of United States Census Publications, 1790–1972,* each recent census has a separate guidebook that defines terms and describes methodologies. To get a sense of the scale of decennial census publishing, there is also the (now discontinued) annual *Census Catalog and Guide,* which lists the available reports from each recent census. For 1990, just the *listing* of decennial census publications spanned over 30 pages.

Within a census volume, the Table Finding Guides, which appear just after the table of contents, are quite useful. With their grids of subjects by geographies, these guides allow users to quickly find the right table.

Suzanne Schulze's three-volume set (1983, 1985, 1988) is also very useful in navigating the library of decennial census volumes from the first decennial census through 1980. Handy grids identify years, volumes, subjects, and geographies, and lead to detailed listings of data by volume.

The most recent census data are best—and increasingly only—accessed online via the American FactFinder (http://factfinder.census.gov) online portal, which provides simpler discovery of data by subject and geography. However, because of "the extremely large file sizes, American FactFinder can only store data from the last two Censuses," (US Census Bureau, Frequently Asked Questions) meaning that the 1990 decennial census data was dropped from American FactFinder when 2010 data was released. Print volumes may be found using the same method as for various older volumes: online as part of the historical census reports website; in local depository libraries; and at State Data Centers.

End of the Long Form: Census 2010 and the American Community Survey

The 2010 census was the shortest and simplest census since the very first one. There was no long form and almost no extra questions: nothing about education, earnings, occupation, transportation, physical features of the dwelling, ancestry, languages, or other detailed socioeconomic and demographic characteristics. There was no sample of the population answering additional questions. Everyone got only the short form, which counts the population, asks about relationships in each household, and gathers data about race and age. The results were the basis of reapportioning Congress; used to distribute shares of billions of federal dollars; and allowed researchers, policy makers, and the public to access basic statistics about the populations of states, cities, counties, and smaller census geographies such as census tracts, block groups, and blocks.

The shift to this throwback census is due to the emergence of the American Community Survey (ACS). Because recent decennial census efforts saw increased difficulty in getting households to fill out the cumbersome long form, as well as ever-rising costs of doing so, the Census Bureau—after years of planning and testing—instituted the ACS to replace the long form. The goal of the ACS isn't only to make the decennial census easier to gather, but also to provide ongoing current data.

The ACS gathers demographic, social, and economic data similar to that previously included on the census long form. Age, race, sex, family relationships, housing characteristics, education and literacy, health and health insurance, employment and income, language, and transportation are all among the subjects of questions asked. Since the ACS is conducted continually instead of once a decade, it provides more current data than the census long form did.

In the ACS, approximately 250,000 households are sampled each month across the nation. This sample is large enough to provide estimates for larger geographies—states, cities, and counties with a population of 65,000 or more—every year instead of every 10 years, as the number of responses to these approximately three million surveys per year will yield statistically valid results. Smaller geographies require more time to accumulate sufficiently sound ACS data: three years for places with 20,000 to 65,000 people; and five years for places with fewer than 20,000 residents. As such, the ACS produces three distinct data sets each year: one-year data sets, three-year data sets, and five-year data sets.

This process—taking multiple years to gather enough data for smaller places—makes the ACS different than the long form in one significant way. Except for those places with more than 65,000 people, which yield yearly data, ACS data is based on moving averages (also known as period averages). This means that if one is looking for data about Gunnison, Colorado, whose population is under 20,000, ACS will have data for the 2005–2009 period, because it takes five years of surveys to gather enough responses for an adequate survey of Gunnison. It will also have data for 2006–2010; 2007–2011; and so on. It will not have data for any single year because not enough residents of Gunnison will receive an ACS in a year to yield useful data. It is, therefore, important to understand that the resulting data is for a period of time, unlike data from the decennial census, which is for a single point in time.

These moving averages do occasionally present confusing options when using the ACS. All places with more than 20,000 people will have multiple ACS figures available. For instance, Syracuse, New York (with a population well over 100,000), will have ACS data for the year 2007, the years 2007–2009, and the years 2005–2009. Each figure will be slightly different. All three are legitimate and useful, one just needs to understand the peculiarities of these moving averages. This is especially tricky when measuring something like prices, which can fluctuate over even short periods. (The Census Bureau is using inflation data to attempt to normalize such statistics.) The importance of comparing census data of similar types and from similar sources should also be stressed. It is generally best to compare 100% data with other 100% data, and sample data with similar sample data (for instance, 3-year ACS samples to other 3-year ACS samples). Herman (2008) offers an excellent overview of the issues surrounding the ACS in general and moving averages in particular.

Online Census Data and American FactFinder

The Census Bureau has now scanned many of its historical census reports, although not comprehensively, and made them available online at www.census.gov/prod/www/decennial.html. Also worth noting is the Historical Census Browser (http://mapserver.lib.virginia.edu), a grant-funded project of the University of Virginia Geospatial and Statistical Data Center that uses an online interface to present a huge amount of historical census data, from 1790 through 1960, although only for counties and larger geographies. The National Historical Geographic Information System (www.nhgis.org) provides a similarly interesting compilation of historical and current census data with advanced geographic capabilities.

Census 2000 was the first census that used the Web as the primary and original data distribution method. The American FactFinder (http://factfinder.census.gov), which was redesigned to coincide with the release of Census 2010 data, is the primary freely available method of accessing contemporary census data. It presents data about the population and economy of the United States and places within: it's simple to enter a state, city, county, place, or even a street address to get data for large or small geographic areas. Likewise, it's fairly straightforward to find and generate tables by navigating through topics using either the advanced or guided search.

The three largest data sources found in American FactFinder are the decennial census, the ACS, and the economic censuses, but it has grown to include the American Housing Survey, additional annual economic surveys from the Census Bureau, the Census of Governments and Annual Survey of Governments, and vintage Population Estimates. If one seeks population or demographic data for a particular state, county, or place, data is available from both decennial censuses and the ACS as well as the other included surveys. For instance, in figure 16.6, data may be accessed for a particular place for either decennial census data or from the Population Estimates program. Options on the left allow for easy access of data by other demographic and socioeconomic characteristics, surveys, topics, and more.

While American FactFinder remains the main source for recent census data, there is a separate page for Census 2010 (www.census.gov/2010census/). Census 2000 and

Census 1990 both also have their own gateway pages, pointing to the data and relevant documentation: www.census.gov/main/www/cen2000.html and www.census.gov/main/www/cen1990.html.

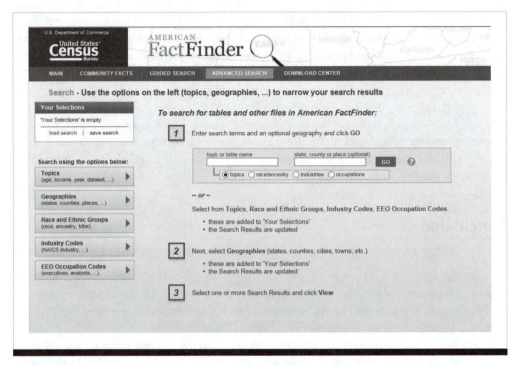

FIGURE 16.6
Using American FactFinder Advanced Search: Note the Options at Left

Decennial Census Microdata and Enhanced Census Data-Based Products

Because advanced researchers often need microdata that they can tabulate to their own specifications, the Census Bureau makes available Public-Use Microdata Samples (PUMS) for both the decennial census and the ACS. These datasets are anonymized samples with records for housing units that include individual response characteristics. PUMS for the 1980–2010 decennial censuses and the ACS are available through the Census Bureau's FTP site (www2.census.gov). 2000 and 2010 decennial census and ACS PUMS are also available in American FactFinder by searching the "topic or table name" for the term PUMS. The ACS PUMS are also available via the Census Bureau's DataFerrett (http://dataferrett.census.gov) data analysis tool. Historic PUMS microdata is available through the Integrated Public Use Microdata Series (IPUMS-USA) (https://usa.ipums.org/usa/), which is a free tool that makes available the data back to the 1850 Census, and from the Inter-university Consortium for Political and Social Research (ICPSR) (www.icpsr.umich.edu).

Decennial census data is also among the most fertile sources for enhanced, privately produced statistical and mapping tools. Since government statistical data is—within the limits of privacy law—under the public domain, third-party developers are able to use the data as the basis of new products. While such reuse is at times somewhat disingenuous—some publishers simply take government documents and reprint them under their own imprint, with perhaps only a new preface as added value—statistical data, especially from the decennial census, has seen some wonderful private development. Census data is behind countless products designed for market research (see chapter 15, Business, Economic, and Consumer Information). For more in-depth research use, companies like Social Explorer (www.socialexplorer.com), SimplyMap (www .geographicresearch.com/simplymap), and PolicyMap (www.policymap.com) use the data to create specialized thematic maps beyond what is possible using American Fact-Finder's mapping options. In 2012, the Census Bureau began providing access to data-sets by API, and the website now includes an app gallery to highlight tools created by the Census Bureau and by third parties.

Conclusion

The unmatched size and scope of the decennial census makes it the most important statistical repository from the government and the most widely used single statistical undertaking in the nation. The ACS, meanwhile, is a groundbreaking effort to provide updated demographic information even for small geographies.

From American FactFinder to census microdata to printed reports, the Census Bureau houses an astonishing amount of statistical data about the nation, available to use in ways designed for all levels of users—from the novice through the professional statistician. The census continues to evolve, and understanding and finding data sources for any particular census requires some research. While access to census data and reports is easier than ever before, it is necessary to know the nature of the statistical effort in order to interpret the results in a meaningful way. A variety of training materials and events are available to help increase one's understanding: Census Bureau-sponsored training events and webinars, Federal Depository Libraries, State Data Centers, and YouTube are often excellent resources for learning more about the census.

Exercises

1. Explore the 1830 census. What statistics are available on race and slavery? Are there statistics by state? By city?
2. Find the population of Phoenix, Arizona, in every census from 1920 to 1990. What further geographic breakdowns exist by decade? When were census tracts introduced?
3. Generate a list of the commuting times to work for all cities in California from Census 2000.

4. For your current address, identify the census tract, block group, and block. What streets or geographic features form the boundaries for your block? What is the population, by age and sex, for your block?

5. What is the most recent median household income for the county you currently reside in? The one you grew up in? For each, what is the specific source of the data?

Sources Mentioned in This Chapter

Sources mentioned in this section do not duplicate the references that follow.

1990 Census, www.census.gov/main/www/cen1990.html.

2000 Census, www.census.gov/main/www/cen2000.html.

2010 Census, www.census.gov/2010census.

2020 Census, www.census.gov/2020census.

American Community Survey, www.census.gov/acs/www.

American FactFinder, http://factfinder.census.gov.

Bureau of the Census. 1974. *Catalog of United States Census Publications, 1790–1972.* Washington, DC: Government Printing Office. http://catalog.hathitrust.org/Record/000732965.

Bureau of the Census. *Census Catalog and Guide.* Annual, 1946–1998. www.census.gov/prod/www/catalogs.html.

DataFerrett, http://dataferrett.census.gov.

Historical Census Browser, http://mapserver.lib.virginia.edu.

Historical Census Reports, www.census.gov/prod/www/decennial.html.

Integrated Public Use Microdata Series (IPUMS-USA), https://usa.ipums.org/usa/.

Inter-university Consortium for Political and Social Research (ICPSR www.icpsr.umich.edu.

National Historical Geographic Information System, www.nhgis.org.

PolicyMap, www.policymap.com.

Public Use Microdata Samples, www2.census.gov.

Schulze, Suzanne. 1983. *Population Information in Nineteenth Century Census Volumes.* Phoenix: Oryx Press.

Schulze, Suzanne. 1985. *Population Information in Twentieth Century Census Volumes, 1900–1940.* Phoenix: Oryx Press.

Schulze, Suzanne. 1988. *Population Information in Twentieth Century Census Volumes, 1950–1980.* Phoenix: Oryx Press.

SimplyMap, www.geographicresearch.com/simplymap.

SocialExplorer, www.socialexplorer.com.

State Data Center Program, www.census.gov/sdc.

US Census Bureau. 2002. *Measuring America: The Decennial Census from 1790 to 2000.* Washington, DC: Government Printing Office.

References

Anderson, Margo J. 1988. *The American Census: A Social History.* New Haven: Yale University Press.

Browning, W. R. F. 2009. "Census." *A Dictionary of the Bible.* New York: Oxford University Press. Oxford Reference Online.

Cassedy, James. 1969. Demography in Early America: Beginnings of the Statistical Mind. Cambridge: Harvard University Press.

Clemetson, Lynette. 2004. "Homeland Security Given Data on Arab-Americans." New York Times, July 30. www.nytimes.com/2004/07/30/politics/30census.html.

Cohn, D'Vera. 2014. "Millions of Americans Changed Their Racial or Ethnic Identity from One Census to the Next." Pew Research Center FactTank, May 5. www.pewresearch.org/fact-tank/2014/05/05/millions-of-americans-changed-their-racial-or-ethnic-identity-from-one-census-to-the-next/.

Colvin, Jill. 2010. "Down for the Count." First Things 202: 39–42.

"Dogs Kill Census Worker, 71, Outside Indiana Cabin." 2000. Los Angeles Times, June 13. http://articles.latimes.com/2000/jun/13/news/mn-40382.

Eckler, A. Ross. 1972. The Bureau of the Census. New York: Praeger.

Gibbs, Nancy. 2010. "Count Me In." *Time*, April 5, 56.

Halacy, Dan. 1980. Census: 190 Years of Counting America. New York: Elsevier/Nelson.

Herman, Edward. 2008. "The American Community Survey: An Introduction to the Basics." Government Information Quarterly 25 (3): 504–519.

Holden, Constance. 2009. "The 2010 Census: America's Uncounted Millions." *Science* 324 (5930): 1008–1009.

Holmes, Steven. 2000. "Report Says Census Bureau Helped Relocate Japanese." New York Times, March 17. www.nytimes.com/2000/03/17/us/report-says-census-bureau-helped-relocate-japanese.html.

Kearns, Brandon. 2012. "Down for the Count: Overcoming the Census Bureau's Neglect of the Homeless." Stanford Journal of Civil Rights & Civil Liberties 8: 155–182.

Kennedy, J. C. G. 1864. Population of the United States in 1860: Compiled from the Original Returns of the Eighth Census under the Direction of the Secretary of the Interior. Washington: GPO.

Long, Quaid. 2011. "Queering the Census: Privacy, Accountability, and Public Policy Implications of Adding Sexual Orientation and Gender Identity Questions to the US Census." *DttP: Documents to the People* 39 (4):15–18.

O'Hare, William. 1998. "Managing Multiple-Race Data." American Demographics 20(4): 42–45.

Orlando, Lucia, and Rebecca Hyde. 2010. "Census 2010: What's the Big Deal?" *DttP: Documents to the People* 38(1): 10–12.

Osborn, Claire. 2013. "Attorney gets 3 years for shooting at census worker." Austin American-Statesman, June 11, www.statesman.com/news/news/local/attorney-gets-3-years-for-shooting-at-census-worke/nYJJQ/.

US Census Bureau, Frequently Asked Questions, https://ask.census.gov/faq.php?id=5000&faqId=9222.

CHAPTER 17

Patents, Trademarks, and Intellectual Property

MARTIN K. WALLACE

Congress shall have power . . . to promote the progress of science and useful arts, by securing for limited times to authors and inventors the exclusive right to their respective writings and discoveries.

—*Article I, Section 8, Clause 8 of the United States Constitution*

Introduction

Neither patents nor trademarks are typical of government information, at least not in the traditional sense, so it may seem strange to find information about them in a book on government information. One usually places items of government information into one of three categories: information about the government, information for the government, or information created by the government (Open Forum Foundation, 2013). Patents and trademarks are, rather, legal agreements between the public—represented by a governing body—and private interests. The content protected by this legal agreement—*the intellectual property*—is neither *about, for,* nor *created by* the government. But patents and trademarks are still, indirectly, government information because they are records of rights acknowledged by the government to those private interests. Plus, surrounding those documents is a vast collection of ancillary information that one could consider *artifacts of doing the business of government*—an oft-overlooked category of government information—such as applications, correspondence, administrative documentation, litigation histories, and bulk data. Approaching this topic more broadly, one must concede that the United States Patent and Trademark Office (USPTO), the patent and trademark-granting authority in the United States, creates and disseminates a lot more information than just the patents and trademarks themselves, and that's largely what will be explored in this chapter.

What Is A Patent?

A patent is a legal agreement giving its owner *the right to exclude others* from manufacturing, using, marketing, selling, offering for sale, or importing an invention for a specified period of time (its term). A national or regional patent-granting authority issues a patent to an inventor if his invention is novel, useful, and nonobvious, and only in return for full public disclosure of how the invention is made and used.

In the United States there are three types of patents; key differences between them are outlined here and summarized in table 17.1:

- Utility patents. These cover novel processes, machines, articles of manufacture, compositions of matter, and new improvements upon any of those. The term of ownership for a utility patent is up to 20 years *from its application date,* so long as the inventor pays periodic maintenance fees. Utility patents are identified by patent numbers (e.g., 8925112). Depending on the search system being employed, this number may be prefixed by a two-letter country code, followed by a document type code, or both (e.g., US8925112 A1). This applies to design and plant patents also.
- Design patents cover new, original ornamental designs for articles of manufacture. Strictly speaking, these are rights for what the article looks like, not what it does. As of May 13, 2015, the term for a design patent is 15 years *from its issue date.* Design patents issued prior to that date have a 14-year term, also from date of issue. Design patents are identified by numbers that begin with the letter D (e.g., D720516).
- Plant patents cover distinct and new varieties of asexually reproduced plants. The term for a plant patent is 20 years *from its application date.* There are no

TABLE 17.1
Key Differences between Utility, Design, and Plant Patents

	Protects	Term Length (in Years)	Term Begins	Maintenance Fees?	Number Prefix
Utility	Novel processes, machines, articles of manufacture, compositions of matter, and new improvements upon any of those	20	Application date	Yes, every 3.5 years from issue date	None (e.g., 8925112)
Design	New, original ornamental designs for articles of manufacture	14 or 15	Issue date	No	D (e.g., D720516)
Plant	Distinct and new varieties of asexually reproduced plants	20	Application date	No	P (e.g., PP25207)

maintenance fees for plant patents. Plant patents are identified by numbers that begin with the letters PP (e.g., PP25207). Since plant patents are considered by many to be a special type of utility patent, nearly everything in this chapter about utility patents will also apply to plant patents unless otherwise noted.

A patent is a negative right, meaning that the holding of the patent does not by itself grant any right to the inventor to manufacture, use, or sell the claimed invention if that activity would infringe another's blocking patent. For example, let's say that Fred holds the patent for a special type of adhesive, and let's say that Sally has just been granted a patent for a novel method of bookbinding. Sally's method of bookbinding relies on Fred's adhesive. Sally can prohibit others from using her new book binding method, but, because Fred's adhesive patent is a blocking patent, she can't practice it herself without Fred's approval. She would need to either wait for Fred's patent to expire, or come to an agreement with Fred that allows her to use the adhesive.

What Is a Trademark?

A trademark is a word, phrase, logo or other graphic symbol, sound, scent, shape, or trade dress used by a manufacturer or seller to distinguish its products or services from those of its competitors. The main purpose of a trademark is to designate the source of the goods or services that the mark is applied to. A trademark registration certificate is a document issued by a trademark-granting authority conferring the right to use the mark and to prohibit others from using the mark or other confusingly similar marks.

Unlike patents, ownership of a trademark right is established upon its first use in commerce, even if it is not registered. In fact, registration of a trademark isn't required for ownership of the mark, and will not be allowed until the mark is actively being used in commerce. While unregistered trademarks are still protected by law, federal registration confers additional legal benefits for an owner trying to defend their trademark against infringement.

> **Federal Registration of Trademarks**
>
> Federal registration confers additional legal benefits for an owner trying to defend their trademark against infringement. These include the presumption that the registrant on file is the mark's owner; presumption that later users infringed; right to sue in federal court; and recovery of profits, damages, and costs in infringement suits with possible triple damages and attorney's fees if the infringement is found to be willful.

Types of Patent and Trademark Information

There is a wide variety of patent- and trademark-related information available to the public. Most obvious are the documents themselves; in the case of patents these would include grants (issued patents) and *published* applications. In the case of trademarks, these would include registration certificates and *published* applications. The word published is emphasized for a reason. There's always some lag time in processing an application before it can be published, but there are some scenarios where a pending application is either not going to be published, or it just hasn't been published yet; some of these scenarios will become apparent later in the chapter.

Along with each application there are sets of ancillary files, often called file wrappers. These include copies of all the documents submitted by the applicant to the patent- or trademark-granting authority, and copies of any correspondence between the author- ity and the applicant or the applicant's legal counsel. For applications filed in multiple jurisdictions, correspondence and related documents shared between multiple granting authorities may also be found.

Then there is the administrative support documentation that is necessary to keep the systems functional. These include things like classification schemas and concordances, examination rules and procedures, and statutory law. Parallel to statutory law, there is also case law and litigation histories that surround infringement suits and a variety of other patent court proceedings.

Lastly, for conducting market research and making important business decisions, hav- ing a document in-hand may be less useful than the data that can be gleaned from large numbers of those documents—things like filing dates, inventor names, assignee contact info, legal status, related or cited documents, classification codes or any number of other data fields. This data can be downloaded in bulk for use in spreadsheets and other visu- alization tools for analysis.

What This Chapter Includes

This chapter includes sources of US patent and trademark information from the cate- gories outlined above. Most patent and trademark information can be located in multi- ple sources. Most of these are freely available, online US government sources, but there are a few exceptions. For those exceptions, other sources—many of which can be found at Patent and Trademark Resource Centers (PTRCs)—are referenced. Important dis- tinctions will be highlighted between what is available online and what may make a trip to a PTRC worthwhile. A list of PTRCs is maintained by the USPTO at www .uspto.gov/learning-and-resources/support-centers/patent-and-trademark-resource -centers-ptrcs. PTRC librarians are not authorized to provide legal assistance or to help with filing patent or trademark applications, but will bend over backward to help a researcher find the information he needs.

This chapter does not include information aimed at patent or trademark applicants. Guides for filing patent and trademark applications, as well as interactive forms, fee pay- ment information, and legal assistance can all be found on the USPTO's website at www .uspto.gov. This chapter also does not include training materials, either for filing applications or for searching the existing and pending registrations. Step-by-step guides to filing patent and trademark applications are also available on the USPTO's website. Tutorials for searching patents and trademarks abound on the open Web and may be found by a simple keyword search in any search engine; to receive the absolute best help with patent or trademark searching, readers should consult their nearest PTRC.

Patents

Granted Patents and Pending Patent Applications

Inventions that are new, useful, nonobvious to someone skilled in the art and accompanied by a written description disclosing how to make and use the invention may be patented. Prior art constitutes all public information in any form before a given date that might be relevant to a patent's claims of originality. Usually the way to determine whether or not an invention is new and nonobvious is by conducting a prior-art search, which includes a search of granted patents and published patent applications (in addition to non-patent literature). This is good practice not only to avoid infringing others' patents, but also because the inventor will gain a better understanding of the state-of-the-art in her industry, and perhaps discover ways to improve on her own or her competitors' inventions.

As a result of the passage of the American Inventors Protection Act of 1999 (AIPA, Title IV of the Consolidated Fiscal Year 2000 Appropriations, P.L. 106-113, 113 Stat. 1501), utility patent applications filed on or after November 29, 2000, are made available to the public, online, within 18 months of their filing dates. This allows researchers to consult not only granted patents, which may have taken years to issue, but also pending applications, which may better represent the current state of the art. Granted patents and pending applications look nearly identical. The quickest way to tell them apart is by their identification numbers. A granted US utility patent always has a prominently displayed patent number consisting of seven or fewer digits (sometimes prefixed by a country code, e.g., US8925112). For the most part, granted patents are numbered sequentially. Post-AIPA applications, on the other hand, are identified by a prominently displayed 11-digit publication number. The first four digits represent the year the application was published and the remaining seven digits are sequential (also sometimes prefixed by a country code, e.g., US20150095116). Pre-AIPA applications were not assigned publication numbers, but are identified by a prominently displayed 2-digit/6-digit application number (e.g., 09/726688). Note that the publication number does not replace the application number in post AIPA applications; the application number is completely different from both the patent number and the publication number; and it will appear on both the published application and the granted patent. Applications prior to November 29, 2000, are available for granted patents only, but are not online. These are discussed later in the section on file wrappers.

US design patents are not subject to this publication rule because in most countries, design patents are governed by a separate system for registering industrial designs and are not treated as patents. Design patents are not published until their issue date and will only have two numbers, their patent number and their application number.

Defensive Publications and Statutory Invention Registrations

Like a patent application, a defensive publication is a technical specification describing an invention; but rather than seeking patent rights on the invention, the inventor

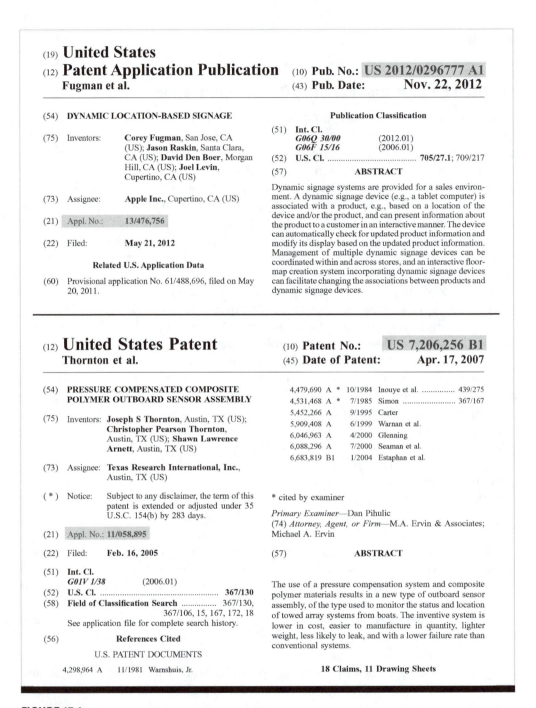

(19) **United States**
(12) **Patent Application Publication**   (10) Pub. No.: **US 2012/0296777 A1**
Fugman et al.   (43) Pub. Date: **Nov. 22, 2012**

(54)   DYNAMIC LOCATION-BASED SIGNAGE

(75)   Inventors: **Corey Fugman**, San Jose, CA
                     (US); **Jason Raskin**, Santa Clara,
                     CA (US); **David Den Boer**, Morgan
                     Hill, CA (US); **Joel Levin**,
                     Cupertino, CA (US)

(73)   Assignee: **Apple Inc.**, Cupertino, CA (US)

(21)   Appl. No.:   **13/476,756**

(22)   Filed: **May 21, 2012**

           Related U.S. Application Data

(60)   Provisional application No. 61/488,696, filed on May
       20, 2011.

Publication Classification

(51)   Int. Cl.
       G06Q 30/00   (2012.01)
       G06F 15/16   (2006.01)
(52)   U.S. Cl. **705/27.1**; 709/217

(57)   **ABSTRACT**

Dynamic signage systems are provided for a sales environment. A dynamic signage device (e.g., a tablet computer) is associated with a product, e.g., based on a location of the device and/or the product, and can present information about the product to a customer in an interactive manner. The device can automatically check for updated product information and modify its display based on the updated product information. Management of multiple dynamic signage devices can be coordinated within and across stores, and an interactive floor-map creation system incorporating dynamic signage devices can facilitate changing the associations between products and dynamic signage devices.

(12) **United States Patent**   (10) **Patent No.:**   **US 7,206,256 B1**
Thornton et al.   (45) **Date of Patent:**   **Apr. 17, 2007**

(54)   **PRESSURE COMPENSATED COMPOSITE
       POLYMER OUTBOARD SENSOR ASSEMBLY**

(75)   Inventors: **Joseph S Thornton**, Austin, TX (US);
                    Christopher Pearson Thornton,
                    Austin, TX (US); **Shawn Lawrence
                    Arnett**, Austin, TX (US)

(73)   Assignee: **Texas Research International, Inc.**,
                    Austin, TX (US)

(*) Notice: Subject to any disclaimer, the term of this
                   patent is extended or adjusted under 35
                   U.S.C. 154(b) by 283 days.

(21)   Appl. No.:   **11/058,895**

(22)   Filed: **Feb. 16, 2005**

(51)   Int. Cl.
       G01V 1/38   (2006.01)
(52)   U.S. Cl. 367/130
(58)   Field of Classification Search 367/130,
                                367/106, 15, 167, 172, 18
       See application file for complete search history.

(56)   **References Cited**

             U.S. PATENT DOCUMENTS

       4,298,964 A   11/1981 Warnshuis, Jr.

       4,479,690 A * 10/1984 Inouye et al. 439/275
       4,531,468 A *   7/1985 Simon 367/167
       5,452,266 A   9/1995 Carter
       5,909,408 A   6/1999 Warnan et al.
       6,046,963 A   4/2000 Glenning
       6,088,296 A   7/2000 Seaman et al.
       6,683,819 B1   1/2004 Estaphan et al.

* cited by examiner

Primary Examiner—Dan Pihulic
(74) *Attorney, Agent, or Firm*—M.A. Ervin & Associates;
Michael A. Ervin

(57)   **ABSTRACT**

The use of a pressure compensation system and composite polymer materials results in a new type of outboard sensor assembly, of the type used to monitor the status and location of towed array systems from boats. The inventive system is lower in cost, easier to manufacture in quantity, lighter weight, less likely to leak, and with a lower failure rate than conventional systems.

18 Claims, 11 Drawing Sheets

FIGURE 17.1
Patent Numbers and Patent Application Numbers

wishes to place the invention into the public domain. Because the defensive publication counts as prior art, the inventor prevents any other party from being granted a patent on the invention. Broadly defined, defensive publications are found in many formats; conference papers, journal articles, and technical reports are all examples of ways inventors seek to publish them. Another common method is to simply post the specification somewhere on the Web where it will be easily located by a patent examiner. Some websites, like www.defensivepublications.org, exist solely for this purpose.

Since April 1968, the USPTO has provided inventors an official means to register their defensive publications. The Defensive Publication Program provided for the technical disclosure and subsequent publication of a pending application where the applicant has waived his rights to an enforceable patent. In May 1985, the Statutory Invention Registration System replaced the Defensive Publication Program. The most important difference between the two programs was that defensibility began with the publication date for the former, but was applied retroactively to the application date for the latter. Since the enactment of the AIPA in 1999, published applications have become de facto defensive publications; the use of statutory invention registration diminished, and the system was repealed completely with the Leahy-Smith America Invents Act of 2011 (P.L. 112-29, 125 Stat. 284, effective Mar. 16, 2013).

Defensive publications (also known as DEFs) and statutory invention registrations (also known as SIRs) are considered to be neither granted patents nor pending applications; but fortunately, they can still be retrieved from the USPTO's search products (and most others) by searching within the Patent Number field. DEF numbers begin with the letter T (e.g., T947001) and SIR numbers begin with the letter H (e.g., H002288). For all intents and purposes, these are treated as patent numbers.

Certificates of Correction, Disclaimers, and Reissue Patents

Once a patent is granted, it can be revised in a number of ways. The simplest is a certificate of correction, which may be requested by a patent's owner, or issued by the patent office, as long as two criteria are met. First, the correction must be of a clerical or typographical nature, or of minor character—adding references to prior art, changing the inventor's name, simple rewording of claims for clarity, and claiming the benefit of an earlier filing date. Second, the correction must not constitute new matter or require reexamination; in other words, the patent owner cannot request additional claims to be added.

Next, a disclaimer is a statement filed by an owner of a patent—or its applicant, if still pending—in which the owner relinquishes certain legal rights to the patent. There are two types of disclaimers: a statutory disclaimer is a statement in which the owner relinquishes legal rights to one or more claims of her patent; a terminal disclaimer dedicates to the public the entire term or the reminder of the term of a patent or application.

Certificates of correction and disclaimers are appended to the back of the patents they correct in the USPTO's search systems, and are both thereafter considered to be part of their original patents. They are not issued numbers independent of their patent or publication numbers, and therefore not searchable by any type of unique identification numbers. Monthly listings of certificates of correction can be found on the USPTO's website at www.uspto.gov/patents-application-process/patent-search/authority-files/certificates-correction. As of this writing, no similar listing is available for disclaimers.

Last, but not least, reissue patents are modified substitutes for patents that have been invalidated. Whenever a patent is deemed wholly or partly invalid, by reason of a defective specification or drawing, or by reason of the patentee claiming more or less than he had a right to claim in the patent, the USPTO can reissue a new patent for the invention disclosed in the original patent for the unexpired part of the term of the original patent. As with corrections and disclaimers, no new matter shall be introduced into the application for reissue. Reissue patents are identified with patent numbers that begin with the letters RE (e.g., RE45317).

For more information on any of the above listed patent types, the *Manual of Patent Examining Procedure* (MPEP), at www.uspto.gov/mpep/, should be consulted. As explained in its Foreword, the *Manual* provides patent examiners, applicants, attorneys, agents, and representatives of applicants with a reference work on the practices and procedures relative to the prosecution of patent applications. It contains instructions to examiners, as well as other material in the nature of information and interpretation, and outlines the current procedures which the examiners are required or authorized to follow in appropriate cases in the normal examination of a patent application.

Patent Families

At its most fundamental level, a patent family is the group of granted patents issued from a single application. For example, an inventor wishing to file in multiple countries may file a Patent Cooperation Treaty (PCT) application and declare that she wants patent protection in the United States, Germany, Japan, China, and South Korea. If the patent is granted in all five countries, the family will include all five of those patents, plus the original application. This is the basic model, but there are others. Some family models will include withdrawn or reissued patents; and there are constructed models that include multiple independently filed applications for the same invention. (For a listing of patent family types, with descriptions, see Zimmerman's Research Guide at https://law.lexisnexis.com/infopro/zimmermans/disp.aspx?z=1816#FAME.)

Information Sources for Patents

USPTO's PatFT and AppFT

The USPTO's web-based database, PatFT, contains the full-text of all patents back to 1976, and is updated every Tuesday with patents granted the previous week. It is keyword-searchable by full-text and field-searchable by an astounding variety of attributes, shown in the sidebar.

High-quality PDF images are available for all US patents, including those dating back to the first US patent in 1790, but PatFT does not, as-of-yet, have digital full-text of pre-1976 patents, and the USPTO has not indexed pre-1976 patents by all of the available fields; these older patents are only field-searchable by Patent Number, Issue Date and Current CPC Classification. (Exceptions to what is available in PDF include unrecovered X-patents, withdrawn patents, or otherwise missing patents. Some of the patents missing from PatFT may be findable by other means; it's recommended that researchers contact their nearest PTRC for help locating known patents that are not available in PatFT. X-patents refer to patents that were lost in the 1836 patent office fire, of which an estimated 2,800 have been recovered.)

List of searchable fields in PatFT.

All Fields	Current US Classification	Prior Published Document Date
Title	Primary Examiner	Referenced By
Abstract	Assistant Examiner	Foreign References
Issue Date	Inventor Name	Other References
Patent Number	Inventor City	Claim(s)
Application Date	Inventor State	Description/Specification
Application Serial Number	Inventor Country	Patent Family ID
Application Type	Government Interest	130(b) Affirmation Flag
Applicant Name	Attorney or Agent	130(b) Affirmation Statement
Applicant City	Parent Case Information	Certificate of Correction
Applicant State	PCT Information	PTAB Trial Certificate
Applicant Country	PCT 371C124 Date	Re-Examination Certificate
Applicant Type	PCT Filing Date	Supplemental Exam Certificate
Assignee Name	Foreign Priority	International Registration Number
Assignee City	Reissue Data	
Assignee State	Reissued Patent Application Filing Date	International Registration Date
Assignee Country		International Filing Date
International Classification	Related US App. Data	International Registration Publication Date
Current CPC Classification	Related Application Filing Date	
Current CPC Classification Class	Priority Claims Date	

PatFT's sister database, AppFT, allows searching of all published, pending, non-provisional *applications* back to March 2001. Like PatFT, AppFT is keyword-searchable by full-text, and field-searchable by most of the same attributes as PatFT (some fields, such as Patent Number, don't apply to pending applications). High-quality PDF images are available for all US applications found in AppFT. Both PatFT and AppFT can be accessed at http://patft.uspto.gov.

When a pending application is granted, it is removed from AppFT and added to PatFT as a granted patent. Provisional patent applications are not published and therefore not available in AppFT. Applicants meeting certain requirements may withhold publication of their applications; these will not be available in AppFT unless their applicants later request publication. For reasons of national security, some applications are withheld from publication due to secrecy orders; those are not available in AppFT unless the secrecy order is lifted.

Resources at the PTRCs

The USPTO provides two other search tools free for public use; however, because they literally connect to the USPTO's network and require a special means for authentication, they are not available on the open Web and require a visit to either the nearest PTRC, or to the USPTO's Public Search Facility in Alexandria, VA. The tools are PubEAST (Public Examiner Automated Search Tool) and PubWEST (Public Web-based Examiner's Search Tool) and they include everything in PatFT and AppFT, plus much more. They include keyword-searchable digital full-text of granted patents back to 1971 and keyword searchable OCR'd (Optical Character Recognition) full-text back to 1920. Inventor names can also be searched back to 1920. These two systems also incorporate additional databases: the USPTO's Foreign Patents Retrieval System (FPRS), European Patent Office (EPO) abstracts, and Japanese Patent Office (JPO) abstracts. Explaining each of these additional databases is beyond the scope of this chapter, but it suffices to say that the PubEAST and PubWEST systems allow searching across granted US patents, pending US applications, and millions of non–US patent documents, all under one roof.

Both systems have far more indexed bibliographic fields than PatFT and AppFT—more than 90 in total. For example, patents that were prosecuted by a specific agent, attorney, or examiner can be searched, or finding out to which art unit at the USPTO a specific patent application has been assigned to can be revealed. Both provide a full suite of Boolean, proximity, truncation, and numerical operators, whereas PatFT and AppFT provide just a few. In addition, while PatFT and AppFT support right-truncation, PubEAST and PubWEST support left, right, and middle truncation. By default, PubEAST and PubWEST will automatically search plurals and some alternate spellings (e.g., color OR colour). This feature can be overridden, but it isn't available at all in PatFT or AppFT. Additionally, both of these search environments can be greatly customized for optimization based on the searcher's needs and habits. Features that are used most can be displayed prominently, while features rarely used can be hidden away. Panes, toolbars and panels can be moved around and displayed in the most convenient locations for the user.

So, what are the differences between PubEAST and PubWEST? Why are there two nearly identical systems? Both of these were originally examiner search systems that were made available to the public years after their initial implementation at the USPTO. The underlying data is exactly the same for both systems and the same documents may be found no matter which system is chosen. PubWEST is the older of the two systems, and while it does look a bit dated, it has a much simpler and more recognizable search interface than PubEAST. Most users will be more at ease with PubWEST.

On the other hand, PubEAST was built from the ground up to closely mimic what examiners do in practice, which is, to quickly review large stacks of patent documents, sort them, mark them for further review, and get irrelevant documents out of their workspace. Its interface is much more sophisticated, and capable of doing quite a bit more. The user's numeric keypad doubles as a navigation keypad which greatly increases the flexibility, speed, and capabilities in reviewing retrieved documents. Single-key tagging of the most relevant documents pertinent to the searcher's target invention automatically creates a new list and allows for many additional capabilities for refinement. The use of Family ID filtering helps the searcher avoid multiple documents describing virtually the same invention by reducing the total number of documents in the results list—all documents in a family are tucked away under the priority document for that family. And, PubEAST uniquely allows for user-annotation of records, or even specific pages of a document, that a searcher finds important. User manuals for both PubEAST and PubWEST, as well as expert advice from a librarian, are available at PTRC locations and at the USPTO's Public Search Facility.

Earlier methods of providing patents to PTRCs included CASSIS (optical discs, through 2011) and microfilm (through 1999), both with complete backfiles. Some PTRCs have chosen to retain their optical discs, and most will still have the microfilm. The microfilm collections are the best archival source for patent images where the electronic version was poorly scanned.

Due to the importance of color rendition of plant patents, those are still printed in color and retained in paper format at PTRCs, back to 1931 (holdings will vary by PTRC location). Plant patents can be searched via PatFT, PubEAST, PubWEST and CASSIS, but the images in those systems are in black and white. As with utility and design patents, the microfilm collections are the best archival source for full-color plant patent images up to 1999. The print volumes held at PTRCs serve as the best source for plant patents published after 1999.

Foreign Patents: Espacenet and Patentscope

One does not need to visit a PTRC and use PubEAST or PubWEST to search for foreign patents—there are two highly recommended, freely available, web-based databases that are designed specifically for international use. The World Intellectual Property Organization (WIPO), the administrative authority for the PCT, has a database called Patentscope (https://patentscope.wipo.int/search/en/search.jsf). Patentscope includes all PCT filings and all resulting granted patents—one for each country where the patent was granted. In addition, it includes non-PCT and pre-PCT collections for many of its member countries, including the United States. The best feature in Patentscope is its two-way translation capabilities. First, Patentscope provides a search-type called Cross Lingual Expansion, available at https://patentscope.wipo.int/search/en/clir/clir.jsf, which translates a query into one or up to a dozen different languages in order to retrieve non-English language documents. See figure 17.2 for a screenshot showing the list of available languages. Second, it can translate those non-English search results into English or up to a dozen other languages. This is the only freely available patents database that provides this feature.

The European Patent Office (EPO), a regional, nongovernmental patent-granting authority, has a database called Espacenet (http://worldwide.espacenet.com/advancedSearch). It is in the EPO's interest to collect all the patent documents of the world, so many non-EPO and non-PCT patent-granting authorities are available. Espacenet is comprised of patent documents from 92 different countries, compared to Patentscope's 148 (EPO, 2011; WIPO, 2013). On the other hand, Espacenet boasts 90-million documents, where Patentscope has only around 45-million (EPO, 2015; WIPO, 2015b). The best feature in Espacenet is its fully integrated implementation of the Cooperative Patent Classification (CPC) system, covered later in this chapter.

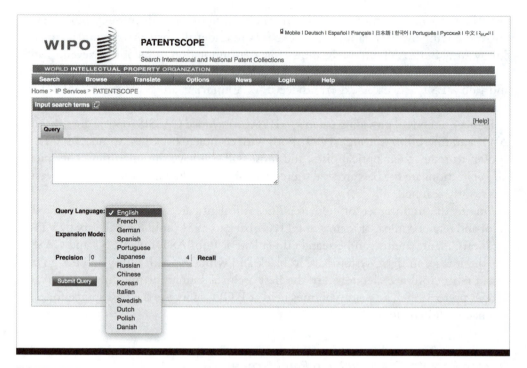

FIGURE 17.2
List of Available Languages in Patentscope's Cross Lingual Expansion
Note: By default it will translate a query into all available languages. If Expansion Mode is set to Supervised, the user can select which languages to use.

Both Patentscope and Espacenet have large pre-digital backfiles: some records will be bibliographic data only, some will have abstracts (translated into English in most cases), and some will have searchable full-text. Most will at least include scans of the original documents, but neither provides OCR full-text from those images.

Google Patent Search

Google is the most recent big player in free online patent databases. Its claim to fame in this crowded market is that it has scanned and OCR'd most of the documents that were previously not available in full-text. Google Patent Search (https://patents.google .com), covers USPTO, EPO, and WIPO documents, so it is a convenient one-stop-shop for all three. It is not without its problems, most obvious being that the OCR quality is fairly poor, and the search options are minimal. It does include an advanced search option that allows searching by patent number, title, inventor, assignee, or classification, found at www.google.com/advanced_patent_search. Google continues to develop new features for its patent search tool. To date, it has been integrated in some interesting ways with Google Scholar, and a Prior Art Finder is available for those who trust Google's algorithms to perform this laborious yet extremely important task. See figure 17.3 for a sample screenshot of the Prior Art Finder.

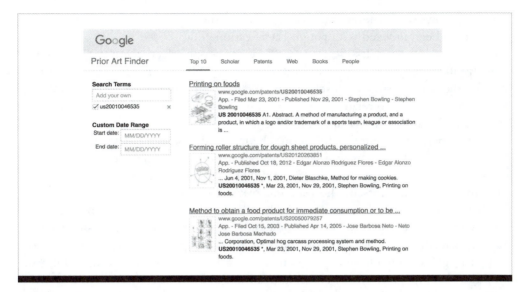

FIGURE 17.3
Prior Art for Application #US20010046535, Printing on Food, Found with Google's Prior Art Finder

Patentscope, Espacenet, and Google Patents Search all include special ways to group families together, but they don't offer a way to tuck them all into one search result like PubEAST does. This could mean the difference of hundreds of redundant documents in search results; this is especially true for Google where there will be hundreds more search results to begin with, due to their database including older documents.

Patent Classification Systems

Patent classification systems are sets of hierarchical taxonomies used to organize inventions by their areas of technology and by specific features within each technology area. This makes them uniquely suited for searching and sorting large collections of patents. Inventions typically receive a primary classification describing the main inventive feature or use, along with one or more additional classifications describing secondary features of the invention. Patent classification systems are living documents that are continually growing to accommodate new areas of technology and refined to better accommodate existing ones.

To be as thorough as possible, a prior art search should not consist of keyword searching alone; a comprehensive prior art search wouldn't be complete without first searching by patent classification. Searching by patent classification avoids the many pitfalls of relying on keywords: vague or inconsistent terminology (e.g., Amusement Device instead of Toy), obsolete names and terms (e.g., water closet), different meanings in different fields (e.g., computer mouse and mouse trap), and synonyms (e.g., rodent extermination device rather than mouse trap). Another huge limitation of relying on keyword searching is that by doing so, the searcher is effectively excluding the large body of earlier patent documents that, while available as images, are not full-text searchable. Classification searching allows the retrieval of all patents back to the 1790s because even the earliest patents have been indexed with patent classification codes.

Cooperative Patent Classification (CPC, www.cooperativepatentclassification.org/index.html) is the system developed and used by the USPTO and the EPO. Its website includes the latest classification scheme with definitions, notices of changes, and concordances from CPC to related classification schemas European Classification (ECLA) and International Patent Classification (IPC).

The Cooperative Patent Classification schema has also been incorporated into many of the patent search systems to greater or lesser degree. Espacenet has fully integrated a classification search type that allows a searcher to begin his search by keyword querying the CPC schema itself. The search algorithm retrieves a relevance-ranked list of possible classification codes, based on the keywords used. Once entry is made into the schema, the searcher can browse, read the definitions, scope notes and cross-references, and then select relevant classification codes to add to the patent search form. Using the form at http://worldwide.espacenet.com/classification is probably the most immediate way to begin a prior art search using classification.

The USPTO website also has the CPC schema (www.uspto.gov/web/patents/classification/), but has not yet integrated a top-level feature like Espacenet's classification search to PatFT or AppFT. The USPTO's site search box can be used to somewhat duplicate Espacenet's classification search by using the keyword pattern: CPC Scheme <keywords>. Similarly, if a searcher wishes to search only definitions of classification symbols, bypassing the schema itself, she can use CPC Definition <keywords>. This will limit site search results to only those from the CPC schema. The searcher then browses the schema, reads the definitions, scope notes and cross-references, and identifies relevant classifications. Once a thorough search of the CPC is conducted, and all relevant classification codes have been identified, the searcher goes to PatFT and AppFT and begins the search with the search field for Current CPC Classification.

The CPC schema is identical on all three of the aforementioned sites (CPC's website, Espacenet, and the USPTO's website); updates are synchronized and there should never be any question as to whether one is more current than the others. However, schema search results may differ between Espacenet and the UPSTO site because they employ different algorithms to retrieve the most relevant classification results.

Both PubEAST and PubWEST do include integrated classification tools, including an index, definitions, and cross references. Using PubEAST, one may conduct a classification search in a similar manner as in Espacenet.

US Patent Classification (USPC) has been discontinued as of January 2015, and is no longer used to classify utility patent documents. The entire backfile of US utility patents has been retrospectively reclassified using CPC, so searching with this new system can retrieve even the oldest documents. The USPC has been frozen and is no longer under development, but is still available for the time being, and is still used for classifying plant and design patents in the United States. Since the pre-2015 backfile of patent documents are classed with USPC, a supplemental search using USPC may be valuable to searchers. The USPC can be browsed in its frozen state at the same URL given for the USPTO's CPC tools, www.uspto.gov/web/patents/classification/.

At the same URL can be found the US Patent Classification (USPC) to IPC concordance, and, while no concordance exists either from or to CPC, a tool to identify the most statistically relevant mapping from USPC to CPC is there. The mapping tool uses a relevancy algorithm to help the user find similar CPC classification symbols based on words in a USPC symbol's definition. For design patents, the USPTO provides the USPC to Locarno Concordance. Locarno is the classification system used by WIPO to organize industrial design registrations which are similar to US design patents.

The Manual of Classification (www.uspto.gov/web/patents/classification/selectnum withtitle.htm), lists the class numbers and descriptive titles of the US patent classes, including design classes. There is also an index to the Manual, the Index to the US Classification System—an alphabetical listing of subject headings referring to specific classes of the classification system found at www.uspto.gov/web/patents/classification/uspcindex/indextouspc.htm.

International Patent Classification (IPC, www.wipo.int/classifications/ipc/en/) is WIPO's system for organizing PCT filings and is the foundation for CPC. IPC is quite general with about 72,000 classification symbols, where CPC is very granular with about 260,000 (EPO & USPTO, 2015; WIPO, 2015a) In contrast, the USPC had about 150,000 codes at its discontinuance. CPC uses the entire IPC schema as a framework, adding additional groups and subgroups with more descriptive definitions.

File Wrappers and Public PAIR

The file wrapper—sometimes called case file, prosecution history, or simply application files—of a patent application is the patent office's official record for the application. A file wrapper is the folder (virtual or literal) into which documents related to a particular patent application are collected and preserved; it contains the complete record of a patent's prosecution—the process of drafting, filing, and negotiating with the USPTO for the grant of a patent—from the initial application to the notice of allowance, or the final notice of disallowance. Some of the most interesting documents found in the file wrappers are the correspondence and office actions that take place between the patent office and the applicant. The file wrapper also includes all related post-grant files, such as maintenance events and changes in legal status.

File wrappers are made public when the patent application is published—up to 18 months after earliest filing date—or when a patent is granted, whichever is first. Since pending applications were not published prior to March 2001, only file wrappers for granted patents are available prior to that date. File wrappers can be found in a number of places, based on their filing date.

Public PAIR (Patent Application Information Retrieval, http://portal.uspto.gov/pair/PublicPair), is used to retrieve granted and pending published application data, transaction history, information about the agent or attorney prosecuting the application, and assignment data. File wrappers are available for most applications published since mid-2003 and are accessed by selecting the Image File Wrapper (IFW) tab in Public PAIR, as shown in figure 17.4. If the wrapper of interest is not included in Public PAIR, a print copy may be requested using an embedded widget. The IFW contents are PDF files that can be downloaded and printed.

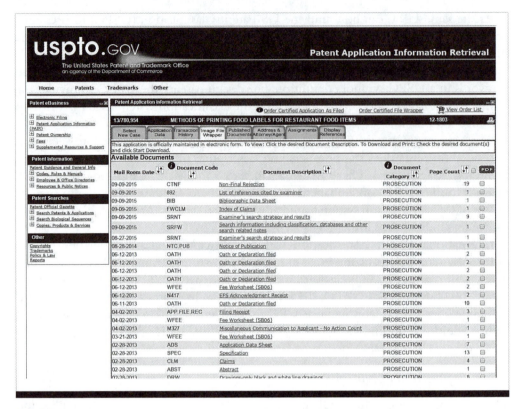

FIGURE 17.4
Image File Wrapper for Application Number 13/780,954, Methods of Printing Food Labels for Restaurant Food Items

The USPTO keeps legal custody of physical file wrappers for 40 years and then transfers custody of those records to the National Archives and Records Administration (NARA, discussed in detail in chapter 18) in College Park, MD. Copies of any file wrapper less than 40 years old and for a patent that was granted but is not available in Public PAIR may be requested for a fee from the USPTO's Public Records Division at http://ebiz1.uspto .gov/oems25p/index.html. On-site access to application files is available at the USPTO's File Inspection Unit located in Randolph Square in Shirlington, VA. Files are stored in off-site repositories, so calling ahead is advised; the telephone number is (703) 756–1100.

NARA has patent application files older than 40 years and back to 1836. All USPTO records at NARA are under Record Group 241. The archived contents are listed at www.archives.gov/research/guide-fed-records/groups/241.html. All requestors are asked to contact the main reference desk, either online at www.archives.gov/research/ or at 1–866–272–6272 to request copies of archived applications and file wrappers.

Official Gazette: Patents

The *Official Gazette of the United States Patent and Trademark Office: Patents,* published since 1872, contains announcements of the patents issued each week, and weekly patent office notices that include certificates of correction, disclaimers, and reissue patents, among others. It can be used to find basic information such as inventor, title, and a short abstract and representative drawing for each patent.

The *Official Gazette* originally contained notices for both patents and trademarks, but was split into two separate publications in July 1971. The *Official Gazette for Patents* ceased print publication in 2002 but continues electronically every Tuesday as the Electronic Official Gazette for Patents (eOG:P) at www.uspto.gov/learning-and-resources/official-gazette/official-gazette-patents. The most recent 52 issues of the Official Gazette: Patents are available there and may be searched by keyword or browsed by geographic origin of the inventor, inventor or assignee name, or classification code. For each notice, a link to the full-text record in PatFT is provided. For patent gazettes older than 52 weeks, but published since 1995, only the notices portion is available on the USPTO's website, at www.uspto.gov/learning-and-resources/official-gazette. However, patent gazettes in their entirety can still be downloaded from the Reed Technology's archive at patents.reedtech.com/pgog.php.

Older Official Gazettes can also be found at most PTRCs and some Federal Depository Libraries (FDLs) on optical discs 1872–2011, and a mixed collection of microfiche and microfilm, 1872–2002. There is also an annual index to the *Official Gazette* provided to FDLs under SuDocs number C 2.5.

Assignments

An assignee is the person or organization to which a patent grant is legally transferred. The Assignment Search database, at http://assignment.uspto.gov, contains all recorded patent assignment information back to August 1980. The data is updated weekly in PatFT, AppFT, and other USPTO search products. These databases reflect the most current assignee data that the USPTO has on record.

Keeping assignment data up-to-date is the responsibility of the assignor and the assignee whenever an assignment transaction takes place. It is considered best practice for assignees to keep the public record up-to-date, but there is no law that says they must do so. When relevant information is given to the USPTO to be recorded in the USPTO's assignment database, the USPTO simply puts the information on the public record and does not verify the validity of the information. Recordation is a ministerial function—the USPTO neither makes a determination of the legality of the transaction nor the right of the submitting party to take the action.

To further complicate matters, entity names are neither normalized nor spell-checked; to retrieve all records for a given assignee, multiple searches may be necessary, and if any assignments were misspelled, those would likely be missed in the search. Note that the assignee indicated on the actual patent document is often not the patent's current assignee of record, as shown in figure 17.5.

Patent Litigation and Case Law

There are various types of legal proceedings surrounding patents. These range from infringement litigation handled by federal courts to other proceedings like pre-grant

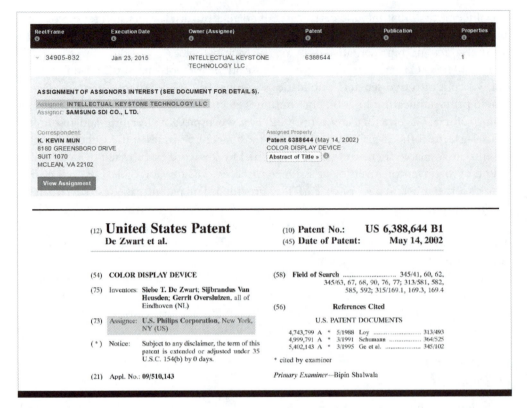

FIGURE 17.5

Detail Comparing the Assignee on the Original Patent Document to the Assignee-of-Record in the USPTO's Assignments Database

and post-grant interferences. Chapter 7, Case Law and the Judicial Branch, applies to all patent litigation cases involving two parties where a patent has been issued (i.e., it's not still pending). Since patent law is federal law, cases involving patent infringement begin in one of the US District Courts. Appeals to these cases are handled at the US Court of Appeals for the Federal Circuit in Washington, DC, circumventing the regional federal appeals courts. If further appeal is sought by either party, a petition for writ of certiorari is submitted to the Supreme Court, who may or may not hear the case (Harris, 2015). For locating dockets and briefs from infringement cases, chapter 7 is also informative.

Pre-grant oppositions and post-grant interferences are also types of patent disputes, but these cases are heard directly by the Patent Trial and Appeal Board (PTAB). Appeals that arise from PTAB decisions are heard by the US Court of Appeals for the Federal Circuit. (As the name implies, the Patent Trial and Appeals Board does also preside over appeals; but here *appeals* refers to something else: appeals made by applicants over adverse decisions of examiners in patent applications and reexamination proceedings, not appeals of decisions made by lower courts.)

Traditionally, oppositions and interferences could only be filed by parties directly affected by a patent allowance (i.e., the potential plaintiff of a patent case), but with the enactment of the America Invents Act of 2011, an interference may now be initiated by any third-party who finds a claim in any pending application or granted patent that he has reason to believe can be invalidated. This principle is called inter partes review—essentially, the public has been invited to submit prior art to the USPTO that may invalidate patents or prevent them from being issued to begin with. It is hoped that this process will increase the quality of patents that are issued. Interferences and oppositions before PTAB will not be found in the usual places as outlined in chapter 7. Instead, PTAB offers its own sources for finding information on these proceedings.

The Patent Review Processing System (PRPS, https://ptabtrials.uspto.gov/) is where information on pending and concluded PTAB proceedings are located. Case histories can be searched by case number, patent number and/or application number, and can be filtered by party name and filing date. Additionally, PTAB offers a portal for both filing and looking up interferences, located at https://acts.uspto.gov/ifiling/. Interferences can be looked up by interference number, patent number, application number, or inventor's name. Lastly, PTAB Decisions (www.uspto.gov/patents-application-process/patent-trial-and-appeal-board/decisions) lists all of PTAB's final decisions, including separate lists of those decisions considered precedential opinions and informative opinions.

In addition to PTAB's resources, the USPTO has another page of patent litigation resources at www.uspto.gov/patents-maintaining-patent/patent-litigation/resources, listing third-party services for finding basic information about patent cases and the parties involved in them. Even though these third-party resources are commercial services, each of them offer a minimal tier of free case information. At the time of this writing, all but one of these services require setting up a free account. Patexia seems to be the only one that doesn't require a user log-in, and it provides quite a bit of free information on patent case histories, comparable to what might be found in a LexisNexis search. It is unknown at this time how comprehensive Patexia or the other commercial products are in comparison with LexisNexis, and it's advised that researchers use the latter if access is available. One significant advantage to using LexisNexis is its support of *Shepard's Citations.* To look up all available court documents on a specific patent, irrespective of the parties involved, one simply needs to type in the magic keyword patno followed by the target patent number into the Shepard's search interface.

For applications published since 2003, all documents issued by PTAB are also added to their respective image file wrappers in Public PAIR. Patent interference case files for historical patent cases are available from NARA in record group 241.

Historical Research

Conducting historical research presents a whole new set of problems from what has been covered thus far. Historians, anthropologists, and genealogists—just to name a few—often need to delve into the murky backfile of the patent literature to find documents for their research. As already mentioned, pre-1976 patents are not searchable by full-text without the use of Google's imperfect OCR'd full-text; and even then, all the problems associated with searching by full-text ring true. It's impossible to find all relevant documents and limit irrelevant documents without a thorough classification search. Fortunately, the entire backfile of US patents has been classified with Cooperative Patent

Classification, and the frozen USPC is still available for additional discovery. Additionally, there are number of finding aides to turn to for assistance.

X patents, also called name and date patents, were the unnumbered patents issued prior to the 1836 fire that destroyed the patent office, along with all the records stored there. Many of the lost patents have been recovered by making new copies from originals provided by the patentees and their heirs. Whenever an X patent is discovered, it is logged, given a number (beginning with the letter X), and processed for inclusion in the various search systems. New copies are made to keep on file at the patent office, and the originals returned to their owners. Notice of the recovered document is included in the weekly Gazette. *Journal of the Franklin Institute,* beginning 1826, also contains information on restored patents.

Subject-matter index of patents for inventions issued by the United States Patent office from 1790 to 1873, inclusive, compiled by M.D. Leggett in 1874 and published by the Government Printing Office, can be found in many libraries, and also scanned pages found in various places online. The *Subject-matter index* provides patent number, date of registration, inventor, and inventor residence. For newer indexes, see the *Index of Patents Issued from the United States Patent and Trademark Office* (General Index of the *Official Gazette*) and *Annual Report of the Commissioner of Patents,* below.

Index of Patents Issued from the United States Patent and Trademark Office includes both a subject index and list of patentees, along with their places of residence. They provide the patent number, registration date, and the volume and page number where it can be located in the *Official Gazette*; these are the most effective methods for starting an investigation of an older patent or inventor. The subject index is arranged by US classification and then alphabetical by subject matter. These volumes once formed the basis for inventor name searching but it ceased publication in paper in 2002. With the ability to search inventor names online back to 1920 in the USPTO's PubWEST, PubEAST, search systems, and the cumulative index of patents included on CASSIS, only the paper indexes for years prior to 1920 are retained by most PTRCs. Some Federal Depository Libraries also retain the indexes under SuDocs C 21.5/2.

Annual Report of the Commissioner of Patents (1837–1999) is the annual fiscal year report of the USPTO. It includes expenditures for restoration of records, models and drawings, and annual grants by state. Note that prior to 1913, the *Annual Report* was synonymous with the aforementioned *Index of Patents.* In 1913 they were divided into two separate volumes. Unlike the *Index of Patents,* the paper reports from 1920 and later are retained by PTRCs. In 2000, this title became *Performance and Accountability Report.* Reports from 1993 to present are available on the USPTO website (www.uspto.gov/about-us/performance-and-planning/uspto-annual-reports). These reports contain some useful statistical data, for example, grants by state or grants by class. Annual Reports back to 1837 are also available in the US *Congressional Serial Set* that can typically be found at Federal Depository Libraries.

Several other finding aids are available in NARA Group 241. Some examples include

- Additional Improvement Patents (1836–1861)
- Patent Interference Case Files (1839–1900) includes general correspondence 1836–1868, case files for patent rights extensions, 1836–1875 and patent application files 1837–1918

- Patent Drawings, 1791–1877 is a collection of 320 rolls of microfilm in five parts
- List of Patents for Inventions & Designs 1790–1847, published at the direction of commissioner Edmond Burke

Last, but not least, the Patent and Trademark Resource Center Association (PTRCA) website lists a wide variety of historical, regional, and specialized databases and other finding aids on its website at http://ptrca.org/history.

Trademarks

Trademarks inhabit a simpler universe than patents; there are fewer types of documents, fewer places to find information about them, and, prosecution from application to registration is more standardized and straightforward.

Trademark Registration Certificates and Applications

As mentioned in the introduction to this chapter, federal trademark registration is optional. Where the USPTO's patents collection is comprised of a near-complete record of all inventions ever patented in the United States, their trademarks collection is but a subset of an unknown larger collection of unregistered marks. The basic trademark document is referred to as its registration certificate, and as with patents, applications for trademark registration certificates begin with the trademark application. Both registration certificates and their applications are publicly available.

Trademarks do not have equivalents to defensive publications or statutory invention registrations; likewise they do not have equivalents of certificates of correction, disclaimers, or reissue patents.

Information Sources for Trademarks
Trademark Electronic Search System (TESS)

TESS, found at www.uspto.gov/trademarks-application-process/search-trademark -database, includes bibliographic records for all active (live) registered and pending federal trademarks, plus nearly all abandoned (dead) registrations. (Roughly 20,000 dead marks, predating modern registration and archiving standards, were never made available in TESS. These missing marks are available at many PTRCs on the discontinued CASSIS optical discs.) TESS offers several options for searching, including a unique Design Code search for finding marks according to their graphical elements. The Design Search Code Manual can be found at http://tess2.uspto.gov/tmdb/dscm/ index.htm. TESS supports many advanced search modifiers (i.e., left, right, and middle truncation, proximity, etc.), allowing users to employ pattern matching techniques that may help identify confusingly similar marks. A librarian at a PTRC may be better suited for design code searching and pattern matching.

Trademark Status & Document Retrieval (TSDR)

TESS is a bibliographic database, but each record in TESS links directly to its application files in the TSDR system located at http://tsdr.uspto.gov/. Here are found the complete electronic records for trademark filings, images of original registration certificates, and other prosecution documents. Applicants may also retrieve status information about their pending trademarks. In addition to linking from TESS, TSDR may be searched by simply entering a valid trademark serial number or registration number.

Official Gazette of the United States Patent and Trademark Office: Trademarks

The *Official Gazette for Trademarks* provides notices of canceled, renewed and newly registered trademarks, and an index of registrants. The *Official Gazette* ceased paper publication in 2012 and has been published on Tuesdays via the USPTO website since 2001. Issues were also distributed to PTRCs on optical discs from July 2, 2002, to December 27, 2011, and are still retained by many PTRC libraries. Complete backfiles on microforms (fiche and/or film) from 1872–2002 are also available at most PTRCs and many FDLs.

The gazette also allows browsing or searching through the bibliographic information and drawings of trademarks published for opposition each week. The most recent 52 issues are available online at www.uspto.gov/learning-and-resources/official-gazette/trademark-official-gazette-tmog and are available at the PTRCs.

Gazettes that are older than 52 weeks, but published since 2002, can still be downloaded in their entirety at www.uspto.gov/learning-and-resources/official-gazette/trademarks/trademark-official-gazette-tmog-archived-editions. For 1995 and later, the Notices portions can be downloaded at www.uspto.gov/learning-and-resources/official-gazette.

Prior to 1995 a consolidated listing of important notices from both the *Official Gazette* and the *Federal Register* in paper is available in either the first or second weekly issue of the *Official Gazette* for January. The consolidated listing shows notices in effect from July 1, 1964, through December of the previous year. These are held at Federal Depository Libraries and PTRC libraries. These are also excerpted and collected at www.uspto.gov/trademark/trademark-updates-and-announcements/trademark-notices-and-comments.

Trademark Assignment Query Menu

As with patents, the assignee indicated on the original registration certificate may not be accurate. Assignees may be searched or assigned using Trademark Assignment Query Menu at http://assignments.uspto.gov/assignments/q?db=tm. Records can be retrieved by serial or registration number, assignor or assignee, or applicant or registrant. TESS and TSDR will reflect the most current assignee that the USPTO has on record. This system contains all recorded trademark assignment information from 1955. Trademark assignments recorded prior to 1955 are maintained at NARA.

State TMs

The USPTO is the granting authority for federal trademark registration certificates in the United States; but because of the time and expense involved, trademark owners will often forgo federal trademark registration if they are not engaged in, or plan to be engaged in, interstate commerce. For these mark holders, many states have their own systems for registering trademarks, and some of them offer online databases for searching. There is no comprehensive listing of state databases; researchers are advised to begin their enquiries on the Secretary of State's website for the target state.

Trademark Litigation and Case Law

The Trademark Trial and Appeal Board (TTAB) is the administrative tribunal responsible for conducting hearings and issuing final decisions on the merits of reexamination appeals, oppositions to, and cancellations of registrations. TTAB is limited to these issues and will not hear cases on unfair competition, criminal conduct, copyrights, or antitrust statutes, even when trademarks are central to them. TTAB doesn't grant damages, issue injunctions, or award costs or fees, but can be much faster and less costly than prosecuting trademark disputes in US District Courts.

TTAB trials are not traditional court trials, but rather trials on paper. Proceedings are prosecuted by submission by the involved parties of documents to TTAB, and follow a strict procedure and time line. TTAB decisions are made by a panel of three administrative judges; a judge who disagrees with a decision may write a dissenting opinion, and a judge who agrees with a decision but doesn't agree with the reasoning behind it may write a concurring opinion. Because the entirety of the proceedings are written, documentation is readily available, as are decisions and dissenting and concurring opinions. All of this can be found in TTABVUE, the Trademark Trial and Appeal Board Inquiry System, at http://ttabvue.uspto.gov/ttabvue/. Proceedings may be searched by proceeding number, by application or registration number, or by party. Pending proceedings can be tracked in real-time. TTAB decisions are also published in the United States Patent Quarterly and in the Official Gazette (Trademarks). TTAB also publishes its Final Decisions at http://e-foia.uspto.gov/Foia/TTABReadingRoom.jsp.

Federal trademark disputes that lie outside of TTAB's purview generally begin federal district courts. Appeals to TTAB decisions are filed in federal circuit courts, but a plaintiff may also begin a new trial from scratch through federal district courts. Chapter 7 of this book discusses how to find proceedings from these courts.

There are three important reference sources for researchers and practitioners wishing to learn more about US trademark law. First, *the Trademark Trial and Appeal Board Manual of Procedure* (TTAB Manual) provides practitioners with basic information generally useful for litigating cases before the Trademark Trial and Appeal Board. It can be found at http://tbmp.uspto.gov/RDMS/detail/manual/TBMP/current/tbmpd1e2.xml. Second, *U.S. Trademark Law: Rules of Practice & Federal Statute* includes a the complete 37 CFR Part 2- Rules of Practice in Trademark Cases, the text of the Trademark Act of 1946, as amended, and related statutory sections. It also lists proposed rules and recent final rules affecting trademark law. It can be found at www.uspto.gov/trademark/laws-regulations. Third, the *Trademark Manual of Examining Procedure* (TMEP) provides the practices and procedures relative to prosecution of applications to register marks in the United States. The *Manual* contains guidelines and materials in the nature of information and interpretation, and outlines the procedures that examining attorneys are required or authorized to follow in the examination of trademark applications. The *Manual* is searchable by keyword, either across the full text, or across the subject index, at http://tmep.uspto.gov/RDMS/detail/manual/TMEP/current/d1e2.xml.

Conclusion

This corpus of patent documents is the largest collection of technical information in the world. To date, there are more than 9 million granted patents and an estimated 1.25 million patent applications pending in the United States; worldwide, there are more than 90 million patent documents (granted and pending) combined. Patents and patent applications include problem-solving information, cutting-edge research, and technical expertise that can't be found anyplace else. They are considered primary sources that are often consulted by researchers in the sciences and engineering, right along with other scholarly literature. The patent literature is also considered to be an authoritative record of the history of technology and is used by historians, genealogists, sociologists, and other researchers who wish to learn more about how society has used technology to solve problems of the past.

The corpus of trademarks, while perhaps not as enthralling at patents, represents a vast collection of business and products information that can't be found anywhere else. There are currently around two million active trademarks in the United States, with several million more dead marks searchable in TESS. Trademark registrations are primary sources with uses in many areas, including history, design, business and more.

For these reasons, the resources outlined in this chapter should be included in the researcher's toolbox for just about any subject. Fortunately, the USPTO and other organizations find them important enough to make them publicly accessible, and even the older information is becoming easier to access.

Exercises

Patents

1. Use PatFT to find out what Tabitha King invented. What is the patent number? What is its Current CPC Class code?
2. Use the Classification Search feature of Espacenet to identify one Cooperative Patent Classification group relevant to dog leashes. Which of its subgroups is most suited for a novel locking mechanism on a retractable leash? Still using

Espacenet, approximately how many patents and patent applications (combined) are classified in this subgroup?

3. Use AppFT to find pending patent applications from inventors in your city or town. What is the application number for the most recent application? What is the publication number?

4. Use Public PAIR to find the application files of patent application number 12/968683. Who was the examiner of this application? What is the status of the application? Which claims were initially rejected in the Non-Final Rejection dated January 21, 2014?

5. Use the USPTO's Assignment Search database to identify the assignee records for patent number 8929911. How many times has this patent been reassigned? Who was the original assignee? Who is the current assignee?

6. Use PRPS to look up information about patent application number 09/744033 (note that you must remove the / for this to work). In the case involving Samsung Electronics (the petitioner) and B. E. Technology (the patent owner), which party was PTAB's final decision in favor of, and why? Who were the presiding administrative judges?

Trademarks

1. Use TESS structured search to find live trademark registrations in your town or city. How many are there? For the most recent registration (at the top of the list), who is the owner? What goods and services are associated with this mark?

2. Use the Design Search Code Manual and TESS structured search to find a trademark that depicts an igloo. What design code did you use? How many live marks include depictions of igloos?

3. Use TESS to find the registration for serial number 77178417. What is the status of this trademark? From within the TESS record, click the TSDR button and look at the documents tab. Why was this trademark abandoned?

4. Use TTABVUE to find TTAB proceedings on registration number 86282348 filed by Windsor Quality Food Company. What is the case number? What is the status of the case? What is the plaintiff's objection to the trademark in this case?

Sources Mentioned in This Chapter

Legislation

American Inventors Protection Act of 1999 (Title IV of the Consolidated Fiscal Year 2000 Appropriations), P.L. 106–113, 113 Stat. 1501.

Leahy-Smith America Invents Act of 2011, P.L. 112–29, 125 Stat. 284.

Trademark Act of 1946, P.L. 79–489, 60 Stat. 427.

US Patent & Trademark Office Sources

Sources listed in this section do not duplicate the references that follow.

Annual Report of the Commissioner of Patents (1837–1999); included in the Serial Set 1837–1925; 1993–present at www.uspto.gov/about-us/performance-and-planning/uspto-annual-reports.

Archive of, www.uspto.gov/learning-and-resources/official-gazette/trademarks/trademark-official-gazette-tmog-archived-editions.

Assignment Search, http://assignment.uspto.gov.

CASSIS (optical discs, through 2011) with complete backfiles (available only at PTRCs).

Certificates of Correction, www.uspto.gov/patents-application-process/patent-search/authority-files/certificates-correction.

CPC (Cooperative Patent Classification) schema, www.uspto.gov/web/patents/classification/.

Final Decisions, http://e-foia.uspto.gov/Foia/TTABReadingRoom.jsp.

Index of Patents Issued from the United States Patent and Trademark Office (General Index of the *Official Gazette*).

Interferences Portal (ACTS), https://acts.uspto.gov/ifiling/.

Manual of (US) Classification, www.uspto.gov/web/patents/classification/selectnumwithtitle.htm.

Manual of Patent Examining Procedure (MPEP), www.uspto.gov/mpep/.

Manual of Procedure, http://tbmp.uspto.gov/RDMS/detail/manual/TBMP/current/tbmpd1e2.xml.

News and notices, www.uspto.gov/trademark/trademark-updates-and-announcements/trademark-notices-and-comments.

Notices only, www.uspto.gov/learning-and-resources/official-gazette.

Official Gazette Notices Search: 1995–Present, www.uspto.gov/learning-and-resources/official-gazette.

Official Gazette: Patents archive, Reed Technology, (July 2, 2002–present) http://patents.reedtech.com/pgog.php.

Official Gazette of the United States Patent and Trademark Office: Patents Electronic Official Gazette for Patents (eOG:P), www.uspto.gov/learning-and-resources/official-gazette/official-gazette-patents.

Patent and Trademark Resource Centers (PTRCs), www.uspto.gov/learning-and-resources/support-centers/patent-and-trademark-resource-centers-ptrcs.

Patent litigation resources, www.uspto.gov/patents-maintaining-patent/patent-litigation/resources.

Patent Trial & Appeals Board (PTAB), www.uspto.gov/patents-application-process/patent-trial-and-appeal-board-0.html.

Patent Trial & Appeals Board, Decisions, www.uspto.gov/patents-application-process/patent-trial-and-appeal-board/decisions.

Patent Review Processing System (PRPS), https://ptabtrials.uspto.gov.

PatFT and AppFT, http://patft.uspto.gov.

Performance and Accountability Reports, www.uspto.gov/about-us/performance-and-planning/uspto-annual-reports.

PubEAST (available only at PTRCs).

PubWEST (available only at PTRCs).

Public PAIR (Patent Application Information Retrieval), http://portal.uspto.gov/pair/PublicPair.

Public Records Division, http://ebiz1.uspto.gov/oems25p/index.html.

Subject-matter index of patents for inventions issued by the United States Patent office from 1790 to 1873, inclusive, http://quod.lib.umich.edu/cgi/t/text/text-idx?c=moa;idno=AGL4739.0001.001.

Trademark Assignment Query Menu, http://assignments.uspto.gov/assignments/q?db=tm.

Trademark Design Search Code Manual, http://tess2.uspto.gov/tmdb/dscm/index.htm.

Trademark Electronic Search System (TESS), www.uspto.gov/trademarks-application-process/search-trademark-database.

Trademark Law: Rules of Practice & Federal Statute, www.uspto.gov/trademark/laws-regulations.

Trademark Manual of Examining Procedure (TMEP), http://tmep.uspto.gov/RDMS/detail/manual/TMEP/current/d1e2.xml.

Trademark Official Gazette, www.uspto.gov/learning-and-resources/official-gazette/trademark-official-gazette-tmog.

Trademark Status & Document Retrieval (TSDR), http://tsdr.uspto.gov.

Trademark Trial and Appeal Board, www.uspto.gov/trademarks-application-process/trademark-trial-and-appeal-board-ttab.

TTABVUE Inquiry System, http://ttabvue.uspto.gov/ttabvue/.

United States Patent and Trademark Office (USPTO), www.uspto.gov.

Other Sources

Sources listed in this section do not duplicate the references that follow.

Cooperative Patent Classification (CPC), www.cooperativepatentclassification.org/index.html.

Defensive Publications, www.defensivepublications.org.

Espacenet, http://worldwide.espacenet.com/advancedSearch.

Classification search, http://worldwide.espacenet.com/classification.

Federal Register, 1994-present, www.federalregister.gov or www.gpo.gov/fdsys/browse/collection.action?collectionCode=FR.

Google Patent Search, https://patents.google.com/.

Advanced, www.google.com/advanced_patent_search.

International Patent Classification (IPC), www.wipo.int/classifications/ipc/en/.

National Archives and Records Administration reference services, www.archives.gov/research/.

Record Group 241, www.archives.gov/research/guide-fed-records/groups/241.html.

Patent and Trademark Resource Center Association (PTRCA) list of historical, regional and specialized databases, http://ptrca.org/history.

Patentscope, https://patentscope.wipo.int/search/en/search.jsf.

Cross Lingual Expansion, https://patentscope.wipo.int/search/en/clir/clir.jsf.

Patexia, www.patexia.com/ip-research.

Zimmerman's Research Guide, https://law.lexisnexis.com/infopro/zimmermans/disp.aspx?z=1816.

References

European Patent Office. (2011). Global Patent Data Coverage. https://data.epo.org/data/data.html.

European Patent Office & United States Patent and Trademark Office. (2015, April 1). List of valid CPC symbols for the 2015.04 CPC Scheme. www.cooperativepatentclassification.org/cpc/interleaved/CPCvalidSymbolsList201504.csv.

Harris, William. (2015). "How Patent Infringement Works." *How Stuff Works.* http://science.howstuffworks.com/innovation/new-inventions/patent-infringement2.htm.

Open Forum Foundation. (2013). *The 20 Basics of Open Government.* http://basics.open4m.org/types-of-gov-info/.

World Intellectual Property Organization. (2013). PCT Applicant's Guide: PCT Contracting States. www.wipo.int/pct/guide/en/gdv011/annexes/annexa/ax_a.pdf.

World Intellectual Property Organization. (2015a). IPC Statistics. www.wipo.int/classifications/ipc/en/
ITsupport/Version20150101/transformations/stats.html.
World Intellectual Property Organization. (2015b). National Collections: Data Coverage. https://
patentscope.wipo.int/search/en/help/data_coverage.jsf.

CHAPTER 18

Historical and Archival Information

CASSANDRA HARTNETT

Introduction

As stewards of collections containing mostly the *published* record of government, librarians recognize those times when our users are really seeking another kind of government content: the inner workings of an agency or the papers of government figures. Primary sources are documentary evidence of an event or moment in time: actual accounts (letters, diaries, news articles, speeches, and more), photographs, artwork, and every manner of records in their original form. Understanding where to find, and how to think about, archival primary sources generated by the activities of the federal government is critical to providing reference and managing government documents collections for the long term. This chapter explores research possibilities using archives, museums, and two important laws: the Freedom of Information Act and the Privacy Act.

Archives, Museums, Libraries: Distinctions Are Fading

In our digital age, many have noted that cultural heritage institutions (see sidebar) are working less and less in isolation (Marty, 2010). Technology as an access tool for exhibits and collections has democratized and helped demystify archives, special collections, and museums—research destinations no longer the exclusive domain of academic scholars. In the pre-Internet era, even enthusiastic public library users were generally unaware of the archives and less well-known museums dotting their local region. The Web has afforded these institutions exposure in ways unimaginable two decades ago.

With their treasures more accessible to the general public via the Web, libraries, archives, and museums are pulling down other barriers for the benefit of their users and their collections. They are sharing resources (technical infrastructure, storage facilities, costs for traveling exhibits); partnering for grants; and venturing into collaborative policy development. Libraries, archives, and museums, especially those that charge no entrance fees, report an increase in patrons despite the economic downturn (American Library Association, 2015). This convergence, comparatively recent and very fluid, signals an increased readiness to look beyond individual repositories. Many archives and museums have developed outreach programs and customized curricula for teachers and middle or high school students, yet another way of revealing their collections. The convergence is good news for librarians, who should not hesitate to contact their colleagues working behind closed doors in archives and museums. For government documents librarians, collaboration and the art of intelligent referrals are not new. With more practice, librarians are starting to overcome the myths and preconceptions of noncirculating, tightly secured archival materials.

Archives

In considering the role of archives, one must start with basic assumptions. We live with the hope that institutions, including governments, keep good records, and that these records are eventually archived and kept accessible for future researchers and historians. As with the preservation of historical artifacts from any era, there is wide variation in practice and circumstances; sometimes records are lost or irrevocably damaged. In the case of the federal government, the agencies themselves are responsible for keeping good records, but their records are (after a time, and on very specific schedules and according to very specific rules) destroyed or transferred to the National Archives and Records Administration (NARA). If one considers an institution—such as one's workplace—one sees that many types of resources are generated as records of activities of the organization (calendars, committee reports, meeting minutes, photos, memos, video and audio recordings, personal notes, letters and e-mail, posters, announcements, and more); these will one day be winnowed down to just the most relevant representative examples. There are also legal, administrative files (personnel files, account statements, and transaction logs, etc.), referred to as administrative records; these will be retained at the agency while still in active use, then transferred to a records center for a certain number of years according to law, and ultimately disposed of—either sent to the archives or destroyed (see figure 18.1 for a records management example from the Department of State). The retaining, transferring, and disposing is not done haphazardly but is based on a records schedule, monitored by records managers within each agency. The idea is to keep only active

Cultural Heritage Organizations

What are cultural heritage organizations and why should libraries and archives work with them? The phrase *cultural heritage* refers to both the tangible components of a society (such as buildings and monuments) as well as intangibles (the dramatic arts, languages, traditional music, and informational, spiritual, and philosophical components) meaningful to a particular people's history and identity. Many institutions manage and preserve cultural heritage resources, including museums, antiquities departments, community cultural centers, and park services. Both government and nongovernmental organizations are involved with cultural heritage management and preservation, from the intergovernmental level—such as the United Nations Educational, Scientific, and Cultural Organization (UNESCO), which designates World Heritage sites—to the smallest local community group (Corbey, 2008).

U.S. Department of State Records Schedule

Chapter 21: Geographic Area Affairs Records

African Affairs-Office of the Assistant Secretary

A-21-010-01a	**Assistant Secretary Files**
Description:	a. Chronological and Subject Files. Arranged partly in chronological order and partly by subject. Telegrams, memorandums, briefing papers and correspondence.
Disposition:	Permanent. Retire to RSC when 3 years old. Transfer to WNRC when 5 years old. Transfer to the National Archives when 30 years old in 5-year blocks.
DispAuthNo:	N1-059-93-18, item 1a Date Edited: 4/1/1999

A-21-010-01b	**Assistant Secretary Files**
Description:	b. Calendar - Appointment Book. Listing of appointments and meetings. No substantive information recorded.
Disposition:	Destroy when no longer needed.
DispAuthNo:	N1-059-93-18, item 1b Date Edited: 4/1/1999

A-21-010-02	**Deputy Assistant Secretaries Files - Arranged both chronologically and by subject**
Description:	Telegrams, memorandums, press releases, copies of speeches, correspondence and other records documenting their activities.
Disposition:	Block files by year. Destroy when 3 years old.
DispAuthNo:	N1-059-93-18, item 2 Date Edited: 4/1/1999

A-21-010-03a	**Staff Assistants Files**
Description:	a. Subject Files. Copies of White House readings, reports, inspection reports, studies, briefing material, Special caption documents, and other documentation needing to be retained for operational purposes.
Disposition:	Block by year. Destroy when one year old.
DispAuthNo:	N1-059-93-18, item 3a Date Edited: 4/1/1999

FIGURE 18.1

The *U.S. Department of State Records Manual* Lists Retention and Disposition Practices for Different Types of Files. *Source: Department of State, 2014.*

records at the agency, whether physical or virtual, and place other materials in a Federal Records Center (FRC) for a predetermined number of years. A number of such centers are maintained by NARA throughout the country, a low-cost, organized alternative to storage at the agency. The federal records management system is described in detail in the "Records Managers" portal at www.archives.gov/records-mgmt/. Further examples of records retention guidance pages at federal agencies include "What Is a Records Schedule?" from the EPA (www.epa.gov/records/what/quest6.htm) and "Geology Discipline Research Records Schedule" from the US Geological Survey (www.usgs.gov/usgs-manual/schedule/432–1-s5/gd.html).

How Archives Differ from Libraries

One easy-to-see difference between government information libraries and archives is that archives tend to be closed-stack collections, allowing visitors access to only a public reading room. In an out-of-sight stack area, print-on-paper materials are housed in acid-free folders and archival boxes, sometimes referred to by the trade name of a predominant manufacturer: Hollinger Metal Edge boxes or simply Hollinger boxes. Electronic media, photographs, and all other imaginable artifacts are stored with care according to preservation standards for that medium. Archivists, a high number of whom are also librarians, often see access and long-term preservation as competing first principles. The more use, the more wear and tear on materials, the greater chance of theft, loss, or damage. An archivist's challenge is to keep collections intact for as many researchers and for as many years as possible. The idea of permanence is no longer part of the archival vocabulary. Unlike most libraries, archives rely heavily on deeds of gift, legal contracts with donors of collections, which may come with restrictions to access or specific preservation requirements. This is less of a concern for governmental archives, as materials tend to be transferred into them based on a regular release schedule. A notable exception: political archives (see later in this chapter), that may contain large amounts of privately donated material. With the archival mission to preserve the historical record, it is important to understand that archives, even government archives, do not and cannot collect everything. Collecting policies are usually made transparent on repository websites. As in libraries, weeding of collections is an accepted archival practice determined by institutional criteria. For more information on specific practices in the government sphere, including the tremendous challenges of managing electronic records, consult the National Association of Government Archives and Records Administrators (NAGARA, www.nagara.org), whose members are practitioners at the local, state, and federal levels.

From a user's point of view, archives and libraries represent a very different experience. Today's users are accustomed to remote digital access to library resources. Using archives (with the obvious exception of purely digital archives) means traveling to a facility with limited hours of operation, requiring a level of preplanning and effort probably unfamiliar to newer researchers. Completely digitized online archival collections are very rare and tangible-to-digitized ratios are high: NARA (as one example), with over 18 billion pages of documents, reported in 2014 that 2 billion of its documents were available digitally (National Archives and Records Administration, 2014). Personal visits to a repository remain the order of the day. Microforms librarian Glenda J. Pearson used the term "captive researchers" to describe individuals whose research compels them to visit a specific facility, such as those with microforms or archives (1988: 288). The benefit of the captive research environment is that it forces the user into an interaction, however minor, with the specialist on hand who may be able to offer significant assistance.

Some of the best advice librarians can give their users is to make contact with an archive before going there for research, confirm that relevant material is available (order it from storage if need be), and prepare as much as possible before making the trip. Archivists Linda Whitaker and Michael Lotstein describe the differences between archives/ special collections and libraries.

> Archives are distinguished from libraries by their rare, unique, original,
> unpublished materials that require security measures such as signing in,
> showing identification, removing back packs, prohibiting food and bever-
> ages, and viewing items under supervision in a reading room. Nothing is
> allowed to be checked out and most archives do not participate in inter-
> library loans. How this material is described bears no resemblance to the
> standard, publication format found in library catalogs. The archives call
> numbers are unique to the repository and reflect many items aggregated
> together. The descriptions are variable and dependent on an archivist to cre-
> ate them. Archives have rituals, customs and a language all their own. If you
> cannot speak the language, you cannot ask the right questions. Understand-
> ing the rules of engagement and the basic differences between a library
> and an archive are fundamental to navigating the system. (Whitaker and
> Lotstein, 2012)

Print-on-paper archives tend to be organized by numbered record group (RG numbers), within which are numbered boxes containing folders of materials. Keeping materials grouped by source and preserving original order are of utmost importance. How are
materials cataloged? Just as Machine Readable Cataloging (MARC) became standard
online encoding of bibliographic cataloging (using AACR and subsequent cataloging
rules), and Dublin Core set standards for metadata, encoded archival description, or EAD,
is today's standard online encoding for archival description, embraced most fully at large
academic institutions. When materials in archives are represented with online finding
guides developed using EAD (generally coded in XML or SGML) this ensures that either
humans or machines can read the guides. To learn more, consult the LC EAD page at
www.loc.gov/ead/eadabout.html or the Encoded Archival Description (EAD) Roundtable at www2.archivists.org/groups/encoded-archival-description-ead-roundtable/.

Online finding guides may also be linked to bibliographic records in library online
catalogs or WorldCat, a useful bridging of the archival and library worlds. Refining a
search by archival material as the format, or even combining a keyword search with the
term *papers,* is sometimes enough to locate such materials in a library catalog. A World-
Cat subject search on *subversive activities,* limited to archival materials, includes a record
for the papers of Elmer Charles Kistler, a Washington State veteran, labor union activist,
and Communist Party member, leading to an online finding aid at http://digital.lib
.washington.edu/findingaids/view?docId=KistlerElmer5347.xml.

Library users expect every individual article or book to be described in an online
catalog or database (piece-level holdings information); researchers using print-on–paper
or microform archives can expect only to see groups of materials described. In the Kistler papers, Box 1, File 29 contains "miscellaneous ephemera, correspondence, and clip-
pings"—one would need to open the folder to see exactly how many or what they are.

Digital archives have broken through this gap in expectations. With digital archives,
whether from the federal government (such as American Memory), the state government (such as the Washington State Digital Archives, www.digitalarchives.wa.gov), a local
city (such as Everett Public Library's Digital Collections, http://epls.org/nw-history/
digital-collections), or a commercial provider (ProQuest's History Vault collections),

there is a chance of being able to navigate down to the individual level, search or count individual items, all using simple search and retrieval techniques. A quality digital archive preserves archival arrangement through the ability to sort by folder or record group, while giving users the ability to search across collections and folders with the metadata and full text. The Digital Public Library of America (http://dp.la) tries to bring together in one user-friendly portal access to all digital library collections, including vast troves of archival material. It is a recommended starting point for those wishing to explore digital archives.

National Archives and Records Administration: A Pivotal Agency

Archives and the archival profession as we know them today had their beginnings with NARA. When the National Archives was founded in 1934 there was no archival profession in the United States. The Archives relied on historians and a small cadre of archivists trained in the small number of state archives that had been founded since the first state archives, in Alabama, in 1901. Within two years, led in large part by National Archives staff, the Society of American Archivists was founded in 1936. The growing number of archivists in the United States needed a common forum to develop both theory and practice for this new line of work. (Jimerson, 2005: 1)

NARA describes itself to the general public this way:

> The National Archives and Records Administration (NARA) is the nation's record keeper. Of all documents and materials created in the course of business conducted by the United States Federal government, only 1%–3% are so important for legal or historical reasons that they are kept by us forever. Those valuable records are preserved and are available to you, whether you want to see if they contain clues about your family's history, need to prove a veteran's military service, or are researching an historical topic that interests you. (National Archives and Records Administration, 2015a)

NARA works directly with agencies to ensure that the entire life cycle of federal record keeping is done according to legal requirements (think of a group of important memos and their creation, use, and disposition, remembering that relatively few—up to 3 percent—are actually transferred to the Archives). For these (hypothetical) memos or papers, if their disposition involves transfer to the Archives, the remainder of their life cycle at Archives includes arrangement and description, preservation, reference, and continuing use by the public (National Archives and Records Administration, 2015b). All of this activity takes place according to federal laws, many of which are codified in 44 U.S.C., and regulations (for details, see www.archives.gov/about/laws/).

NARA has two impressive research facilities in the Washington, DC area: the neoclassical National Archives Building (Archives 1) adjacent to the National Mall (a marble palace holding originals of the Constitution and Declaration of Independence), and the modern National Archives at College Park, Maryland (Archives 2) that opened in 1994. NARA has about 20 other facilities across the United States in locations as diverse as Long Island and Riverside, California—all with original material. These geographically dispersed collections contain records of federal agencies in their multistate areas (see sidebar) and can help users order reproductions of materials from other NARA facilities.

The NARA website makes the shifting world of massive federal archival content seem remarkably simple and straightforward. NARA staff members continually add finding aids and newly digitized content, providing users with more and more of an educated stab at what they might be likely to find deep in NARA's collections. On the splash page, a horizontal array of five photographic thumbnails grabs attention: Research Our Records, Veterans' Service Records, Teachers' Resources, Our Locations, and Shop Online. Research Our Records further subdivides into online and in-person research, and well-designed tutorials. Throughout much of archives.gov, the bottom navigation area contains a standard and very useful set of links to News and Social Media features and Research Guides, and further faceting by broad topic, type of research and type of researcher. Under Search Online, a standard reference work, the three-volume *Guide to Federal Records in the National Archives of the United States,* provides a master list of record groups. The resource has been converted into a simplified online format at www.archives.gov/research/guide-fed-records. Entries include historical notes on each agency or activity (such as inclusive dates) and brief descriptive notes (type and extent of records available).

The top link under Search Online is the National Archives Catalog (www.archives .gov/research/search/). Although a disclaimer points out that only a fraction of NARA's holdings are represented here, just searching the catalog and using its search help screens is an education. A search on mcaffrey AND photographs yielded dozens of results, including one for *Record Group 385: Records of the Naval Facilities Engineering Command, 1948–1999* that included Operation Safe Haven Photographs ca. 1994,

> a disassembled album of photographs documenting construction of housing for Cuban refugees at the Rodman Naval Station in Panama during Operation Safe Haven. The photographs show construction battalion personnel (Seabees) erecting tents and fencing and putting cots together at Navy Camp Number Three on Empire Range Six. Also pictured are volunteers, camp staff, the arrival of Cubans, refugees being greeted by General Barry McCaffrey, and recreational activities. (National Archives and Records Administration, 2015)

Under the Catalog search box, one finds information about a new public API to allow users to reuse content and contribute catalog data in powerful new ways.

If one were searching for materials from the Yokohama War Crimes Trials, as another example, either the *Guide to Federal Records* or the Archival Research Catalog (ARC) would be a logical starting place. A search in the *Guide* for the control word *yokohama* brings five results, each representing different record groups (RGs). The identical search in the ARC brings 1,505 results; refining the search to *yokohama & war crimes* reduces the results to a more manageable 35, including a cache of materials within RG 338: *Yokohama War Crimes Trials Case Dockets, compiled 1946–1949.* With the archival description for this item, the "Archived Copies" tab describes the exact physical extent of the material, where it is located (College Park, MD), and how users can order reproductions, with a link on how to obtain copies of records: www.archives.gov/research/order.

NARA departments specialize in still pictures (images like Lewis Hine's documentation of child labor, the National Parks photos of Ansel Adams, and much more—see figure 18.2); motion pictures, sound and video recordings; and cartographic and architectural records. NARA's Access to Archival Databases (http://aad.archives.gov/aad) allows direct searching of federally compiled records databases. Examples include databases like *Records for Passengers Who Arrived at the Port of New York During the Irish Famine . . . 1/12/1846–12/31/1851* (similar files exist for those arriving from Germany, Russia, and Italy) and *Records About Worker- Initiated Strikes and Employer-Initiated Lockouts . . . 1953–1981.*

NARA's leadership in historic preservation is noteworthy as well. NARA's preservation department creates guidelines and resources useful to any cultural heritage organization. Consult www.archives.gov/preservation/technical/ to learn about everything from solvents and peels used by conservators to digital imaging, electronic records storage, and preservation standards that inform national and international practice.

> **NARA Gems May Be Found Locally**
>
> The NARA facility in Seattle contains original records from federal agencies in Washington, Oregon, Idaho, and parts of Montana, with microfilm holdings from other areas. For example, the holdings from the Bureau of Prisons include over 100 years of records from Washington State's federal penitentiary (on remote McNeil Island), with such items as prisoner and staff publications, staff journals, expense records, inmate case files, and mug shots.
>
> *Source: Guide to Archival Holdings at NARA's Pacific Alaska Region (Seattle), www.archives.gov/pacific-alaska/seattle/holdings/rg-100–199.html#129.*

Political Archives

There are many different archives across the United States holding the papers of those who have served in national elective offices (see www.archives.gov/legislative/repository -collections). NARA administers the national system of presidential libraries, addressed in chapter 8. Congress has its own historians (the Senate Historical Office and US House of Representatives Office of the Historian), but what happens to the papers of former members of Congress once they leave office? The story is not entirely straightforward: consider the challenge of stewarding congressional material, the kinds of resources that start accumulating with the opening of every elected member's office. Congressional staffers trained in best practices of office and records management are essential. Both the secretary of the Senate and the clerk of the House are busy managing the records of Congress, including materials from committees and reports required to and from Congress. Members and their office staffs are supplied with the Records Management Manual for Members (Office of the Clerk, 2010).

1893-42. Puget Sound Navy Yard. 7 September 1942.
Miss Margaret A. Christenson making weld on keel of BDE 40.
Fire Watch Mrs. Ruth E. Hefta.

FIGURE 18.2
Women Welders during World War II, Washington State

In 2008, the passage of House Concurrent Resolution 110–307 was a tremendous leap forward, welcomed by congressional papers archivists, as it spells out the importance of members' papers, makes it clear that their maintenance and organization is every member's responsibility, and encourages members to "arrange for the deposit or donation of the Member's own noncurrent Congressional papers with a research institution that is properly equipped to care for them, and to make these papers available for educational purposes at a time the Member considers appropriate" (H. Con. Res. 110-307, 2008: 1). It is important to note that this resolution supports voluntary donations of papers. A member may retain his or her papers or donate them at will. Time will tell the effectiveness of this new law, but archivists are hopeful for this movement in the right direction.

So the answer to the question "Where do members' papers end up?" is actually the last item on the to-do lists of federal legislators as they leave office. Sometimes a member woos an institution, sometime an institution woos a member—but in either case, with few exceptions, the member or the repository must raise enough money to allow for the accessioning and processing of his or her papers. Congressional papers collections, especially those of senators, are notoriously large and difficult to process. Former

Speaker Thomas "Tip" O'Neill's papers are at Boston College, Senator Barry Goldwater's are at the Arizona Historical Foundation, and the late Senator Robert Byrd's (at his death, the longest-serving senator in US history) are at Shepherd University in Shepherdstown, West Virginia. For those members who do not designate a specific institution for their papers, their materials can go to NARA's Center for Legislative Archives (www.archives.gov/legislative/), which preserves members' materials as well as committee, caucus, and oversight records. Congressional materials stored here are generally opened to the public after 30 years, unless a member specifies an earlier waiting period. Two excellent guides are available for any librarian interested in legislative archives: *Managing Congressional Collections* (Miller, 2008) and *An American Political Archives Reader* (Paul et al., 2009), both published in conjunction with the Society of American Archivists.

Museums

The federal government is home to an array of museums, starting with 15 listed on USA.gov. The list is deceptively short, however, as both the Smithsonian Institution and the National Park Museums represent groupings of museums. The National Park Service's "Discover History" page is a reminder that our nation's history can be found in the almost 400 national parks as well as every American town, with sites ranging from the evidence of ancient civilizations, to US presidents' childhood homes, to battlefields, to civil rights memorials (National Park Service, 2015). The USA.gov portal also links to numerous state museums. Museum collections are one important means for scholars to supplement the resources they might find in a library or archive. Museums, notes Jennifer Trant,

> are most often subject-based collections of exceptional objects or specimens. For all but the most senior scholar, an encounter with a museum collection is a highly mediated experience. Unique artifacts are presented in an exhibition space, assembled according to a curatorial thesis and sequenced to support an argument or illustrate a theme. (Trant, 2009: 371)

Curators and other museum professionals collect not only artifacts but information resources. Most museums, especially the larger ones, maintain libraries and archives to support their collections and the research of curators, docents, and visitors. These may be open to the public or may require special permission to use. Seattle's Wing Luke Museum of the Asian Pacific American Experience includes the Governor Gary Locke Library and Community Heritage Center (http://db.wingluke.org/), a repository that goes beyond traditional boundaries of museum collections and libraries by combining the two. Kansas City's renowned Nelson-Atkins Museum of Art houses the 155,000-volume Spencer Art Reference Library (www.nelson-atkins.org/education/Library.cfm). The McCracken Research Library at the Buffalo Bill Center of the West in Cody, Wyoming (www.bbhc.org/mccracken/), collects materials about the American West, including *Concessions in National Parks: Hearings before the Sub-Committee on Public Lands* (1948).

The digital convergence of libraries, archives, and museums has created a buzz in the professional literature, resulting in collaborative theme issues on this topic in *Library Quarterly 80, no. 1* (2010), *Archival Science 8, no. 4* (2008), and *Museum Management and Curatorship 24, no. 4* (2009). Librarians interested in honing their government information skills must learn to get out of the house and learn more about other kinds of heritage organizations. Making a regular practice of visiting archives and museums—or better yet, performing research there to get a feel for the user experience—is a commonsense way to start. Also recommended is the work of the America Library Association/ Society of American Archivists/American Alliance of Museums Committee on Archives, Libraries, and Museums (CALM), www.ala.org/groups/ committees/joint/jnt-saa_ala, which has been working on these joint concerns since the early 1970s.

Federally Affiliated Museums Listed at USA.gov
American Art Museum
Cooper-Hewitt, National Design Museum
Freer Gallery of Art and Arthur M. Sackler Gallery
Hirshhorn Museum and Sculpture Garden
Holocaust Museum
National Arboretum
National Gallery of Art
National Museum of African Art
National Museum of American History
National Museum of Natural History
National Museum of the American Indian
National Park Museums
National Portrait Gallery
National Postal Museum
Smithsonian Institution

Source: www.usa.gov/Citizen/Topics/ History_Museums.shtml.

National Libraries

Since this chapter mostly explores primary resources in museums and archives, why mention libraries? The United States is unique in supporting five national libraries: LC, the National Agricultural Library, the National Library of Education, the National Transportation Library, and the National Library of Medicine (addressed in chapter 11). Most of these libraries also serve archival and museum roles, acquiring and preserving thousands of unique and rare materials, creating internationally respected exhibits, and using their web pages to promote their holdings.

The LC is in a league of its own, containing 160 million items as of 2014, including 37 million books, 69 million manuscript items, "the largest rare book collection in North America; and the world's largest collection of legal materials, films, maps, sheet music, and sound recordings" (Library of Congress, 2015). To educators, students, and anyone interested in history, it contains American Memory, the prototypical digital archive, piloted in 1990, allowing users to explore many different kinds of primary sources online, all documenting the American experience. American Memory is a public-private collaboration, with content contributed from many different museums. LC leads the National Digital Information Infrastructure and Preservation Program (NDIIPP), funded by Congress in 2000 to preserve digital content (web pages, sound and video files, geospatial files and much more), build technical infrastructure, develop policies, and establish institutional collaborations. A more recent LC initiative, the

National Digital Stewardship Alliance (www.digitalpreservation.gov), brings NDIIPP's digital preservation work to even more partners.

The National Agricultural Library (www.nal.usda.gov) has two facility locations: Beltsville, Maryland and Washington, DC. It is the nation's premier agricultural archive and library, a coordinative body for the agricultural collections at land grant university libraries and USDA field libraries. Its extensive website has a Visual Arts and Agricultural History section and a top notch digital collection, both pointing to much primary source material. The National Library of Education (http://ies.ed.gov/ncee/projects/nle) serves the public, the federal government, and the education community, housing a collection of 60,000 volumes and 800 journal subscriptions, primarily government literature. Reference assistance is available on-site, via phone or e-mail, but the library does not offer a portal-style website to its collections at the time of this writing. The National Transportation Library (NTL) (http://ntl.bts.gov) was founded to collect materials in support of government decision making on transportation matters. In 2008 it merged with the US Department of Transportation Library. Its fastest area of collection growth is in digital material (statistical, policy, and technical) deposited by government agencies from the federal, state, local, and tribal levels.

Historical Biographical Information

Genealogy

One clear trend in archives and special collections is the growth of a large, enthusiastic user group: genealogists (Hedegaard and Melrose, 2008). Information useful for family histories can be found in both published and unpublished government documents. Historically, genealogical collections and services in libraries tend to be segregated from mainstream services. Most academic libraries do not usually offer deep resources for searching family history; this has typically fallen to public libraries, state and local historical societies, church organizations, state and regional archives, and the private sector. Technology has disrupted this configuration, as the digitization of government resources, newspapers, and archival sources has led to some rich sources for searching personal history and new interconnectedness between different kinds of primary resources. Academic librarians, including government documents librarians, now acknowledge that the same skills used to research family history are good for general biographical and historical research and vice versa. And the medical information field overlaps with genealogy, as well; a recent study of family historians showed that over half of the responding households collect some kind of ancestral medical data. These data typically come from death certificates, obituaries, and word-of-mouth or family records and might be useful in promoting increased awareness and surveillance of health risks, both individual and societal (Case, 2008).

A very selective sample of government information useful for genealogical research would include:

- Congressional publications, such as the *Serial Set* (as stated in chapter 3, it is worth traveling to use a library that subscribes to the commercially digitized

Serial Set, congressional hearings, or *Congressional Record*): a family member may have been cited by Congress, testified, been under investigation, or filed a claim against the federal government, or may be listed in one of the military directories.

- General Land Office patents: a family member may have purchased or home-steaded land from the federal government; see www.glorecords.blm.gov or www.archives.gov/genealogy/land/.

- NARA offers immigration records, military service records, and a Resources for Genealogists guide (www.archives.gov/research/genealogy/).

- The Social Security Administration Death Master File (SSDMF) (https://www.ssdmf.com) allows fee-based searching; various commercial sites allow unlimited searching as part of their offerings, such as http://search.ancestry.com/search/db.aspx?dbid=3693. These services provide full name, birth date, death date, Social Security number, state of birth and last residence of the deceased, 1935 until three years before the current date.

- Patent and Trademark Office: a family member may hold a patent (www.uspto.gov).

- Copyright Office: a family member may have copyrighted an original work (http://cocatalog.loc.gov).

- Census Questionnaires: after 72 years census questionnaires become available on microfilm at NARA facilities and large centers for genealogy; digital editions (fee based) are available through Ancestry.com, HeritageQuest.com, and on privately sponsored government sites like http://1940census.archives.gov (sponsored by archives.com).

- Citizenship and Immigration Services: users may write to obtain immigration and naturalization records of deceased family members, for a reasonable fee (https://genealogy.uscis.dhs.gov).

- Birth, death, marriage, and divorce certificates are available via state and/or county vital records offices, county clerks, or county courts. See *Where to Write for Vital Records,* www.cdc.gov/nchs/w2w.htm.

More detailed lists may be found in Constance Reik's *Bibliography for Farmers, Soldiers and Sailors for Family Research and Historical Research* (Reik, 2008) and in a 48-page bibliography from the Oklahoma Department of Libraries titled *Genealogical Resources in U.S. Federal Depository Libraries* (Oklahoma Department of Libraries, 2006).

Ancestry.com and HeritageQuest.com are two subscription services that have managed to prevail in the genealogical research marketplace. Both are available as individual or institutional subscriptions, and all types of libraries are now subscribing to one or the other. In a Reference Backtalk column in *Library Journal,* aptly titled "Why I Love Ancestry.com," the author answers her question with two simple replies: because it works and because we need it (Kundanis, 2008). Kundanis attributes its success in the library market to Ancestry's inclusion of US and UK census, birth, marriage, death, immigration, and military records, as well as school yearbooks, ancestral charts, and family group sheets, all at an affordable rate. HeritageQuest (www.heritagequestonline.com), produced by ProQuest, allows the searching of US federal census materials; a sizable genealogy article database; Revolutionary War pension and warrant files; and memorials, petitions, and private relief actions culled from the *Serial Set*. It would be hard to argue that these commercial products have not significantly increased the usefulness and discovery of historical government data. Surely genealogy as a topic area will continue finding its way into every librarian, archivist, and curator's day-to-day work.

Directories

Knowing who worked in a government agency and when can provide significant context for historical research. Those seeking a deeper look inside a federal agency, such as detailed staff and office listings, should consult a commercially produced guide or directory. Once a staple in many kinds of libraries, these directories today seem most apt to be held by law, corporate, archival, and government collections. Librarians who have managed to collect and retain copies of the *Federal Yellow Book* have a valuable historical resource at their fingertips. Produced by Leadership Directories, Inc., it is an annual subscription (with new editions delivered quarterly) that allows users to search for tens of thousands of federal employees by name, organization, or subject, even annotating entries by type of political appointment. Print directories offer a fixed, permanent record for a sequence of years, with more detail than one might find with constantly updated agency directory databases on the Web (although Leadership Directories now supplies its resources online as well, updated daily, for nearly three times the print subscription price). ABC-CLIO/Greenwood offers *The United States Executive Branch: a Biographical Directory of Heads of State and Cabinet Officials* covering 1789–2000. From 1816 to 1959, the government itself issued the *Official Register of the United States* (many years of which are available via FDsys and the HathiTrust), the directory of choice for finding federal employees when the government workforce was much smaller. Many agencies published their own directories, such as the Department of Health and Human Services *Telephone Directory* (HE 1.28:), and while these are valuable, they generally lack advanced indexing features. The hefty *Biographical Directory of Congress* (http://bioguide .congress.gov) provides authoritative summaries of congressional careers and notes the holding institution for members' papers when known. The biennial *Congressional Pictorial Directory* (http://catalog.hathitrust.org/Record/000535814 and http://catalog .hathitrust.org/Record/000535816) offers photos of House and Senate members in volumes going back as far as 1951.

Requesting Government Records Using FOIA and the Privacy Act

Congress passed the Freedom of Information Act, or FOIA (P.L. 89-554, 80 Stat. 378) in 1966; it went into effect the following year and was amended in 1974 (P.L. 93-502, 88 Stat. 1561), 1996 (P.L. 104-231, 110 Stat. 3048), 2002 (P.L. 107-306, 116 Stat. 2383), and 2004 (P.L. 108-136, 117 Stat. 1392). This groundbreaking law gives any individual or group the opportunity to request previously unreleased records from executive branch agencies. Citizens' rights under FOIA are frequently mentioned along with rights

under the Privacy Act (P.L. 93–579, 88 Stat. 1896), a 1974 act outlining how executive branch agencies gather, maintain, and release personal information about citizens
and legal permanent residents. The Privacy Act protects individuals against other members of the public accessing their government files and allows individuals to correct
information appearing in their own government files. Journalists, researchers, activists,
investigators, people seeking to clear their names, and others use FOIA and the Privacy
Act to request files, including files on themselves. Agencies must release the requested
information unless it falls under one of nine exemptions and three exclusions (see sidebar). The agency has 20 working days to acknowledge a request in writing and may
extend that for an additional 10 working days, with notification to the requester. The
Department of Justice oversees FOIA compliance, and the Office of Management and
Budget (OMB) oversees Privacy Act compliance.

There are two major caches of FOIA information on the government web: FOIA
.gov, and the Department of Justice Office of Information Policy (OIP) FOIA Resources
page, www.justice.gov/oip/foia-resources/. FOIA.gov is the better bet for quick information, for those wanting to file a request, or for students of middle school level and up.
Much of the FAQs are delivered via narrative explanations (a paragraph or so each) followed by video tutorials. A dashboard approach means that the public can see how many
FOIA requests have been filed, responded to (and by which agency), or backlogged,
back to FY 2009. It is impressive to see FOIA quantified: 714,231 requests handled in
FY 2014 alone! The OIP page is geared to FOIA practitioners within government and
law, with reference materials, court decisions, regulations, best practices, a FOIA calendar, and a directory of agency FOIA sites. The OMB brings together a complicated
set of Privacy Act guidelines at www.whitehouse.gov/omb/inforeg_infopoltech#pg/.

The three exclusions, rarely used, pertain to especially sensitive law enforcement and
national security matters. The FOIA does not apply to Congress, the courts, or the central
offices of the White House, nor does it apply to records in the custody of state or local
governments. However, all state governments have their own FOIA-type statutes (see
a list from the National Freedom of Information Coalition, www.nfoic.org/state-foi
-laws). "The FOIA does not require a state or local government or a private organization or business to release any information directly to the public, whether it has
been submitted to the federal government or not. However, information submitted to
the federal government by such organizations or companies may be available through
a FOIA request if it is not protected by a FOIA exemption, such as the one covering trade secrets and confidential business information" (United States General Services
Administration, 2015: 2).

Fulfilling requests may take months or even years. The person making the request
must pay for all research ($15 to $40 per hour) and photocopying fees involved (min-
imally 10 cents per page) (General Services Administration, 2015: 9). Every agency is
required to maintain a public FOIA reading room (so that requestors may view materials in person), a link on its agency web page providing FOIA contacts, instructions, and
an electronic reading room displaying materials already released. The FBI's electronic
reading room is the most famous, with many celebrity files and historically significant cases available for perusal. One random foray into a file mentioning illegal drugs
and the Grateful Dead (http://foia.fbi.gov/foiaindex/gratefuldead.htm) also turns up a

What Information Is Available under the FOIA?

The Freedom of Information Act provides public access to all federal agency records except for those records (or portions of those records) that are protected from disclosure by any of nine exemptions or three exclusions (reasons for which an agency may withhold records from a requester). The exemptions are as follows:

1. Information that is classified to protect national security.

2. Information related solely to the internal personnel rules and practices of an agency.

3. Information that is prohibited from disclosure by another federal law.

4. Trade secrets or commercial or financial information that is confidential or privileged.

5. Privileged communications within or between agencies, including:

   a. Deliberative Process Privilege

   b. Attorney-Work Product Privilege

   c. Attorney-Client Privilege

6. Information that, if disclosed, would invade another individual's personal privacy.

7. Information compiled for law enforcement purposes that:

   7 (A). Could reasonably be expected to interfere with enforcement proceedings

   7 (B). Would deprive a person of a right to a fair trial or an impartial adjudication

   7 (C). Could reasonably be expected to constitute an unwarranted invasion of personal privacy

   7 (D). Could reasonably be expected to disclose the identity of a confidential source

   7 (E). Would disclose techniques and procedures for law enforcement investigations or prosecutions

   7 (F). Could reasonably be expected to endanger the life or physical safety of any individual

8. Information that concerns the supervision of financial institutions.

9. Geological information on wells.

Source: http://FOIA.gov/faq.html.

reference to the Shelter Half, a 1970s-era Tacoma, Washington, coffeehouse geared toward GIs opposed to the Vietnam War—see figure 18.3. Exempt information is blacked out, or redacted, and numbers along the side provide the reason for the redaction: b7c in fig. 18.3 means that names were withheld because of "records or information compiled for law enforcement purposes . . . [that] could reasonably be expected to constitute an unwarranted invasion of personal privacy" (5 U.S.C. § 552).

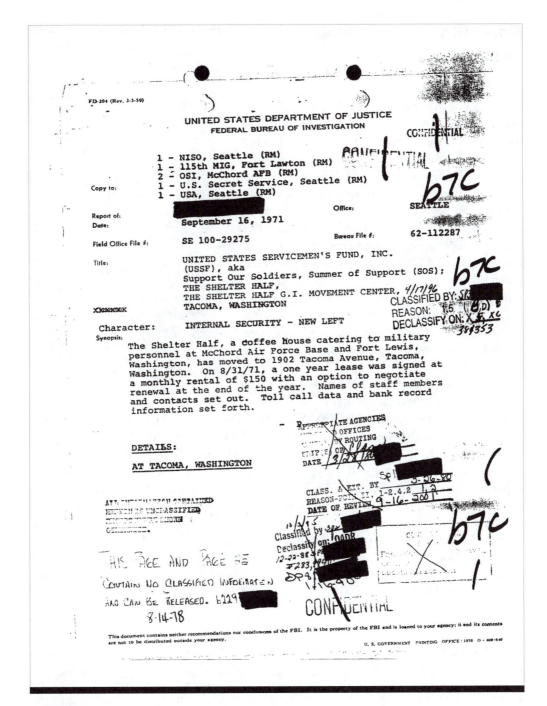

FIGURE 18.3

Sample Page, Concerning a Tacoma, Washington, Coffeehouse, from a 14-Page FBI File on the Grateful Dead

More FOIA Agencies, Projects, and Products

A handful of other resources merit special attention in the FOIA realm. The Office of Government Information Services (OGIS) within NARA (http://ogis.archives.gov) mediates FOIA disputes, reviews policies, and recommends policy changes, serving as the government-wide FOIA ombudsperson. The National Security Archive, a project of George Washington University committed to collecting declassified documents, offers an outstanding set of FOIA guides at www.gwu.edu/~nsarchiv/nsa/foia/guide.html. Here are detailed ways to make FOIA work for you: follow a sample request through the process; understand the related areas of classification, declassification, reclassification, and redeclassification; and learn about FOIA guidance, history, and news. Of special note is their *Follow a Request through the FOIA Process* at http://nsarchive.gwu.edu/nsa/foia/foia _flowchart.pdf. The Digital National Security Archive (DNSA), hosted by ProQuest, makes available a growing collection of documents acquired chiefly by the National Security Archive through FOIA requests. Gale/Cengage offers the Declassified Documents Reference Service (DDRS), a subscription service of over 116,000 digitized declassified documents, regularly harvesting materials as they are declassified on schedule from agencies, the National Archives, and the presidential libraries. (Special tip: adding the word "translation" into a DDRS search retrieves selected materials of the Foreign Broadcast Information Service, discussed in chapter 9.) The Declassification Project at Columbia University (https://industry.datascience.columbia.edu/project/declassification-engine) performs big data analysis and text mining on declassified materials from DDRS.

Feast or Famine in the World of FOIA

Professor David H. Price of St. Martin's University filed over 600 FOIA requests during the course of his research on the intelligence community and anthropologists. In an appendix to *Threatening Anthropology: McCarthyism and the FBI's Surveillance of Activist Anthropologists,* Price offers specific advice from his years of filing requests and appealing FOIA denials. He points out that some agencies, such as the National Security Agency, denied all of his requests (by law, such denials must be based on exemptions). The Department of Energy gets high marks for requests fulfilled within weeks, whereas the FBI frequently takes six or more years to send records or denials of records (Price, 2004).

Conclusion

This chapter examined diverse sources for primary source material from the government. Special attention has been paid to the convergence of libraries, archives, and museums as trusted repositories working to improve access to government information in the digital age. NARA is a particular focus, with its central role in preserving the unpublished record of the federal government. As with other chapters, the structures and services explored on the federal level have local parallels in the form of state, county, and municipal archives and museums. The role of museums and national libraries has been considered, along with the blossoming field of genealogy and its relationship to government documents. We concluded our review by considering FOIA and Privacy Act requests as a further line of inquiry into the riches of the federal government.

Exercises

1. Find the nearest congressional papers collection—your own institution may very well serve as one. Check the Center for Legislative Studies, www.archives .gov/legislative/repository-collections/. If you cannot visit a collection in person, locate one with a well-established collection of digitized material. What does the collection reveal about the controversies of the day?

2. Using 1940Census.gov, look for historic census questionnaires filled out a) by someone with your own last name or a similar last name, b) a family member, or c) someone from your town. How did the census code this individual's race? Occupation? Who else lived in the same household?

3. Find the nearest NARA facility, and name three agencies whose materials are housed there.

4. Pick a federal agency and find its FOIA electronic reading room. What kinds of materials are there, and is it well organized? What happens when you look for FOIA information from a similar agency on the state level?

5. What is the oldest federal government-produced video content you can discover on the open Web? Are you able to view it, and what is the topic?

Laws Mentioned in This Chapter

Expressing the Sense of Congress that Members' Congressional Papers Should Be Properly Maintained and Encouraging Members to Take All Necessary Measures to Manage and Preserve These Papers, House Concurrent Resolution 110-307 (2008).

Freedom of Information Act (FOIA), P.L. 89-554, 80 Stat. 378 (1966).

FOIA Amendments: P.L. 93-502, 88 Stat. 1561 (1974), P.L. 104-231, 110 Stat. 3048 (1996), P.L. 107-306, 116 Stat. 2383 (2002), and P.L. 108-136, 117 Stat. 1392 (2004).

Privacy Act, P.L. 93-579, 88 Stat. 1896 (1974).

Sources Mentioned in This Chapter

Sources mentioned in this section do not duplicate the references that follow.

1940 Census: Official 1940 Census Website, http://1940Census.archives.gov/.

About EAD, www.loc.gov/ead/eadabout.html.

Access to Archival Databases (AAD), http://aad.archives.gov/aad/.

American Library Association/Society of American Archivists/American Alliance of Museums Committee on Archives, Libraries, and Museums (CALM), www.ala.org/groups/committees/joint/jnt-saa_ala/.

An American Political Archives Reader. 2009. Karen Dawley Paul, Glenn Gray, L. Rebecca Johnson Melvin, and Congressional Papers Roundtable (Society of American Archivists). Lanham, MD: Scarecrow.

Ancestry.com, www.ancestry.com.

Biographical Directory of Congress, http://bioguide.congress.gov.

Center for Legislative Archives, www.archives.gov/legislative/.

Citizenship and Immigration Service Genealogy Page, https://genealogy.uscis.dhs.gov.

Congressional Pictorial Directory, http://purl.access.gpo.gov/GPO/LPS11679/.

Congressional Record. 1873–. Washington, DC: Government Printing Office.

Copyright Office, http://cocatalog.loc.gov.

Declassified Documents Reference Service (DDRS), (description) http://gdc.gale.com/products/declassified-documents-reference-system/.

Digital National Security Archive (DNSA), www.proquest.com/products-services/databases/dnsa.html.

Digital Public Library of America, http://dp.la.

Encoded Archival Description (EAD) Roundtable, www2.archivists.org/groups/encoded-archival-description-ead-roundtable/.

Federal Staff Directory. 2015. Thousand Oaks, CA: CQ Press.

Federal Yellow Book. 2015. New York and Washington, DC: Leadership Directories.

FOIA.gov, www.foia.gov.

Follow a Request through the FOIA Process, http://nsarchive.gwu.edu/nsa/foia/foia_flowchart.pdf.

Freedom of Information Act (Department of Justice), www.justice.gov/oip/foia-resources.

General Land Office Patents, www.glorecords.blm.gov.

Geology Discipline Research Records Schedule, www.usgs.gov/usgs-manual/schedule/432–1-s5/gd.html.

Guide to Federal Records in the National Archives of the United States, www.archives.gov/research/guide-fed-records/.

HeritageQuest.com (description), http://proquest.libguides.com/heritagequestonline/.

Library of Congress, www.loc.gov.

Miller, Cynthia. *Managing Congressional Collections.* 2008. Chicago: Society of American Archivists.

National Agricultural Library, www.nal.usda.gov.

National Archives and Records Administration, www.archives.gov.

National Archives Catalog, www.archives.gov/research/catalog/.

National Association of Government Archives and Records Administrators (NAGARA), www.nagara.org.

National Digital Stewardship Alliance, www.digitalpreservation.gov.

National Freedom of Information Coalition, www.nfoic.org.

National Library of Education, http://ies.ed.gov/ncee/projects/nle/.

National Security Archive FOIA Guide, www.gwu.edu/~nsarchiv/nsa/foia/guide.html.

Office of Government Information Services, https://ogis.archives.gov.

Official Register, www.gpo.gov/fdsys/search/searchresults.action?st=title%3a%220fficial+Register+of+the+United+States%22 or http://catalog.hathitrust.org/Record/002137439/.

Online Research Tools and Aids, www.archives.gov/research/start/online-tools.html.

Patent & Trademark Office, www.uspto.gov.

Preservation: Specifications and Research, www.archives.gov/preservation/technical/.

Privacy Act Guidance, www.whitehouse.gov/omb/inforeg_infopoltech#pg/.

ProQuest History Vault (description only), www.proquest.com/products-services/historyvault.html.

Records Managers, www.archives.gov/records-mgmt/.

Resources for Genealogists, www.archives.gov/research/genealogy/.

Sobel, Robert, and David B. Sicilia. 2003. *The United States Executive Branch: A Biographical Directory of Heads of State and Cabinet Officials.* Westport, CT: Greenwood.

Social Security Administration Death Master File, 1935–2014 (last three years will now be embargoed), http://search.ancestry.com/search/db.aspx?dbid=3693 or www.ssdmf.com/ (both fee-based).

United States Executive Branch: A Biographical Directory of Heads of State and Cabinet Officials. 2003. Santa Barbara, CA: ABC-CLIO/Greenwood.

US *Congressional Serial Set.* 1817–. Washington, DC: Government Printing Office.

Washington State Digital Archives, www.digitalarchives.wa.gov.

What is a Records Schedule? www.epa.gov/records/what/quest6.htm.

Where to Write for Vital Records, www.cdc.gov/nchs/w2w.htm.

References

American Library Association. 2015. *ALA Library Fact Sheets,* www.ala.org/tools/libfactsheets/.

Case, Donald O. 2008. "Collection of Family Health Histories: The Link Between Genealogy and Public Health." *Journal of the American Society for Information Science and Technology* 59, no. 14: 2312–2319.

Corbey, Raymond. 2008. "Cultural Heritage." In *New Encyclopedia of Africa,* John Middleton and Joseph C. Miller, eds. 2nd ed., vol. 2. Detroit: Thompson, Gale, 550–555.

Department of State. 2014. *U.S. Department of State Records Schedule.* Chapter 21: Geographic Areas Affairs Records. http://foia.state.gov/_docs/RecordsDisposition/A-21.

Federal Bureau of Investigation. 2001. FBI Records: The Vault. The Grateful Dead Part 1 of 1. https://vault.fbi.gov/The%20Grateful%20Dead%20/.

General Services Administration. 2015. Your Right to Federal Records: Questions and Answers on the Freedom of Information Act and the Privacy Act. www.gsa.gov/graphics/staffoffices/Your_Right _to_Federal_Records.pdf.

Guide to the Elmer Charles Kistler Papers, example of finding guide, http://digital.lib.washington.edu/ findingaids/view?docId=KistlerElmer5347.xml.

Hedegaard, Ruth, and Elizabeth Anne Melrose. 2008. *International Genealogy and Local History: Papers Presented by the Genealogy and Local History Section at IFLA General Conferences 2001–2005.* IFLA publications series, 130. Munchen: K G Saur.

Jimerson, Randall. 2005. "Notes from the 20th Anniversary of the National Archives and Records Administration Panel Discussion." May 20. web.archive.org/web/20130401000000*/http://www .archives.gov/about/history/anniversary/panel/randall-jimerson.html.

Kundanis, Barb. 2008. "Why I Love Ancestry.com." *Library Journal* 133, no. 17: 98. lj.libraryjournal .com/2008/10/ljarchives/why-i-love-ancestry-com.

Library of Congress. 2015. "About the Library." www.loc.gov/about/generalinfo.html.

Marty, Paul. 2010. "An Introduction to Digital Convergence: Libraries, Archives, and Museums in the Digital Age." *Library Quarterly* 80, no. 1 (January): 15.

National Archives and Records Administration. 2009. *The National Archives in the Nation's Capital: Information for Researchers.* Washington, DC: National Archives and Records Administration.

National Archives and Records Administration. 2010. "Operation Safe Haven Photographs, compiled ca. 1994–ca. 1994" (Archival Description, Scope & Content Note). ARC Identifier 637550/Local Identifier 385-SH. http://research.archives.gov/description/637550/.

National Archives and Records Administration. 2014. "Strategy for Digitizing Archival Materials for Public Access, 2015–2024." www.archives.gov/digitization/strategy.html.

National Archives and Records Administration. 2015a. "What is the National Archives?" www.archives .gov/about/.

National Archives and Records Administration. 2015b. "What's a Record?" www.archives.gov/about/
info/whats-a-record.html.

National Park Service. 2015. "Discover History and Historic Preservation in the National Park Service."
www.nps.gov/history/.

Office of the Clerk, House of Representatives. 2010. *Records Management Manual for Members.* Publication
M–1. www.docstoc.com/docs/45018198/Records-Management-Manual-for-Members/.

Oklahoma Department of Libraries, US Government Information Division. 2006. *Genealogical
Resources in U.S. Federal Depository Libraries.* Last revised July 23. www.odl.state.ok.us/usinfo/
GenealogicalResources.pdf.

Pearson, Glenda J. 1988. "Government Publications on Microform: Integrating Reference Services."
Microform Review 15, no. 5, 286–291.

Price, David H. 2004. *Threatening Anthropology: McCarthyism and the FBI's Surveillance of Activist Anthropologists.* Durham: Duke University Press.

Reik, Constance. 2008. *Bibliography for Famers* [sic], *Soldiers and Sailors for Family Research and Historical
Research.* www.fdlp.gov/file-repository/outreach/events/depository-library-council-dlc-meetings/
2008-meeting-proceedings/fall-dlc-meeting-arlington-va-3/157-bibliography-for-famers-soldiers-and
-sailors-for-family-research-a-historical-research/.

Society of American Archivists. 2016. So You Want to Be an Archivist: An Overview of the Archives
Profession. www2.archivists.org/profession/.

Trant, Jennifer. 2009. "Emerging Convergence? Thoughts on Museums, Archives, Libraries, and Professional Training." *Museum Management and Curatorship* 24, no. 4: 369–387.

USA.gov. 2015. "Museums." www.usa.gov/Citizen/Topics/History_Museums.shtml.

Whitaker, Linda, and Michael Lotstein. 2012. "Pulling Back the Curtain." In *Doing Archival Research in
Political Science,* Scott A. Frisch, Douglas B. Harris, Sean Q. Kelly, and David C. W. Parker. Amherst,
NY: Cambria Press.

About the Authors and Contributors

CASSANDRA HARTNETT began her career shelving fiction books at the Plattsburgh Public Library. She received her Master of Library and Information Studies from the University of Michigan. She has been employed at the University of Michigan Library (Research Library Residency Program), the University of Michigan School of Information, and Detroit Public Library. She currently serves as US Documents librarian, University of Washington Libraries. She also serves as affiliate faculty at the University of Washington Information School, teaching LIS 526 (Government Information). She is a cofounder of the Northwest Government Information Network (NGIN) and was 2008–2009 chair of the American Library Association's Government Documents Round Table.

ANDREA L. SEVETSON began her library career checking in periodicals at Macalester College. She received her Master of Arts in Library and Information Studies from the University of Wisconsin-Madison, and has since been employed as a government documents librarian at the University of California, Berkeley; the US Census Bureau; LexisNexis, and is currently employed as a trainer with ProQuest. She has served as the chair of the American Library Association's Government Documents Round Table, and was appointed to the US Depository Council to the Public Printer and served as its chair. She is the recipient of the CIS/GODORT/ALA "Documents to the People" Award and the James Bennett Childs Award for distinguished contributions to documents librarianship. She is the author of many articles and editor of *The Serial Set: Its Make-up and Content* (Bethesda, MD: ProQuest, 2013).

ERIC J. FORTE began his library career writing SuDoc call numbers on congressional documents for the regional federal depository at the Texas State Library in Austin. He holds a Masters in Library and Information Science from the University of Illinois at Urbana-Champaign and has worked as a librarian with government information at Western State College of Colorado, the University of California at Santa Barbara, and Boise State University. He has taught government documents at the University of Illinois, and presented and written about government information in various venues. He currently works with OCLC.

Peggy Roebuck Jarrett (chapters 4, 5, and 7) is reference and collection development librarian at the Gallagher Law Library, University of Washington School of Law. She is the federal depository coordinator and the selector for federal, state, and international government publications. She earned her Master of Science in Library and Information Science from The Catholic University of America, and started her career working in law firm libraries. She is active in the American Association of Law Libraries, currently serving as chair of the Government Relations Committee. She has also served as a member of the Depository Library Council to the Public Printer.

Amy West (chapter 10) served as the Librarian for Data Services at the University of Minnesota until June 2015.

Ann Glusker (chapter 11) is the Consumer Health Librarian at The Seattle Public Library, and has worked as a medical librarian at a large health cooperative, and as an epidemiologist at Public Health—Seattle & King County, answering data requests. She has a PhD in Sociology/Demography, a Master's degree in Public Health and a Master's degree in Library and Information Science, all from the University of Washington. Her dissertation was published as a book, titled *Fertility Patterns of Native- and Foreign-Born Women: Assimilating to Diversity*. She loves to work with health data and information, and writes a wellness blog for SPL staff.

Susan Edwards (chapter 12) is head of the Library's Social Sciences Division of the University of California, Berkeley where she also received her Master of Library and Information Science degree. She has connected users with information in government documents for over 30 years, and remains passionate about the importance of access to information.

Kathryn Tallman (chapter 13) is a Government Information Librarian at the University of Colorado-Boulder. She received her Master of Science in Library and Information Science from the University of Illinois at Urbana-Champaign and has been with the University of Colorado-Boulder since 2012.

Jesse Silva (chapter 14) is the Librarian for Federal and State Government Information, Political Science, Public Policy and Legal Studies at the University of California, Berkeley. Previously he worked at the University of North Texas, Innovative Interfaces, San Jose State, and UC Santa Cruz. He holds an MLIS from San Jose State University and is a coauthor of the book *Legal Executions in California: A Comprehensive Registry, 1851–2005* (McFarland Press, 2006).

Lucia Orlando (chapter 14) is the librarian for Government Information, Social Sciences, and Arts and Humanities at the University of California, Santa Cruz. She holds an MLIS from San Jose State University.

Jessica Jerrit (chapter 15) is a business research and instruction librarian at the University of Washington, where she also received her MLIS. In addition to working with the business school, she is also liaison to the Department of Economics.

Kelly L. Smith (chapter 16) is the Government Information and Urban Studies & Planning Librarian at UC San Diego. She previously worked at the Indiana University-Purdue University Indianapolis (IUPUI) University Library and holds an MLIS from San Jose State University.

Annelise Sklar (chapter 16) is Social Sciences Collection Coordinator and Librarian for Political Science, Environmental Policy, Law & Society, International Government Information, and Social Sciences Data at UC San Diego. She previously worked at the University of New Mexico and has an MSLS from the University of North Carolina at Chapel Hill.

Martin Wallace (chapter 17) is the Maker Literacies and Engineering Liaison Librarian at the University of Texas at Arlington. He holds an MLIS from the University of North Texas and an MS in Information Systems from the University of Maine. He has been a liaison to various academic departments in engineering and the sciences for over ten years. He specializes in patent information, has taught courses on patent searching, and for nine years served as the University of Maine's representative to the USPTO's Patent and Trademark Resource Centers Program. In his current role, he provides patent search consultations for clients of UTA's Office of Technology Management and for members of EpicMavs, UTA's community entrepreneurship program.

Index

A

F

S

W

X

Y